Jasenovac Concentration Camp

This book presents state-of-the-art discussions around the concentration camp Jasenovac. Initially one of the largest camps of the Second World War, Jasenovac became a symbol of supra-national unity during the Yugoslav period and in the 1990s re-emerged as a contested symbol of narrational victimhood. By analyzing some of the most controversial topics related to the Second World War in south-eastern Europe – the Holocaust, the genocide of Serbs and Roma, the issues of political prisoners and state-sponsored crimes, censorship during Communist Yugoslavia, the use of memory in war propaganda, and representation of tragedies in museums and art – the book allows for a greater understanding of the development of intergroup violence in the former Yugoslavia. It will be of interest to scholars and students of history, genocide studies, memory studies, and sociology as well as professionals working in the field of conflict resolution and reconciliation.

Andriana Benčić Kužnar is an assistant professor of Military Sociology at the Faculty of Humanities and Social Sciences, University of Zagreb (Croatia). She published the book *Memory of the Croatian War of Independence* in 2020. Her research interest lies in the intersection of nationhood and identity with collective memories of war and political uses of the past.

Danijela Lucić is an assistant professor of Military Sociology at the Faculty of Humanities and Social Sciences, University of Zagreb (Croatia). She published the book *State Terrorism* in 2019, and three co-authored books in the fields of war studies, security studies, and qualitative and quantitative research.

Stipe Odak is a researcher and lecturer at the Université catholique de Louvain (Belgium). He received his PhD in Political and Social Sciences from UC Louvain and a doctorate in Theology from KU Leuven (Belgium). His research focuses on the intersections of memory, religion, and conflicts.

Routledge Studies in Genocide and Crimes against Humanity

The Routledge Series in Genocide and Crimes against Humanity publishes cutting-edge research and reflections on these urgently contemporary topics. While focusing on political-historical approaches to genocide and other mass crimes, the series is open to diverse contributions from the social sciences, humanities, law, and beyond. Proposals for both sole-authored and edited volumes are welcome.

Edited by Adam Jones, University of British Columbia in Kelowna, Canada.

Preventing Mass Atrocities
Policies and Practices
Edited by Barbara Harff and Ted Robert Gurr

Cultural Genocide
Law, Politics, and Global Manifestations
Edited by Jeffrey Bachman

Historical Dialogue and the Prevention of Mass Atrocities
Edited by Elazar Barkan, Constantin Goschler and James E. Waller

A Cultural Interpretation of the Genocide Convention
Kurt Mundorff

From Discrimination to Death
Genocide Process Through a Human Rights Lens
Melanie O'Brien

In the Shadow of Genocide
Justice and Memory within Rwanda
Stephanie Wolfe, Matthew Kane, Tawia B. Ansah

Jasenovac Concentration Camp
An Unfinished Past
Edited by Andriana Benčić Kužnar, Danijela Lucić and Stipe Odak

Jasenovac Concentration Camp
An Unfinished Past

Edited by Andriana Benčić Kužnar,
Danijela Lucić and Stipe Odak

LONDON AND NEW YORK

First published 2023
by Routledge
4 Park Square, Milton Park, Abingdon, Oxon OX14 4RN

and by Routledge
605 Third Avenue, New York, NY 10158

Routledge is an imprint of the Taylor & Francis Group, an informa business

© 2023 selection and editorial matter, Andriana Benčić Kužnar, Danijela Lucić and Stipe Odak individual chapters, the contributors

The right of Andriana Benčić Kužnar, Danijela Lucić and Stipe Odak to be identified as the authors of the editorial material, and of the authors for their individual chapters, has been asserted in accordance with sections 77 and 78 of the Copyright, Designs and Patents Act 1988.

All rights reserved. No part of this book may be reprinted or reproduced or utilised in any form or by any electronic, mechanical, or other means, now known or hereafter invented, including photocopying and recording, or in any information storage or retrieval system, without permission in writing from the publishers.

Trademark notice: Product or corporate names may be trademarks or registered trademarks, and are used only for identification and explanation without intent to infringe.

British Library Cataloguing-in-Publication Data
A catalogue record for this book is available from the British Library

Library of Congress Cataloging-in-Publication Data
Names: Odak, Stipe, editor. | Kužnar, Andriana Benčič, 1987– editor. | Lucić Danijela, 1986– editor.
Title: Jasenovac Concentration Camp : an unfinished past / edited by Stipe Odak, Andriana Benčič Kužnar, an Danijela Lucić.
Other titles: Jasenovac – manipulacije, kontroverze i povijesni revizionizam. English
Description: Updated, second (English) edition. | Abingdon, Oxon ; New York, NY : Routledge, 2023. |
Series: Routledge studies in genocide and crimes against humanity |
Includes bibliographical references and index.
Identifiers: LCCN 2022054919 (print) | LCCN 2022054920 (ebook) | ISBN 9781032353791 (hardback) | ISBN 9781032353890 (paperback) | ISBN 9781003326632 (ebook)
Subjects: LCSH: Jasenovac (Concentration camp) | Jasenovac (Concentration camp)–Historiography. | World War, 1939–1945– Prisoners and prisons, Croatian. | World War, 1939–1945–Atrocities–Croatia.
Classification: LCC D805.5.J37 J2813 2023 (print) | LCC D805.5.J37 (ebook) | DDC 940.54/724972–dc23/eng/20221115
LC record available at https://lccn.loc.gov/2022054919
LC ebook record available at https://lccn.loc.gov/2022054920

ISBN: 978-1-032-35379-1 (hbk)
ISBN: 978-1-032-35389-0 (pbk)
ISBN: 978-1-003-32663-2 (ebk)

DOI: 10.4324/9781003326632

Typeset in Times New Roman
by Newgen Publishing UK

Contents

List of Figures	vii
List of Tables	ix
List of Editors and Contributors	xi
Acknowledgements	xiv
Preface	xv

PART I
Naming 1

1 Jasenovac Uses and Misuses of the Past: Manipulations and Historical Revisionism Surrounding the Biggest WWII Camp in the Balkans 3
STIPE ODAK, ANDRIANA BENČIĆ KUŽNAR AND DANIJELA LUCIĆ

2 The Road to 'Serbian Yad Vashem': Manipulations of the History of the Sajmište and Jasenovac Camps 33
JOVAN BYFORD

3 Racial Laws in the Independent State of Croatia: Social and Legal Aspects 55
NATAŠA MATAUŠIĆ

4 Crime and Punishment, or – What is the Connection between Jasenovac and Bleiburg? Biographical Excerpts on War Criminals from the Jasenovac Camp 74
IVO GOLDSTEIN

PART II
Counting 95

5 Jasenovac and Bleiburg between Facts and Manipulations 97
VLADIMIR GEIGER AND MARTINA GRAHEK RAVANČIĆ

6 Jasenovac Concentration Camp and Its Role in the Destruction of the NDH People: Calculation of the Possible Number of Victims Based on the Partially Revised 1964 Census 138
DRAGAN CVETKOVIĆ

7 Forgotten Victims of World War II: The Suffering of Roma in the Independent State of Croatia, 1941–1945 188
DANIJEL VOJAK

PART III
Describing 225

8 Contested Cultural Memory in Jasenovac: A Post-Communist/Post-Socialist Memorial Museum in an Era of Historical Revisionism 227
VJERAN PAVLAKOVIĆ

9 Jasenovac on Film: Manipulations of Identities and the Performance of Memory 255
ANA KRŠINIĆ-LOZICA

10 The International Committee of the Red Cross and Camps on the Territory of the Independent State of Croatia with Special Review of the Jasenovac Concentration Camp 276
MARIO KEVO

Index 298

Figures

6.1	Yugoslavia, civilians – losses according to territorial affiliation	140
6.2	Yugoslavia, civilians – participation in the population and participation in losses according to territorial affiliation	141
6.3	NDH, civilians – the dynamic of suffering	141
6.4	NDH, civilians – percentage in the loss of civilians according to nationality	142
6.5	NDH – national structure of population and the civilian losses according to nationality	143
6.6	NDH, civilians – the dynamic of losses over years	145
6.7	NDH, civilians – national structure according to circumstances of death	147
6.8	NDH, civilians – the participation of Jasenovac in total losses	148
6.9	NDH, civilians – the participation of Jasenovac in total losses	149
6.10	NDH, civilians – the participation of Jasenovac in total losses according to the year of suffering	151
6.11	NDH, civilians – the dynamics of losses in Jasenovac and according to the year of suffering	151
6.12	NDH, civilians – the participation of Jasenovac in the losses suffered at concentration camps	153
6.13	NDH, civilians – the dynamics of losses in camps	153
6.14	National structure of victims in Jasenovac camps	154
6.15	NDH, civilians – percentage in the population and percentage in the losses in the Jasenovac camp	156
6.16	NDH, civilians – national structure of total casualties and casualties at Jasenovac camp	158
6.17	NDH, civilians – national structure according to the location of suffering	159
6.18	NDH, civilians – the participation of Jasenovac in the losses suffered at concentration camps according to nationality	160

6.19	NDH, civilians – participation in the losses at concentration camps according to nationality	161
6.20	NDH, Jasenovac – the dynamic of losses according to nationality	164
6.21	NDH, Jasenovac – national structure according to the year of suffering	164
6.22	NDH, civilians, Serbs – the participation of victims at Jasenovac in total losses according to the year	167
6.23	NDH civilians, Serbs – the dynamic of suffering according to the location	167
6.24	NDH, civilians, Jews – the participation of losses at Jasenovac in the total losses according to the year of suffering	170
6.25	NDH, civilians, Jews – dynamics of suffering according to the location	170
6.26	NDH, civilians, Roma – the participation of losses at Jasenovac in total losses according to the year	172
6.27	NDH, civilians, Roma – dynamics of losses according to the location	172
6.28	NDH, civilians, Croats – the participation of losses at Jasenovac in total losses according to the year	175
6.29	NDH, civilians, Croats – dynamics of losses according to the location	175
6.30	NDH, civilians, Muslimans – the participation of losses in Jasenovac in the total losses according to the year	177
6.31	NDH, civilians, Muslims – dynamics of losses according to the location	177

Tables

5.1	Fatalities in the Jasenovac and Stara Gradiška camps according to different estimates, computations and lists	119
5.2	Fatalities on Bleiburg and the "Way of the Cross," 1945, according to different estimates, computations and lists	120
6.1	NDH, civilians – the dynamic of losses over years	142
6.2	NDH, civilians – percentage in the population and percentage in the loss of civilians according to nationality	143
6.3	NDH, civilians – national structure of losses according to the year of losses	144
6.4	Circumstances of suffering according to nationality	146
6.5	NDH, civilians – the participation of Jasenovac in total losses	148
6.6	NDH, civilians – the participation of Jasenovac in losses suffered at concentration camps	149
6.7	NDH, civilians – the role of Jasenovac in the destruction of civilians according to the year of suffering	150
6.8	NDH, civilians – the role of Jasenovac in the destruction of civilians in concentration camps according to the year of death	152
6.9	Camp Jasenovac – national structure of losses	155
6.10	NDH, civilians – the role of Jasenovac in the destruction of civilians according to ethnicity	157
6.11	NDH, civilians – the role of Jasenovac in the destruction of civilians in concentration camps according to ethnicity	160
6.12	Jasenovac camp – national structure according to the year of suffering	163
6.13	NDH civilians, Serbs – the role of Jasenovac in destruction according to the year of suffering	166
6.14	NDH, civilians, Jews – the role of Jasenovac in destruction according to the year of suffering	169

6.15	NDH, civilians, Jews – the role of Jasenovac in destruction according to the year of suffering	171
6.16	NDH, civilians, Croats–the role of Jasenovac in destruction according to the year of suffering	174
6.17	NDH, civilians, Muslims–the role of Jasenovac in extermination according to the year of suffering	176

Editors and Contributors

Andriana Benčić Kužnar is an assistant professor of Military Sociology at the Faculty of Humanities and Social Sciences, University of Zagreb. She has been a research fellow at the United States Holocaust Memorial Museum (2014/2015), Yad Vashem International Institute for Holocaust Research (2017), Amsterdam School for Heritage, Memory and Material Culture, University of Amsterdam (2016–2019). She has published articles and has given presentations at various conferences in the field of Holocaust and genocide studies, collective memory of war conflicts and politics of memory and identity.

Jovan Byford is a senior lecturer in Psychology at the Open University, Milton Keynes, UK. His main research interests lie in the interdisciplinary study of social and psychological aspects of shared beliefs and social remembering, especially in relation to conspiracy theories, antisemitism, and Holocaust remembrance. He is also interested more generally in the relationship between psychology and history.

Dragan Cvetković is an advisor at the Genocide Victims Museum, Belgrade. His areas of interest are World War II in Yugoslavia, human losses, genocide, and the Holocaust. His research spectrum ranges from the losses suffered in settlements and municipalities to the total losses of Yugoslavia. In 2020 he published the book, *From "Topovske šupe" Concentration Camp to "Sajmište" Concentration Camp. Quantitative Analysis of the Holocaust in Occupied Serbia.*

Vladimir Geiger is a scientific advisor at the Croatian Institute of History, Zagreb. As a researcher at the Institute he dealt with various topics, including twentieth-century Croatian history, especially with the period of World War II and its aftermath, with emphasis on the question of human losses during that period. He has published numerous scientific papers as well as monographs and collections of documents in regard to the question of those losses.

Ivo Goldstein is a Croatian historian and diplomat of Jewish origin. He is a professor at the Department of History, Faculty of Humanities and Social

Sciences, University of Zagreb. He has been a Croatian ambassador to France (2013–2017). Independently, or with his father, Slavko Goldstein, he has published widely about the Holocaust, World War II, Jews in Zagreb and Croatia, and Croatian modern history.

Martina Grahek Ravančić is a senior scientific associate at the Croatian Institute of History, Zagreb. She is interested in subjects concerning World War II and its aftermath: Particularly topics of victims/casualties during the war, the question of repatriations, and the role of the Yugoslav judicial system after 1945.

Mario Kevo is an associate professor and the head of the Department of History at the Catholic University of Croatia, Zagreb. He has published extensively on the subjects of World War II, adoption and implementation of the International Law of Armed Conflict, and on the work of the International Committee of the Red Cross during World War II and its aftermath.

Ana Kršinić–Lozica is an art critic, curator, and a PhD candidate at the Faculty of Humanities and Social Sciences, University of Zagreb. In her thesis, she deals with transformations of memory on the Jasenovac camp as traced through its representations in visual arts, film, literature, and architecture from 1945 until today. Recently she completed a long-term project as a research leader on the heritage of modern sculptor Vera Dajht-Kralj, coordinated by Zivi Atelje DK and the Croatian Museum of Architecture of the Croatian Academy of Sciences and Arts, and in 2018 published the monograph *Beyond Visible: The Public Sculpture of Vera Dajht Kralj*.

Danijela Lucić is an assistant professor of Military Sociology at the Faculty of Humanities and Social Sciences, University of Zagreb. She published the book *State Terrorism* (2019) as well as three co-authored books and numerous articles in the fields of security studies, terrorism, business intelligence, and quantitative and qualitative research.

Nataša Mataušić is a retired museum advisor at the Croatian History Museum, Zagreb. She has published widely in the area of the Holocaust in Croatia and the former Yugoslavia. She has been a long-term president of the Jasenovac Memorial Site board of directors, as well as the Croatian member of International Holocaust Remembrance Alliance (IHRA).

Stipe Odak is a lecturer and post-doctoral researcher at the Université Catholique de Louvain (Belgium). He received his PhD in Political and Social Sciences from UC Louvain (Belgium) and a doctorate in Theology from KU Leuven (Belgium). He is a published poet and a member of PEN International center in Bosnia and Herzegovina.

Vjeran Pavlaković is an associate professor at the Department of Cultural Studies at the University of Rijeka, Croatia. He received his PhD in

History in 2005 from the University of Washington, and has published articles on cultural memory, transitional justice in the former Yugoslavia, and the Spanish Civil War. He is a co-editor of the volume *Framing the Nation and Collective Identity in Croatia* (Routledge, 2019); other recent published work includes "The Legacy of War and Nation-Building in Croatia since 1990," in *Balkan Legacies: The Long Shadow of Conflict and Ideological Experiment in Southeastern Europe* (Purdue UP, 2021), and "Memory Politics in the Former Yugoslavia" in the 2020 *Yearbook of the Institute of East-Central Europe*. He was the lead researcher on the Memoryscapes project as part of Rijeka's European Capital of Culture in 2020 and a co-founder of the Cres Summer School on Transitional Justice and Memory Politics. Current research includes transnational muralization of conflict and a history of Dalmatian immigrants in the American Southwest.

Danijel Vojak is a senior research associate at the Ivo Pilar Institute of Social Sciences, Zagreb. He has published scientific papers in international and domestic scientific publications, mostly on history of Roma, and he is the author of educational publications on the history of Roma suffering in World War II in Croatia. Vojak has collaborated on several domestic and international scientific projects related to Roma history and he is the author of several exhibitions on the history of the Roma in World War II.

Acknowledgements

This book comes as a result of a long process of collaboration inspired by a common desire to acknowledge and understand past tragedies as a way toward social betterment. We would like to thank Jasenovac Memorial Site, which continuously supported us in this process. Likewise, we wish to extend our gratitude to the Croatian Ministry of Culture and Media, which contributed financially to this publication. Above all, we would like to express our deepest appreciation to all the co-authors, collaborators, translators, and reviewers who invested time and effort into this book. Finally, we are really grateful to Routledge's editors who recognized the significance of our work and accepted it for publication.

Preface

Why Is it Important to Talk about Jasenovac Camp?

In the last four years, the success of this volume is continually being confirmed by its sales in the Croatian language, thousands of downloads, and now by its English translation. Even though time has elapsed since the first edition, in 2018, de facto, not a lot has changed in the (inter)disciplinary domain of Eastern European Holocaust Studies in regard to the Jasenovac camp. Manipulations, controversies, and historical revisionism, nowadays repeatedly conceptualized as Holocaust distortion, which also inspired the Croatian title of this volume (in translation: *Jasenovac Manipulations, Controversies and Historical Revisionism*), are still main (meta)concepts that burden the case of Jasenovac nationally and internationally. Despite being a relatively narrow subject in Eastern European Holocaust studies, the controversial and contested theme of Jasenovac camp, and primarily the camp's human losses, including the suffering of Jews and Roma along with its exaggeration and/or downsizing, remains universal.

Accordingly, this translation and update of the first Croatian edition was highly inspired and supported by our editors from Routledge. Guided and driven by their valuable and insightful comments and recommendations, we decided to change a conceptual frame for presenting the scientific components of this volume, as well as to add and reorganize articles in substantial ways.

This Preface to the second edition is intended to explain these changes, along with emphasising the global and contextual importance of Jasenovac camp in the field of Holocaust and genocide studies, memory studies (specifically in dealing with the traumatic past), Balkan studies, nationalism studies, and sociology of war and violence, so that the reader might better understand and appreciate the comprehensive value of this new edition.

In the history of World War II, every concentration camp is simultaneously a part of the same system of terror and is a unique tragedy. The story of Jasenovac is, in many ways, specific. As the largest complex of concentration, incarceration, forced labor, and death camps in the Balkans, it was a place of unimaginable suffering and death for tens of thousands of people. Most contemporary estimates consider the number of Jasenovac victims to vary between 80–120 thousand.

The tragedy of Jasenovac is thus one of those traumas that escape closure; it is a painful past that refuses to become history. However, unlike other World War II concentration camps, the story of Jasenovac continued well after the end of the war. Four decades after 1945, with two full generations having reached maturity in an entirely different system of government, Jasenovac had its dark redux. Socialist Yugoslavia represented Jasenovac as a place of unity in suffering, as a universal lesson against internecine violence addressed to Yugoslav people of all ethnicities and nationalities (as it was commonly phrased at the time). Jasenovac was meant to be a permanent memento of the atrocities that inter-ethnic violence brings. Its most prominent monument – a concrete flower facing the sky – was equally conceived as a metaphor for the whole society that grew as an indestructible flower of life from soil soaked in blood and violence.

Unfortunately, the history of terror was about to take another chapter. It is not an exaggeration to say that the real wars in the former Yugoslavia were preceded by memories of wars in which Jasenovac played the most prominent role. In the nationalist propaganda during the reign of Slobodan Milošević in Serbia, Jasenovac was painted not as a symbol of unity but precisely the opposite – as the ultimate proof that Serbs and Croats cannot live together, and that another genocide against the Serbs was being prepared. Serbs, targeted in World War II on the basis of their nationality, undoubtedly constituted the largest group that was victim to the genocidal policies of the Independent State of Croatia (Nezavisna Država Hrvatska, NDH), a Nazi-allied puppet state that existed from 1941 to 1945. Together with Jews and Roma, Serbs comprised most of the victims of Jasenovac. This painful legacy of suffering, unfortunately, was not articulated in the spirit of open social discussion. Suddenly, in the late 1980s and early 1990s, two major shortcomings coalesced. The first one was state-dictated censorship of free research on World War II crimes. Since Jasenovac was, in the eyes of the state, a symbol of common suffering, then more victims meant more sacrifice. Thus, the number of victims was intentionally inflated in official publications and encyclopedias. This was supported by economic incentives: the Yugoslav state based their demands for reparation from Germany on the number of victims; thus more victims of Jasenovac meant higher demands for reparations and stronger victimhood claims in the international fora. The second was the change of framework. In the Serbian propaganda after 1987, Jasenovac lost the significance of the universal tragedy and became the symbol of Serbian suffering. Previous manipulation with the numbers of the victims of Jasenovac found particularly fertile ground in such an atmosphere. Thus the long shadow of Jasenovac that had started in 1941 stretched well into the 1990s, becoming one of the motivating factors for war and subsequent crimes that occurred on the territories of Croatia and Bosnia and Herzegovina. The tragic story of Jasenovac, however, has another chapter, which is still being written. After the end of the Croatian War of Independence (1991–1995), Jasenovac continues to be a contested subject, not only among historians but also on the inter-state level. Mutual processes before the International Court of Justice between Croatia and Serbia for their violations of the Genocide Convention (filed respectively in 1999 and in 2010) featured extended discussion on Jasenovac. Schoolbooks and educational materials on World War II cannot avoid the controversies of Jasenovac. Even purely religious processes (such as canonizations) cannot escape the shadow of Jasenovac when it comes to individuals who were active during World War II. The best example is the case of former Archbishop of Zagreb, Alojzije Stepinac, whose canonization was halted after suspicions were raised about his reluctance to speak openly against the Ustaše regime.

Still today, controversies around Jasenovac do not cease. In the last two decades, there were certain advances among Serbian and Croatian historians regarding the consensus around historical facts related to Jasenovac. In the same period, however, there was a rise in revisionist publications. Since Jasenovac was such a prominent symbol in the 1940s and 1990s, it became a synecdoche of suffering on the one hand, and guilt on the other. In Croatian nationalist circles, new theories arose that aimed to rewrite the story of Jasenovac entirely. Already in the 1990s, right-wing Croatian nationalists and Holocaust deniers attempted to downgrade the number of Jasenovac victims and the nature of the camp. More recently, they suggested that Jasenovac was a postwar communist camp housing a higher number of prisoners than the Ustaše camp, even though the main complex of Jasenovac camps, so-called camp III Brickworks, was already demolished in 1945. In the deniers' view, its whole tragic legacy was misconstrued and needed to be revalued as a story of Croatian suffering and victimhood.

The memorialization of the Jasenovac tragedy is not divided only symbolically, but even geographically. After the establishment of state borders in the 1990s, one part of the former Jasenovac concentration camp ended up on the territory of the Republic of Croatia (now a part of the EU). The second part is placed at the territory of Republika Srpska (a federal entity of Bosnia and Herzegovina with a Serbian majority). A new permanent exhibition on Jasenovac was opened in 2006 at the Jasenovac Memorial Site, located on the Croatian side. There, the central piece of the exhibition were victims, each listed by their name. Those names (currently 83,811) were collected from different historical sources. Aside from having an ethical value of commemorating each individual by their name, they were also meant to establish a baseline for scientific discussions about the number of victims of Jasenovac, which is still a highly controversial topic. On the Republika Srpska side, Donja Gradina Memorial Site encapsulates the largest mass killing and mass burial site of the Jasenovac complex, with more than 150 marked and unmarked graves. The site still informs visitors that 700,000 people were murdered in Jasenovac, an unfounded figure based on the aforementioned state-sponsored propaganda in Yugoslavia, which was later instrumentalized during the war in the

1990s. In the contemporary politics of Republika Srpska, Jasenovac is further instrumentalized as a legitimation for its existence as a separate entity within Bosnia and Herzegovina. In the words of Milord Dodik, their most prominent politician, Republika Srpska is the bulwark against any new genocide on Serbs. Regrettably, for the political establishment of Republika Srpska, Jasenovac is not a gateway to acknowledge their collective responsibility for the genocides in Bosnia and Herzegovina perpetrated by the Serbs. On the contrary, Jasenovac is used as a diversion from a true and responsible discussion about the tragic past. Needless to say, such political instrumentalizations and revisionist publications only deepened social cleavages. Jasenovac is therefore both a symbol and a symptom. It is a symbol of an immense tragedy; it is a symptom of continuous frustrations caused by unsuccessful processes of coming to terms with the past.

So, why is it important to talk about Jasenovac? As we tried to show, its story reveals, arguably more than anything else, how tragic memories can be transmitted over generations and continually cause new violence. The camp's story also illustrates how remembrance of tragedies requires continuous ethical vigilance. Aside from being a lesson for future generations against the dangers of violence, they have equal potential to become elements of war propaganda. Social memories do not construct themselves spontaneously; they result from group processes. For that reason, it is particularly important to talk once again about Jasenovac, hoping that its long legacy will eventually become conducive for intergroup understanding and compassion.

This volume is divided into three thematic units: Naming, Counting, Describing. As explained in the initial chapter, those three strategies are used as a way to overcome the central problem of every large-scale tragedy: How to represent something that escapes standard means of representation. In the case of Jasenovac, the strategies of naming the crimes, counting the victims, and describing the tragedies were also the main axes of controversies that developed from the end of World War II until today.

Our goals were therefore threefold: (1) to present the most important historical controversies related to Jasenovac; (2) to explore the area of broader scientific consensus and the main causes of disagreement; and (3) to take a step forward by contributing to consensus-finding and clarification of vagueness through new scientific research and insights. While controversies about the past will always exist, our aim is to point out which legitimate doubts are caused by a possible lack of historical sources, by a lack of evidence, or by still insufficient research, and which 'controversies' are created by selective, imprecise, or tendentious interpretation of historical facts and sources. For this reason, we wanted to gather a team of renowned scholars, primarily historians, who have distinguished themselves by the quality of their scientific work, and a number of young scholars who offer new perspectives on the topic of Jasenovac. We also aimed to represent the topic from the perspective of different disciplines. The works can thus be classified into the disciplines of history, sociology, political science, and comparative literature, as well as into interdisciplinary fields of Holocaust and Genocide studies, memory studies, Balkan studies, and sociology of war and violence. When choosing associates, we tried to select experts who, in addition to their rich research work, have dealt with the issues related to Jasenovac camps. Of course, we are aware that it is not possible to give a comprehensive and thorough overview of all the historical controversies related to Jasenovac in one volume. It should therefore be read not as a conclusion, but as one step in the direction of conducting a responsible conversation about a difficult past.

The volume begins with the chapter by Stipe Odak, Andriana Benčić Kužnar, and Danijela Lucić: "Jasenovac Uses and Misuses of the Past: Manipulations and Historical Revisionism Surrounding the Biggest WWII Camp in the Balkans." In this introductory chapter, the aim of the authors is to analyze two main questions: (1) Why Jasenovac became a central element of historical contestation in the territory of the former Yugoslavia, and (2) which elements of the Jasenovac story-telling are specifically contested. Putting the problem of Jasenovac within the larger framework of social memory construction, the authors suggest that discursive construction of Jasenovac cannot be perceived outside its foundational historical events – events of immense human suffering that is ultimately inexpiable. The challenge of 'describing the indescribable,' yielded strategies of conceptual, numeric, and descriptive representation of the past – strategies that unravel a wide scope of propagandistic and revisionist narratives surrounding Jasenovac. Each of them, as frequently demonstrated in this introductory chapter, has also produced a host of struggles and debates, predominantly in Croatia and Serbia, which have strong emotional communal appeal, but questionable historical veracity. This introductory chapter is followed by Jovan Byford's "The Road to 'Serbian Yad Vashem': Manipulations of the History of the Sajmište and Jasenovac Camps." Byford's work on constructions of memory politics analyzes various connections between the Sajmište (Fairground camp) and Jasenovac, presenting various forms of manipulation with both of these former camps. The intention of the author is to scrutinize the "wars of remembrance" between Serbian and Croatian nationalists, who shortly before and during the wars of the 1990s skilfully manipulated the past of the Sajmište and Jasenovac camps, in the context of mutual accusations of "proneness to genocide," participation in the Holocaust, and anti-Semitism. The third work, titled "Racial Laws in the Independent State of Croatia – Social and Legal Aspects," and written by Nataša Mataušić, summarizes the problems of racial laws passed by the Ustaša authorities, particularly in 1941. While mentioned in numerous works, as Nataša Mataušić points out, there has so far been only one academic paper dedicated exclusively to the problem of racial laws in the Independent State of Croatia. In this chapter, the author first gives a brief overview of the history of the Ustaša movement.

Presenting quotations from the Ustaša constitution, Mataušić demonstrates that the Ustaša movement initially directed its hatred towards Serbs, and that racial laws against Jews and Roma were copied from German legislation. Mataušić provides information on how the NDH was established outside the parliamentary elections and underlines that it was recognized by only 13 states, which were satellites of the Triple Alliance. Legal provisions were based on the Poglavnik's (Leader's) personal decisions, and not on deliberations of any representative or legislative body.

The closing chapter of Part I offers a historical description of the Jasenovac tragedy by invoking ten biographies of Ustaša criminals whom, the author rightly considers, the public should be reminded of in an atmosphere of *negationist* revision of history. Thus, in the work by Ivo Goldstein, "Crime and Punishment (or – what is the connection between Jasenovac and Bleiburg): Biographical excerpts on War Criminals from the Jasenovac Camp," the terms "Jasenovac" and "Bleiburg" (understood in both a narrower and a broader sense) are briefly explained, and the author points out their interconnectedness. The author emphasizes that for a long time both topics have been manipulated, in historiography as well as in the general public. As an example of the manipulations with the theme of Jasenovac camp in the postwar period, the author mentions the exaggeration of the number of camp victims (allegedly 700,000 of them), but also warns of abuses of the Jasenovac camp from the 1990s to the present day – abuses that stem from the efforts to minimize or deny Ustaša crimes. The author states that the abuse of the Bleiburg theme began among Croatian emigrants, and in the 1990s it spread to their homeland, where, in the author's words, "it served political propaganda much more than the deserved reverence for the Bleiburg victims." Along with some alternative perspectives on an already analysed topic, on Jasenovac and Bleiburg, the focus of this chapter clearly stays grounded in horrifying atrocities committed by Ustaše perpetrators in the Jasenovac camp.

The first in several chapters on a most controversial Jasenovac theme, here conceptualized as "Counting," is "Jasenovac and Bleiburg between Facts and Manipulations" by Vladimir Geiger and Martina Grahek Ravančić. The authors contrast, in relation to numbers, real scholarly views on the Jasenovac camp and the Bleiburg case with the positions of self-proclaimed experts. The chapter presents a critical reading of a series of works to date, especially those related to the victims of World War II, focusing in particular on the number of victims and victims' lists. Grahek Ravančić and Geiger agree with the thesis of Mihael Sobolevski that, in the cases of Jasenovac and Bleiburg, the research of human losses was very often not founded on reality and left it to the individual and collective imaginations. Extreme situations have been created on the basis of extreme traumas. By critiquing "mythomaniac," selective, and one-sided claims, in both the Serbian and Croatian contexts, this chapter provides an important contribution to the study of Bleiburg and Jasenovac.

Dragan Cvetković's chapter, "Jasenovac Concentration Camp and its Role in the Destruction of the NDH People – Calculation of the Possible Number of Victims Based on the Partially Revised 1964 Census," provides in-depth analysis of this most controversial topic related to World War II – the number of Jasenovac camp's victims. Based on the partially revised Yugoslav victim list from 1964, the author presents his estimations of the number of civilians killed in the NDH, and civilian victims of the Jasenovac camp. The victims are also stratified according to their national structure, the dynamics of casualties between 1941 and 1945, and numerous other criteria. As a reference point for comparison, he uses demographic data on the population in the territory of the Kingdom of Yugoslavia, and later in the territory of the Independent State of Croatia. Cvetković also supports the obtained results with archival sources and research articles, as well as with nonfiction prose. According to the author, his focus was placed on civilian victims who died in the "complex and layered war fought on the territory of the NDH, in which several warring parties participated (...), [those were the] repressive and military forces of the NDH, and insurgents who eventually divided themselves into Partisans and Chetniks." The results presented in the article single out Serbs, Jews and Roma as national/ethnic groups exposed to the greatest persecution. Those groups also had the most casualties in proportion to their share of the total population. Dragan Cvetković's work is a particularly valuable contribution to understanding the nature of the suffering in World War II, the Independent State of Croatia, and the Jasenovac concentration camp, about which there are still extremely pronounced disagreements on the Croatian and Serbian sides.

The last in the chapters on "Counting," as well as an important contribution to the Roma Holocaust in NDH is Danijel Vojak's "Forgotten Victims of World War II, or the Suffering of the Roma in the Independent State of Croatia, 1941–1945." Based on historiographical and journalism, archives, and the press, this chapter displays and explains the suffering of the Roma during World War II in the NDH. In the introductory discussion, the author reviews the topic of Roma victims in Croatian and European historiographies and discusses public attitudes towards Roma victims from the postwar period to the present day. It was emphasized that Roma victims became the subject of research in the Yugoslav historiography quite late, in the mid-1980s. Later in the chapter, the author deals with numerous phenomena important for the genesis and understanding of the persecution and suffering of Roma in the NDH. In this overview, Vojak goes from the enactment of racial laws through attempts to enumerate the Roma, over the alleged solution of the "Gypsy issue" by colonizing and exempting "White Roma" from persecution, to the deportation of the Roma population to the Jasenovac camp and their mass losses. The question on human losses of the Roma population in Jasenovac camp is extensively discussed.

When it comes to describing a Jasenovac tragedy, the present volume brings an important contribution by Vjeran Pavlaković, titled "Contested Cultural Memory in Jasenovac: A Post-Communist/Post-Socialist Memorial Museum in an Era of Historical Revisionism." This chapter discusses the role of the memorial in Jasenovac as a space of cultural memory (institutionalized memory) and its (lack of) success to be an instrument and space of education about World War II. The author raises additional questions related to the absence of successful examples of such institutions in Croatia and the absence of a deliberate public debate. Instead, as per Pavlaković, there is constant turmoil over World War II memories, especially when important commemorations take place. The author presents a broader set of difficulties related to prospects of World War II museums, highlighting that they should competently deal with ethnic and national cleavages during the war and afterwards, and contribute to development of a national culture of memory. In Croatia, oversaturated with politics of memory, it would therefore be crucial for political elites and museologists to harmonize the design of permanent exhibitions dealing with the twentieth century so that they convey pluralistic narratives about the past, in line with the European paradigms of coming to terms with the legacy of the Holocaust, World War II, and the Communist dictatorship.

The work of Ana Kršinić–Lozica, "Jasenovac on Film: Manipulations of Identities and the Performance of Memory," is a valuable contribution to "Describing." The chapter analyzes four documentaries, which approach Jasenovac in different, often conflicting and mutually contradictory ways when it comes to memory politics and identity construction. The films analysed are: "Jasenovac" directed by Gustav Gavrin and Kosta Hlavaty (1945), "Jasenovac" by Bogdan Žižić (1966), "Blood and Ashes of Jasenovac" by Lordan Zafranović (1983), and "Jasenovac – the Truth" by Jakov Sedlar (2016). The works are strongly grounded in concrete examples, persuasively pointing to the power of documentaries in the construction of collective memories and identities. Ultimately, an analysis of documentaries shows that this genre does not only serve the representation of memory, but above all is a memory act in itself.

The last of the chapters in the present volume is the work of Mario Kevo: "The International Committee of the Red Cross and Camps on the Territory of the Independent State of Croatia with Special Reference to the Jasenovac Camp." This chapter stands as an important contribution to the discussion of revisionism understood as Holocaust denial. Based on original material from the Archives of the International Committee of the Red Cross at Geneva, as well as on research literature, memoirs, and other primary sources, the chapter provides very interesting information about the relationship between the NDH and the International Committee of the Red Cross (ICRC) as well as ICRC's assistance to the Jasenovac camp detainees, especially those left without any institutional protections, which is one of the most important controversies related to Jasenovac.

Finally, we bring to all interested readers this updated, second (English) edition in our sincere desire to finally contribute to better historical transparency of Jasenovac camp and thus to enable future research. At the same time, we feel obliged to warn about general Holocaust distortion, which has not bypassed Croatia and neighbouring countries. We also believe that this second edition, which attempted to offer a more general context on Jasenovac camp within Holocaust and genocide studies, memory studies, and nationalism studies, will thereby find its true value in these areas of research.

Andriana Benčić Kužnar, Stipe Odak and Danijela Lucić
Editorial Board

Part I
Naming

1 Jasenovac Uses and Misuses of the Past

Manipulations and Historical Revisionism Surrounding the Biggest WWII Camp in the Balkans

Stipe Odak, Andriana Benčić Kužnar and Danijela Lucić

Introduction: Understanding and Communicating Traumatic Past

For decades the horrors of World War II have been challenging our abilities for understanding and representation. Writing about the Holocaust, Susan Sontag indicated that it was an event that escapes intelligibility, a tragedy that cannot be comprehended.[1] Churchill's famous claim that frightful cruelties on the Eastern Front were "a crime without a name"[2] pointed to a perplexing characteristic of something that appeared so excessive that it goes beyond standard concepts of language. *Having no name* does not imply a lack of existence. To the contrary, the 'crime without a name' existed to such a degree that it challenged all previous ways of understanding social order and its disintegration, moving closer to the theoretical extreme of Arendt's 'radical evil.'[3] The ability to understand, represent, communicate, and share a common past lies at the heart of social life. Therefore, positioning oneself within a community implies positioning oneself within a narrative[4] that the community shares about its past – not just any past, however, but the past that 'matters,' the past that is organically tied to social life and has a bearing on it.[5]

It does not surprise us that social memories of groups are often marked with collective memories of tragedies, phenomena that Alexander terms 'cultural traumas.' Unlike individual traumas, which are frequently suppressed and denied, collectives react to traumas by constructing stories, framing, and symbolic representations. Therefore, collective traumas are inseparable from the sense of community (the "we"),[6] solidarity, and responsibility.[7] It follows that collective traumas are, to a lesser degree, replications of actual painful past events and much more a shared framework of understanding the past and future. "Rather than descriptions of what is," collective traumas are according to Alexander, "arguments about what must have been and what should be."[8] In practical terms, what differentiates cultural trauma from a 'dispassionate description' is the element of intentionality that every cultural trauma

DOI: 10.4324/9781003326632-2

contains. By constructing cultural traumas, groups "not only cognitively identify the existence and source of human suffering but may also take on board some significant responsibility for it."[9] Cultural trauma is, succinctly put, a "symbolic – cum – emotional representation" shared within a collective.[10] What to do, however, when such a past needs to be transmitted, but contains elements that are almost unfathomable, events that dramatically question all our previous worldviews, representations that cast doubt upon our very notions of a community and a possibility thereof? From a historical perspective, there seem to be three principal strategies to cope with the challenges of understanding and representations of the past: (1) developing new concepts; (2) presenting the scale of suffering in numeric terms; (3) describing the scale of horror mimetically through linguistic or visual means. All of these categories, however, had their particular predicament of being employed in a factual as well as a symbolic way. It is not a surprise that the main 'battles' over memory and representation have concentrated in three areas, those of *naming*, *counting*, and *describing*. Furthermore, it is essential to notice that the battles of representation are never equally dispersed over the whole scope of history. Instead, they are concentrated around several axial events or *topoi* that are perceived as gravitating centers of larger processes. Auschwitz, as the central representational axis of the Holocaust, is one such example. In the context of former Yugoslavia, Jasenovac had a similar status.[11] In both historiography and collective memory, Jasenovac became a *pars–pro–toto* of all horrors committed during World War II in the territories of the Independent State of Croatia (Nezavisna Država Hrvatska, henceforth: NDH), but also a synecdoche of guilt and responsibility for those crimes.

Jasenovac: The Symbolic Center of the Traumatic Past

Already during World War II, Jasenovac was recognized as a particularly dark spot in Croatian history, the symbolic place of shame for the crimes of the regime. In his report to the *US Office of Strategic Services*, Croatian cleric in exile Augustin Juretić wrote that "the story of Jasenovac is the blackest page of the pro-Nazi Ustaše regime."[12] Even some high-ranking officials of the NDH viewed Jasenovac with shame. Vinko Nikolić, an emigre to Argentina after the war, asserted in 1969 that "Jasenovac is a great Croatian wound, and an even greater shame, for which even today our souls ache and our faces burn for shame."[13] During the Yugoslav period, Jasenovac received different symbolic meanings. In Perica's words, it became "a shrine of the civil religion of brotherhood and unity and a memorial to the Partisan struggle in which all ethnic groups and minorities took part and suffered."[14] Mojzes concurs, stating that "for the former Yugoslavia, Jasenovac is a symbol subsuming all the horrendous genocidal actions that transpired primarily against Serbs, Jews, and Roma but also against the political enemies of the Nezavisna Država Hrvatska (NDH)."[15] Dissolution of Yugoslavia, preceded with rising inter-ethnic tensions, led to another rendering of Jasenovac in historiography and collective memory. Among Serbian nationalists, Jasenovac was matched only by Kosovo in its symbolic power to represent national tragedy. Due to its importance, it also became a tool of war propaganda directed against Croats.[16] On the other hand, amidst Croatian nationalists, it was presented as the founding stone of anti-Croatian 'myths' and sometimes described as a place of Croatian martyrhood. In its campaign program for 1992 elections, the right-wing party in Croatia, Hrvatska Stranka Prava (Croatian Party of Rights), thus characterized Jasenovac as "the greatest symbol of the enduring discrimination against dead and living Croats ... Jasenovac is the monument of the Great Serbian myth about the genocide [committed by] Croats. It was raised at the place of a wartime prison camp in which several hundred people of various nationalities [among which the largest number were Croats] were killed."[17]

Even professional historians, who were trying to counter ideological misuse of Jasenovac, sometimes used this name both in its concrete and metaphorical sense. Serbian demographer Bogoljub Kočović, for instance, in an interview from 1998 thus explained that in one of his approximations of war victims, he used Jasenovac as a symbol for all other Ustaša concentration camps.[18] The aftermath of the wars in the 1990s did bring some improvement in historical clarifications regarding Jasenovac. The symbolic use of the word *Jasenovac* nonetheless persisted. In a recent review of a comic novel, *Ponori Zla* (Abysses of Evil), Serbian historian Dević stated that Jasenovac became "for all times the symbol of all the horrors that Serbs suffered" over different territories in Croatia and Bosnia and Herzegovina.[19] On the other hand, Croatian publicist Blanka Matković wrote recently that Jasenovac is "the symbol of all lies we have been stuffed with over the last 70 years."[20]

Problems with the Symbolic Use of Jasenovac

The problem with the symbolic use of places of terror becomes visible in tendencies to instrumentalize *terrorscapes*[21] for other purposes, for example, rejecting or defending the idea of statehood. "Using the name Jasenovac as a symbol," Mojzes claims,

> many Serbs overreached by rejecting the very idea of an independent Croatian state and regarded all who favored the idea [...] as being guilty of the genocide. [...] In their zeal for self–defense, the Catholic Church and many Croats have found themselves accused of being Holocaust deniers or genocide deniers, as they fall way short of acknowledging responsibility where it would be morally appropriate to do so.[22]

Therefore, the contestation around Jasenovac seldom places a clear focus on the concrete system of World War II camps in the vicinity of the eponymous town. More often, this contestation is the only introduction into larger debates about statehood, ideology, ethnic identity, or even current political legitimacy – resulting in a situation that can (perhaps cynically) be described as follows: Who rules the representation of Jasenovac, rules the representation of national history. Consequently, lines between historical facts and community narratives can become blurred or even entirely erased. The main predicament of such a situation is the loss of the ability to reach mutual understanding and ethical consensus. If the past is presented predominately through community narratives, then there is no common ground around which those narratives can gravitate. To be clear, we do not hold that it is possible to present history and memory as diametrically opposite extremes along the objectivity-bias axes. We argue instead that both history and memory should be perceived as two different modes of approaching the past and be used as mutual correctives. While history in some cases can be manipulated from 'above' leaving memories and oral histories as a more reliable deposits of past events, memories are perpetually in danger of becoming biased, self-exculpatory, and exclusionary narratives.

In summary, our main argument is that continuous struggles over Jasenovac stem from three main sources: (1) inability to justly represent the immense scope of historical tragedy; (2) merging of emotional, symbolic, and factual discourse in construction of collective traumas; and (3) frequent use of Jasenovac as a symbol for larger phenomena. In practice, those struggles were manifested in contestation over *naming* (i.e., whether Jasenovac was a part of a genocidal policies of NDH or 'merely' a labor camp for state prisoners); *numbers* (i.e., how many victims died in Jasenovac Camp); and *descriptions* (i.e., museological representations of the conditions in the camp). In the following paragraphs, we will focus more closely on these elements.

Past and Current Struggles around Jasenovac

The historiography around Jasenovac is a complex one, and it went through different phases. The first phase was marked with a state-controlled historical discourse on Jasenovac, which lasted, broadly speaking, from 1945 until the second half of 1980s. The second phase was a period of the rise of nationalist discourse surrounding Jasenovac in Serbia (second half of the 1980s onwards) that coincided with first waves of deliberate independent research about the number of victims of Jasenovac. The third phase was characterized with the rise of nationalist discourse about Jasenovac in Croatia (the early 1990s onwards), followed by the publishing of an ever-larger amount of independent historiographical research about Jasenovac in Croatia and Serbia (late 1990s/early 2000s onwards). And, finally, we can detect a new reactionary phase of historical revisions concentrated in the mid- and late 2010s. The first phase of state-controlled discourse about Jasenovac cannot be called revisionism, since there was virtually no independent historical research that could yield a broader consensus among researchers. Subsequent phases of nationalist historiography in Serbia and Croatia could only be tentatively termed historical revisionism, since this historiography mostly reacted against, or reused, previous state-controlled Yugoslav narratives, adapting them to their political agendas, while ignoring more scientifically sound literature published abroad. Perhaps a more opportune term for that period would be 'historical manipulations,' since standards of truly independent academic research were only to be established afterward. In contrast, a new phase of 'reinterpretation' of history, which appeared in the mid- and late 2010s, can be described as proper historical revisionism that challenges facts around which there is already overwhelming consensus among experts. Although Jasenovac has the most prominent place in historical debates in Croatia and Serbia, those debates occur in different contexts. In Croatia, broader topics that involve Jasenovac include the rehabilitation of the NDH, Communist repression that crosses into strong anti-Communism with nationalist connotations, the role of religious communities during the war, and competition for victimization narratives between Serbs and Croats.[23]

The revisionist current in Croatia has its roots in the mid-1990s.[24] Namely, the first wave of publications that challenged previous statements about Jasenovac appeared with the establishment of the Croatian state, after bloody wars that followed the fall of Yugoslavia. Yet, in the recent five years, we are witnessing an actual rise of historical revisionism in Croatia, a rise resulting in a considerable amount of literature that not just outstrips its predecessors, but also draws the attention of the international scientific community to the Holocaust and genocide in NDH.[25] Thus, there is certainly a strong need to warn, to examine, and to outline the most important determinants of contemporary revisionist voices in Croatia regarding Jasenovac, as well as to try to understand and to explain which social circumstances spur those voices' existence.

Approximately in the century's second decade, and especially accentuated in most recent years, a rather heterogeneous group consisting mostly of professional historians and scientists from other disciplines in Croatia, have claimed that Jasenovac camp was not a death camp nor a concentration camp whatsoever. In their view, Jasenovac was just a collection and labor camp. They also insist that the majority of deaths were committed by Communists in the subsequent Communist/Socialist period, after 1945,[26] thus suggesting that the camp continued to function after 1945 (against historical consensus). This group also implies that one cannot speak, in the strict sense, of the Holocaust against Jews and the genocide against Serbs and Roma, thus relativizing the organized character of the crimes. In Croatian revisionist narrative, the NDH ultimately was not a repressive, racial, and genocidal (puppet) state, but the legitimate state that has taken counterinsurgency operations against Croatian and Serbian Communists and Serbian Chetniks, which Croatian revisionists identify as the main and most numerous victims of the NDH.[27] Although revisionism in Croatia stays outside the mainstream of the academic community and is not supported by ruling political elites, the authors of revisionist books and articles are not on the margins of the society. Some of these authors are employed in influential Croatian scientific and cultural institutions, and their books are supported by well-established publishing houses.[28] Therefore

Croatian revisionists gained a visible social platform, especially through social media, and they gathered themselves around existing and newly founded NGOs that from the beginning were openly, and extremely right-wing, politically oriented. Even though Croatia always showcased difficulties in trying to establish a stable and balanced historical narrative on Jasenovac, which is therefore still not easily translated into political memory by the state,[29] the common attitude within Croatia towards Jasenovac camp and today's site of memory rests on the opinion that Ustaša terror together with Jasenovac as its most prominent expression, were the biggest shame in Croatian history. This is in line with the internationally adopted historical narratives on Ustaše and their closeness to Nazi Germany. As recently highlighted by Kasapović in *Encyclopedia of Genocide*, NDH is placed into the category as one of the 15 deadliest regimes of the twentieth century.[30] Also, in *The Historiography of the Holocaust*, the NDH is listed among especially active executors of the Holocaust in Eastern Europe.[31]

In the Serbian context, the phase of 'historical manipulations' was marked with frequent use of exaggerated approximations of the number of victims in Jasenovac camp. In the last decade in Serbia, there were significant improvements in scientific research of that issue and, consequently, one can detect, at least among mainstream historians, a certain distancing from previous historiography. At the same time, almost all high-ranking politicians still refuse to refer to those discoveries. Jasenovac thus remains an axial point of national victimhood identity, but also a symbol that is used to vindicate nationalist political programs (past and present). Even though in both cases (Croatian and Serbian) a strong anti-Communist sentiment is present, they are differently voiced. Croatian revisionists present Communists as a group that simply continued to use the premises of the former camps for imprisonment and execution of new political enemies, while those revisionists place only a symbolic 'burden' of guilt on Ustaše, whom they perceive as those who desired an independent Croatian state. In the case of Serbian revisionism or manipulations with Jasenovac, Communists are seen as historically irresponsible ideologues who covered up the terror of past crimes in the interest of the utopian ideal of 'brotherhood and unity.'[32] Many controversial issues surrounding World War II and NDH might have led to constructive dialogue if approached argumentatively and scientifically. However, when brought to the social arena by revisionist historians and publicists with less than ideal respect for historical facts, they rather lead to new 'memory firestorms.' In such situations, Jasenovac remains the most potent symbol that continues to fuel ideological and ethnonational divisions domestically and regionally. On the international plan, the rise of revisionism undermines better understanding of World War II in the Balkans and has a negative influence on the broader culture of remembrance.

In the following paragraphs we will now turn to a more specific analysis of the aforementioned strategies of 'battles' over Jasenovac: *naming*, *counting*, and *describing*.

Naming

Speaking about her experiences in the 1940s, Ruth Kluger, a concentration camp survivor, wrote that the Holocaust "had no name yet, and hence it wasn't even an idea, only an event,"[33] adding that "[a] concept without a name is like a stray dog or feral cat. To domesticate it, you have to call it something."[34] It is not a surprise then that such evil required a new name, a new concept coined by Lemkin as 'genocide.' Very soon, the word 'genocide' received a specific aura of exclusivity, becoming the term to describe the most extreme violations of legal norms. In the 1985 *Report on the Question of the Prevention and Punishment of the Crime of Genocide*, prepared by the UN Special Rapporteur Benjamin Whitaker, genocide represents "the ultimate crime and the gravest violation of human rights it is possible to commit."[35] However, aside from its legally defined aspects, the concept of genocide carries specific moral connotations and is often used as an emotionally laden metaphor that aims to underline the scope of a collective tragedy. In some cases, as Totten remarks, the term 'genocide' is used "to capture the ear of even the most blasé public" or to 'hype' the cause they advocate.[36] The term *Holocaust*, intended to describe a very specific and unprecedented attempt to entirely destroy the whole Jewish population,[37] had a similar fate of frequent appropriations and issues. Bruce McDonald criticizes the 'competition' in the Balkans to have their own 'Holocaust' and 'genocide.'[38] The Balkans is by no means an exceptional case. In one of his last interviews, Raul Hilberg describes the problematic use of the terms 'Holocaust' and 'genocide' that are decontextualized to such a point that even cruelty to animals is presented as a 'Holocaust.'[39] In short, the very terms of 'genocide,' 'Holocaust,' and 'Auschwitz' have all been matters of contestation when it comes to Jasenovac.

For historical revisionist on the Croatian side, it is thus important to present Jasenovac 'merely' as a camp for those who were political enemies of the state, therefore detaching it from the term 'genocide.' Although cases of politicide in their scope and horror can be completely comparable to those of genocide, on the symbolic and emotional-evocative level the execution of political enemies seems to create an impression of a less-serious crime. On the other side, certain Serbian authors insisted on strong parallels between the Holocaust and Jasenovac, without proper contextualization.[40] Thus, in both Croatian and Serbian, the concrete terms are symptoms of a larger and long-term struggle over the representations of tragedies, as will be illustrated in the following paragraphs.

Jasenovac: Part of a Genocidal Strategy or a Political Prison?

In June 2014, a group of Croatian historians established an NGO entitled *Društvo za istraživanje trostrukog logora Jasenovac* (Society for Research of the Triple Camp Jasenovac).[41] Their main premise, mentioned in the title, is to prove the continuity of the Jasenovac concentration camp well beyond the end of World War II, arguing that the terrors of the Communist-controlled camp exceeded those that took place during the period of NDH. However, a main thrust of their research is to oppose claims of genocidal actions of NDH. In a 2015 article, for instance, they claim that "nobody was killed in Jasenovac just because the person was a Serb or Orthodox," presenting executions in the camp only as a matter of ad-hoc revenge.[42] The article, censoriously, does not mention legal provisions (Croatian: *zakonske odredbe*) that precisely targeted ethnic and racial groups, enacted within the first weeks of NDH. Razum, a member of the society, however, acknowledges the provisions' existence but argues that NDH only partially and unwillingly included racial laws in their legislation and that these laws were not "a product of Croatian people," but only a consequence of alignment with then-existing legislations in Germany, Italy, Hungary, and so forth. Consequently, according to Razum, those legal provisions did not cause anyone's persecution just because the person was a Jew or a Roma.[43] Razum and Jonić, as Mataušić demonstrates in her contribution to the present volume, also stated that the juridical status of legal provisions was lesser than laws, and that Jews and Roma did not suffer due to those legal provisions on racial purity but because of the "general regulations about the treatment of undesirable individuals or wrongdoers (in other words regulations that treated Jews and non-Jews equally) or in worse cases, often without the backing of any regulations."[44] In reality, as Croatian historians Geiger and Mataušić separately argue, so-called legal provisions had very clear strength and force of law in the NDH,[45] and the NDH was among the first puppet states that included harsh racial laws/legal provisions on Jewish claims of citizenship (4 June 1941) and seizure of Jewish property (adopted on 27 August 1941; 9 October 1941; 30 October 1942) soon after establishment of the NDH.[46] Kasapović underlines that the real consequences of these laws/provisions and NDH policies resulted in the deaths of 75–80 percent of Jews who in 1941 lived in the NDH, which is among highest percentages of Jewish deaths in Nazi-occupied Europe.[47] In short, there is a large amount of evidence that the crimes against certain ethnic and religious groups in NDH amount to what we currently know as the crime of genocide. However, a certain number of historians in Croatia attempt to deny the appropriateness of that term and describe racial laws merely as ineffective and externally imposed by part of the legislature, as stated above. Substantially, revisionists in Croatia are continuously aiming to relativize the shameful place that Jasenovac holds in the national and Yugoslav history, stating that Jasenovac is rather continuously used as a part of symbolic arsenal for embarrassing Croats and putting shame on Croatian history. In the already mentioned revisionist view, which is denying any genocidal nature of the Jasenovac camp, and consequently the genocidal nature of the NDH itself, Jasenovac is seen as immense burden set over Croats – one which puts in question all the aspects of a Croatian 'heroic' past. As stated earlier, among Croatian nationalists and revisionists, Jasenovac is seen as the foundation stone of anti-Croatian 'myths' and as the greatest symbol of an enduring discrimination against Croats. Having in mind the central revisionist assumption that the whole history of the embarrassment of the Croatian past is narrowed down to Jasenovac camp, it is also easy to see that the main revisionist idea is therefore to deconstruct what they call "Jasenovac myth," over which they aim to relativize and finally deny the Holocaust and genocide committed in the NDH. And Jasenovac camp is beyond doubt, the most prominent substantive and symbolic expression of NDH racial and genocidal politics.[48]

On the other hand, in the Serbian political context, the term genocide is occasionally used in an extended and symbolic sense that goes beyond the historical and legal meaning of the term. In the first issue of the newsletter of the Jasenovac Research Institute, Simo Brdar, curator of the Donja Gradina Memorial Area, thus mentions "spiritual genocide" over Serbian people, referring to the destruction of churches.[49] President of Republic of Srpska (BiH) Željka Cvijanović stated in May 2019, during the commemoration of camp victims in Donja Gradina (former part and the biggest mass killing field of the Jasenovac complex of concentration camps), that the suffering that took place in Donja Gradina was even "more than genocide." In her words: "Neither legal nor moral terminology contains the term appropriate to qualify the crimes, lack of humanity and outrageous nature of execution methods or the ideological–political concept that stood behind them."[50] At the same time, she used the occasion to legitimize the existence of the Republic of Srpska as an institution that in the 1990s protected Serbian people from even greater suffering during the war. Use of the term *genocide* for direct political purposes was yet clearer in the speech of former President of the Republic of Srpska Milorad Dodik, during 2017 commemoration in Donja Gradina, when he asked the following:

> How could we allow to be sided by the ideology that aimed to present Serbian suffering not as genocide, [the ideology which] now allows to some followers of the criminals to say that those were victims of war, thus equating suffering on all sides?[51]

In the same speech, Dodik presented the Republic of Srpska as a safeguard against suffering, saying: "If in 1941 we had had the Republic of Srpska, Jasenovac would not have happened. That is why the Republic of Srpska is created."[52] Cvijanović's insistence that crimes that took place to require a new concept for something that is "more than genocide" illustrates how struggles over *naming* are far from being politically neutral. The direct political use of the term is even more visible in Dodik's representation of the Republic of Srpska as an entity that was allegedly established to prevent a new 'Jasenovac,' that is, genocide over the Serbian population.

Counting

A number of victims is arguably the most consistent red thread of all discussions about Jasenovac. From the end of World War II up until recently, different approximations of the number of the camp's victims varied from several thousand to over a million, which is a significant discrepancy (to put it mildly).[53] One cannot but wonder as to why the number of victims became such a central question to the Jasenovac tragedy, and why estimates of the number differs to such an extent. A clue can be found in the initial problem that we represented – that of the excessive tragedies that escape representations.

Numbers, simply put, can be a useful strategy to capture the immense; they can serve as a condensed representation of the suffering, as a memento that can be easily recalled and visualized. The essential characteristic of numbers is their scalability, which was then translated to the nature of suffering – the higher the numbers, the greater the suffering. Although people generally subscribe to the idea that "even one innocent victim is too much," some comparison is often unavoidable. Therefore, the scale of the tragedy and, consequently, the scale of suffering and trauma becomes expressed in numbers. At that point, numbers of victims are no longer playing a merely pragmatic role; they become 'symbolic truths,' shorthand for the suffering in its entirety. For that reason, changing the numbers implies redaction of the tragedy itself. Numbers thus are not merely perceived as a documentary statement but can have a symbolic role as well. Although it is difficult to test this claim empirically, it could also be the case that rounded numbers – such as 'six million' or 700,000 – are easier to remember and be used as a representation of collective suffering than any non-rounded number of victims that might change over time due to new discoveries. As it was extensively presented in the contribution of Geiger and Grahek Ravančić, manipulation of the number of victims in Jasenovac came from different sources. Immediately after the war, the number of victims was linked to the claims for bigger wartime reparations that Yugoslavia presented during the International Tribunal in Nürnberg and the Paris Conference on Reparations. In that context, the Federal People's Republic of Yugoslavia reported 1.7 million individual human losses, out of which at least 600,000 victims were said to have been killed in Jasenovac.[54] A report of the 1946 State Commission for the Investigation of Crimes Committed by the Occupiers and their Collaborators presented a similar approximation of Jasenovac victims, without any clear methodological basis for those claims. As Geiger and Grahek Ravančić assert, this report was the "source on which the myth about Jasenovac is based."[55] Since subsequent state commissions that aimed at preparing a comprehensive list on individual victims could not corroborate those approximations, they were put under publication embargo, while the number of 700,000 victims of Jasenovac, according to Pavlaković, "was considered sacrosanct in Communist-era Yugoslavia."[56] The struggle around the number of victims especially escalated during the late 1980s, when certain Serbian nationalist historians used unrealistic numbers of up to two million "Serbian victims of Jasenovac" as a part of war propaganda that provoked opposite reactions among Croatian nationalist currents that tried to minimize the numbers.[57] At the same time, as of the late 1980s, there also have been growing efforts to establish the number of victims based on censuses and statistical approximations and, when those sources became available, on individual victims' lists. The most important census was prepared by the Federal Yugoslav Commission for the Registration of War Victims in 1964.[58] In the 2000s, the Jasenovac Memorial Site in Croatia and the Museum of Genocide Victims in Serbia, independently prepared lists of individual victims based on the said census, that is, the register of individual victims from 1964, and a number of additional sources.[59] Those two databases generally converge around the number of victims that ranges between 80,000 and 130,000, which was at the same time significantly less than the previously promoted number of 700,000 in Serbia, and yet much bigger than certain nationalist circles in Croatia would want. In order to deny genocidal crimes of the NDH committed against Serbs, Roma, Jews, Croatian anti-fascists, political enemies, and victims of other nationalities, revisionist authors in Croatia clearly centered their attacks, especially from 2012 to 2016, on the database containing the name list of Jasenovac victims, conducted by the Jasenovac Memorial Site.[60] In line with the afore-mentioned revisionist stance that Jasenovac rather stands as a symbol of "all lies Croats have been stuffed with over the last 70 years,"[61] downsizing of Jasenovac camp casualties continued to occupy the scope of Croatian nationalist and revisionist narratives. As an illustration, more than thirty articles were published in the Croatian weekly, *Hrvatski tjednik*, from December 2015 until December 2017, all to generally discredit the Jasenovac victim database. Bringing mocking titles such as "New Jasenovac Victims from 21st Century;"[62] or "United States Holocaust Memorial Museum in Jaws of Jasenovac Myth,"[63] when referring to the USHMM's decision to take over the Jasenovac list of victims and include it in their database, revisionists attended to demonstrate that the entire Jasenovac victim database is false, citing numerous individual examples of human lives that have been lost in different camps or places. Yet, the Jasenovac Memorial Site itself stated that the database is incomplete and asked everyone who has information about victims to refer to the institution in order to improve data.[64] Regardless, the intention of revisionists to claim the entire Jasenovac Memorial Site's victim list database is false and feeds the thesis that in the NDH Serbs, Jews and Roma were not killed, but that Partisans and Communists were killing 'Croatian patriots' in the immediate postwar period, after 1945.[65] They also often accentuate that only a few thousand victims died within Jasenovac camp during World War II,[66] mostly due to various diseases, the most prominent of which was typhus.[67] On the Serbian side, manipulation with numbers is primarily visible in the still-ongoing insistence on symbolic numbers of 700,000 victims of Jasenovac that Stefan Radojković, collaborator of the Museums of Genocide Victims in Belgrade recently described as "mythical," underlying the necessity of objective findings based on the individual victims' registers.[68] However, still in 2008, Milan Bulajić, president of the Fund for Genocide Research and former director of the same Museum of Genocide Victims, insisted that the number of 700,000 is not the 'symbolic' number, but the number of real victims, simply referring to approximations of survivors and the fact that the same number appeared even in some Croatian publications.[69] Jasenovac Research Institute, situated in New York, as Geiger and Grahek Ravančić stress,[70] used to promote the same number. However, the situation seems to change over time. While some members of that Institute put forward a number of more than half a million victims in the first phase of World War II, other members seem to have a more moderate discourse. For instance, in the first newsletter of the revisionist Jasenovac Research Institute, Miletić stated this:

> Estimates of the number killed in the Jasenovac concentration camp vary from 80,000 to 750,000, and when, in addition to this figure, are added the 180,000 people who were driven from their homes and the 240,000 people who were forcibly converted to Roman Catholicism, one gets a full picture of the genocidal crimes committed in the Independent State of Croatia by the Ustaše regime.[71]

However, even in the same publication, Simo Brdar, the curator of the Donja Gradina Memorial Area writes the following: "Facts indicate that from April 1941 until mid-August 1942 around 600,000 Serbs were killed in the NDH in the most brutal manner. Around 180,000 Serbs were deported to Serbia during the war."[72] Moreover, Srboljub Živanović, president of another NGO, entitled the International Commission for the Truth on Jasenovac, repeatedly insisted on the number of 700,000 victims.[73]

In short, the individual list of victims of Jasenovac concentration camp, an ongoing research project that is constantly updated, became one of the main targets of revisionist attacks both from Croatian and Serbian side. Often, the very fact that the number of victims changes in light of new discoveries (which is from the perspective of historiography, a usual and expected process) is perceived as a sign of unreliability and/or falsification. This does not surprise if we carry in mind the difference between historical/analytical approach to victimhood and a communal construction thereof. Nevertheless, attempts to exaggerate or reduce the number of victims inevitably carry ethical problems that stem precisely from the status of the victims. Mojzes notes,

> [i]n the case of exaggeration, we are at least symbolically destroying additional, though illusory, members of the victim group. By reducing the numbers, we are denying the very real suffering, torture, and deaths that did occur, pretending as if these people never lived. The effect is destroying them twice – once when they died and now annihilating them and their memory again.[74]

Describing and Exhibiting

The third mode of representation of tragedies is a description of particular horrors that took place during World War II. In some internationally known cases, such as the one of Nazi soap bars made of human fat, with abbreviations

RIF, horrific images of torture were proven to be fabricated.[75] It could be that those narratives were created out of a desire to underline even stronger the inhuman nature of the Nazi regime. However, the same narratives that later fail the test of historical research are then used by historical revisionists to cast doubt on the historiography as a whole, arguing that one 'myth' is only a part of larger 'mythology.' A parallel problem arises when it comes to museological representation of terrors. Virtually all museums of the Holocaust had their institutional history and debates over the optimal ways to represent the terrors. While common goals of all museological institutions are historical accuracy, veracity, and responsibility in representing past tragedies, the solid methods of representation can vary from informative panels to concrete exhibits of alleged human remains, as was the case in Buchenwald with the notorious lampshade made of human skin that later became removed from the current permanent exhibition.[76] While there is a general consensus that traumatic events should be represented, it is not as evident that the best strategy for achieving it is the 'mimetic' representation of trauma through new trauma, that is, by creating an experience of shock among visitors. The role of memorial museums, as it is stated in the International Memorial Museums Charter,[77] is to nourish pluralistic culture of remembrance, especially of "public crimes against minorities." Moreover, their humanitarian and educational mission requires them to encourage empathy with the victims avoiding any commemoration "in the form of revenge, hate and resentments between different groups of victims."[78] When it comes to representation of perpetrators, the aim is not to 'demonize' them but rather to demonstrate how their actions stemmed from "their ideology, aims and motives." The curators of the new Buchenwald exhibition presented their aim as a desire to show "how it could have happened" but "without patronizing, moralizing or emotionally overpowering" visitors.[79] The main issue with retraumatization through images of terror is the fact that the state of shock can effectively prevent understanding and ethical reasoning. Inga Clendinnen speaks about the "Gorgon effect," which amounts to "the sickening of imagination and curiosity and the draining of the will, which afflicts so many of us when we try to look squarely at the persons and processes implicated in the Holocaust."[80] In view of the fact that processes that took place during the Holocaust could have parallels elsewhere, it is not sufficient to be emotionally appalled, but also to understand, in a dual way, how it was possible before, and how it is relevant today. Both of those processes of understanding require not only empathic identification with the victims but also the faculty of judgment and reasoning.

Jasenovac had its own complex history of representation. The third permanent museum exhibition, in particular, aimed to move away from direct representation of massacred bodies and weapons towards victim-oriented narratives, partly motivated by the negative experience with the previous permanent exhibition that was used for ideological and propagandistic purposes in the late 1980s and during the war in the 1990s.[81] That move, however, did not remain without critics.[82] Thus, representations of suffering including the selection of cases, their description and narration, are by no means neutral, and they are currently a major element of contestation between revisionist groups. Revisionist groups in Croatia that desire to represent Jasenovac in a more 'humane' way, just as a collection and labor camp with decent conditions, paint it as a camp in which social and economic life flourished, accompanied with cultural events such as concerts and operettas.[83]

On the other side, groups in Serbia that desire to represent Jasenovac as the most extreme concentration and extermination camp, insist on claims that it was unmatched in cruelty in the whole of human history. In one of the publications of Jasenovac Research Institute, authors desire to present Jasenovac as an unprecedented place of suffering, stating, "By horrors and atrocities committed by the Ustaše, it is without precedent in the history of mankind"[84] and "German camps practiced industrial genocide, but in Jasenovac men, women and children were killed in the most bestial way, the sort of which has never been recorded in history of mankind."[85] Aside from the horrific images of torture and terror, one of the common things is the insistence on historically dubious production of soap from human remains in Donja Gradina. Brdar thus states: "[I]n Donja Gradina Ustaše produced soap out of fat parts of corpses of inmates. The remains that were created by such a process Ustaše dumped into these graves or transported by railway to the right bank of the Sava and dumped them there."[86] Similarly, Živojinović asserts the following: "[W]e will never find out how many Serbs were killed in caldrons for soap production in Donja Gradina, a witness to which is material evidence that is still there."[87]

In January 2018, Israeli historian Gideon Greif curated a propagandistic exhibition on Jasenovac, shown in the United Nations (UN) building in New York, and entitled "Jasenovac – A Right Not to Forget." Even though the exhibition was held on UN premises, the UN stated that the content was exclusively under the authority of organizers, and that its maintenance on UN premises does not imply that UN accepts it.[88] On the basis of the exhibition, Greif published the book *Jasenovac: Auschwitz of the Balkans*, which on the very first pages contains this description: "The Ustaše opened a pregnant women's belly and took out her child (fetus) and they opened up the belly of another woman and they shoved the child (fetus) in."[89] Hence, the title of the book as well as its content, do not differ from previous Serbian revisionist and historically completely inaccurate writings. Greif's narrative might be considered as a copy of *Jasenovac. Balkan Auschwitz*, Milan Bulajić's narrative.[90] Bulajić, as mentioned earlier, was one of the most determined advocates attesting to the genocidal nature of the Croats and the hundreds of thousands of victims of the Jasenovac camp, most of them Serbs. Descriptive presentation of horrors was not without political connotations. Upon the closing of the mentioned exhibition on Jasenovac, Aleksandar Pajić, assistant to the Serbian minister of education, rhetorically asked about the message of the photographs, objects, and letters of victims and responded that they "tell about our civilization, about where we were before and which unethical and inhuman methods we used to create some other states."[91] The current of presenting the nature of the camp through extremely sadistic images has precedent in the late 1980s, when images of dismembered bodies and macabre presentations on torture in Jasenovac were used as a tool of war propaganda. Jovičić thus describes how certain images of historical atrocities, collected in a mobile exhibition, *Dead Opening the Eyes of the Living*, were presented in a Yugoslav barracks just before the war in Yugoslavia, preparing a way to subsequent revenge crimes.[92] The same exhibition was later used as a reference during the genocide case before the International Court of Justice between Croatia and Serbia.[93]

As we can see once again, the contestation is not about the existence of Jasenovac, but the nature of tragedies that happened there, and those tragedies can appear either as minor or as the worst possible, depending on the mental images that the representation of horrors produce. It is a difficult ethical question as to whether such emotionally charged events, such as genocides, can (or should) be represented in an 'objective' or dispassionate way. Nevertheless, one needs to remember that traumas of the past cannot be recreated in the present time, and that every presentation is always a mosaic of the much larger image. While concentration camps were, without a doubt, places of the most horrible dehumanization and macabre innovation centers of torture techniques, they were also places of resistance on the side of victims, no matter how seemingly insignificant it was in the larger scope of the events. Silencing entirely one or another is therefore tantamount to willful misrepresentation.

Conclusion

In this introductory chapter, we aimed to analyze two main questions: (1) why Jasenovac became the central element of historical contestation in the territory of the former Yugoslavia, and (2) which elements of the Jasenovac storytelling are specifically contested. Putting the problem of Jasenovac within the larger framework of social memory construction and – consequently – construction of social reality,[94] we have suggested that discursive construction of Jasenovac cannot be perceived outside its foundational events, those of immense human suffering which is ultimately inexpiable and beyond representation. The challenge of 'describing the indescribable,' yielded in strategies of *conceptual, numeric,* and *descriptive* representation of the past. Each of them, as frequently demonstrated in this article, has also produced a host of debates, predominantly in Croatia and Serbia, which have strong emotional–communal appeal, but questionable historical veracity.

First, at the conceptual level (i.e., *naming*), the focus is on terms 'genocide' and 'Holocaust.' On the one hand, Croatian revisionists try to diminish and relativize the scale of evil and crime by presenting Jasenovac as a camp organized for political enemies (thus negating the term *genocide*. On the other side, certain Serbian authors insist on strong parallels between *Holocaust* and Jasenovac, where Jasenovac, as a matter of fact, is a synonym for the most extreme 'genocide.' In some political discourses, it is even presented as a phenomenon that is "more than genocide." Moreover, individuals on the Croatian side are trying to deconstruct what they call "Jasenovac myth" and to deny altogether the Holocaust and genocide committed in the NDH by placing in question the relevance of racial laws in NDH. According to their claims, Jasenovac is a symbol of enduring discrimination against Croats and a foundation stone of anti-Croatian 'myths.' On the Serbian side, particularly in the political context, the term *genocide* is often used in an extended and symbolic sense that goes beyond the historical and legal meaning of the term: sometimes for destruction of sacral objects, which is deemed "spiritual genocide." The term is also used to promote current political projects, such as legitimization of the Republic of Srpska, especially commemorations in Donja Gradina Memorial Area. Second, *counting* is indisputably the most contentious element of all discussions about Jasenovac. Numbers are frequently seen as convenient to represent suffering, and the logic of the *counting* strategy seems to be the following: the higher the numbers, the greater the suffering. Although approximations of the number of victims have been significantly improved over time thanks to independent research projects, the previous number of 700,000 victims is still frequently used in Serbia. Despite all evidence that convincingly denies that number, many authors on the Serbian side persist and promote hundreds of thousands of victims. On the other side, Croatian revisionists endure in their downsizing of Jasenovac camp casualties, claiming that only a few thousand victims died within Jasenovac camp during World War II. They also insist that predominant causes of those deaths were different diseases not direct executions. The third strategy for representing the terrors of the past, *describing,* also reflects continuous and highly contested (often enraged) history and memory battles over Jasenovac. While revisionist groups in Croatia are trying to paint Jasenovac in a more 'humane' way, as a collection and labor camp with decent living conditions and where cultural and economic life flourished, groups in Serbia try to represent Jasenovac as the most extreme concentration and extermination camp in Europe. In their effort to be as convincing as possible, in their *descriptions* both sides are using misleading stories or historically dubious statements for which there is no conclusive evidence – stories that are nevertheless very vivid and potentially can stir up strong public influence.

Referring to the recent contestations over Jasenovac, which include all of the mentioned strategies (*naming, counting* and *description*), it is obvious (even from a brief overview of the recent past) that Croatian revisionist circles persist in leaning on individuals, associations, and publications that minimize the Jasenovac past by denying the genocidal politics surrounding it, downscaling the number of victims, and presenting the living conditions as decent. In the Serbian context, however, revisionism is detectable in the exaggerated number of victims, the often imprecise and decontextualized use of the word *genocide*, and insistence on descriptions of torture methods that are not always reliable. Those elements are also reflected in daily social and political life, sometimes directly used to promote political projects of Serbian nationalist parties. Ultimately, this volume is a contribution to the complex history of Jasenovac, which has a new opportunity to guide future research and to bring more clarity into different *conceptual, numeric*, and *descriptive* representations of Jasenovac. We cannot predict whether this research project will help to decrease the Holocaust and genocide denial, resistance to responsible dealing with the traumatic past, and manipulation of victims and of historical tragedies. We can, however, restate our conviction that dedicated scientific work is the only viable base in the long process of finding balanced narratives and broad consensus on past traumas. In the context of Jasenovac, if future consensus were reached, the positive ramifications would prove the vast importance of learning lessons from the difficult past of World War II.

Notes

1 Susan Sontag, *Against Interpretation and Other Essays*, Penguin Modern Classics (London: Penguin, 2013), pp. 124.
2 Winston Churchill, "Prime Minister Winston Churchill's Broadcast to the World about the Meeting with President Roosevelt," www.ibiblio.org/pha/timeline/410824awp.html (accessed August 11, 2019).
3 Hannah Arendt, *The Human Condition* (Chicago: University of Chicago Press, 1998), pp. 241.
4 As MacIntyre famously postulated, people in their actions and practices are essentially tellers. Story-telling is first and foremost a social activity, a process of continuous interaction between individuals and groups since: "I can only answer the question 'What am I to do?' if I can answer the prior question 'Of what story or stories do I find myself a part?'" Cf. Alasdair C. MacIntyre, *After Virtue: A Study in Moral Theory*, 3rd ed. (Notre Dame, IN: University of Notre Dame Press, 2007), pp. 216.
5 See: Jeffrey K. Olick, "Collective Memory," in: *International Encyclopedia of the Social Sciences*, 2nd ed., William A. Darity, ed., *Macmillan Social Science Library* (Detroit, MI: Macmillan Reference, 2008), pp. 7.
6 "Suffering collectivities–whether dyads, groups, societies, or civilizations – do not exist simply as material networks. They must be imagined into being. The pivotal question becomes not who did this to me, but what group did this to us?" Jeffrey C. Alexander, *Trauma: A Social Theory* (Cambridge: Polity, 2012), pp. 2.
7 Ibid., pp. 3.
8 Ibid., pp. 4.
9 Ibid., pp. 6.
10 Ibid., pp. 2.
11 See: Stipe Odak and Andriana Benčić, "Jasenovac – A Past That Does Not Pass: The Presence of Jasenovac in Croatian and Serbian Collective Memory of Conflict," *East European Politics and Societies*, vol. 30, no. 4 (2016), pp. 805–829. https://doi.org/10.1177/0888325416653657.

12 Quoted in: Jozo Tomasevich, *War and Revolution in Yugoslavia, 1941-1945: Occupation and Collaboration* (Stanford, CA: Stanford University Press, 2001), pp. 400.
13 Slavko Goldstein, *1941: The Year That Keeps Returning* (New York: New York Review Books, 2013), pp. 80. Quoted in: Tomasevich, *War and Revolution in Yugoslavia, 1941-1945*, pp. 400.
14 Vjekoslav Perica, *Balkan Idols: Religion and Nationalism in Yugoslav States, Religion and Global Politics* (Oxford: Oxford University Press, 2002), pp. 148.
15 Paul Mojzes, *Balkan Genocides: Holocaust and Ethnic Cleansing in the Twentieth Century* (Lanham, MD: Rowman & Littlefield, 2011), pp. 46.
16 See for instance: David B. MacDonald, *Balkan Holocausts?: Serbian and Croatian Victim-Centred Propaganda and the War in Yugoslavia* (Manchester, and New York: Manchester University Press, 2002), pp. 149–50.
17 *Izborna deklaracija Hrvatske stranke prava* (Election Declaration of the Croatian Party of Rights) (1992), pp. 3, quoted in: Jill A. Irvine, "Ultranationalist Ideology and State-Building in Croatia, 1990–1996," *Problems of Post-Communism*, vol. 44, no. 4 (1997), pp. 35, https://doi.org/10.1080/10758216.1997.11655740.
18 Bogoljub Kočović, "Još jednom o žrtvama Drugog svjetskog rata, genocidu i Jasenovcu," *Hrvatska ljevica*, vol. 5, no. 10 (1998), pp. 36.
19 Jadovno, "Ponori zla: strip u kome je opisana burna istorija Hercegovine," http://jadovno.com/ponori-zla-strip-u-kome-je-opisana-burna-istorija-hercegovine/ (accessed August 11, 2019).
20 In original (Croatian), pp. "Jasenovac je simbol svih laži kojima smo kljukani u zadnjih 70 godina." Blanka Matković, "Jasenovac je simbol laži, kojima smo kljukani u zadnjih 70 godina," www.hkz-kkv.ch/matkovic-jasenovac_simbol_lazi.php (accessed August 11, 2019).
21 For broader discussions on contested places of terror see the works of the Terrorscapes research network, available at: www.terrorscapes.org (accessed July 29, 2019).
22 Mojzes, *Balkan Genocides*, pp. 46.
23 For a recent review, see: Mirjana Kasapović, "Genocid u NDH: Umanjivanje, banaliziranje i poricanje zločina," *Politička misao*, vol. 55, no. 1 (2018), pp. 7–33; also see: Andriana Benčić Kužnar and Vjeran Pavlaković, "Exhibiting Jasenovac: Controversies, Manipulations and Politics of Memory," in: Zuzanna Dziuban (ed.) *Accessing Campscapes: Inclusive Approaches to European Contested Pasts* (Amsterdam: Amsterdam University Press, 2021), forthcoming.
24 See: Ljubica Štefan, *Srpska pravoslavna crkva i fašizam* (Zagreb: Globus, 1996); Ljubica Štefan, *Poslijeratni Titov logor Jasenovac 1945.-47./48* (Zagreb: Hrvatsko žrtvoslovno društvo and Narodne novine, 1998); Josip Pečarić, *Srpski mit o Jasenovcu* (Zagreb: Dom i svijet, 1998); Josip Jurčević, *Nastanak jasenovačkog mita* (Zagreb: Hrvatski studiji Sveučilišta u Zagrebu, 1998); Petar Vučić, *Židovstvo i hrvatstvo. Prilog istraživanju hrvatsko židovskih odnosa* (Zagreb: Croatiaprojekt, 2001). For a recent criticism of revisionist currents in Croatia, also see: Kasapović, "Genocid u NDH: Umanjivanje, banaliziranje i poricanje zločina."
25 Pål Kolstø, "The Croatian Catholic Church and the Long Road to Jasenovac," *Nordic Journal of Religion and Society*, vol. 24, no. 1 (2011), pp. 37; Mirjana Kasapović, "Genocid u NDH: Umanjivanje, banaliziranje i poricanje zločina," pp. 25.

26 Vladimir Horvat, "Tri jasenovačka logora," in: Vladimir Horvat, Igor Vukić, Stipo Pilić and Blanka Matković (eds.) *Jasenovački logori–istraživanja* (Zagreb: Društvo za istraživanje trostrukog logora Jasenovac, 2015), pp. 11–54; Stipo Pilić and Blanka Matković, "Poslijeratni zarobljenički logor Jasenovac prema svjedočanstvima i novim arhivskim izvorima," in: Vladimir Horvat, Igor Vukić, Stipo Pilić and Blanka Matković (eds.) *Jasenovački logori–istraživanja* (Zagreb: Društvo za istraživanje trostrukog logora Jasenovac, 2015), pp. 145–235; Stipo Pilić and Blanka Matković, "Poslijeratni zarobljenički logor Jasenovac prema svjedočanstvima i novima arhivskim izvorima," in: *Radovi Zavoda za povijest HAZU u Zadru*, 56 (2014), pp. 323–408; Mladen Ivezić, *Titov Jasenovac* (Zagreb: Samizdat, 2014).
27 Igor Vukić, "Sabirni i radni logor Jasenovac, 1941–1945," in: Vladimir Horvat, Igor Vukić, Stipo Pilić and Blanka Matković (eds.) *Jasenovački logori–istraživanja* (Zagreb: Društvo za istraživanje trostrukog logora Jasenovac, 2015), pp. 55–144; also see Dr. Stjepan Razum: Nema dokaza za masovne ustaške zločine u Jasenovcu, ali ima za partizanske!, www.braniteljski-portal.com/dr-stjepan-razum-nema-dokaza-za-masovne-ustaske-zlocine-u-jasenovcu-ali-ima-za-partizanske (accessed 10 July 2019).
28 See: Mirjana Kasapović, "Genocid u NDH: Umanjivanje, banaliziranje i poricanje zločina," pp. 10.
29 See: Andriana Benčić Kužnar and Vjeran Pavlaković, "Exhibiting Jasenovac: Controversies, Manipulations and Politics of Memory," in: Zuzanna Dziuban (ed.) *Accessing Campscapes: Inclusive Approaches to European Contested Pasts* (Amsterdam: Amsterdam University Press, 2021), forthcoming.
30 Mirjana Kasapović, "Genocid u NDH: Umanjivanje, banaliziranje i poricanje zločina," pp. 16; Israel Charny (ed.), *Encyclopedia of Genocide* (Santa Barbara: ABC-Clio, 1999), pp. 27, I.
31 Dean Stone (ed.), *The Historiography of the Holocaust* (Basingstoke: Palgrave Macmillan, 2014), pp. 120.
32 For a broader context of debates, see: Zdenko Radelić, *Hrvatska u Jugoslaviji 1945.-1991.: od zajedništva do razlaza* (Zagreb: Školska knjiga–Hrvatski institut za povijest, 2006); Sabrina P. Ramet, *The Three Yugoslavias: State–building and Legitimation, 1918–2004* (Bloomington, IN: Woodrow Wilson Center Press.; Chesham, UK: Indiana University Press, 2006). One of the recent example of the revisionist publications that insists on the unfounded claims of over 700,000 victims in Jasenovac is Gideon Greif's book *Jasenovac–Auschwitz of the Balkans: The Ustasha Empire of Cruelty* (Belgrade: Knjiga komerc, 2018).
33 Ruth Kluger, *Still Alive: A Holocaust Girlhood Remembered* (New York: Feminist Press at the City University of New York, 2003), pp. 180. Quoted in: Jill Stauffer, *Ethical Loneliness: The Injustice of not Being Heard* (New York: Columbia University Press, 2015), pp. 12.
34 Ibid.
35 Benjamin Whitaker, "Revised and Updated Report on the Question of the Prevention and Punishment of the Crime of Genocide," 5, www.legal-tools.org/doc/99c00c/pdf/ (accessed August 11, 2019).
36 Samuel Totten, "'Genocide,' Frivolous Use of the Term," in: Israel W. Charny (ed.) *Encyclopedia of Genocide* (Santa Barbara, CA, Oxford: ABC-CLIO, 1999), pp. 35.

37 See the Interview with Yehuda Bauer: Yad Vashem, "An Interview with Prof. Yehuda Bauer: Interviewer: Amos Goldberg," 45, www.yadvashem.org/odot_pdf/Microsoft%20Word%20-%203856.pdf (accessed July 16, 2019).
38 MacDonald, *Balkan Holocausts?*, pp. 160–178.
39 *Logos Journal*, "Is There a New Anti-Semitism? A Conversation with Raul Hilberg," last modified May 21, 2007, www.logosjournal.com/issue_6.1-2/hilberg.htm (accessed August 11, 2019).
40 See: Jovan Byford, "When I Say 'The Holocaust,' I Mean 'Jasenovac': Remembrance of the Holocaust in contemporary Serbia," *East European Jewish Affairs*, vol. 37, no. 1, 2007, pp. 51–74, https://doi.org/10.1080/13501670701197946.
41 Društvo za istraživanje trostrukog logora Jasenovac, https://drustvojasenovac.wordpress.com/ (accessed July 11, 2019).
42 See: Društvo za istraživanje trostrukog logora Jasenovac, "Zašto tvrdimo da nitko u Jasenovcu nije ubijen zato što je bio Srbin ili pravoslavac." https://drustvojasenovac.wordpress.com/2015/06/06/zasto-tvrdimo-da-nitko-u-jasenovcu-nije-ubijen-zato-sto-je-bio-srbin-ili-pravoslavac/ (accessed July 11, 2019).
43 Stjepan Razum, „Nekorofilski antifašisti i njihove laži o NDH i ustašama," *Hrvatski tjednik*, 25 February 2016.
44 In original (Croatian), pp. "općih propisa o postupanju s nepoćudnim osobama ili prijestupnicima (dakle, propisa koji su se jednako odnosili na Židove i na nežidove) ili još gore, nerijetko i bez neposrednog oslonca na ikakve propise." Tomislav Jonjić u povodu knjige *Dragutin Gjurić–Životnim putem Hrvatske Tomislava Đurića*. Available on: www.tomislavjonjic.iz.hr/V_20_previranja.html (accessed July 20, 2019). Quoted in: Nataša Mataušić, "Rasni zakoni u NDH–društveni i pravni aspekti," in: Andriana Benčić, Stipe Odak, and Danijela Lucić (eds.) *Jasenovac: manipulacije, kontroverze i povijesni revizionizam* (Jasenovac: Spomen područje Jasenovac, 2018), pp. 221–245.
45 Marko Samardžija, *Hrvatski jezik, pravopis i jezična politika u Nezavisnoj Državi Hrvatskoj* (Zagreb: Hrvatska sveučilišna naklada, 2008), pp. 470, quoted in: Vladimir Geiger, "Dokon pop i jariće krsti," www.historiografija.hr/?p=1991 (accessed July 11, 2019); Nataša Mataušić, "Rasni zakoni u NDH–društveni i pravni aspekti," in: Andriana Benčić, Stipe Odak, and Danijela Lucić (eds.) *Jasenovac: manipulacije, kontroverze i povijesni revizionizam* (Jasenovac: Spomen područje Jasenovac, 2018), 221–45.
46 *Naredba o promjeni židovskih prezimena i označavanju Židova i židovskih tvrtki* from 4. June 1941; *Odredba o preuzimanju i upravi židovskih zgrada i imanja* from 27 August 1941; *Zakonska odredba o podržavljenju imetka Židova i židovskih poduzeća* from 9 October 1941; *Zakonska odredba o podržavljenju židovske imovine* from 30 October 1942. Quoted in: Vladimir Geiger, "Dokon pop i jariće krsti," www.historiografija.hr/?p=1991 (accessed July 11, 2019); Nataša Mataušić, "Rasni zakoni u NDH–društveni i pravni aspekti," in: Andriana Benčić, Stipe Odak, and Danijela Lucić (eds.) *Jasenovac: manipulacije, kontroverze i povijesni revizionizam* (Jasenovac: Spomen područje Jasenovac, 2018), pp. 221–245.
47 Mirjana Kasapović, "Genocid u NDH: Umanjivanje, banaliziranje i poricanje zločina," pp. 16; Tomislav Dulić, "Mass Killing in the Independent State of Croatia, 1941–1945: a Case for Comparative Research," *Journal of Genocide Studies*, vol. 8, no. 3 (2006), pp. 255.
48 Mirjana Kasapović, "Genocid u NDH: Umanjivanje, banaliziranje i poricanje zločina," pp. 10–21.

49 Simo Brdar, "An Introduction to Donja Gradina: The Largest Execution Site of the Jasenovac Concentration Camp," *Jasenovac Research Institute*, vol. 1, no. 1 (2005), pp. 6. www.jasenovac.org/res/doc/jasenovac1.pdf (accessed July 16, 2019).
50 In original (Serbian), pp. "Stradanje koje se ovde desilo više je od genocida, a ni pravna, ni moralna terminologija ne poznaju primerenu kvalifikaciju za zlodela, neljudskost i svirepost metoda kojima su vršene egzekucije ili za ideološko-politički koncept koji je iza toga stajao." See: Kurir.rs, "Cvijanović: Stradanje u Jasenovcu više je od genocida," www.kurir.rs/region/bosna-i-hercegovina/3247195/cvijanovic-stradanje-u-jasenovcu-vise-je-od-genocida (accessed July 20, 2019).
51 In original (Serbian), pp. "Kako smo mogli dozvoliti da nas potisne ideologija koja je išla za tim da ne prikaže stradanje Srba kao genocid, nego sada dozvoljava nekima koji su sljedbenici zločinaca da ovdje pričaju da se radi o žrtvama rata izjednačavajući jednako stradanje na svim stranama." See: Glas Srpske, "Dodik: Stradanja ne bi bilo da smo 1941. imali Republiku Srpsku," www.glassrpske.com/lat/novosti/vijesti_dana/dodik-stradanja-ne-bi-bilo-da-smo-1941-imali-republiku-srpsku/235114 (accessed July 20, 2019).
52 In original (Serbian), pp. "Da smo 1941. godine imali Republiku Srpsku ne bi doživjeli Jasenovac. Zato je Republika Srpska i stvorena." See: Glas Srpske, "Dodik: Stradanja ne bi bilo da smo 1941. imali Republiku Srpsku," www.glassrpske.com/lat/novosti/vijesti_dana/dodik-stradanja-ne-bi-bilo-da-smo-1941-imali-republiku-srpsku/235114 (accessed July 20, 2019).
53 For an extensive presentation of the discussions and manipulations with numbers of victims of Jasenovac Concentration Camp, see the contribution of Vladimir Geiger and Martina Grahek Ravančić in this volume. For an overview of the debates about the numbers of victims, also see: Vladimir Geiger, "Numerical Indicators of the Victims of the Jasenovac Camp, 1941–1945 (Estimates, Calculations, Lists)," *Review of Croatian History*, vol. 9, no. 1 (2013), pp. 170–185.; Vladimir Geiger, "Ljudski gubici Hrvatske u Drugom svjetskom ratu koje su prouzročili ́okupatori i njihovi pomagači ́. Brojidbeni pokazatelji (procjene, izračuni, popisi)," *Časopis za suvremenu povijest*, vol. 43, no. 3 (2011), pp. 724–727; and Vladimir Geiger and Martina Grahek Ravančić, "Jasenovac i Bleiburg između činjenica i manipulacija," in: Andriana Benčić, Stipe Odak, and Danijela Lucić (eds.) *Jasenovac: manipulacije, kontroverze i povijesni revizionizam* (Jasenovac: Spomen područje Jasenovac, 2018), pp. 19–63. The *Jasenovac Memorial Site* has information on over 83,000 individual victims. See: Spomen područje Jasenovac/Jasenovac Memorial Site, "List of Individual Victims of Jasenovac Concetretion Camp," www.jusp-jasenovac.hr/Default.aspx?sid=6711 (accessed July 20, 2019). The US Holocaust Memorial Museum estimates between 56,000 and 97,000 victims. See: United States Holocaust Memorial Musuem, "Jasenovac," https://web.archive.org/web/20090916030858/http://www.ushmm.org/wlc/article.php?lang=en&ModuleId=10005449 (accessed July 2, 2019). For earlier demographic estimates, see: Bogoljub Kočović, *Žrtve Drugog svetskog rata u Jugoslaviji* (London: Veritas Foundation Press, 1985); and Vladimir Žerjavić, *Gubici stanovništva Jugoslavije u drugom svjetskom ratu* (Zagreb: Jugoslavensko viktimološko društvo, 1989), pp. 179–182.
54 Vladimir Geiger and Martina Grahek Ravančić, "Jasenovac i Bleiburg između činjenica i manipulacija," pp. 24.
55 Ibid., pp. 21.

56 Vjeran Pavlaković and Davor Pauković, "Framing the Nation: An Introduction to Commemorative Culture in Croatia," in: Vjeran Pavlaković and Davor Pauković (eds.) *Framing the Nation and Collective Identities: Political Rituals and Cultural Memory of the Twentieth Century Traumas in Croatia, 1st Edition* (London and New York: Routledge, 2019), pp. 12.

57 Vladimir Geiger and Martina Grahek Ravančić, "Jasenovac i Bliburg između činjenica i manipulacija," pp. 29. Vladimir Geiger, "Numerical Indicators of the Victims of the Jasenovac Camp, 1941–1945 (Estimates, Calculations, Lists)," pp.162; Ozren Žunec, *Goli život* (Zagreb: Demetra, 2007), pp. 393–395.

58 The previously reported number of 600,000 and 700,000 fatalities of the Jasenovac camp, mainly Serbs, started to unravel in 1998 when the Bosnian Institute released an individual name list of victims from the Yugoslav Census Commission of 1964 (see: *Jasenovac. Žrtve rata prema podacima Statističkog zavoda Jugoslavije*, edited by Meho Visočak i Bejdo Sobica, Zürich–Sarajevo, 1998; Žrtve rata 1941–1945. godine. Rezultati popisa, Beograd, 1966, Beograd, 1992). When those strictly protected data, until then under embargo, were published, it became obvious that the exaggerated numbers were completely ungrounded. See: Vladimir Geiger, "Numerical Indicators of the Victims of the Jasenovac Camp, 1941–1945 (Estimates, Calculations, Lists)," in: *Review of Croatian History*, vol. 9, no. 1 (2013), pp 165; Bogoljub Kočović, *Nauka, nacionalizam i propaganda (Između gubitaka i žrtava Drugoga svetskog rata u Jugoslaviji)* (Paris: Editions du Titre, 1999), pp. 143–144; Davor Kovačić, "Jasenovac–žrtve rata prema podacima Statističkog zavoda Jugoslavije; Sarajevo–Zurich 1998, 1171. str.," *Časopis za suvremenu povijest*, vol. 32, no. 1 (2000), pp. 219–224.

59 For the list prepared by *Jasenovac Memorial Site* see: Spomen područje Jasenovac/ Jasenovac Memorial Site, "Survey and Search of the List of Individual Victims of Jasenovac Concentration Camp List of individual victims of Jasenovac concentration camp," www.jusp-jasenovac.hr/Default.aspx?sid=7620 (accessed July 11, 2019).
www.jusp-jasenovac.hr/Default.aspx?sid=7620 (accessed August 6, 2019). For the list prepared by the *Museum of Genocide Victims*, see contribution of Dragan Cvetkovic to this volume.

60 See also: *Spomen područje Jasenovac/Jasenovac Memorial Site*, "Survey and Search of the List of Individual Victims of Jasenovac Concentration Camp List of individual victims of Jasenovac Concentration Camp," www.jusp-jasenovac.hr/Default.aspx?sid=7620 (accessed July 11, 2019).

61 In original (Croatian), pp. "Jasenovac je simbol svih laži kojima smo kljukani u zadnjih 70 godina." ibid.

62 "Nove jasenovačke žrtve iz 21. stoljeća," *Hrvatski tjednik*, no. 42, 26 October 2017, pp. 42–45.

63 "Komunistički autogol: Američki muzej holokausta u raljama jasenovačkog mita koji je sprdnja sa zdravim razumom," *Hrvatski tjednik*, no. 38, 12 October 2017, pp. 38–41.

64 It is important to clarify that we are not arguing that the victims list from 1964 is comprehensive or without inconsistencies. See: Vladimir Geiger, "Numerical Indicators of the Victims of the Jasenovac Camp, 1941–1945 (Estimates, Calculations, Lists)"; Vladimir Geiger and Martina Grahek Ravančić, "Jasenovac i Bleiburg između činjenica i manipulacija"). In that respect, certain comments that indicated repeated names on more than one list of concentration camp

victims around Europe are entirely legitimate and some seem to be used to improve Jasenovac victim lists. However, what in our view could be considered as a form of historical revisionism is an attempt to put the whole victim list into question based on a smaller number of inaccuracies which are entirely understandable when taking into account 20 years of distance between the original events and the period of documentation and, less than optimal quality of original documents, missing sources and, moreover, the fact that certain victims were registered in more than one concentration camp before losing their lives.

65 Vladimir Mrkoci and Vladimir Horvat, *Ogoljela laž Jasenovca* (Zagreb: Naklada Čić, 2008); Stjepan Razum, "Evo što smo dosad otkrili istražujući Jasenovac," *Hrvatski tjednik*, November 12, 2015, pp. 18.

66 Tjedno.hr, "Od ukupno 18.600 ogoraša u Jasenovcu umrlo njih 1360," www.tjedno.hr/od-ukupno-18-600-logorasa-u-jasenovcu-je-umrlo-njih-1360/ (accessed August 7, 2019).

67 Igor Vukić, "Sabirni i radni logor Jasenovac, 1941.–1945.," pp. 73–76.

68 Museum of Genocide Vicitims, "Doprinos mlađih stručnih saradnika Muzeju žrtava genocida," www.muzejgenocida.rs/85-novosti/542-doprinos-mladih-stru%C4%8Dnih-saradnika-muzeja %C5%BErtava-genocida.html (accessed August 7, 2019).

69 Interview with Milan Bulajic, available at: www.politika.rs/sr/clanak/48701/Specijalni-dodaci/Stvarne-zrtve-a-ne-mit (accessed August 12, 2013).

70 Vladimir Geiger and Martina Grahek Ravančić quoted that "the virtual *Jasenovac Research Institute* based in Brooklyn, New York" was a "proponent of the mystification and obscuration of the facts on Second World War human losses in Yugoslavia and Croatia" and for that purpose they used a number from the 1964 Wartime Victim Census Commission of 597,323 fatalities and casualties of WWII in Yugoslavia's as the Jasenovac victim list. See: Vladimir Geiger and Martina Grahek Ravančić, "Jasenovac i Bliburg između činjenica i manipulacija," pp. 32; Vladimir Geiger, "Numerical Indicators of the Victims of the Jasenovac Camp, 1941–1945 (Estimates, Calculations, Lists)," pp. 165. The *Institute* on its webpage initially promoted number of 700,000 victims of Jasenovac concentration camp, rather than numbers from the 1964 Wartime Victim Census Commission stated above, but later those numbers were moved from the webpage. See current webpage: Jasenovac Research Institute, "What was Jasenovac?" http://jasenovac.org/what_was_jasenovac.php (accessed August 6, 2019).

71 Antun Miletic, "Why Jasenovac?" *Jasenovac Research Institute*, vol. 1., no. 1 (2005), pp. 3. www.jasenovac.org/res/doc/jasenovac1.pdf (accessed July 10, 2019).

72 Simo Brdar, "An Introduction to Donja Gradina: The Largest Execution Site of the Jasenovac Concentration Camp," pp. 6.

73 See: Srboljub Živanović, "Jasenovac System of Croatian Concentration Camps for Extermination of Serbs, Jews and Roma–1941–1945," www.serb-victims.org/en/content/view/299/29/ (accessed August 7, 2019).

74 Paul Mojzes, "Examination of Genocide: Truth and Justice Instead of Political and Economic Gain," 5, http://forel.idn.org.rs/tekstovi/clanci/EXAMINATION%20OF%20GENOCIDE.pdf (accessed July 16, 2019).

75 Holocaust Controversies, "Nazi shrunken heads, human skin lampshades, human soap, textiles from human hair? Sorting out the truth from the legends," http://holocaustcontroversies.blogspot.com/2017/11/nazi-shrunken-heads-human-skin.html (accessed August 11, 2019).

76 See: Stiftung Gedenkstätten Buchenwald und Mittelbau-Dora, "Stimmt es, dass die SS im KZ Buchenwald Lampenschirme aus Menschenhaut anfertigen ließ?" www.buchenwald.de/en/1132/ (accessed August 11, 2019).
77 International Holocaust Remembrance Alliance, "International Memorial Museums Charter," www.holocaustremembrance.com/international-memorial-museums-charter (accessed August 11, 2019).
78 Ibid.
79 "wie es dazu kommen konnte," jedoch ohne oberlehrerhaft zu bevormunden, zu moralisieren oder (emotional) zu überwältigen." Stiftung Gedenkstätten Buchenwald und Mittelbau-Dora, "Konzeption & Gestaltung," www.buchenwald.de/1455/ (accessed August 11, 2019).
80 Inga Clendinnen, *Reading the Holocaust* (Cambridge: Cambridge University Press, 2006), pp. 4.
81 See for instance: Odak and Benčić, "Jasenovac – A Past That Does Not Pass: The Presence of Jasenovac in Croatian and Serbian Collective Memory of Conflict," pp. 812–816.
82 Efraim Zuroff, the director of The Simon Wiesenthal Center described it, for instance, as a "postmodern fog." Quoted in: Rob van der Laarse, "Beyond Auschwitz? Europe's Terrorscapes in the Age of Postmemory," in: *Memory and Postwar Memorials: Confronting the Violence of the Past*, ed. Marc Silberman and Florence Vatan (New York: Palgrave Macmillan, 2013), pp. 82. For the director's view on the concept of the third exhibition, see: Nataša Jovičić, "Jasenovac Memorial Museum's Permanent Exhibition–the Victim as an Individual," *Review of Croatian History*, vol. 2, no. 1 (2006).
83 Mirjana Kasapović, "Genocid u NDH: Umanjivanje, banaliziranje i poricanje zločina," pp. 12–13.
84 Simo Brdar, "An Introduction to Donja Gradina: The Largest Execution Site of the Jasenovac Concentration Camp," Jasenovac Research Institute 1, no 1 (2005), pp. 6. www.jasenovac.org/res/doc/jasenovac1.pdf (accessed July 16, 2019).
85 Ibid.
86 Ibid., pp. 9.
87 Srbija Danas, "Srbe u Jasenovcu kuvali žive u kazanima za sapun: Ispovest patologa koji je brojao žrtve u zloglasnom logoru!," www.srbijadanas.com/vesti/drustvo/potresna-ispovest-srbe-u-jasenovcu-zive-kuvali-u-kazanima-za-sapun (accessed August 8, 2019). The official site of Donja Gradina Memorial Site the following is stated: "In March of 1993, a British ITN television crew, led by Clive Gordon, visited Donja Gradina. At his suggestion and by a random sample method, one grave at the grave field "Topola" (near the soap factory) was opened. Mainly osteological remains of feet, hands, forearms and lower legs were found. It was obvious that inmate bodies were cut here for soap production. Since that time, this grave is called the 'Cutting Grave.'" (www.jusp-donjagradina.org/en/research-in-donja-gradina/ (accessed July 16, 2019). However, in e-mail correspondence with Clive Gordon, leader of the team, he stated the following: "We were not really the 'initiators' of the excavation in 1993, we were simply a film crew covering the war in Bosnia. We were aware that excavations at Jasenovac were on-going and asked for permission to film an excavation in progress. The possible use of human remains for soap was, as far as I can remember, never referred to in the film and we certainly had no video evidence that this was, 'obviously' or not, the case." (e–mail correspondence between Stipe Odak and Clive Gordon on July 28, 2019).

88 See: Dnevnik.hr, "Dačić se oglasio o izložbi o Jasenovcu: 'Ona je uperena protiv zločinaca i onih koji žele da se to zaboravi i izbriše,'" https://dnevnik.hr/vijesti/svi jet/ivica-dacic-se-oglasio-o-izlozbi-jasenovac-pravo-na-nezaborav---504467.html (accessed July 23, 2019).
89 Gideon Greif, *Jasenovac Auschwitz of the Balkans* (Israel: Garey Tikva, 2018). Also quoted in: Andriana Benčić Kužnar and Vjeran Pavlaković, "Exhibiting Jasenovac: Controversies, Manipulations and Politics of Memory," in: *Accessing Campscapes: Inclusive Approaches to European Contested Pasts*. Zuzanna Dziuban (ed.) (Amsterdam: Amsterdam University Press, 2021), forthcoming.
90 See: Milan Bulajić, *Jasenovac. Balkan Auschwitz. System of Croatian Nazi-Ustasha Genocide Camps for Serbs, Jews and Gypsies*.
91 In original (Serbian), pp. "Govori o našoj civilizaciji i o tome gde smo nekada bili i kakvim nečasnim i neljudskim metodama smo se služili da bismo napravili neke druge države," http://rs.n1info.com/Vesti/a247709/Javni-cas-o-Jasenovcu-u-skupst ini.html, emphasis ours (accessed August 3, 2019).
92 Nataša Jovičić, "Jasenovac Memorial Site," 14–17, www.bideo.info/buesa/image nes/seminario_croacia.pdf (accessed July 3, 2013).
93 Odak and Benčić, "Jasenovac – A Past That Does Not Pass: The Presence of Jasenovac in Croatian and Serbian Collective Memory of Conflict."
94 Peter L. Berger and Thomas Luckman, *The Social Construction of Reality: A Treatise in the Sociology of Knowledge*. (Reprinted in Penguin Books Limited, 1991).

Bibliography

Alexander, Jeffrey C. *Trauma: A Social Theory*. Cambridge: Polity, 2012.
Arendt, Hannah. *The Human Condition*. Chicago: University of Chicago Press, 1998.
Benčić Kužnar, Andriana and Vjeran Pavlaković. "Exhibiting Jasenovac: Controversies, Manipulations and the Politics of Memory," in: Zuzanna Dziuban (ed.) *Accessing Campscapes: Inclusive Approaches to European Contested Pasts*. Amsterdam: Amsterdam University Press, 2021, forthcoming.
Berger, Peter L. and Thomas Luckman. *The Social Construction of Reality: A Treatise in the Sociology of Knowledge*. Reprinted in Penguin Books Limited, 1991.
Brdar, Simo. "An Introduction to Donja Gradina: The Largest Execution Site of the Jasenovac Concentration Camp." *Jasenovac Research Institute* 1, no. 1, 2005, pp. 6–9. www.jasenovac.org/res/doc/jasenovac1.pdf (accessed July 16, 2019).
Bulajić, Milan. *Jasenovac. Balkan Auschwitz. System of Croatian Nazi-Ustasha Genocide Camps for Serbs, Jews and Gypsies*. Beograd: Muzej žrtava genocida, 2001.
Byford, Jovan. "When I Say 'the Holocaust,' I Mean 'Jasenovac': Remembrance of the Holocaust in contemporary Serbia." *East European Jewish Affairs* 37, no. 1, 2007, pp. 51–74. https://doi.org/10.1080/13501670701197946.
Churchill, Winston. "Prime Minister Winston Churchill's Broadcast to the World about the Meeting with President Roosevelt." www.ibiblio.org/pha/timeline/410824 awp.html. Accessed July 15, 2019.
Clendinnen, Inga. *Reading the Holocaust*. Cambridge: Cambridge University Press, 2006.
Dnevnik.hr. "Dačić se oglasio o izložbi o Jasenovcu: 'Ona je uperena protiv zločinaca i onih koji žele da se to zaboravi i izbriše.'" https://dnevnik.hr/vijesti/svijet/ivica-dacic-se-oglasio-o-izlozbi-jasenovac-pravo-na-nezaborav---504467.html. Accessed July 23, 2019.

Društvo za istraživanje trostrukog logora Jasenovac. "Zašto tvrdimo da nitko u Jasenovcu nije ubijen zato što je bio Srbin ili pravoslavac." https://drustvojaseno vac.wordpress.com/2015/06/06/zasto-tvrdimo-da-nitko-u-jasenovcu-nije-ubijen-zato-sto-je-bio-srbin-ili-pravoslavac/. Accessed July 11, 2019.

Dulić, Tomislav. "Mass Killing in the Independent State of Croatia, 1941–1945: a Case for Comparative Research." *Journal of Genocide Studies* 8, no. 3, 2006, pp. 255–281.

Geiger, Vladimir. "Dokon pop i jariće krsti." www.historiografija.hr/?p=1991. Accessed July 11 2019.

———. "'Ljudski gubici Hrvatske u Drugom svjetskom ratu koje su prouzročili 'okupatori i njihovi pomagači.' Brojidbeni pokazatelji (procjene, izračuni, popisi)." *Časopis za suvremenu povijest* 43, no. 3, 2011, pp. 699–749.

———. "Numerical indicators of the victims of the Jasenovac camp, 1941–1945 (estimates, calculations, lists)." *Review of Croatian History* 9, no. 1, 2013, pp. 151–187.

Geiger, Vladimir and Martina Grahek Ravančić. "Jasenovac i Bliburg između činjenica i manipulacija," in: Andriana Benčić, Stipe Odak and Danijela Lucić (eds.) *Jasenovac: manipulacije, kontroverze i povijesni revizionizam*. Jasenovac: Spomen područje Jasenovac, 2018, pp. 19–63.

Glas Srpske. "Dodik: Stradanja ne bi bilo da smo 1941. imali Republiku Srpsku," www.glassrpske.com/lat/novosti/vijesti_dana/dodik-stradanja-ne-bi-bilo-da-smo-1941-imali-republiku-srpsku/235114. Accessed July 20, 2019.

Goldstein, Slavko. *1941: The Year That Keeps Returning*. New York: New York Review of Books, 2013.

Greif, Gideon. *Jasenovac Auschwitz of the Balkans*. Israel: Garey Tikva, 2018.

Holocaust Controversies. "Nazi shrunken heads, human skin lampshades, human soap, textiles from human hair? Sorting out the truth from the legends." http://holocaustcontroversies.blogspot.com/2017/11/nazi-shrunken-heads-human-skin.html. Accessed July 16, 2019.

Horvat, Vladimir. "Tri jasenovačka logora," in: Vladimir Horvat, Igor Vukić, Stipo Pilić and Blanka Matković (eds.) *Jasenovački logori–istraživanja*. Zagreb: Društvo za istraživanje trostrukog logora Jasenovac, 2015, pp. 11–54.

Institute for Research on Suffering of the Serbs in XX c. "Jasenovac System of Croatian Concentration Camps," www.serb-victims.org/en/content/view/299/29/. Accessed August 7, 2019.

International Holocaust Remembrance Alliance. "International Memorial Museums Charter." www.holocaustremembrance.com/international-memorial-museums-charter. Accessed July 16, 2019.

"Interview with Milan Bulajic." www.politika.rs/sr/clanak/48701/Specijalni-dodaci/Stvarne-zrtve-a-ne-mit. Accessed July 20, 2019.

Irvine, Jill A. "Ultranationalist Ideology and State-Building in Croatia, 1990–1996." *Problems of Post- Communism* 44, no. 4, 1997, pp. 30–43. https://doi.org/10.1080/10758216.1997.11655740.

Ivezić, Mladen. *Titov Jasenovac*. Zagreb: Samizdat, 2014.

Jadovno. "Ponori zla: strip u kome je opisana burna istorija Hercegovine." http://jadovno.com/ponori-zla-strip-u-kome-je-opisana-burna-istorija-hercegovine/. Accessed July 16, 2019.

Jasenovac. Žrtve rata prema podacima Statističkog zavoda Jugoslavije. prir. Meho Visočak i Bejdo Sobica, Zürich–Sarajevo, 1998.

Jasenovac Research Institute. "What was Jasenovac?" http://jasenovac.org/what_was_jasenovac.php. Accessed August 6, 2019.

Jovičić, Nataša. "Jasenovac Memorial Museum's Permanent Exhibition–the Victim as an Individual." *Review of Croatian History* 2, no. 1, 2006, pp. 295–299.

———. "Jasenovac Memorial Site." www.bideo.info/buesa/imagenes/seminario_croacia.pdf. Accessed July 3, 2013.

Jurčević, Josip. *Nastanak jasenovačkog mita*. Zagreb: Hrvatski studiji Sveučilišta u Zagrebu, 1998.

Kasapović, Mirjana. "Genocid u NDH: Umanjivanje, banaliziranje i poricanje zločina." *Politička misao* 55, no. 1, 2018, pp. 7–33.

Kočović, Bogoljub. *Nauka, nacionalizam i propaganda (Između gubitaka i žrtava Drugoga svetskog rata u Jugoslaviji)*. Paris: Editions du Titre, 1999.

———. *Žrtve Drugog svetskog rata u Jugoslaviji*. London: Veritas Foundation Press, 1985.

———. "Još jednom o žrtvama Drugog svjetskog rata, genocidu i Jasenovcu." *Hrvatska ljevica* 5, no. 10, 1998, pp. 35–37.

Kolstø, Pål. "The Croatian Catholic Church and the Long Road to Jasenovac." *Nordic Journal of Religion and Society* 24, no. 1, 2011, pp. 37–56.

"Komunistički autogol: Američki muzej holokausta u raljama jasenovačkog mita koji je sprdnja sa zdravim razumom." *Hrvatski tjednik*, 12 October 2017, pp. 38–41.

Kovačić, Davor. "Jasenovac–žrtve rata prema podacima Statističkog zavoda Jugoslavije; Sarajevo–Zurich 1998, 1171. str." In: *Časopis za suvremenu povijest* 32, no. 1, 2000, pp. 219–224.

Kurir.rs. "Cvijanović: Stradanje u Jasenovcu više je od genocida." www.kurir.rs/region/bosna-i-hercegovina/3247195/cvijanovic-stradanje-u-jasenovcu-vise-je-od-genocida. Accessed July 20, 2019.

Logos Journal. "Is There a New Anti-Semitism? A Conversation with Raul Hilberg." Last modified May 21, 2007. www.logosjournal.com/issue_6.1-2/hilberg.htm. Accessed June 27, 2019.

MacDonald, David B. *Balkan Holocausts?: Serbian and Croatian Victim-Centred Propaganda and the War in Yugoslavia*. Manchester and New York: Manchester University Press, 2002.

MacIntyre, Alasdair C. *After Virtue: A Study in Moral Theory*. 3rd ed. Notre Dame, IN: University of Notre Dame Press, 2007.

Mataušić, Nataša. "Rasni zakoni u NDH–društveni i pravni aspekti," in: Andriana Benčić, Stipe Odak, and Danijela Lucić (ed.) *Jasenovac: manipulacije, kontroverze i povijesni revizionizam*. Jasenovac: Spomen područje Jasenovac, 2018, pp. 221–245.

Matković, Blanka. "Jasenovac je simbol laži, kojima smo kljukani u zadnjih 70 godina." www.hkz-kkv.ch/matkovic-jasenovac_simbol_lazi.php. Accessed July 16, 2019.

Miletić, Antun. "Why Jasenovac?" *Jasenovac Research Institute* 1, no. 1, 2005, pp. 1–3. www.jasenovac.org/res/doc/jasenovac1.pdf. Accessed July 10, 2019.

Mojzes, Paul. "Examination of Genocide: Truth and Justice Instead of Political and Economic Gain." http://forel.idn.org.rs/tekstovi/clanci/EXAMINATION%20OF%20GENOCIDE.pdf. Accessed July 16, 2019.

———. *Balkan Genocides: Holocaust and Ethnic Cleansing in the Twentieth Century*. Lanham, MD: Rowman & Littlefield, 2011.

Mrkoci, Vladimir, and Horvat, Vladimir. *Ogoljela laž logora Jasenovac*. Zagreb: Naklada Čić, 2008.

Museum of Genocide Vicitims. "Doprinos mlađih stručnih saradnika Muzeju žrtava genocida," www.muzejgenocida.rs/85-novosti/542-doprinos-mladih-stru%C4%8Dnih-saradnika-muzeja%20%C5%BErtava-genocida.html. Accessed August 7, 2019.

"Nove jasenovačke žrtve iz 21. Stoljeća." *Hrvatski tjednik*, 26 October 2017, pp. 42–45.

Odak, Stipe, and Andriana Benčić. "Jasenovac – A Past That Does Not Pass: The Presence of Jasenovac in Croatian and Serbian Collective Memory of Conflict." East European Politics and Societies 30, no. 4, 2016, pp. 805–829. https://doi.org/10.1177/0888325416653657.

Olick, Jeffrey K. "Collective Memory," in: William A. Darity (ed.) *International Encyclopedia of the Social Sciences. 2nd ed. Macmillan social science library, 7–8.* Detroit: Macmillan Reference USA, 2008.

Pavlaković, Vjeran and Davor Pauković. "Framing the Nation: An Introduction to Commemorative Culture in Croatia," in: Vjeran Pavlaković and Davor Pauković (ed.) *Framing the Nation and Collective Identities: Political Rituals and Cultural Memory of the Twentieth Century Traumas in Croatia, 1st Edition.* London and New York: Routledge, 2019, pp. 1–29.

Pečarić, Josip. *Srpski mit o Jasenovcu*. Zagreb: Dom i svijet, 1998.

Perica, Vjekoslav. *Balkan Idols: Religion and Nationalism in Yugoslav States. Religion and Global Politics.* Oxford: Oxford University Press, 2002.

Pilić, Stipo and Blanka Matković. "Poslijeratni zarobljenički logor Jasenovac prema svjedočanstvima i novim arhivskim izvorima," in: Vladimir Horvat, Igor Vukić, Stipo Pilić and Blanka Matković (eds.) *Jasenovački logori–istraživanja.* Zagreb: Društvo za istraživanje trostrukog logora Jasenovac, 2015, pp. 145–235.

Pilić, Stipo, and Blanka Matković "Poslijeratni zarobljenički logor Jasenovac prema svjedočanstvima i novima arhivskim izvorima." *Radovi Zavoda za povijest HAZU u Zadru*, 56, 2014, pp. 323–408.

Radelić, Zdenko. *Hrvatska u Jugoslaviji 1945.-1991.: od zajedništva do razlaza.* Zagreb: Školska knjiga–Hrvatski institut za povijest, 2006.

Ramet, Sabrina P. *The Three Yugoslavias: State-building and Legitimation, 1918–2004.* Woodrow Wilson Center Press. Bloomington, IN and Chesham, UK: Indiana University Press, 2006.

Razum, Stjepan. "Dr. Stjepan Razum: Nema dokaza za masovne ustaške zločine u Jasenovcu, ali ima za partizanske!" www.braniteljski-portal.com/dr-stjepan-razum-nema-dokaza-za-masovne-ustaske-zlocine-u-jasenovcu-ali-ima-za-partizanske. Accessed July 10, 2019.

———. "Evo što smo dosad otkrili istražujući Jasenovac." *Hrvatski tjednik*, 12 November 2015.

———. "Nekorofilski antifašisti i njihove laži o NDH i ustašama," *Hrvatski tjednik*, 25 February 2016.

———. "Dr. Stjepan Razum: Nema dokaza za masovne ustaške zločine u Jasenovcu, ali ima za partizanske!," www.braniteljski-portal.com/dr-stjepan-razum-nema-dokaza-za-masovne-ustaske-zlocine-u-jasenovcu-ali-ima-za-partizanske. Accessed July 10, 2019.

Sontag, Susan. *Against Interpretation and Other Essays.* Penguin Modern Classics. London: Penguin, 2013.

Spomen područje Jasenovac/Jasenovac Memorial Site. "List of Individual Victims of Jasenovac Concentration Camp." www.jusp-jasenovac.hr/Default.aspx?sid=6711. Accessed July 20, 2019.

———. "Survey and Search of the List of Individual Victims of Jasenovac Concentration Camp List of individual victims of Jasenovac Concentration Camp," www.jusp-jasenovac.hr/Default.aspx?sid=7620. Accessed July 11, 2019.

Srbija Danas, "Srbe u Jasenovcu kuvali žive u kazanima za sapun: Ispovest patologa koji je brojao žrtve u zloglasnom logoru!" www.srbijadanas.com/vesti/drustvo/potresna-ispovest-srbe-u-jasenovcu-zive-kuvali-u-kazanima-za-sapun. Accessed August 8, 2019.

Stauffer, Jill. *Ethical Loneliness: The Injustice of not Being Heard.* New York: Columbia University Press, 2015.

Stiftung Gedenkstätten Buchenwald und Mittelbau-Dora. "Stimmt es, dass die SS im KZ Buchenwald Lampenschirme aus Menschenhaut anfertigen ließ?" www.buchenwald.de/en/1132/. Accessed July 16, 2019.

———. "Konzeption & Gestaltung." www.buchenwald.de/1455/. Accessed July 16, 2019.

Stone, Dean (ed.). *The Historiography of the Holocaust.* Basingstoke: Palgrave Macmillan, 2004.

Štefan, Ljubica. *Srpska pravoslavna crkva i fašizam.* Zagreb: Globus, 1996.

———. *Poslijeratni Titov logor Jasenovac 1945.-47./48.* Zagreb: Hrvatsko žrtvoslovno društvo i Narodne novine, 1998.

Tjedno.hr. "Od ukupno 18.600 ogoraša u Jasenovcu umrlo njih 1360," www.tjedno.hr/od-ukupno-18-600-logorasa-u-jasenovcu-je-umrlo-njih-1360/. Accessed August 7, 2019.

Tomasevich, Jozo. *War and Revolution in Yugoslavia, 1941–1945: Occupation and Collaboration.* Stanford, CA: Stanford University Press, 2001.

Totten, Samuel. "'Genocide,' Frivolous Use of the Term," in: Israel W. Charny (ed.) *Encyclopedia of Genocide.* Santa Barbara, CA, Oxford: ABC-CLIO, 1999, pp. 35–36.

United States Holocaust Memorial Museum. "Jasenovac," https://web.archive.org/web/20090916030858/ www.ushmm.org/wlc/article.php?lang=en&ModuleId=10005449. Accessed July 2, 2019.

van der Laarse, Rob. "Beyond Auschwitz? Europe's Terrorscapes in the Age of Postmemory," in: Marc Silberman and Florence Vtan (ed.) *Memory and Postwar Memorials: Confronting the Violence of the Past.* New York: Palgrave Macmillan, 2013, pp. 71–92.

Vučić, Petar. *Židovstvo i hrvatstvo. Prilog istraživanju hrvatsko-židovskih odnosa.* Zagreb: Croatiaprojekt, 2001.

Vukić, Igor. "Sabirni i radni logor Jasenovac, 1941.-1945," in: Vladimir Horvat, Igor Vukić, Stipo Pilić and Blanka Matković (eds.) *Jasenovački logori–istraživanja.* Zagreb: Društvo za istraživanje trostrukog logora Jasenovac, 2015, pp. 55–144.

Whitaker, Benjamin. "Revised and Updated Report on the Question of the Prevention and Punishment of the Crime of Genocide." www.legal-tools.org/doc/99c00c/pdf/. Accessed July 16, 2019.

Yad Vashem. "An Interview with Prof. Yehuda Bauer: Interviewer: Amos Goldberg." www.yadvashem.org/odot_pdf/Microsoft%20Word%20-%203856.pdf. Accessed July 16, 2019.

Žerjavić, Vladimir. *Gubici stanovništva Jugoslavije u drugom svjetskom ratu.* Zagreb: Jugoslavensko viktimološko društvo, 1989.

Živanović, Srboljub. "Jasenovac System of Croatian Concentration Camps for Extermination of Serbs, Jews and Roma–1941-1945," www.serb-victims.org/en/content/view/299/29/. Accessed August 7, 2019.

Žrtve rata 1941–1945. godine. Rezultati popisa, Beograd, 1966, Beograd, 1992.
Žunec, Ozren. *Goli život*. Zagreb: Demetra, 2007.
www.jasenovac.org (Jasenovac Research Institute). Accessed July 15, 2019.
www.jusp-jasenovac.hr (Javna ustanova Spomen područje Jasenovac). Accessed July 15, 2019.
www.terrorscapes.org (Terrorscapes. Transnational Memory of Totalitarian Terror and Genocide in Postwar Europe). Accessed July 29, 2019.

2 The Road to 'Serbian Yad Vashem'
Manipulations of the History of the Sajmište and Jasenovac Camps

Jovan Byford

In late September 2017, Serbian media reported that a bill had been finalized that would finally turn the site of the former Nazi camp, Sajmište (Fairground), in Belgrade into a memorial complex. This was announced by Goran Vesić, the city manager of Belgrade, after the session of the commission that had been working for several years on the design of the future memorial at Sajmište. Considering that the drafting of the mentioned law and its sending to the parliamentary procedure had already been announced (the first version of the law was leaked to the public already at the end of 2016, and the final version was announced in June 2017), this news would not have attracted special attention had it not been for one interesting detail. The session of the commission for Sajmište was held in Jasenovac, Croatia, 300 km away from the place where the announced memorial complex was supposed to be located.

The chairman of the commission for Sajmište was the bishop of Pakrac–Slavonia, Jovan Ćulibrk, in whose diocese Jasenovac is located. One might have thought that the reason for holding the session in Jasenovac was that Bishop Jovan, due to other obligations, was unable to travel to Belgrade, or that he simply wanted to host members of the commission in his diocese. However, the real reasons were very different. As Goran Vesić explained to the media, "the connection between Jasenovac and Sajmište in Belgrade is very strong," and "Sajmište cannot be understood without understanding Jasenovac." Moreover, Vesić continued, "The Jasenovac Memorial Complex is not large enough, given the number of people who died there, and it is very important for us that Sajmište becomes a central memorial site when it comes to remembering the victims of World War II." Finally, he concluded: "That is why it is important that the commission is sitting in Jasenovac today."[1]

This short statement for the media contains three interrelated assumptions about Sajmište and Jasenovac that are often taken for granted in Serbia today. The first is that there is an essential, historical connection between these two camps; second, that Sajmište is a natural place for a "central" memorial complex dedicated to the victims of genocide in the Independent State of Croatia; and, third, that the complex – a kind of "Serbian Yad Vashem," a memorial to Serbian victims of genocide – constitutes the appropriate response to the shortcomings of the existing, "insufficiently large" memorial in Jasenovac

DOI: 10.4324/9781003326632-3

itself. In this chapter, I will delve into the origins of these three theses, which are rooted in a long tradition of manipulation of the history of both Sajmište and Jasenovac in Serbia. I will also show that controversial interpretations of the history of the Sajmište camp in Serbia today are partly the legacy of the "war of remembrance" between Serbian and Croatian nationalists, fought just before and during the actual wars of the 1990s. At the time of the collapse of Yugoslavia, Sajmište, like Jasenovac, was a significant symbolic battleground in the war of words between Serbian and Croatian nationalists, who equally skillfully manipulated the history of these places as they accused each other's nations of being 'genocidal', of participating in the Holocaust or being inherently anti-Semitic. Disputes over Sajmište and its connection with Jasenovac, which survive to this day, can therefore be seen as another example of the longstanding connection, and interplay, between Serbian and Croatian nationalist discourses, which for thirty years have jointly resisted the development of a historically informed memory of the victims of World War II in Yugoslavia. Finally, through the story of the evolution of the idea of a Serbian "Yad Vashem" (Israel's official memorial to the victims of the Holocaust) at Sajmište, I will try to draw attention to the deep mark that the events of the 1990s have left on historical memory in Serbia when it comes to the Holocaust and other crimes committed in Yugoslavia in the period from 1941 to 1945.

A Brief Overview of the History of the Sajmište Camp

Between 1941 and 1944, close to 20,000 people died in the concentration camp at Sajmište in Belgrade. Located in the pavilions of the prewar Belgrade Fairgrounds, on the left bank of the Sava River, the Sajmište camp was not only the largest camp established by the German occupation authorities in Serbia during World War II, but also one of the first Nazi camps in Europe created for the mass internment of Jews. Between December 1941 and March 1942, about 7,000 Jews, mostly women, children, and the elderly, were brought to what was officially known as *Judenlager Semlin* – the Jewish camp in Zemun. This was almost half of the prewar Jewish population of the part of Serbia that in 1941 found itself under direct occupation by the German Reich. In the spring of 1942, in just six weeks, almost all Jewish inmates were systematically killed in a deadly gas van. Shortly afterwards, Serbia was declared *Judenrein* – cleansed of Jews – and Sajmište was turned into *Anhaltelager*, a temporary detention camp mainly for Serb hostages, political prisoners and captured Partisans, most of whom were later deported to Norway, Germany, or smaller labor camps in central Serbia. In the spring of 1942, the Third Reich had a constant shortage of labor, so Sajmište, located near the Danube River and next to an important railway junction, became the key distribution center of forced labor from all over the former Yugoslavia. From 1942 until the dissolution of the camp in July 1944, about 32,000 detainees (mostly Serbs from the territory of the Independent State of Croatia) were brought to the Anhaltelager. Of this number, about a third died in the camp, mostly from starvation and disease, or they were killed by guards and members of the camp's internal administration. Others were transported to labor camps, usually after a brief stay at Sajmište.[2]

Sajmište remained under the control of German authorities until May 1944. After some of the camp buildings were damaged during the Allied bombing raid on Belgrade in April 1944, most detainees were transferred to other camps, and control over Sajmište and the small number of detainees who remained there was handed over to the Zemun office of the General Directorate for Public Order and Security of the Independent State of Croatia. Three months later, on July 26, 1944, Sajmište was officially abandoned.

After the end of World War II, the ruins of the camp remained deserted until 1947, when the construction of New Belgrade began.[3] Since the pavilions that survived the bombing of 1944 were at that time the only larger building structures on the left bank of the Sava River, the area of the former camp, which was now referred to as *Staro Sajmište* – the Old Fairground – was converted into the headquarters of youth brigades, who were entrusted with the first phase of construction. The brigades remained at Sajmište until 1950, and after their departure most of the smaller buildings erected after the war were adapted into apartments allocated to poor families as social housing, while smaller prewar pavilions were given to the Association of Fine Artists of Serbia in 1952. The interiors of these buildings were turned into modest studios for young artists, who also used them as their residences. This state of affairs persisted for the next sixty years: Staro Sajmište is still a neglected and impoverished settlement with several hundred families, who often maintain dilapidated buildings and unpaved paths at their own expense. Over the years, a number of businesses have sprung up as well – car-repair shops, warehouses and workshops – but also a high school, a travel agency, a bookshop, a restaurant, even a small concert venue which, despite growing opposition, has been staging rock concerts, boxing matches, theater performances and dance parties.

As with most camps in the former Yugoslavia, before the 1960s there were no major initiatives to adequately mark the tragic history of Sajmište. In postwar Yugoslavia, concentration camps were not "functional" within the dominant discourse of public memory, as they did not fit into the "narrative of glorious resistance or equally glorious Partisan struggle" of the Yugoslav peoples.[4] However, in 1960, with the establishment of the Section of Former Inmates of Sajmište, which operated within Yugoslavia's main veterans' association, the Union of Fighters of the People's Liberation Wars, this situation gradually changed. Over time, and thanks to the efforts of surviving detainees, Sajmište came to be recognized as an important symbolic space and historically significant site. Still, the first serious initiative to turn Sajmište into a representative place of remembrance did not appear until after Tito's death in 1980. At the time, sociopolitical organizations such as the Union of Fighters of the People's Liberation Wars and the Coordinating Committee for the Preservation of Revolutionary Traditions sought to combat the societal challenges of the post–Tito period with "new revolutionary engagement," which included the promotion of the memory of "heroes of the anti-fascist struggle." It is in that context that Sajmište became the subject of official, institutionalized, and public remembrance, and the place of large scale annual commemorations. There were also increasingly vocal calls for the inhabitants of Sajmište to be evicted, and for the site to be turned into a memorial center of "pan-Yugoslav significance." This thinking informed the decision of the Belgrade City Assembly in 1987 to include "Staro Sajmište – the site of the Gestapo camp during World War 2" in the official register of important heritage sites in the city.

Until the late 1980s, Sajmište was, therefore, primarily viewed as a monument to anti-fascism: regular commemorations held on 9 May, for example, were dedicated exclusively to Belgrade's "revolutionary past" and the memory of the "victims of fascism." Their goal was "the reaffirmation of the moral and social values of the People's Liberation War and the socialist revolution," and they were dominated by motifs that reflected the symbolic order of socialist Yugoslavia: "resistance," "defiance," "heroism," and "revolution." And perhaps most importantly, the motif of the common suffering of the Yugoslav peoples permeated the representations of the camp. Ever since 1946, when the Yugoslav State Commission for the Investigation of the Crimes of the Occupiers and Their Accomplices published a report entitled "Sajmište, the place of suffering of the People of Yugoslavia," the "Yugoslav" nature of the camp had occupied a central place in its interpretation. In the early 1980s, this aspect of the memory of Sajmište gained in importance, as one of the purposes of the commemorations at Sajmište was the fight against Serbian and other nationalisms, which were seen at the time as the main form of "counter-revolutionary activity" in Yugoslavia and the main threat to Yugoslav unity.[5] Few could have predicted then that only a few years later, the maligned forces of the "counter-revolution" would turn their attention to Sajmište, and, by seeking to appropriate it, leave a lasting mark in the way that the Serbian public perceives its tragic history.

From the Place Where Yugoslavs Suffered to the Symbol of Serbian Martyrdom: Sajmište as "Serbian Yad Vashem"

During the late 1980s, at a time when ideological motifs and priorities set by the likes of the Union of Fighters and the Coordinating Committee for the Preservation of Revolutionary Traditions still dominated the memorial activities at Sajmište, an alternative interpretation of World War II history began to appear in public discourse in Serbia. The new perspective not only encompassed new themes and foci – primarily the genocide in the Independent State of Croatia between 1941 and 1945 – but it also marked the emergence of a new culture of remembrance, with its own institutional basis and commemorative practices. Its main exponent was the nationalist elite in Serbia.

In November 1988, a conference entitled "Jasenovac 1945–1988" was held at the Serbian Academy of Sciences and Arts (Serbian acronym: SANU). The gathering was organized by a special committee, founded on the initiative of the historian Vladimir Dedijer in 1984, which collected "material on the genocide of Serbs and other Yugoslav peoples in the twentieth century."[6] The creation of the Genocide Committee (as it was known within SANU) reflected the growing belief among historians at the Academy that "in our country no one writes about genocide from a scientific point of view, and even fewer books with historical material intended for the international audience have been printed."[7] Among the members of the committee appointed in 1984 were academics Vladimir Dedijer, Radovan Samardžić, Dobrica Ćosić and Milorad Ekmečić, as well as two historians who were not members of the Academy – Andrej Mitrović and Branko Petranović. The committee was later joined by Smilja Avramov and the self-proclaimed "Serbian Simon Wiesenthal," Milan Bulajic, who had been appointed in 1986 as an official observer, on behalf of the SANU, at the Zagreb trial of Ustaša war criminal Andrija Artuković.

In the early stages of its work, the Genocide Committee adopted, at least publicly, a pan-Yugoslav approach: it sought to collect material on genocides "against all the peoples of Yugoslavia" including against Muslims in eastern Bosnia in 1943. Nevertheless, despite these initial "pan-Yugoslav" pretensions, the Genocide Committee played an important role in the rise of Serbian nationalism, a development in which the Academy of Sciences as a whole was heavily implicated.[8] Thanks to the efforts of the members of the Genocide Committee and other prominent academics from the Historical Section of SANU, by the second half of 1988 the history of the genocide in the Independent State of Croatia had become an obsession in Serbian public discourse.[9] The role of the Genocide Committee in fueling the public excitement became even more pronounced after Dedijer's death in November 1990, when two prominent nationalists, academician Radovan Samardžić and his deputy Milan Bulajić, took the helm. It was then that several people from outside the Academy who were preoccupied with the suffering of Serbs were invited to join the committee. Among them were Archimandrite (and future bishop) Atanasije Jevtić, Srboljub Živanović, Dragoje Lukić, Đuro Zatezalo, and others. The committee also established links with the Serbian Orthodox Church, with which it organized, in 1991, a series of the highly publicized exhumations of mass graves of Serbs murdered fifty years earlier by the Ustasha. Over time, the Genocide Committee became the principal instrument for combating what they saw as the policy of "organized oblivion" of Serbian suffering in the Independent State of Croatia.[10] It developed an openly propagandistic, and nationalist remit: genocide in other parts of Yugoslavia (especially against Muslims in eastern Bosnia) was no longer mentioned, let alone investigated.

The "Jasenovac 1945–1988" conference reflected the Committee's increasingly pronounced nationalist orientation and its focus on Serb victims. One of the main topics of the gathering was the number of victims in Jasenovac. Milan Bulajić, who was the spokesman for the Genocide Committee, insisted that the exact number of victims of this camp had never been established, which was true, but he did so in a way that insinuated that the official figure of between 500,000 and 700,000 victims (originally put forward by the State Commission for the Investigation of Crimes of the Occupiers and Their Accomplices), is probably an underestimate. After all, the whole point of the supposed "conspiracy of silence" surrounding Serbian suffering, which many Serbian nationalists believed in at the time, was to hide, or minimize the real number of Serbian casualties, which was estimated by some to have exceeded one million dead.

In response to the "manipulations" over Jasenovac in official Yugoslav historiography, Milan Bulajić proposed a project aimed at finally breaking the "taboo" surrounding the camp, resisting the "ban on investigating World War II victims," and enabling the truth about Serb victimhood in the Independent State of Croatia to be finally revealed to the world. The project would involve the creation of a "database on victims of genocide," compiled by a separate institution, the "Museum of Genocide" dedicated to the victims of the Yugoslav "Holocaust–genocide" or "Yugoslav Holocaust."[11]

Bulajić's initiative to establish a "Museum of Genocide" was immediately endorsed by a wider stratum of the nationalist elite in Serbia who saw such an institution as a significant means by which Serbia would affirm its then reestablished status as a nation state. The museum would also help forge a new "nationalized" memory of World War II focused on Serbian suffering, and in doing so affirm Serbia's role as the bastion of the Serbian people. Authorities in Serbia, including Slobodan Milošević and Vojislav Šešelj, promptly offered their support.[12] Interest in the Museum of Genocide intensified after the publication of *Wastelands of Historical Reality,* a revisionist book by the historian and future president of Croatia, Franjo Tuđman. The "Museum of Genocide, similar to the one built by the Jews in Jerusalem a long time ago" was seen as the best way to refute the allegations of Croatian nationalists that the number of victims in Jasenovac was only 40,000.[13]

Shortly afterwards, the question was raised about the location of the proposed museum. In February 1990, during a public round-table discussion, Milan Bulajić proposed that the museum, which he occasionally referred to by the eerie title "Museum of the Dead," could be located at "the place of remembrance of the Nazi camp Sajmište in Belgrade." The idea was immediately endorsed by other speakers at the event, who announced the creation of a "Serbian Yad Vashem," where it would be noted that "the Serbian people are one of the biggest victims of genocide" in history.[14] The appeal of Staro Sajmište as a place for the future museum lay in the fact that the relatively large area occupies a prominent position on the left bank of the Sava River near the city center, and the fact that it had already been earmarked for development as a memorial complex. Notably, in the deliberations regarding the future location of the "Museum of Genocide," Staro Sajmište figured as an empty symbolic and geographical space, devoid of its unique and tragic history. The victims of the Sajmište camp were practically excluded from the history of the site, giving way to a new object of remembrance, the Serbian victims of the Ustaša genocide.

The final decision to build the museum (officially named the "Museum of Genocide Victims") at Sajmište was made in December 1991, at a meeting held at the Belgrade municipal council.[15] Although it was clear to those involved that the opening of the museum was a long-term goal – residents of Sajmište needed to be evicted, and the buildings restored – the 'Law on the Establishment of the Museum of Genocide Victims' was swiftly drafted and passed by the Serbian Parliament in July 1992.[16] The Museum began operating in 1995, in temporary offices in the center of Belgrade, where it is located to this day, still awaiting a suitable space for a permanent exhibition.

Sajmište as "Part of a Wider Circle of Death" around Jasenovac

To present Sajmište as the most logical place for the future Museum of Genocide Victims and a place where a memorial center dedicated primarily to the victims of Ustaša terror should be set up, Milan Bulajić often emphasized the connection between Sajmište and Jasenovac camps. This is important because, with the exception of the conclusion of a communiqué on Sajmište issued in 1945 by the State Commission for the Investigation of the Crimes of the Occupiers and Their Accomplices, where Ustaša leaders Ante Pavelić and Dido Kvaternik were mentioned among the persons responsible for the crimes perpetrated in the Sajmište camp, Sajmište was not known as part of the history of the Independent State of Croatia. Therefore, the logic behind the proposal to locate the Museum of Genocide Victims there was not obvious. To address this, Bulajić promoted a selective and often historically unfounded interpretation of Sajmište, all with the aim of "exporting" the camp to the Independent State of Croatia, and connecting it with Jasenovac, the symbol of Serbian suffering and the core object of memory in the future Museum of Genocide Victims. This strategy involved emphasizing several peripheral aspects of the history of the Sajmište camp, or tendentiously focusing on carefully selected instances of the suffering of its victims.

At an event organized by SANU shortly after the Museum of Genocide Victims was founded, Milan Bulajić offered two reasons why this museum should be located in Belgrade, more precisely at the Sajmište. First, Bulajić stated, "corpses from the Independent State of Croatia, from the Ustaša death camp Jasenovac, floated down the Sava River to its banks in Belgrade." Thus, the Sava River and its banks symbolically connect the Serbian capital with Jasenovac. Second, "detainees were sent to Jasenovac from Sajmište," which represents another unbreakable bond between these two camps.[17] Two more arguments were added later: first, that Sajmište was formally located "on the territory of the NDH," that is, it was "formed on the basis of an agreement between the Nazi command in Belgrade and the Croatian Ustaša authorities," and, second, that the worst period of suffering in this camp was between May and July 1944, when control was handed over to the General Directorate for Public Order and Security of the Independent State of Croatia and the Ustaša police in Zemun.[18] Together, these four claims provided Bulajić with proof that Sajmište was in fact "part of a wider circle of the Nazi–Ustaša system of the Jasenovac death camp."[19] The Jasenovac camp itself was only the "first circle" of death; the surrounding smaller Ustaša camps were the "second circle"; while the third, broadest circle, included "the entire territory of the Ustaša Independent State of Croatia (NDH)," including the Sajmište camp.[20]

It is important to point out that each of Bulajić's four arguments contains a grain of truth. It is true that Sajmište was formally located on the territory of the Independent State of Croatia, whose eastern border was the left bank of the Sava River in Belgrade. It is true that groups of detainees from the Independent State of Croatia, including those from Jasenovac, were transported to Sajmište, from where some were sent back to the Ustaša instead of to labor camps in Germany or Norway, and were then liquidated in Jasenovac. This was the fate of about 4,000 mostly Serb detainees who were transported from Jasenovac to Sajmište in August 1942. After they were declared "unfit for work," about a thousand of them were executed at Sajmište, while the rest were returned to the NDH on September 1, 1942. Only 2,400 detainees survived the transport back to Jasenovac, and they were executed upon arrival at the killing sites in Donja Gradina.[21] It is also true that the corpses of victims from the NDH floated down the Sava River all the way to Belgrade, just as it is true that the Ustaša took command of the Sajmište camp in May 1944. However, all this does not mean that Bulajić's conclusions stand up to scrutiny. Throughout its existence, Sajmište was exclusively a *Nazi* camp and was part of the history of that region of Serbia that was under the direct occupation of Nazi Germany, not the NDH. The agreement between the German command in Belgrade and the authorities in Zagreb, which placed the pavilions of the former Belgrade fairgrounds under the jurisdiction of the German security apparatus in Belgrade, was a mere formality and, until May 1944 the camp was guarded exclusively by German soldiers under the command of German authorities in Serbia. Likewise, the fate of the detainees who were returned to the Ustaša in no way justifies the qualification that Sajmište was part of the Jasenovac camp system.[22] The number of detainees returned to the NDH was not only relatively small in relation to the total number of victims of Sajmište, but their tendentious prioritization diverts attention from the fact that there were many more equally exhausted deportees from Croatia and Bosnia and Herzegovina who were executed at Sajmište by German guards and members of the camp administration, or who died of starvation and disease. In Bulajić's version of events, however, the return of detainees to Jasenovac in September 1942 represents a seminal moment in the wartime history of Sajmište, and the proof of the connection that exists between this camp and the suffering of Serbs in the Independent

State of Croatia. As for the corpses that the River Sava brought to Belgrade, their actual number (about four hundred) was much lower than the 15,000 that Bulajić mentions in his books, and they were certainly not victims from Jasenovac, located about 300 km upstream from Belgrade. Finally, Bulajić's claim that the period May–July 1944, when the camp was taken over by the Ustaša, was a time of special brutality is inaccurate. According to Bulajić, at Sajmište, the Ustašas – led by camp commander Petar Brzica, who was "sent to this post from Jasenovac where he won a competition in 'who was going to slaughter more detainees" – "beat" detainees even more often than was the case under German administration.[23] However, Milan Koljanin (author of the only detailed study of the Sajmište camp) claims that in the last months of the camp's existence there was a milder regime compared to the period when there were many more detainees, and when the camp was under German command. In addition, even after Sajmište was taken over by the Ustaša, this camp was not an "Ustaša" camp in the way that Jasenovac had been throughout its existence. The detainees at Sajmište, even between May and July 1944, were primarily "German detainees" and people whom the "German police [...] counted on to be sent to work in the Third Reich."[24]

Although in his works he emphasized the connections between Sajmište and Jasenovac, Milan Bulajić did not completely forget the status of this camp as "a Nazi creation and the place of suffering of Jews" from the territory of occupied Serbia.[25] Therefore, this was not an instance of complete rewriting of the history of Sajmište and the suppression of the Holocaust committed on the territory of occupied Serbia. But, in the overall narrative of the genocide in World War II expounded by Bulajić and other advocates of the Museum of Genocide Victims, the facts about the Judenlager occupied a peripheral place.[26] In fact, in his public appearances, Bulajić tended to "remember" the Jewish dimension of Sajmište's history, either in the presence of Jews, or when he expected the Israeli government or Jewish organizations around the world to provide funding for the project of the "Serbian Yad Vashem" at Sajmište. Unfortunately, this trend has survived to this day.

Serbo–Croatian Propaganda War and the Interpretations of the History of Sajmište

The interpretation of Sajmište and its history in the early 1990s was influenced by, among other things, the disputes between Zagreb and Belgrade about the attitude of Serbs and Croats towards Jews during World War II. On the Croatian side, the most active in this war of words were authors such as Tomislav Vuković, Ljubica Štefan, Josip Pečarić, Ante Knežević and the American publicist Philip Cohen.[27] In their works, they tried to present the Serbs as a "genocidal people," whose collaborators during World War II, acting with the blessing of the Serbian Orthodox Church, committed much more terrible crimes than the Ustaša, and that they cleansed Serbia of Jews. Like their Serbian counterparts, Croatian authors claimed that there was a "conspiracy of silence" in socialist Yugoslavia, but one that covered up the genocidal character of *Serbian* nationalism and its bloody legacy. Thus, the anti-Serbian propaganda abundantly borrowed from, and inverted the arguments of Serbian nationalists, who were the first to write about the "conspiracy of silence" surrounding Ustasha crimes, the genocidal nature of (Croatian) nationalism, the role of the (Catholic) Church in the genocide committed in World War II. On the Serbian side, the main protagonists in the debates were Milan Bulajić, the authors of the book *The Truth About "Serbian Anti-Semitism,"* Andrija Gams and Aleksandar Levi, and Jaša Almuli, at that time one of the spokesmen of the controversial and nationalist Serbian–Jewish Friendship Society.[28] In response to the various "accusations" from Zagreb, they generally sought to completely deny the existence of anti-Semitism in Serbia, emphasizing instead its widespread presence in Croatia, both in the past and today.

Eventually various ministries (the Ministry of Culture and Information in Serbia and the Ministry of Foreign Affairs in Croatia), as well as the regime media in both countries, joined in the polemic, thus elevating it to the level of state propaganda. Also, the works of the above-mentioned authors were translated and published into English,, in part or in whole, which means that they were intended not only for the domestic audience, but also for international public opinion as part of a marketing project of national reputation management.[29] The fact that the attitude towards Jews featured prominently in the international propaganda of the two countries is interesting in itself and could be attributed, at least partly, to the belief in the power of Jewish public opinion in America, which was apparent on both sides.[30]

The polemics in the early 1990s are important for the topic of this chapter, because from the very beginning, Sajmište was one of the main symbolic battlegrounds in the war of words between Serbian and Croatian quasi historians. It is impossible to determine who "started first," but already in the late 1980s, authors in Serbia increasingly made the argument that Sajmište was located on the territory of the Independent State of Croatia. The intention was not necessarily to "blame" Croatia for the victims of this camp, but to point out that the Serbian collaborationist government had no influence on the events in the camp. Because Sajmište was under German administration and on the territory of another state, some authors in Serbia claimed that Nedić's collaborationist government in Belgrade could not bear responsibility for the Holocaust. This argument was not new because it was used by collaborationists themselves in postwar trials.[31] However, in the late 1980s, it was reintroduced into public discourse as part of the story of the impeccable tradition of Serbian–Jewish friendship, and in an effort to divert public attention from the role Nedić's government played in implementing anti-Jewish measures in the early stages of occupation, in the appropriation of Jewish property, in the internment of Jews in the Topovske Šupe and Banjica camps, and so on.[32] However, there were also those who saw in the fact that Sajmište was formally located on the territory of the Independent State of

Croatia proof that it was an Ustaša camp. As early as 1990, in an article in *Politika*, Sajmište was mentioned, along with Jasenovac and Jadovno, as a place of Ustaša crimes against Serbs, Jews, and Roma.[33]

Croatian authors responded to such claims with a counterattack. Apart from disputing the claim that Sajmište was an Ustaša camp (especially not at the time when Jews were imprisoned there), they tried to prove that the biggest killers at Sajmište were in fact Serbs. Their writings give the impression that only the outer perimeter of the camp was secured by German guards, and that the Serbian authorities had control over the camp itself. In the book *Review of Serbian Anti-Semitism*, Tomislav Vuković and Edo Bojović promoted the notorious kapo in the Anhaltelager, Radivoje Kisić, to "Yugoslav [sic.] camp commander," and other kapos, recruited from the ranks of detainees, to Serbian "policemen."[34] The killing of Jews in the camp was attributed to "Serbian-German allies." In the book *Serbian Orthodox Church and Fascism*, Ljubica Štefan also states that Sajmište was "run by the Germans and the Serbian police of Milan Nedić, led by Dragi Jovanović."[35] This, of course, is not true, given that, when Sajmište was handed over to the German military administration in Belgrade, the NDH government set an explicit condition that there could be no Serb guards or police officers in the camp.

The hitherto unknown "facts" about Sajmište were presented by Croatian authors as a significant discovery that had been hidden for decades by the "conspiracy of silence." Štefan alleged that the truth about Sajmište had been hidden in order to present Serbia as "pure and innocent" on the issue of the Holocaust, and to put all the blame on the Croats. In this case, Štefan drew on an argument identical to that found in the literature on Jasenovac published in Belgrade at the time. She claimed that "liberators," namely Partisans, deliberately destroyed every trace of the crimes committed at Sajmište and that the camp was "erased from history – intentionally, systematically."[36] The fact that after the war "never, absolutely never was any commemoration held at (Sajmište)" was also attributed to the conspiracy.[37] Of course, neither of these two claims is correct.

Another thing that made Sajmište especially attractive for Croatian propaganda was that with a fairly simple numbers game, this camp could be presented not only as a Serbian counterpart to Jasenovac, but also as a worse place of suffering than the largest camp in the NDH. For example, in the book *Serbian Myth about Jasenovac*, Josip Pečarić cites the findings of the State Commission for the Investigation of the Crimes of the Occupiers and Their Accomplices, according to which "more than 40,000 victims" perished at Sajmište. In addition, he states that the actual number of victims is most likely even higher, given that Yugoslav authorities supposedly concealed the real number of Jewish victims of Sajmište, which, according to Pečarić, exceeded 11,000. However, when it came to the number of victims of Jasenovac, Pečarić was not nearly as inclined to rely on the findings of the State Commission and the literature from the era of socialist Yugoslavia. On the contrary, he devoted a significant number of pages in the book to the 'evidence' that the number of victims in Jasenovac was much smaller than the alleged 600,000, and he endorsed Tuđman's view that the number of victims was around 40,000. It is not difficult to see where this argument leads. If the highest estimates of the suffering at Sajmište are compared with the numbers Jasenovac found in Croatian revisionist literature, it turns out that Sajmište was a larger camp than Jasenovac, and that the biggest crime on the territory of Yugoslavia was committed not in the Independent State of Croatia, but in occupied Serbia. Therefore, in the writing of Croatian authors, the effort to prove that Serbia was not "pure and innocent" when it comes to the Holocaust, quickly morphed into a campaign to prove that Serbia was in fact the main perpetrator of the Holocaust and genocide in the Balkans and that no one knew about this because of the systematic "hiding of the truth about the Belgrade concentration camps." Ljubica Štefan even insinuates that an injustice was done to Croatia when Jasenovac was included among the 22 camps whose names are inscribed in a mosaic of memories in Yad Vashem in Israel, and suggested that Sajmište should have occupied that spot.

Mutual accusations of 'genocidality', which involved the distortion of historical facts, raised tensions on both sides in the 1990s, and fueled nationalist passions, animosity, and resentment among the general public. In the context of war propaganda, that after all was the purpose of these debates. Unfortunately, in both Serbia and Croatia, some of the arguments have taken root and persist to the present day. In Serbia, when it comes to the Holocaust, many things are still explained away and justified by the claim that "Sajmište was in the Independent State of Croatia." Meanwhile, there are some in Croatia today who still believe that there were camps in Belgrade that can be compared to Jasenovac in terms of the number of victims and the horrors that took place there, and that, therefore, in the Yugoslav context, the NDH was not uniquely evil. However, what is especially important when it comes to the memory of Sajmište is that, thanks to the debates with their Croatian counterparts, Bulajić and his associates perfected the arguments about Sajmište as part of the history of the NDH, and in doing so became even more convinced that the site of this camp is an ideal place for a memorial center dedicated to the Serbian suffering in the Independent State of Croatia.[38]

Monument at Sajmište and Selective Remembrance of the Victims of World War II

In anticipation of the eviction of the residents of Staro Sajmište and its restoration for the needs of the "Serbian Yad Vashem," a monument was erected at the site in April 1995. The imposing, abstract sculpture, the work of the Belgrade sculptor Miodrag Popović, was laid on a pedestal on the left bank of the Sava River, at the spot that supposedly marked the line along which ran the barbed wire perimeter around the camp. The sculpture, in the shape of a "cracked form of a circle, one part of which symbolizes life and the other death" was chosen as far back as in 1987, at a time when Sajmište symbolized the common suffering of Yugoslavs, and was meant to represent resistance to fascism. The original intention was for the monument to be unveiled on May 9, 1989, as part of the annual anti-fascist commemoration at Sajmište. However, for technical and financial reasons, the monument was erected six years later.

In those six years, a lot had changed in Serbia. The monument was not unveiled on May 9, 1995, which would have been highly appropriate given that the 50th anniversary of the end of World War II was being celebrated throughout Europe that year. Instead, the ceremony was held two and a half weeks earlier, on Friday, April 21. This date was not chosen at random; it marked an important change in the commemorative calendar of the Republic of Serbia. April 22 is the day when in 1945 a group of about six hundred detainees organized a breakout from Jasenovac, after which the camp practically ceased to exist. Since 1992, that date had been officially commemorated in the Republic of Serbia as the Day of Remembrance for the Victims of Genocide in Yugoslavia. The unveiling of the monument at Sajmište was conceived by the organizers as an event with a dual meaning, marking two important dates – the Day of Genocide Victims and the 50th anniversary of the victory over fascism. In that sense, the ceremony simultaneously signified continuity with the ceremonies at Sajmište of the 1980s, and the drive to promote new historical dates and objects of remembrance.

The dual meaning of the event was reflected also in the inscription on the monument, which was ceremoniously unveiled that day. The sculpture, which was designed in 1987 as a monument to "victims and casualties of the resistance to the Gestapo and their camp police," now had a much broader meaning:[39]

> In this place, in a Nazi concentration camp at the Old Fairground, during the occupation of Yugoslavia from 1941 to 1944, war crimes and genocide were committed against nearly one hundred thousand patriots, participants in the National Liberation War, women, children and old people. Every second prisoner was killed in the camp or at execution sites in Jajinci, Bežanijska Kosa, Jabuka and Ostrovačka Ada. Many were taken to German death camps throughout occupied Europe. Most of the victims were Serbs, Jews or Gypsies. This monument is dedicated to them, and also to the victims to the notorious Ustasha camp in Jasenovac and the victims of Hungarian occupying forces, who were brought to Belgrade by the waves of the Sava and Danube. To the brave people who resisted Nazi terror and to all victims of genocide in Yugoslavia.
>
> Belgrade, April 22, 1995 on the Day of Remembrance of the Victims of Genocide and the 50th anniversary of the victory over fascism.

The first two sentences directly reflect the representations of Sajmište from the time of socialist Yugoslavia. They would have been included even if the monument had been unveiled in 1989 as originally planned. "Patriots" and "participants in the national liberation struggle" are given priority in the hierarchy of victims, and the object of memory is situated in the context of the "Nazi occupation of Yugoslavia." Mentioned also are "resistance to Nazi terror" and *Yugoslav* victims of genocide. The inclusion of these motives was undoubtedly a concession to the members of SUBNOR (Savez udruženja boraca narodnooslobodilačkog rata Jugoslavije; "Federation of the Association of Veterans of the National Liberation War of Yugoslavia"), who in previous decades advocated that Sajmište get such a monument. However, already in the third sentence, it is not the Yugoslavs, but the triad "Serbs, Jews, and Roma" who are mentioned as victims honored at Sajmište. This marked the transition to a culture of remembrance typical of the 1990s. Clearly, the monument was not only dedicated to the victims of Sajmište, but also to victims of Jasenovac and those killed by the Hungarian occupiers. Among the victims "brought to Belgrade by the waves of the Sava and the Danube" are those who led Milan Bulajić to characterize the riverbank near Sajmište as "the third circle of death around Jasenovac," although on this occasion the victims of the notorious Novi Sad raid in January 1942 were added.

The "geography of memory" implicit in the reference to Sajmište as a place that symbolically, at the confluence of the two rivers, connects the suffering of "Serbs, Jews, and Roma" in different parts of the country, reflected the view promoted at the time by supporters of the Museum of Genocide Victims, and much of the Serbian nationalist elite. The final sentence of the inscription summarizes the dual role of the monument: it pays tribute to "the brave people who resisted Nazi terror," and "to all the victims of the genocide in Yugoslavia."

A particularly interesting feature of the unveiling ceremony at Sajmište in April 1995, was that suffering in Jasenovac was hardly mentioned. Although the event marked the anniversary of the day of the breakout from Jasenovac, this camp, or the Serbian victimhood in the Independent State of Croatia more generally, were barely mentioned in the speeches, the recital, or the commentary during the live broadcast on Serbian state television. The connection between Sajmište and Jasenovac, which had been so insisted upon in previous years, was visible only in the inscription on the monument (which was read out at the very beginning of the ceremony), and the date when the whole event was organized. Such selective memory was a reflection of the political moment. In April 1995, the fate of the Republic of Serbian Krajina – the self-proclaimed state-like entity created by Serb rebels in Croatia – was uncertain. The monument was being unveiled just a week before the start of "Operation Flash," a large-scale military action during which parts of the rebel-held area that included Jasenovac – which had been under Serb control since October 1991 – was re-occupied by the Croatian army. Authorities in Serbia were aware of the upcoming operation and probably realized that Serb martyrdom in Jasenovac and historical ties to Serbs in Croatia were topics that are best avoided. Therefore, the historical parallels that the regime media had insisted on in previous years, such as that between Tuđman's Croatia and the Independent State of Croatia, or the genocide from 1941–1945 and the one allegedly being committed against Serbs in Croatia at the time, were nowhere to be found. The brutality of German occupation and the heroism of the population, rehearsed during the ceremonies held at Sajmište during the 1980s, but updated with new motifs such as the emphasis on Serbs as the main victims and bearers of resistance, offered a more "usable" version of the past. Zoran Lilić, the then president of Yugoslavia – a state that, throughout the Yugoslav conflict of 1991–1995, insisted that it was "was not at war" – conveyed a message of peace and humanity in his speech, and mentioned Serbs in Croatia and Bosnia in a single sentence. A week before "Operation Flash," he sent them a message (if not a warning) that they could expect (only) "moral, political, and humanitarian support" from Serbia.

Sajmište as a Memorial Outpost of Jasenovac

In the period after 1995, the monument at Sajmište began to play a significant role as a memorial to the victims of genocide in the Independent State of Croatia. Commemorations were held at the site each year on April 22. The day would begin with an early-morning wreath-laying ceremony at Sajmište, followed by a short walk across the bridge to the Cathedral Church of St. Michael the Archangel (Saborna Crkva), where a liturgy was held. The liturgy was followed by an afternoon event, usually an exhibition, a round table discussion, a conference, or a *svečana akademija*, a type of formal recital. These events, just like the liturgy, were dedicated to the genocide in the Independent State of Croatia: in 1997 there was a round table discussion on Jasenovac, in 1998 and 2000 an exhibition entitled "The System of Ustaša Death Camps Jasenovac," and so on.[40] Although these were not mass events, it was clear that, in the context of marking the Day of Genocide Victims, Sajmište and the monument from 1995 represented a place of remembrance primarily for the Serb victims of genocide in the Independent State of Croatia. In the following years, the emphasis on Jasenovac began to prevail to such an extent that it occasionally led to the complete neglect of the memory of Jews from the territory of occupied Serbia, who lost their lives in the Sajmište camp. This was especially evident in 2005, when, a few weeks before the Day of Remembrance for the Victims of Genocide, the Ministry of Culture of the Republic of Serbia issued a statement informing the public about the upcoming celebration of the double jubilee: "90th anniversary of the genocide of Armenians and Greeks, and the 60th anniversary of the genocide committed by the Ustašas against Serbs, Jews, and Roma in Jasenovac."[41] So, in the year in which the world marked the 60th anniversary of the end of the Holocaust – and, more importantly, in a statement announcing a series of events beginning with the laying of wreaths at Sajmište – the only example of genocidal violence committed between 1941 and 1945 considered worthy of commemoration in Serbia was the one committed against Serbs, Jews, and Roma in the NDH. The memory of the "victims of genocide" was clearly limited, both spatially and symbolically, to the Independent State of Croatia. The Jews who lost their lives in Serbia under Nazi occupation, including at Sajmište, were once again forgotten.

After the year 2000, the campaign to create a Museum of Genocide Victims at Sajmište was renewed. In 2002, on the tenth anniversary of the founding of the museum, Milan Bulajić submitted the project "Museum of Genocide Victims – Sajmište" to the Belgrade Land Development Public Agency.[42] In the end, however, nothing came out of this initiative. In the first years after the fall of Milošević, there was not much support for Bulajić's ambitious plans. Shortly after, the government of Zoran Đinđić decided to remove Milan Bulajić from the post of director of the Museum of Genocide Victims.

However, in 2003, in the aftermath of the assassination of Zoran Đinđić and the rise to power of the more conservative politician, Vojislav Koštunica, the Museum of Genocide Victims project once again gained currency. Especially after 2006, when the new permanent exhibition of the Memorial Museum in Jasenovac opened. Many in Serbia, but also in Croatia and beyond, were of the view that the exhibition downplays the horrors of Jasenovac and is insulting to the memory of the victims.[43] In the Museum of Genocide Victims, many saw an opportunity for the Republic of Serbia to set the record straight, and offer a riposte to the inappropriate exhibition in Jasenovac. Among the advocates of this solution were Milan Bulajić's old "comrades-in-arms," but also representatives of the Association of Former Detainees of Jasenovac, who considered the museum a place where "people from all over the world" would learn about the suffering in the Independent State of Croatia: that is, about the facts that are suppressed in the new exhibition in Jasenovac.[44] The memorial museum at Sajmište was also discussed during a five-day Israeli–Serbian scientific exchange dedicated to the study of the Holocaust, organized in 2006 by the Ministry of Culture of the Republic of Serbia. On that occasion, the museum at Sajmište was once again discussed in the context of the controversy surrounding the new museum exhibition in Jasenovac.[45] Therefore, just as in 1989, when Croatian revisionism was the trigger for the idea of building a Museum of Genocide Victims at Sajmište, in 2006–2007, the memorial center was seen as little more than a tool in the ongoing skirmishes with Croatia over Jasenovac. This remains the case to the present day, in that the media, politicians, and the general public in Serbia still tend to "remember" Jasenovac only in the context of polemics with, and criticism of some action of Serbia's western neighbor. As a result, Sajmište, long seen as a memorial "outpost" of Jasenovac, remains a significant symbolic battleground in the "war of memories" between Belgrade and Zagreb.

There is, however, another dimension to the latest drive to create a memorial center at Sajmište. In 2007, under the auspices of the Municipality of New Belgrade, a very different initiative related to Sajmište was launched, aimed at creating a memorial center specifically dedicated to the history of the Sajmište camp, and to the Holocaust.[46] The effort to establish such a memorial and educational center in Belgrade was, at least to some extent, a reaction of the progressive political elite and civil society in Serbia to the then very prominent revisionist tendencies in Serbian society (primarily the attempt to rehabilitate collaborationist politicians Milan Nedić and Dimitrije Ljotić), and the almost complete neglect of the Holocaust in public memory. An expert group formed in 2013 by then-mayor of Belgrade from the ranks of the Democratic Party, Dragan Ðilas, worked on the realization of this project, which was aimed at creating a new, evidence-based and historically informed culture of memory.[47] However, the work of this group was doomed from the start. A memorial to victims of the Holocaust and all those who perished at Sajmište was incompatible with the dominant discourse of remembrance of World War II in Serbia, one that remains focused on Serbian suffering, and which, therefore, does not recognize the Holocaust as an event that, in its own right, is worthy of memory and respect.[48] Therefore, already in 2014, shortly after the Serbian Progressive Party of Aleksandar Vučić took over power in Belgrade, the composition of the committee had changed, and Serbian suffering in the Independent State of Croatia was once again placed center stage.

As things stand, Serbia will eventually get the "Serbian Yad Vashem" at Sajmište, of the kind that Milan Bulajić imagined in the late 1980s.[49] The current Serbian president, Aleksandar Vučić, promised as much in September 2021 when he announced that the Museum of Genocide Victims will be allocated suitable exhibition space at Sajmište, and will be tasked with "demonstrating to the whole world the suffering of Serbs." The riverbank adjacent to the site of the former camp, Vučić added, will be named "The Bank of the Victims of Jasnovac" and from there, Serbia will show the world "what the Serbian people went through eighty years ago."[50]

Of course, the need to have a memorial center dedicated to Serbian victims of genocide in the capital of the Republic of Serbia is not in question. The Serb victims of the Ustaša regime certainly deserve such a place of remembrance, especially given that the scale and scope of the genocide of Serbs in the Independent State of Croatia is still frequently being overlooked and sometimes even denied in Croatia. However, such a memorial center has no place in Sajmište, which has its own unique history and tragic past. The memory of the victims of Jasenovac cannot be built at the cost of marginalizing the Holocaust of Serbian Jews.

Thus, instead of a worthy memorial to the victims who perished there, Sajmište will become a lasting reminder of the extent to which the controversial politics of memory from the 1980s and 1990s still defines the attitude towards the past in Serbia. The country will clearly have to wait a bit longer for the kind of memorial that the victims of both Sajmište and Jasenovac undoubtedly deserve.

Notes

1 Dragana Biberović, "Vesić: Izrađen Nacrt zakona o Starom Sajmištu," *Radio Televizije Srbije* website, www.rts.rs/page/stories/sr/story/125/drustvo/2880615/vesic-izradjen-nacrt-zakona-o-starom-sajmistu.html (accessed September 23, 2017).
2 On the history of the Sajmište camp, see: Milan Koljanin, *Nemački logor na Beogradskom sajmištu* (Beograd: Institut za savremenu istoriju, 1992).
3 A detailed analysis of the post–war history of Sajmište is the topic of my book Staro sajmište: mesto sećanja, zaborava i sporenja, on which one part of this text is based (cf. Jovan Byford, *Staro sajmište: mesto sećanja, zaborava i sporenja*, Beograd: Beogradski Centar Za Ljudska Prava, 2011). The book can be downloaded electronically at: http://oro.open.ac.uk/33501/.
4 Heike Karge, "Mediated remembrance: Local practices of remembering the Second World War in Tito's Yugoslavia," *European Review of History*, vol. 16, no. 1 (2009), pp. 55.
5 "Nurturing revolutionary traditions in the function of achieving the current program goals of the Socialist Alliance of Belgrade with reference to the implementation of conclusions in this area, adopted at the presidency of GK SSRN and GO SUBNOR in 1982, 1983 and 1985" April, 1988. Arhiv Jevrejskog istorijskog muzeja, Beograd, K.KSO–20, 410/88, pp. 1.
6 Slobodan Kljakić, "Kratka istorija Odbora SANU za sakupljanje građe o genocidu nad srpskim narodom i drugim narodima Jugoslavije u XX veku," in Predrag Dragić-Kijuk (ed.) *Catena Mundi II* (Kraljevo: Ibarske Novosti & Matica Srba i Iseljenika Srbije, 1992), pp. 498–512.
7 "Pismo Vladmira Dedijera Izvršnom odboru SANU," ibid., pp. 499.
8 Olivera Milosavljević, "Zloupotreba autoriteta nauke," in Nebojša Popov (ed.) *Srpska strana rata: Trauma i katarza u istorijskom pamćenju* (Beograd: Samizdat B92, 2002), pp. 340–374.
9 Jasna Dragović-Soso, *Saviours of the Nation* (Montreal: McGill-Queen's University Press, 2002), pp. 113.
10 See: "Zapisnik sa sednice Odbora za sakupljanje građe o genocide protiv srpskog naroda i drugih naroda Jugoslavije u XX. veku, 24. XII 1990. godine" in Slobodan Kljakić (ed.) *Kratka istorija Odbora SANU*, pp. 512.
11 "Okrugli sto–Muzej žrtava genocida," *Svet*, April 1, 1990, pp. 5.
12 Milan Bulajić, "Genocid nad pravoslavnim Srbima u Drugom svjetskom ratu," in Milan Bulajić (ed.) *Genocid nad Srbima u II svetskom ratu* (Beograd: Srpska književna zadruga, 1995), pp. 12.
13 Ditto, pp. 3.
14 A. Brkić, "Srbi ne znaju koliko ih nema," *Svet*, April 1, 1990, pp. 65.
15 D. Đurđević, "Suprotstavljanje neistinama," *Politika*, December 19, 1991, pp. 8.
16 Milan Bulajić, "Uvodno izlaganje," in Milan Bulajić and Radovan Samardžić (eds.) *Ratni zločini i zločini genocida, 1991–1992*. (Beograd: Srpska akademija nauka i umetnosti. Odeljenje istorijskih nauka, 1993), pp. 21.
17 Ditto, 21–22.
18 See: Milan Koljanin, *Nemački logor na Beogradskom sajmištu*, pp. 51.
19 Milan Bulajić, *Jasenovac: ustaški logor smrti, srpski mit?: hrvatski ustaški logori genocida nad Srbima, Jevrejima i Ciganima* (Beograd: Stručna knjiga, 1999), pp. 159.

The Road to 'Serbian Yad Vashem' 51

20 Milan Bulajić, *Jasenovac: Uloga Vatikana u nacističkoj Hrvatskoj* (Beograd: Pešić i sinovi, 2007), pp. 283–284.
21 Ditto, pp. 286.
22 Milan Koljanin, "Veze između nemačkog logora na Beogradskom sajmištu i logora NDH Jasenovac i Stara Gradiška" in Jelka Smreka (ed.) *Jasenovac 1986* (Round table) (Jasenovac: Spomen područje Jasenovac, 1986), pp. 177.
23 Milan Bulajić, *Jasenovac: ustaški logori smrti, srpski mit?* pp. 164.
24 Milan Koljanin, *Nemački logor na Beogradskom sajmištu*, pp. 443.
25 Milan Bulajić, *Deset godina Muzeja žrtava genocida* (Beograd: Fond za istraživanje genocida, 2003), pp. 469. For a critical analysis of Bulajić's treatment of the Holocaust, see: Jovan Byford, "When I say 'the Holocaust', I mean 'Jasenovac': Remembrance of the Holocaust in contemporary Serbia," *East European Jewish Affairs*, vo. 37, no. 1 (2011), pp. 51–74.
26 Milan Bulajić, *Jasenovac: uloga Vatikana u nacističkoj Hrvatskoj*, pp. 11.
27 Tomislav Vuković and Edo Bojović, *Pregled srpskog antisemitizma* (Zagreb: Alatir, 1992); Anto Knežević, *Analysis of Serbian Propaganda* (Zagreb: Domovina, 1992); Ljubica Štefan, *Srpska pravoslavna crkva i fašizam* (Zagreb: Hrvatski institute za povijest, 1996); Josip Pečarić, *Srpski mit o Jasenovcu: Skrivanje istine o beogradskim konc-logorima* (Zagreb: Dom i svijet/Hrvatski informativni centar/Hrvatski institut za povijest, 1998); Philip Cohen, *Serbia's Secret War: Propaganda and the Deceit in History* (Texas: College Station, 1996).
28 Andrija Gams and Aleksandar Levi, *The Truth about Serbian Anti-Semitism* (Beograd: Ministarstvo informisanja Republike Srbije, 1994); Jaša Almuli, "Creating Big Lies About Serbia and Serbs," feuilleton, *Politika*, December 26, 1993–January 25, 1994. The Serbian-Jewish Friendship Society was founded in 1988 by a group of public figures, Serbs and Jews, with the aim of promoting good relations between the two peoples as well as between Serbia and Israel. However, his work was primarily in the function of nationalist propaganda in the late 1980s. It is important to emphasize that the Serbian-Jewish Friendship Society was never officially accepted by the Association of Jewish Communities of Yugoslavia, and was not its official body. Moreover, many within the Jewish community in Serbia have openly criticized the Society's activities and described it as a "functionalization" of Jews and their history, motivated by propaganda goals. See: Laslo Sekelj, *Vreme beščašća: Ogledi o vladavini nacionalizma* (Beograd: Akademia Nova Bgd, 1995) and Paul Gordiejew, *Voices of Yugoslav Jewry* (New York: Suny Press, 1999).
29 See: David Bruce Macdonald, *Balkan Holocausts? Serbian and Croatian victim-centred propaganda and the war in Yugoslavia* (Manchester: Manchester University Press, 2002).
30 See: Jovan Byford, "When I say 'the Holocaust', I mean 'Jasenovac'," op. cit.
31 "Branilac Alkalaj optužuje za ubistvo 9,000 jevrejskih žena i dece," *Politika* (Beograd), April 21, 1946, pp. 6.
32 See: Jovan Byford, "The collaborationist administration and the treatment of Jews in Nazi-occupied Serbia," in Sabrina Ramet and Ola Listhaug (eds.) *Serbia and Serbs in the Second World War* (Basingstoke: Palgrave Macmillan, 2011), pp. 109–126.
33 Quoted from Renaud de la Brosse, *Political propaganda and the plan to create a "State for all Serbs,"* Report compiled at the request of the Office of the Prosecutor

of the International Criminal Tribunal for the Former Yugoslavia, pp. 24, http://hague.bard.edu/reports/de_la_brosse_pt2.pdf (accessed February 20, 2018).
34 Tomislav Vuković and Edo Bojović, *Pregled srpskog antisemitizma*, pp. 95–97.
35 Ljubica Štefan, *Srpska pravoslavna crikva i fašizam*, pp. 263–264.
36 Ditto, pp. 269.
37 Ibid.
38 See, for example, Bulajić's polemic after Pečarić in *Jasenovac: ustaški logori smrti, srpski mit?* pp. 753–818.
39 Boško Novaković, "Sećanja za budućnost: Koncentracioni logor Sajmište," *Godišnjak grada Beograda* vol. 42 (1995), pp. 160.
40 Milan Bulajić, *Dani sećanja na žrtve genocida 2005/2006* (Beograd, 2006).
41 "Istina o genocidu–uslov mira i stabilnosti," Serbian Government Press Release, March 28, 2005.
42 Milan Bulajić, *Deset godina Muzeja žrtava genocida*, pp. 517–519.
43 Ljiljana Radonić provided a scientifically based and serious criticism of the exhibition in the work "Slovak and Croatian invocation of Europe: The Museum of the Slovak National Uprising and the Jasenovac Memorial Museum," *Nationalities Papers: The Journal of Nationalism and Ethnicity*, vol. 42, no. 3. (2014), pp. 489–507.
44 Smilja Tišma, "Sajmište ispunjava sve uslove," in *Beogradsko Staro sajmište, 3+1* (Beograd: Urbanistički zavod Beograda, 2008), pp. 193; Tomislav Zečević, "Jasenovačka logorašica Smilja Tišma: Živi sam svedok srpske tragedije," *Dveri srpske*, vol. 13, no. 47–50 (2011), pp. 78–79; Slobodan Kljakić, "Falifikovanje istine," *Politika*, March 27, 2006, pp. 9.
45 *Jasenovac: Proceedings and Speeches of the 4th international Conference on Jasenovac, Banja Luka–Donja Gradina, May 30–31, 2007*, Banja Luka, 2008, pp. 121.
46 President Ožegović spoke with Gojko Marčeta, President of the Municipal Board of SUBNOR, Information Service of the City Municipality of New Belgrade, January 25, 2008.
47 The author of the present text was also a member of this group.
48 See: Jovan Byford, "When I say 'the Holocaust'," op. cit.
49 On the shortcomings of the proposed law, see: Jovan Byford, "Disputed Law on the Old Sajmište," Peščanik.net, February 11, 2011, http://pescanik.net/sporni-zakon-o-starom-sajmistu/ (accessed December 20, 2020).
50 "Vučić sa patrijarhom: Svesrpsko svetilište biće izgrađeno na najtužnijem mestu u Donjoj Gradini," website of the Serbian Radio Television, 10 September 2021, available at www.rts.rs/page/stories/sr/story/125/drustvo/4507404/vucic-patrijarh-jasenovac-konferencija-za-novinare.html (Accessed 21 September 2021).

Bibliography

Almuli, Jaša. "Stvaranje velikih laži o Srbiji i Srbima," feuilleton *Politika*, Beograd, December 26, 1993–January 25, 1994.
"Branilac Alkalaj optužuje za ubistvo 9,000 jevrejskih žena i dece," *Politika*, Beograd, April 21, 1946.
Brkić, A. "Srbi ne znaju koliko ih nema," *Svet* (Beograd), April 1, 1990.
Bulajić, Milan. "Uvodno izlaganje," in Milan Bulajić and Radovan Samardžić (eds.) *Ratni zločini i zločini genocida, 1991–1992*. Beograd: Srpska akademija nauka i umetnosti. Odeljenje istorijskih nauka, 1993, pp. 7–32.

——, Milan. "Genocid nad pravoslavnim Srbima u Drugom svjetskom ratu," in Milan Bulajić (ed.) *Genocid nad Srbima u II svetskom ratu*. Beograd: Srpska književna zadruga, 1995, pp. 1–32.
——, Milan. *Jasenovac. Ustaški logor smrti. "Srpski mit?" Hrvatski ustaški logori genocida nad Srbima, Jevrejima i Ciganima*. Beograd: Stručna knjiga, 1999.
——, Milan. *Deset godina Muzeja žrtava genocide*. Beograd: Fond za istraživanje genocida, 2003.
——, Milan. *Dani sećanja na žrtve genocida 2005/2006*. Beograd: Pešić i sinovi, 2006.
——, Milan. *Jasenovac: Uloga Vatikana u nacističkoj Hrvatskoj*. Beograd: Pešić i sinovi, 2007.
Byford, Jovan. "When I say 'the Holocaust', I mean 'Jasenovac': Remembrance of the Holocaust in contemporary Serbia." *East European Jewish Affairs*, vol. 37, no. 1, 2007, pp. 51–74.
——. "Sporni zakon o Starom sajmištu." *Peščanik.net*, Beograd, February 11, 2011, http://pescanik.net/sporni-zakon-o-starom-sajmistu. Accessed February 20, 2018.
——, Jovan. "The collaborationist administration and the treatment of Jews in Nazi-occupied Serbia," in Sabrina Ramet and Ola Listhaug (eds.) *Serbia and Serbs in the Second World War*. Basingstoke: Palgrave Macmillan, 2011, pp. 109–126.
——, Jovan. *Staro sajmište: mesto sećanja, zaborava i sporenja*. Beograd: Beogradski Centar Za Ljudska Prava, 2011.
Cohen, Philip. *Serbia's Secret War: Propaganda and the Deceit in History*. Texas: College Station, 1996.
de la Brosse, Renaud. *Political propaganda and the plan to create a "State for all Serbs."* Report compiled at the request of the Office of Prosecutor of the International Criminal Tribunal for the Former Yugoslavia, http://hague.bard.edu/reports/de_la_brosse_pt2.pdf. Accessed February 20, 2018.
Biberović, Dragana. "Vesić: Izrađen Nacrt zakona o Starom Sajmištu," *Radio Televizije Srbije*, September 23, 2017, www.rts.rs/page/stories/sr/story/125/drustvo/2880615/vesic-izradjen-nacrt-zakona-o-starom-sajmistu.html. Accessed February 20, 2018.
Dragović-Soso, Jasna. *Saviours of the Nation*. Montreal: McGill-Queen's University Press, 2002.
Đurđević, D. 'Suprotstavljanje neistinama', *Politika* (Beograd), December 19, 1991.
Gams, Andrija and Aleksandar Levi. *The Truth about Serbain Antisemitism*. Beograd: Ministarstvo informisanja Republike Srbije, 1994.
Gordiejew, Paul. *Voices of Yugoslav Jewry*. New York: Suny Press, 1999.
Heike, Karge. "Mediated remembrance: local practices of remembering the Second World War in Tito's Yugoslavia," *European Review of History*, vol. 16, no. 1, 2009, pp. 49–62.
Jasenovac: Proceedings and Speeches of the 4th international Conference on Jasenovac, Banja Luka–Donja Gradina, May 30–31, 2007. Banja Luka, 2008.
Kljakić, Slobodan. "Kratka istorija Odbora SANU za sakupljanje građe o genocide nad srpskim narodom i drugim narodima Jugoslavije u XX veku," in Predrag Dragić-Kijuk (ed.) *Catena Mundi II*. Kraljevo: Ibarske Novosti & Matica Srba i Iseljenika Srbije, 1992, pp. 498–512.
——, Slobodan. "Falifikovanje istine," *Politika* (Beograd), March 27, 2006.
Knežević, Anto. *Analysis of Serbian Propaganda*. Zagreb: Domovina, 1992.
Koljanin, Milan. "Veze između nemačkog logora na Beogradskom sajmištu i logora NDH Jasenovac i Stara Gradiška," in Jelka Smreka (ed.) *Jasenovac 1986* (Round table). Jasenovac: Spomen područje Jasenovac, 1986, pp. 173–180.

Koljanin, Milan. *Nemački logor na Beogradskom sajmištu.* Beograd: Institut za savremenu istoriju, 1992.
Macdonald, David Bruce. *Balkan Holocausts? Serbian and Croatian victim-centred propaganda and the war in Yugoslavia.* Manchester: Manchester University Press, 2002.
Milosavljević, Olivera. "Zloupotreba autoriteta naukem," in Nebojša Popov (ed.) *Srpska strana rata: Trauma i katarza u istorijskom pamćenju.* Beograd: Samizdat B92, pp. 340–374.
Novaković, Boško. "Sećanja za budućnost: Koncentracioni logor Sajmište," *Godišnjak grada Beograda,* vol. 42, 1995, pp. 157–163.
"Okrugli sto–Muzej žrtava genocida," *Svet,* April, 1, 1990.
Pečarić, Josip. *Srpski mit o Jasenovcu: Skrivanje istine o beogradskim konc-logorima.* Zagreb: Dom i svijet/Hrvatski informativni centar/Hrvatski institut za povijest, 1998.
Radonić, Ljiljana. "Slovak and Croatian invocation of Europe: The Museum of the Slovak National Uprising and the Jasenovac Memorial Museum," *Nationalities Papers: The Journal of Nationalism and Ethnicity,* vol. 40, no. 3, 2014, pp. 489–507.
Sekelj, Laslo. *Vreme beščašća: Ogledi o vladavini nacionalizma.* Beograd: Akademia Nova Bgd, 1995.
Štefan, Ljubica. *Srpska pravoslavna crkva i fašizam.* Zagreb: Hrvatski institut za povijest, 1996.
Tišma, Smilja. "Sajmište ispunjava sve uslove," in *Beogradsko Staro sajmište, 3+1.* Beograd: Urbanistički zavod Beograda, 2008.
Vuković, Tomislav and Edo Bojović. *Pregled srpskog antisemitizma.* Zagreb: Alatir, 1992.
Zečević, Tomislav. "Jasenovačka logorašica Smilja Tišma: Živi sam svedok srpske tragedije," *Dveri srpske,* vol. 13, no. 47–50, 2011, pp. 78–79.

3 Racial Laws in the Independent State of Croatia
Social and Legal Aspects

Nataša Mataušić

The word *Ustaša* was originally used for participants in an insurrection or mutiny. During the insurrections against the Turks in the nineteenth century, it was used both for Croats and for Serbs. It was only since the 1930s, and especially during World War II, that the term came to be used primarily for members of Pavelić's organisation.[1] "The first recorded use of the Ustaša name for Pavelić's organisation was in the title of the emigrant magazine *Ustaša* in May 1930."[2] The beginnings of the Ustaša Organisation (since April 1941 the Ustaša Movement) are associated with Croatian political emigrants in Italy. It has, therefore, never been a parliamentary political party or organisation of any other kind in the Kingdom of Yugoslavia. The nature and intentions of the Ustaša Organisation are expressed in its two main policy documents:

1. *The Constitution of Ustaša, the Croatian Revolutionary Organisation* from 1932 (Croatian acronym: UHRO)
   The first article of the Constitution says, "The aim of Ustaša, the Croatian Revolutionary Organisation is to free Croatia from foreign servitude, to make her a fully independent and autonomous state in her entire national and historic territory."[3] From this article we can conclude that this was a militant and revolutionary organisation (revolutionary in its fighting methods, but not in the sense of striving to change the social and political system), and that its anti-Yugoslavian stance ("foreign servitude") was synonymous with anti-Serb sentiment.
2. *The Ustaša–Domobran Principles*, 1933

Article 11 of the *Principles* says, "No one should be allowed to decide about Croatian national and state matters who is not by ancestry, and by blood, a member of the Croatian people, nor should any foreign peoples or states be allowed to decide the destiny of the Croatian people and the Croatian state,"[4] pointing to a consistent anti-Serb sentiment, because although this is not directly stated, the mention of foreign peoples and states clearly implies Serbs. At the time the *Principles* were written – and, indeed, since 1918 – the Serbian royal dynasty, Karađorđević, had been deciding about all "state matters," including those that concerned the "Croatian people," in the

DOI: 10.4324/9781003326632-4

Kingdom of Serbs, Croats and Slovenes/Kingdom of Yugoslavia. Dr. Ante Pavelić openly wrote about the methods he would use to fulfil his goal (the foundation of an independent Croatian state) in the magazine *Ustaša, vjesnik hrvatskih revolucionara* (*Ustaša, the Herald of Croatian Revolutionaries*) from February 1932 in his article *No more slavery*: "The knife, the revolver, the bomb and the time fuse, these are the idols … the machine gun and the time fuse, these are the bells that will proclaim the new dawn and the resurrection of the Independent State of Croatia."

A consistent anti-Serb sentiment and a sense of national exclusivity that portrayed Serbs as the historic enemies of any Croatian state had been constantly present in the organisation since its foundation; as early as then, they announced they would take radical steps against Serbs once Croats are in power.[5] Anti-Semitism only appeared in the second half of the 1930s, especially after the start of the war instigated by National Socialism. Since their very beginnings, the Ustaša strived to create a "pure Croatian living space," above all "clear" of Serbs, political enemies and non-Aryans.[6] In contrast to the genocide against the Serb Orthodox population, which was planned in advance during the emigration period, their policy towards Jews (and the Roma) changed gradually through several phases, following the already-tested Nazi methods involving an excommunication, concentration, and extermination phase.[7] However, it took the Nazis eight years to get from the excommunication to the extermination phase (1933–1941), while the Ustaša government did this in only four months (April–July 1941).

The Foundation of the Independent State of Croatia

The Independent State of Croatia (Croatian acronym: NDH) was proclaimed on April 10, 1941 on Zagreb radio.[8] Slavko Kvaternik, a retired Austro-Hungarian colonel and the head of the homeland branch of the Ustaša Organisation, read out a statement about the state's "resurrection" in the name of Ante Pavelić, "the Poglavnik of the Ustaša Organisation."[9] At the time, Pavelić was in Pistoia, near Florence, Italy, where Ustaša members living in Italy had been gathering in order to return to the homeland together. The news about the foundation of NDH was given to Pavelić by his wife, Mara. It was by this act that the Independent State of Croatia was established, bypassing regular democratic parliamentary elections and without the knowledge of the future prime minister, Pavelić. The Ustaša Organisation "came to power primarily because of events that happened in its vicinity and over which it had no control, and not because of its own strength and conviction to establish the Independent State of Croatia by itself."[10] Pavelić arrived in Zagreb on April 15, and "as early as April 16 1941 Pavelić changed and republished the most important Ustaša documents, the Ustaša constitution and the Ustaša principles that became the foundation for the political system of the new state. Through these changes, the former UHRO grew into "Ustaša – the Croatian Liberation Movement."[11]

NDH was recognised by 13 states all together: the Axis powers, their allies and the occupied countries in which puppet governments were established. However, even though Italy and Germany recognised NDH as a sovereign state, German and Italian documents mentioning NDH usually mention "occupation zones" and "occupying forces." Therefore, we can conclude that it was a German–Italian protectorate of sorts and, after the capitulation of Italy in 1943, solely a German protectorate. The United Kingdom, the United States and the Soviet Union still recognised the Kingdom of Yugoslavia and its government in exile, and likewise its territorial integrity. The first article of the Montevideo Convention lists the generally accepted legal criteria for a state: "The State as a person of international law should possess the following qualifications: (a) a permanent population; (b) a defined territory; (c) government; and (d) capacity to enter into relations with the other States."[12]

In this paper I will focus on the concept of state government. The aspects of state government are: legislative: usually the parliament (*sabor* in Croatian), but often also the government and the president if they have the right to make directives and rulings with legislative power; judicial: the courts, their jurisdiction ranging from local to statewide, with the Supreme Court as the highest judicial body in the state; and executive: the government, with the president of the government (the prime minister) at its head, tasked with running the state. The members of the government are ministers, appointed and chosen by the prime minister. What were these aspects of government like in NDH? The highest-ranking person in the government of the Independent State of Croatia, formed on April 16, 1941, the head of state with the title Poglavnik (this title, used for the leader of the Ustaša Organisation, became the title of the head of state), the commander in chief of the military forces, and the first minister of foreign affairs was Pavelić. All the power in the state was, therefore, concentrated in the hands of one man.[13]

A legal provision from January 24, 1942 established and assembled an institution called the Croatian State Parliament. Its role was largely advisory, and it held no real political power. It assembled for sessions on several days in February, April, and December 1942, and all the members were invited and appointed by Ante Pavelić himself. This Parliament, by definition, should have been suggesting and passing laws, only existed during the year 1942 and held 13 sessions, but never passed or declared a single law. Since the state had no representative, legislative body to decide on a constitution, the inner system of the state was based on various laws and statutory provisions, made – just like all other external and internal political decisions – by Ante Pavelić (as the holder of sovereignty) and the ministers he appointed. But, as Vladimir Geiger rightly points out in his paper "Dokon pop i jariće krsti,"[14] these laws and statutory provisions still held all the weight of law; they were not treated as inferior to laws passed by votes in parliament. According to the *Statutory Provision on the Names of Legal and Other Regulations and Local Resolutions* from October 20, 1941, "Provisions can only be given by the Poglavnik of the Independent State of Croatia. Provisions can be: (1) statutory provisions, which are legal in nature; (2) general provisions, used to regulate general matters, which are not legal in nature; (3) special provisions, which regulate special (individual) matters that only the Poglavnik may legally decide upon.

All of the Poglavnik's statutory provisions are cosigned by the ministers in charge. Provisions of general and special nature, appointments and provisions given by the Poglavnik as the commander in chief of the armed forces do not need to be cosigned."[15] Geiger also points out the explanation for "Law and statutory provision" given by the Croatian State Bureau for Language (The Croatian Language Bureau), which states that "in the Independent State of Croatia regulations are given in the form of statutory provisions and of orders. The former are passed by the Poglavnik as the holder of legislative government, and the latter by various administrative bodies, starting from ministries, but based on authority given to them by the legislative government (laws or statutory provisions). A statutory provision is a law in the true sense of the word, that is, it holds the same strength as a law; in other words, in the hierarchy of regulations it is above an order. There is therefore no reason to refer to a statutory provision as a law in its own context where the nature of the matter demands so. For example, were the Poglavnik to proclaim a new civil code by way of a statutory provision, his own text should refer to "this law" and not to "this statutory provision." The same is true of criminal law, securities law, and even of university law (A)."[16]

The Ministry for Law and Worship was established immediately after the foundation of the Independent State of Croatia by the Poglavnik's order on appointing the first Croatian state government from April 16, 1941. Its first minister was Mirko Puk, replaced in 1942 by Andrija Artuković.

Racial Legislation

Legislation in NDH complied to German and Italian legislation; this included the laws and statutory provisions about racial and national exclusiveness, as illustrated by the similarity between the names of these laws: *Decree on the Protection of the Italian Race* (Italy), *Law on Protection of Aryan Blood and Honour* (Germany), *Legal provision on the Protection of the Aryan Blood and Honour of the Croatian People* (Independent State of Croatia). These racial laws discriminated, dehumanised and denied legal protection to people who were not of *"deutsches oder artverwandtes Blut"* (in Germany), *"razza Italiana"* (in Italy) or "Aryan origin" in Croatia. Mile Budak, the minister for worship and education in NDH, said this during his trial in Zagreb in 1945:

> All the laws concerning non-Aryans were written by an expert committee following the Poglavnik's orders, and we did not discuss the law as such, but we had often discussed the subject. All the members of the government held an anti-semitic position. We were guided by our experience that Jews in Croatia had always carried out anti-Croatian policies and supported such regimes.[17]

Budak said government's anti-semitism was, however, partly tempered by the fact that among the Jews "there were many exceptions who were ideologically on the Croatian side, and those we attempted to help."[18]

Only two days after his arrival in Zagreb, on April 17·, Pavelić "prescribed and declared" his *Legal Provision on the Defence of the Nation and State*.[19] It stated that anyone "who in any way harms, or has harmed in the past, the honour and livelihood of the Croatian people or in any way endangers the survival of the Independent State of Croatia or the state government, even if only in attempt, is guilty of criminal high treason,"[20] and "whoever is found guilty of the crime in article 1 is to be punished by death."[21] This legal provision became the basis for a regime of terror. However, whether by accident or on purpose, the provision did not elaborate on what was to be considered high treason, or what harming and endangering the "honour and livelihood of the Croatian people" entailed. In addition to this, the provision introduced "special people's courts"; by a subsequent legal provision from May 17, they became court martials. *The Statutory Provision on Court Martials*[22] only allowed for one punishment: death by firing squad.[23] There was no legal recourse against the ruling of a court martial. At first most of the convicted were Serbs and Jews; later they included all opponents of the Ustaša regime. In December the provision was somewhat mitigated to state that "in less severe cases the court may pass a prison sentence, three years at least, instead of the death penalty.[24] Statutory provisions from July 5 and 10, 1941, specify in more detail the acts to be prosecuted by court martials: anyone who "by way of writing, drawing, publishing and disseminating books or newspapers"[25] mocks the regime, speaks out against the Poglavnik, spreads Communist propaganda, as well as "anyone who listens to forbidden wireless channels (the BBC above all) or disseminates news from such channels."[26] On the suggestion of his minister of internal affairs, on April 30, Pavelić "prescribed and proclaimed" three statutory provisions that formed the basis of racial legislation: the *Statutory Provision on Citizenship*,[27] the *Statutory Provision on Race*[28] and the *Statutory Provision on the Protection of the Aryan Blood and Honour of the Croatian People.*[29] According to article 1 of the *Statutory Provision on Citizenship*, to be considered a citizen of NDH one needs to be "an individual of Aryan ancestry who is proven not to have hindered the efforts of the Croatian people towards liberation and who is willing to serve the Croatian people and NDH readily and faithfully."[30] Only such an individual "stands protected by NDH."[31] Article 2 implies that Jews and Roma, and also Serbs, are not entitled to citizenship and to the protection of the state. The "Explanations of racial statutory provisions" and "Comments on certain legal articles" published in the newspaper *Hrvatski narod* on May 3 point out: "This legal provision is made in accordance with the German legal provision. The German law speaks of '*deutsches oder artverwandtes Blut*' (German or kindred blood), and the Italian law of '*razza italiana*' (the Italian race). 'Blood' does not signify 'ancestry' in the Croatian language in the same way it does in German. 'Blood' in the sense of 'ancestry' is a metaphorical expression, considering that blood has, biologically, nothing to do with inheritance. There is no special Croatian race, for the Croats are, just like all other European peoples, a mixture of the Nordic, Dinaric, Alpine, Baltic, and Mediterranean races, with small tinges of other races. The best expression is, therefore, Aryan ancestry. *Aryan race* would also be incorrect, as we can conclude from the definition in article 1 of the statutory provision."[32]

The *Statutory Provision on Race* defined which individuals were to be considered to be of Aryan, and which of non-Aryan origin. Aryan origin was defined as being "descended from ancestors who are members of the European group of races, or from descendants of this group of races outside Europe. It was proved by a certificate of baptism (birth) and a wedding certificate for first- and second-degree ancestors (parents and grandparents)."

But while the definition of a Jew is precisely elaborated (article 3) in 5 sub-articles, the definition of a Roma (article 4) consisted of one sentence only. Basically, Jews were defined as all "individuals descended from at least three second degree ancestors (grandparents) who are of the Jewish race. Grandparents are to be counted as Jews if they belong to the religion of Moses or if it was the religion of their birth." Article 5 of this law announced, "in alliance with the Ministry for Internal Affairs," the establishment of a "racial-political committee that would create and consider suggestions in all doubtful cases of racial affiliation," and that the final decision in all doubtful cases of racial affiliation would be made by the minister for internal affairs. According to the aforementioned "Explanations of racial statutory provisions," this statutory provision contains definitions to be used by all special orders, "which would be passed when necessary,"[33] and "Article 1 includes the definition of Aryan origin. On 'deutches oder artverwandtes Blut',"[34] According to the German commentary of the law, it refers to all European peoples except for Jews and Gypsies. "Jews as well as Gypsies each make up their own racial group. [...] Jews have remained outside the European group because of their religious and racial exclusiveness, and Gypsies because of their social status, each having for centuries married only inside their own community."[35] Article 3, which includes the definition of a Jew, is explained as follows: "This definition is not strict, because it allows for an individual who is half-Jewish to be counted as Aryan. The same definition is used in German and Italian law. [...] The legal provision uses the words Moses's blood rather than Jewish blood in order to emphasise that the word *Jew* refers to a member of the Jewish race regardless of religion."[36] Article 6, which allows for certain Jews to hold Aryan rights (because of a sufficient quantity of Aryan chromosomes, as stated in the explanation for this article of the law), says "Individuals who prior to April 10, 1941, have proven themselves of merit to the Croatian people, especially for the liberation thereof, and their spouses, if the marriage took place before this law was passed, as well as the descendants from such a marriage [...] can be granted by the head of state all the rights enjoyed by individuals of Aryan ancestry, beyond what is prescribed in this order."[37] A similar order was given in the "First Regulation to the Reich Citizenship Law of November

14, 1935" in article 7, which stated that the Führer and the chancellor could grant exemptions from the regulations laid down in the law. The *Statutory Provision on the Protection of the Aryan Blood and Honour of the Croatian People* forbade intermarriage with Jews and other individuals of non-Aryan ancestry.

Article 1 of this statutory provision forbids a person "that in addition to Aryan ancestors has one second-degree ancestor who is a Jew or other European non-Aryan"[38] with an individual "of the same racial ancestry,"[39] and article 3 also forbids "extramarital sexual intercourse of a Jew or other non-Aryan individual with a woman of Aryan ancestry."[40] Severe punishments are imposed on those who disobey this order and commit the "crime of race defilement"[41] – "jail or prison,"[42] – and "for especially severe cases, such as rape of a chaste girl," also the death penalty. The "Explanations of racial statutory provisions" state that "the ultimate goal of every Aryan nation-state has to be ridding itself of non-Aryan elements, especially of Jews, who constantly attempt to reach positions of power, to influence the people with their political and moral views and to take material advantage of them. To achieve this goal, it is necessary to prohibit a biological relationship between an Aryan and a non-Aryan."[43] The explanations for the concepts of "race," "racism" and "racial legislation" are worth noting. "A race is a group of people with corresponding major inherited characteristics. [...] Only members of the racial group that constitutes a people can successfully collaborate in the development of the authentic cultural heritage of this people. Only they can enjoy full citizenship of a nation-state, unlike individuals, groups and peoples who are racially of a different ethnicity, of different character and social structure. Racially foreign elements should not meddle in matters of ruling a people and promoting a national culture, for their effect will be destructive and they will sway life from the national direction. [...] For this reason, a people that wishes to preserve its national individuality cannot give individuals of foreign race the same rights it gives to individuals of shared ancestry and racial structure."[44]

It is further stated that "there are two racial groups living as minorities among the Croatian nation that significantly differ from it by their racial characteristics. One of them is of high social standing – the Jews – and the other is of low social standing – the Gypsies. When we speak of Jews, we do not mean those who belong to the religion of Moses, but those who belong to the Jewish racial group, for the essence of the Jewish community is not religion – it is its racial structure and its biological heritage from long ago,"[45] and "by emphasising the meaning of race in the citizenship law, it is affirmed once and for all that the Independent State of Croatia is a nation-state and that only Aryans have the right to assume positions of authority in it and to govern its fate."[46] In addition to the explanation of the concept of race, the introductory part of the "Explanations of racial statutory provisions" published in *Narodni list* on May 3, 1941, places considerable emphasis on the explanation of the concept of racism. The explanations offered for these two concepts make the reasons this statutory provision was passed easy to discern. Nonetheless, a covert "apology" of sorts also seems to be present. On racism, it is stated,

> It has often been said that racism is a doctrine contrary to the teachings of the Catholic faith and, consequently, to one of the foundations of Croatian spiritual culture. Racism is the belief that a certain race is elevated above all other races, which are of lesser value, and for this reason is chosen by fate to govern all other races. This belief has no foundation in biological facts. Biological science does not differentiate by value; it merely states the existing facts. Every living being is adapted as well as possible to the environment and the conditions in which it lives, and in the same way every human race is adapted as well as possible for its own living conditions and, in itself, of equal value to all others. [...] True racism is only found in Jews. Their religious books, which also form the basis of their national life, depict Jews as a people chosen by God to whom all other peoples should be subordinated. [...] Racial legislation does not dictate racist derision and contempt for other nations, but merely the will of our nation to be culturally and economically self-reliant again and to continue bettering itself following its own spirituality. Racial statutory provisions are purely the expression of the wish for the State of Croatia, its destiny and its spiritual and economic culture to be governed in the national spirit and solely to the benefit of the Croatian people.[47]

Siegfried Kasche, the German ambassador to the NDH government, wrote in his letter from May 3, 1941, concerning the situation in NDH, which included legislation:

> (2) Legislation: the publishing of the laws has now been administered. These legal measures deserve to be pointed out and acknowledged: (a) on citizenship, Jews and the protection of blood (considerably adapted to German statutory provisions). [...] The legislation is still significantly deficient in a technical sense. Much is prescribed, but without organising the matters of authority and implementation. It can still be said, generally, that work is carried out according to plan and towards consolidation.[48]

Concerning the matter of "how much input the Germans had in the formation of these laws" (racial laws), Nada Kisić Kolanović does not offer a final answer, but she quotes statements made by certain Ustaša and German high officials. According to Vladimir Židovec,[49] among Pavelić's more radical ministers who during the second emigration period "avoided any discussion of the anti-Jewish measures like the plague" there was a tendency to paint the passing of the anti-Jewish laws as done "under pressure and suggestion by the Germans."[50] At his trial in Zagreb in 1947, Kasche stated that he "assumed that the legislation on the civic standing of the Jewish population was influenced by the German measures,"[51] and the state treasurer, Vladimir Košak, claimed that these laws were "not as far-reaching" because otherwise they would threaten the elementary family identity of the Ustaša leaders whose wives were of Jewish or half-Jewish origin (Pavelić, Kvaternik, Budak, Žanić, Oršanić, Perčević and others). It was not a matter of transplanting the German orders, but rather of the Ustaša 'complying with their allies'."[52]

The first three racial laws were followed by a profusion of other statutory provisions and orders through which Jews were completely disenfranchised: the *Statutory Provision on Religious Conversion* from May 3, 1941,[53] which in effect banned conversion from Judaism to Catholicism, and the *Statutory Provision on the Ban of Employment of Female Individuals in Non-Aryan Households* from May 6.[54] The order by the Ministry for National Economy of NDH that all Jews are to be discharged from public service was being implemented as early as May 17.[55] Article 1 of the *Statutory Provision on the Protection of the National and Aryan Culture of the Croatian People*, from June 4,[56] prohibited Jews from taking part in any activities, organisations and institutions of the "social life, youth, sports and culture of the Croatian people in general, and especially in literature, journalism, visual and musical arts, urbanism, theatre and film."[57] This was followed by the *Order on the Changing of Jewish Surnames and the Marking of Jews and Jewish Companies*, from June 4,[58] the *Order on Determining the Racial Affiliation of State and Self-Governing Officials and of Independent Academics*, also from June 4,[59] and the *Order on Preventing the Concealment Jewish Property*, from June 5.[60] These statutory provisions were accompanied by numerous prohibitions: for example, of visiting coffee houses, inns and movie theatres, of walking in parks, of going to the market prior to 10 a.m. A strong anti-Jewish propaganda in the media, and concrete actions such as discharge from jobs, eviction from apartments and the confiscation of property, and even the first individual killings, soon became everyday occurrences.[61] Compulsory wearing of an identifying Jewish sign was introduced in some towns in Croatia as early as April 1941. Since they were prescribed by the local Ustaša administrations, they differed from town to town.[62] In Zagreb, the Jewish Department of the Ustaša Police Committee prescribed on May 22 that all Jews regardless of age (therefore, including infants) should wear a Jewish sign consisting of two pieces of yellow cloth with a drawing of a Jewish star. Very soon, on June 4, this order was made obsolete, and the yellow patch was replaced by a round, yellow metal plate with the imprinted capital letter Ž (for "Židov," the Croatian word for Jew), which had to be worn by all Jews older than 14. This was the only anti-Jewish measure in NDH that preceded the corresponding measure in the Third Reich (September 1, 1941).[63]

In conclusion: racial laws and statutory provisions "prescribed and proclaimed" by the holder of statehood of NDH, that Ante Pavelić had the power of law. They followed the example of similar laws passed in Nazi Germany and Fascist Italy, emphasising the Aryan origin of Croats. Their purpose was to protect the Croatian Aryan population from non-Aryans – Jews and Roma. Their consequence was that Jews and Roma were completely disenfranchised, deprived of citizenship, and therefore of the protection of the state. The extent to which the Germans participated in devising the NDH racial laws is difficult to ascertain on the basis of the available archive documents and written memoirs from this period of Croatian history, and systematic scientific research on this matter is yet to be taken. Still, there is no basis and merit to the (entirely futile) suggestions by some authors, such as Stjepan Razum[64] and Tomislav Jonjić,[65] that the racial laws "were not passed as laws but as the Poglavnik's *statutory provisions* and other lower-ranking regulations (!)," and that it is easy to "ascertain that the 'racial legislation' did not contain any regulations on apprehension, detention in concentration camps or shooting."[66] Jonjić points out as a positive and exclusive point that, in the *Statutory Provision on Race*, "Article 6 allowed for the possibility that 'non-Aryans' should be accorded full rights of citizenship, making them what was colloquially known as 'honorary Aryans'."[67] Jonjić claims that Croatian Jews were not persecuted (sent to concentration camps or sentenced to death) because of racial laws, but rather based on

> general regulations about the treatment of undesirable individuals or wrongdoers (in other words regulations that treated Jews and non-Jews equally) or in worse cases, often without the backing of any regulations, by government institutions exceeding their authority or by individuals and groups acting against the law, under direct or indirect pressure by the Germans, in an anti-Jewish climate created by propaganda pamphlets.[68]

without mentioning whether those who had exceeded their authority by sending Jews to the Ustaša camps (and to certain death) were ever punished for this. In addition to this, of course, he happens to forget that there is a plethora of documents, both original and published, that show Jews and Roma being sent to concentration camps for no other reason than being Jews and Roma.[69] Between April 1941 and August 1942, dealing with the "Jewish problem" was a task left to the NDH authorities. Of around 39,000 Jews living in NDH at the time, around 24,000 were killed in Ustaša camps and other places of execution. Have all of these people been undesirable individuals or wrongdoers, as Jonjić suggests, or intellectual instigators of felonies by unknown perpetrators, or have perhaps sexual liaisons between Jews and women of Aryan ancestry suddenly become widespread in spite of the severe punishments? In the summer of 1942 and spring of 1943 around 7,000 Jews were taken by the SS, with help from the Ustaša, to various Nazi camps, most of them to Auschwitz. Only about 8–9,000 Jews survived, mostly those living in areas under Italian rule, those who had joined Partisan forces or lived in territories under Partisan rule, and those who were saved with the help of Croatian citizens.[70]

The Nationalisation of Jewish Property: Racial Legislation in Matters of Property Law

The nationalisation of Jewish property was carried out in several phases, with legal basis in several statutory provisions. [71] I will list these statutory provisions without elaborating in detail on their contents. They can be considered a part of racial – in this case, anti-semitic – legislation, because they dealt solely with Jews and their property. Soon after NDH was founded, on April 18, 1941, the *Statutory Provision on the Preservation of Croatian National Property*[72] made void all legal agreements between Jews or between a Jew and a non-Jew in the two months prior to the establishment of NDH. This provision became the basis for the economic and financial devastation of Jews in Croatia. The government explained this measure as a manifestation of the protection of national interests in the NDH economy, which needed to be in the hands of Croatian manufacturers and merchants, not Jews. As early as April 20, governors or commissioners were placed in all Jewish companies. The *Statutory Provision on the Prevention of Hiding Jewish Property*[73] prescribed from one to five years in prison and the confiscation of property for anyone who participated in the hiding of Jewish property or conducted any legal agreements on behalf of Jews. This was only the prelude to measures that were to follow. The *Statutory Provision on Marking Jewish Businesses* from June 4[74] made it obligatory for all Jewish-owned businesses to display a yellow tablet or sheet of yellow paper (in the middle of the shop window and above the entrance) with the inscription "Jewish company."

The first phase of the nationalisation of property was the identification of property, a segregation process that singled out Jewish property in order to ascertain Jewish-owned wealth in its entirety. *The Statutory Provision on the Obligatory Registration of Property Owned by Jews and Jewish Companies*[75] from June 5, 1941, made it obligatory for Jews to register their property at the Trade Renovation Bureau of the Ministry for National Economy within 20 days. Property taken between April 10 and June 5 had to be registered as well. This obligation also affected Aryan individuals married to Jews. Disobeying this statutory provision was punished by 1–10 years of "severe prison," and the confiscation of property. The statutory provision defined Jewish business companies as "business companies owned by Jews in their entirety"[76] or those "with one or more Jewish individuals as members of the administration or management."[77] These companies had to register their property as well, and those that failed to do so or "withheld it entirely or in part" were to be punished by "one to five years in prison and a monetary fee of up to 10 million dinars."[78] All companies confiscated on the basis of this statutory provision were given to the state to "run them directly, lease them, sell them or liquidate them in favour of the treasury."[79] *The Order on the Implementation of the Statutory Provision on the Obligatory Registration of Property Owned by Jews and Jewish Companies*[80] clarified who was under obligation to register their property:

> all Jews of both sexes that are members of this state, as well as those Jews from foreign states who were on the territory of the Independent State of Croatia on the day when the Statutory Provision on the Obligatory Registration of Property Owned by Jews and Jewish Companies was passed.[81]

The next phase was the confiscation of property (which meant the property was taken in the name of the state, with no compensation). The two basic statutory provisions on the nationalisation of Jewish property were the *Statutory Provision on the Nationalisation of the Wealth of Jews and Jewish Companies*[82] passed on October 9, 1941 and the *Statutory Provision on the Nationalisation of Jewish Property*[83] from October 30, 1942. The first invested the State Directorate "for the purpose of the national economy [to]... confiscate the wealth of every Jew and every Jewish company, with or without reimbursement, for the benefit of the Independent State of Croatia."[84] The second made the state the formal owner of all Jewish property: according to article 1,

> all the wealth and all the property rights of individuals who are considered Jews according to article 3 of the Statutory Provision on race from April 30, 1941, as well as all legacy left by such individuals who died after February 10, 1941, are now the property of NDH.[85]

All individuals who had illegally come into possession of such property were requested to return it by the end of November 1941 with no legal repercussions, but after this date such an action would be considered a crime.

Until the Bureau for Nationalised Property was established in January 1942, there was a succession of often-changing government bodies for the management, buying, and selling of confiscated or abandoned Jewish property that had passed into the possession of the state. On June 24, 1941 the State Directorate for Renovation had been established.[86] It dealt with relocating the population and with the takeover, assessment, selling, and management of the real estate and property of relocated individuals, and its work was supervised by the government. It is interesting to note that, unlike numerous other statutory provisions, it was possible to file complaints against the Directorate's decisions to the government administration.[87] A few days later, the State Directorate for the Renovation of Economy was established.[88] The selling of nationalised Jewish property, especially manufacturing companies, was placed in its authority. In September 1941 all matters to do with nationalisation were consolidated in one institution named the State Directorate for Renovation. In January 1942 all matters to do with nationalisation were passed over to the Treasury (governed by the aforementioned Vladimir Košak), where the Bureau for Nationalised Wealth was established for this purpose.

There were significant problems with the direct implementation of these statutory provisions. Large amounts of gold and silver ended up in private pockets. Plundering happened in various ways, and especially when keys taken from Jews deported to concentration camps were handed to the authorities only after the house or apartment was plundered. The largest number of merchant and craft companies was sold via the economic cooperatives "Hrvatski radiša" ("Croatian worker") from Zagreb and "Napredak" ("Progress") from Sarajevo. The State Bureau for Nationalised Wealth was gradually losing control over the nationalised property as it was handed over to cooperatives, which allowed for further plundering and looting of Jewish property. Vladimir Košak, the Treasury Minister, stated during the investigation in 1946 that the plundering of Jewish property was committed by "numerous Ustaša, police, and military officials" and that the state had attempted to create a new class of Croatian businessmen by this "Aryanisation of the economy," but all it had achieved was that a handful of people "became rich overnight, knowing no methods of trade other than smuggling and the black market."[89]

The question of the total value of nationalised Jewish property, if we count movables, valuables, real estate, manufacturing companies, trade companies, crafting companies, and securities (shares, bond certificates, debentures, insurance policies and deposit books) might not have a final answer. According to a report by the Bureau for Nationalised Wealth from September 15, 1943, the value of nationalised property taken from Jews was 6.7 billion kuna.[90]

Conclusion

Soon after the establishment of NDH, a legislative system was created based on statutory provisions and orders with the strength of law. The three racial laws that formed the basis for all later anti-Jewish legal regulations were passed as early as April 30, 1941. They were modelled after similar laws in Nazi Germany and Fascist Italy. The extent to which the Germans influenced the "prescribing and proclaiming" of these laws is difficult to ascertain, and further systematic scientific research is yet to be undertaken. The racial laws left Jews and Roma without state protection and citizenship and, as a consequence, a large number of Jews and Roma perished in Ustaša jails and concentration camps and, since May 1942, also in German concentration camps throughout occupied Europe. The racial laws concerning property law nationalised almost all Jewish real estate and movables – ostensibly for the economic growth of NDH, but in reality, clearly for the sake of misusing and plundering these assets.

Notes

1 Aleksa Đilas, *Osporavana zemlja, Jugoslavenstvo i revolucija* (Beograd: Književne novine, 1990), pp. 155.
2 Mario Jareb, *Ustaško–domobranski pokret od nastanka do travnja 1941* (Zagreb: Hrvatski institut za povijest/Školska knjiga, 2005), pp. 115.

3 *Ustav Ustaše,* 1932, pp. 1.
4 Mario Jareb, *Ustaško–domobranski pokret*, pp. 128.
5 For more on this topic, see: Nataša Mataušić, *Jasenovac 1941.–1945. Logor smrti i radni logor* (Jasenovac-Zagreb: Javna ustanova Spomen područje Jasenovac, 2003), pp. 14–15; Fikreta Jelić Butić, *Ustaše i Nezavisna Država Hrvatska* (Zagreb: Liber, 1977), pp. 162–178.
6 According to the Polexis encyclopaedia, Aryans ("the noble ones") are the descendants of Indo-European or Indo-Iranian tribes, or members of the peoples who speak Indo-European languages. In the nineteenth century, Joseph Arthur de Gobineau postulated that the Aryan race was a higher, more pure white race. The Nazis adopted this meaning of the word and added an anti-semitic aspect when passing their racial laws. Count Arthur the Gobineau's book *An Essay on the Inequality of the Human Races* (1854) was a significant source of information for the Nazis with its "scientific" explanation of the human races. He claims that there are three basic human races, the white, black and yellow race, and that the white race is the superior among them. The superior race should dominate the other races and must by no means mix with them, because miscegenation can strengthen the weaker races and weaken the strong. Furthermore, Gobineau claims that the Aryans are the jewel of the white race, and that the Germans are the best among the Aryans. That was the part of his book that had the largest influence on the creation of the National Socialist theories. See: Vanja Golberger, "Rasni zakoni u Trećem Reichu," http://povijest.net/rasni-zakoni-u-trecem-reichu/ (accessed February 2, 2018).
7 Ivo Goldstein, *Holokaust u Zagrebu* (Zagreb: Novi Liber, 2001), pp. 124.
8 Communist historiography after World war II uses the phrase "so-called Independent State of Croatia."
9 We can state with certainty that there is no official document about the founding of NDH. None of the three main participants in this event – Dr Vladko Maček, Slavko Kvaternik and Edmund Veesenmayer – mention such a document. Vladko Maček, *Struggle for Freedom* (University Park, PA, 1957), pp. 228–229; Veesenmayer's report to the German ministry of foreign affairs, in: US State Department, *Documents on German Foreign Policy*, 1918–1945, Series D, vol. 12, pp. 515–517; Slavko Kvaternik, *NDH i dr. Pavelić, Sjećanja* (manuscript), HDA, Dossier Ante Pavelić, MUP RH, 013.0/4, 1324–1554. The manuscript was published in Nada Kisić Kolanović, *Vojskovođa i politika* (Zagreb: Golden marketing, 1997).
10 Mario Jareb, *Ustaško-domobranski pokret od osnutka do travnja 1941. godine* (Zagreb: Hrvatski institut za povijest/Školska knjiga, 2006), pp. 570.
11 Ibid, pp. 594.
12 The Montevideo Convention, originally titled *The Montevideo Convention on the Rights and Duties of States,* was signed in Montevideo, Uruguay, on December 6, 1933, during the Seventh International Conference of American States.
13 Since 1932 Pavelić had been using the title Poglavnik (chief, leader) in his signature, after the examples of Mussolini (Duce) and Hitler (Führer).
14 Vladimir Geiger, "'Dokon pop i jariće krsti' ili jesu li postojali rasni zakoni u NDH? Reagiranje na tekst dr. sc. Stjepana Razuma 'Nekrofilski antifašisti i njihve laži o NDH i ustašama' objavljenog u *Hrvatskom tjedniku* br. 596 od 25. veljače 2016." www.historiografija.hr/?p=1991 (Accessed February 20, 2018).
15 Josip Junašević and Miroslav Šantek (eds.) *Zbornik zakona i naredaba Nezavisne Države Hrvatske*, pp. 789.

16 Marko samardžija (ed.) *Jezični purizam u NDH. Savjeti Hrvatskoga državnog ureda za jezik* (Zagreb: Hrvatska sveučilišna naklada, 1993), pp. 45.
17 HR HDA, MUP RH 013.0.52. Mile Budak, pp. 16.
18 Ibid.
19 *Zakoni zakonske odredbe i naredbe proglašene od 11. travnja do 26. svibnja 1941*, book 1, vol 1–10 (Zagreb, n. d.), pp.15. *Narodne novine,* April 17, 1941, no. 4.
20 Ibid.
21 Ibid.
22 Ibid, pp. 288–291; *Narodne novine*, May 20, 1941, no. 32.
23 Ibid.
24 "Zakonska odredba od 12 prosinca 1941, o preinaci i dopuni zakonske odredbe o proširenju nadležnosti prijekog suda i pokretnog priekog suda od 22. rujna 1941," in *Zakoni zakonske odredbe i naredbe proglašene od 7. prosinca do 31. prosinca 1941.*, book 10, vol. 91–100. (Zagreb, n. d.) pp. 42–43.
25 Goldstein, *Holokaust u Zagrebu*, pp. 118.
26 Ibid.
27 *Zakoni zakonske odredbe i naredbe proglašene od 11. travnja do 26. svibnja 1941,* book 1, vol. 1–10 (Zagreb, n. d.), pp. 109–112; *Narodne novine*, April 30, 1941, no. 16. In Germany, two laws defining "citizenship of the Reich" were passed on September 15, 1935. The law on citizenship prescribed that only Germans and those of "kindred" blood were to be considered citizens of the Reich, being the only ones entitled to civic and political rights.
28 *Zakoni zakonske odredbe i naredbe proglašene od 11. travnja do 26. svibnja 1941,* book 1, vol. 1–10 (Zagreb, n. d.), pp. 107–109; *Narodne novine*, April 30, 1941, no. 16. The chief interpreter of the government's policies, the minister for worship and education Mirko Puk, saw the laws on race and on the protection of the Aryan blood and honour of the Croatian people as a logical result of the Ustaša model of government – the "one leader, one ruling nation" principle. The gist of his interpretation of the law from the aspect of NDH legislation was that "Jews are excluded from all public and self-governing services, their private legal activities in the sphere of economy are limited, and marriage between a Jew and an Aryan is forbidden in order to remove their harmful influence on the Croatian people." See: Nada Kisić Kolanović, "Podržavljenje imovine Židova u NDH," *Časopis za suvremenu povijest*, XXX/1998, no. 3, pp. 432.
29 *Zakoni zakonske odredbe i naredbe proglašene od 11. travnja do 26. svibnja 1941,* book 1, vol. 1–10 (Zagreb, n. d.), pp. 113–115; *Narodne novine*, April 30, 1941, no. 16.
30 Ibid.
31 Ibid.
32 *Hrvatski narod*, no. 80, May 3, 1941.
33 Ibid.
34 Ibid.
35 Ibid.
36 Ibid.
37 *Zakoni zakonske odredbe i naredbe proglašene od 11. travnja do 26. svibnja 1941,* book 1, vol. 1–10 (Zagreb, n. d.), pp. 107–109; *Narodne novine*, April 30, 1941, no. 16.
38 *Zakoni zakonske odredbe i naredbe proglašene od 11. travnja do 26. svibnja 1941,* book 1, vol. 1–10 (Zagreb, n. d.), pp. 113–115; *Narodne novine*, April 30, 1941, no. 16.

39 Ibid.
40 Ibid.
41 Ibid.
42 Ibid.
43 *Narodne novine*, April 30, 1941, no. 16.
44 Ibid.
45 Ibid.
46 Ibid.
47 Ibid.
48 Bogdan Krizman, *Pavelić između Hitlera i Mussolinija* (Zagreb: Globus, 1980), pp. 27–28.
49 Dr Vladimir Židovec, a jurist from Karlovac, was the first Croatian special minister and assignee in Sofia (1941–1943).
50 Nada Kisić Kolanović, "Podržavljenje imovine Židova u NDH," *Časopis za suvremenu povijest*, vol. 30, no. 3 (1998), pp. 433.
51 Ibid., pp. 434.
52 Ibid., pp. 435.
53 *Zakoni zakonske odredbe i naredbe proglašene od 27. svibnja do 30. lipnja 1941*, book 2, vol. 11–20 (Zagreb, n. d.), pp. 131–132; *Narodne novine*, June 7,1941, no. 46; Ibid, pp. 157; *Narodne novine*, May 5, 1941, no. 19.
54 *Zakoni zakonske odredbe i naredbe proglašene od 27. svibnja do 30. lipnja 1941*, book 1, vol. 1–10 (Zagreb, n. d.), pp. 161–163; *Narodne novine*, May 6,1941, no. 20.
55 Goldstein, *Holokaust u Zagrebu*, pp. 146.
56 *Zakoni zakonske odredbe i naredbe proglašene od 27. svibnja do 30. lipnja 1941*, book 2, vol. 11–20 (Zagreb, n. d.), pp. 40.
57 Ibid.
58 Ibid., pp. 54–60.
59 Ibid., pp. 105–118.
60 Ibid., pp. 73–75.
61 For more information see Goldstein, *Holokaust u Zagrebu*, pp. 125–131.
62 Ibid.
63 The Germans first prescribed the wearing of the "Jewish sign" in the *Generalgouvernement* area (occupied Poland, formally a part of the Third Reich). Following the Nazi practice, the Ustaša adopted this measure before it was expanded to the entire area of the Reich.
64 Stjepan Razum, "Nekrofilski antifašisti i njihove laži o NDH i ustašama," *Hrvatski tjednik* no. 596, February 25, 2016.
65 Tomislav Jonjić, "U povodu knjige *Dragutin Gjurić–Životnim putem Hrvatske Tomislava Đurića*," www.tomislavjonjic.iz.hr/V_20_previranja.html (Accessed February 2, 2018).
66 Ibid.
67 Ibid.
68 Ibid.
69 See: Antun Miletić, *Koncentracioni logor Jasenovac 1941–1945. Dokumenta*, book I–II (1986); book III (1987); book IV (Beograd-Jagodina: Narodna knjiga/Gambit, 2007), pp. 2500.
70 Righteous Among the Nations is a honorific used for a person who saved Jews from Nazi persecution during World War II, risking their own life and the lives of their family members. Over 23,000 people from around the world have received

this medal, the highest Israeli state honour for non-Jews; 104 of them are from Croatia.
71 See: Nada Kisić Kolanović "Podržavljenje imovine Židova u NDH," *Časopis za suvremenu povijest*, vol. 30, no. 3 (1998), pp. 425–640; Zlata Živković Kerže, "Podržavljenje imovine Židova u Osijeku u NDH," *Časopis za suvremenu povijest*, vol. 39, no. 1 (2007), pp. 97–116; Vladimir Šadek, "Postupanje ustaškog režima s imovinom Židova i Srba u kotarima Koprivnica i Đurđevac," *Podravina*, vol. 14, no. 28 (2015), pp. 5–16.
72 *Narodne novine*, no. 43, 1941.
73 *Zakoni zakonske odredbe i naredbe proglašene od 27. svibnja do 30. lipnja 1941*, book II, vol. 11–20 (Zagreb, n. d.), pp. 73–75.
74 Ibid., pp. 54–60.
75 Ibid, pp. 75–79.
76 Ibid.
77 Ibid.
78 Ibid.
79 Ibid.
80 Ibid., pp. 79–105.
81 Ibid.
82 *Zakoni zakonske odredbe i naredbe proglašene od 1. do 29. listopada 1941*, book 7, vol. 61–70 (Zagreb, n. d.), pp. 93–95.
83 *Zakoni zakonske odredbe i naredbe proglašene od 27. listopada do 14. studenog 1941*, book 15, vol. 241–250 (Zagreb, n. d.), pp. 133–142.
84 *Zakoni zakonske odredbe i naredbe proglašene od 1. do 29. listopada 1941*, book 7, vol. 61–70 (Zagreb, n. d.), pp. 93.
85 *Zakoni zakonske odredbe i naredbe proglašene od 27. listopada do 14. studenog 1941*, book 15, vol. 241–250 (Zagreb, n. d.), pp. 133.
86 *Narodne novine*, no. 58, June 24, 1941.
87 *Narodne novine*, no. 60, June 26, 1941.
88 *Narodne novine*, no. 70, July 8, 1941.
89 Nada Kisić Kolanović, "Podržavljenje imovine Židova u NDH," *Časopis za suvremenu povijest*, XXX/1998, no. 3, pp. 444.
90 Ibid., pp. 453. During WWII the exchange rate of NDH Kuna against the US Dollar was 50:1, meaning that 1 NDH Kuna was valued at 0.02 US Dollar (1 NDH Kuna = 0.02 USD). The corresponding amount of 6,711,369,971 kuna would thus amount to 134,227,399.42 dollars. Accounting for inflation, the same amount would be valued at $2,122,554,160.53 in today's US dollars (the calculation has been made by using the US Inflation Calculator at the: www.usinflationcalculator.com and comparing 1943 and 2021).

Bibliography

Blažević, Robert and Amina Alijagić. "Antižidovstvo i rasno zakonodavstvo u fašističkoj Italiji, nacističkoj Njemačkoj i ustaškoj NDH," *Zbornik Pravnog fakulteta Sveučilišta u Rijeci*, vol. 31, no. 2, 2010, pp. 879–916.
Đilas, Aleksa. *Osporavana zemlja, Jugoslavenstvo i revolucija*. Beograd: Književne novine, 1990.
Documents on German Foreign Policy, 1918–1945., seria D, vol. 12, 515–517; SAD, State Department.

Geiger, Vladimir. "Dokon pop i jariće krsti" ili jesu li postojali rasni zakoni u NDH?" www.historiografija.hr/?p=1991. Accessed February 20, 2018.
Goldberger, Vanja. "Rasni zakoni u trećem Reichu." http://povijest.net/rasni-zakoni-u-trecem-reichu/. Accessed February 20, 2018.
Goldstein, Ivo. *Holokaust u Zagrebu*. Zagreb: Znanje, 2001.
HR HDA, MUP RH, 013.0/4., Ante Pavelić. 1324–1554.
HR HDA, MUP RH 013.0.52., Mile Budak, 16.
Hrvatski narod, no. 80, May 3, 1941.
Jareb, Mario. *Ustaško-domobranski pokret od nastanka do travnja 1941*. Zagreb: Hrvatski institute za povijest/Školska knjiga, 2006.
Jelić-Butić, Fikreta. *Ustaše i Nezavisna Država Hrvatska*. Zagreb: Sveučilišna naklada Liber, 1977.
Jonjić, Tomislav. "U povodu knjige Dragutin Gjurić–Životnim putem Hrvatske Tomislava Đurića." www.tomislavjonjic.iz.hr/V_20_previranja.html. Accessed February 20, 2018.
Junašević Josip and Miroslav Šantek (eds.) *Zbornik zakona i naredaba Nezavisne Države Hrvatske, Godina 1941.*, vol. 1–12. Zagreb, 1941.
Kolanović Kisić, Nada. "Podržavljenje imovine Židova u NDH," *Časopis za suvremenu povijest*, vol. 30, no. 3, 1998, pp. 425–640.
Kolanović Kisić, Nada. *Vojskovođa i politika*. Zagreb: Golden Marketing, 1997.
Krizman, Bogdan. *Pavelić između Hitlera i Mussolinija*. Zagreb: Globus, 1980.
Maček, Vlado. *Struglle for Freedom*. Pennsylvania: University Park, 1957.
Mataušić, Nataša. *Jasenovac 1941.–1945., Logor smrti i radni logor*. Jasenovac: Spomen područje Jasenovac, 2003.
Miletić, Antun. *Koncentracioni logor Jasenovac 1941–1945. Dokumenta, I–III, Beograd, 1986. i 1987., IV*. Jagodina: Gambit, 2007.
Narodne novine, no. 4, April 17, 1941.
Narodne novine, no. 16, April 30, 1941.
Narodne novine, no. 19, May 5, 1941.
Narodne novine, no. 32, May 20, 1941.
Narodne novine, no. 46, June 7, 1941.
Narodne novine, no. 58, June 24, 1941.
Narodne novine, no. 60, June 26, 1941.
Narodne novine, no. 70, July 8, 1941.
Razum, Stjepan. "Nekrofilski antifašisti i njihove laži o NDH i ustašama," *Hrvatski tjednik* no. 596, February 25. 2016.
Šadek, Vladimir. "Postupanje ustaškog režima s imovinom Židova i Srba u kotarima Koprivnica i Đurđevac," *Podravina*, vol. 14, no. 28, 2015, pp. 5–16.
Samardžija, Marko (ed.) *Jezični purizam u NDH. Savjeti Hrvatskoga državnog ureda za jezik*. Zagreb: Hrvatska sveučilišna naklada, 1993.
Ustav Ustaše. 1932, pp. 1.
Zakoni zakonske odredbe i naredbe proglašene od 11. travnja do 26. svibnja 1941, book 1 (vol. 1–10). Zagreb (without year mark).
Zakoni zakonske odredbe i naredbe proglašene od 27. svibnja do 30. lipnja 1941, book 1 (vol. 11–20). Zagreb (without year mark).
Zakoni zakonske odredbe i naredbe proglašene od 1. do 29. listopada 1941, book 7 (vol. 61–70). Zagreb (without year mark).

Zakoni zakonske odredbe i naredbe proglašene od 7. prosinca do 31. prosinca 1941, book 10 (vol. 91–100). Zagreb (without year mark).
Zakoni zakonske odredbe i naredbe proglašene od 27. listopada do 14. studenog 1942, book 25 (vol. 241–250). Zagreb (without year mark).
Živković Kerže, Zlata. "Podržavljenje imovine Židova u Osijeku u NDH," *Časopis za suvremenu povijest*, vol. 39, no. 1, 2007, pp. 97–116.

4 Crime and Punishment, or – What is the Connection between Jasenovac and Bleiburg?

Biographical Excerpts on War Criminals from the Jasenovac Camp

Ivo Goldstein

Jasenovac and Bleiburg, that is, "Jasenovac" and "Bleiburg," have grown in the last quarter of a century into two topoi of Croatian history and national memory, but in most of the literature no causal relationship has ever been established between them. In this text, I would attempt to explain how this relationship is established – primarily in the sense that a good part of Jasenovac criminals were punished at Bleiburg and the "Way of the Cross," or at postwar trials. Over the past decades, the name "Jasenovac," in addition to denoting the Prisavlje settlement near the Sava River and the Ustaša camp, has taken on a third, symbolic, meaning: it has become the notion for Ustaša genocidal crime and political terror, most systematically carried out in Jasenovac camps and 30 other Ustaša camps. In a broader sense, the term "Jasenovac" is sometimes applied to all the Ustaša crime committed during the regime of the Independent State of Croatia.[1] Bleiburg is a small town in the south of Austria, near the Austrian–Slovenian border. In the final battles of World War II, the majority of the army of the defeated Independent State of Croatia [NDH] broke through on May 15, 1945, to the field in front of Bleiburg, intending to capitulate in front of the Eighth Army units of the British Army. British commanders refused to accept the surrender of the NDH army. At that time, a small part of Ustaša officers and soldiers fled to the nearby forests and hills, while most of the army surrendered to Yugoslav Army units and Slovenian Partisans. The disarmed prisoners were taken to Maribor and Celje, where some larger groups were immediately set aside for liquidation, and the rest were sent on long marches to distant prison camps, some even as far as Macedonia. Along the way, they were massively abused, often killed, or died of exhaustion and diseases. These torturous marches were called the "Way of the Cross."[2] Of the members of the NDH army that capitulated that May on the Bleiburg field, barely half of them lived to see a general amnesty in the camps on August 3, 1945, according to which they were sent to serve in the Yugoslav Army or released, and some were taken before the judicial authorities of the new Yugoslav government. The totality

DOI: 10.4324/9781003326632-5

of the crimes committed against the prisoners of the NDH army in the first postwar months, was given the common name "Bleiburg."

In postwar Yugoslavia, all the way to its breakup – a full 45 years – the Bleiburg syndrome had to be kept silent in public. In the homes of the victims, sad memories were quietly nurtured, scarce knowledge was retold with bitterness, and family legends sprouted. Lonely attempts to investigate and tell the full truth were vigorously prevented and punished by the authorities. Forced amnesia was imposed on Bleiburg.[3] On the contrary, in the Ustaša emigration, Bleiburg became the central myth of collective bitterness and political gathering. Ustaša officers and officials who fled the Bleiburg field on the eve of the capitulation or escaped by other means managed to settle down all over the world after many vicissitudes. Scattered around the world, divided by different interpretations of their military and political defeat, many quarreling with each other as well, they nevertheless became connected by the common theme of Bleiburg. It was therefore a matter of unity in suffering and in resentments towards the victor. With the apotheosis of their own suffering, the suffering inflicted on everyone else was suppressed into oblivion, and Bleiburg tried to cover up Jasenovac.

There are also the roots of Bleiburg mythology: The number of victims has multiplied ten times over the numbers in the real tragedy, and annual commemorations have been turned into political rallies with inflammatory messages soaked in hatred. Due piety to victims was thus disrespected. During its 45 years, the Ustaša emigration produced many hundreds of memoirs, articles, and books about Bleiburg, among which there were shocking and convincing testimonies about details, but not a single historiographical work that would analyze the causes and the course of Bleiburg events and give the reader a complete picture free of political one-sidedness. In general, everything was very superficially and schematically reduced to hatred towards Croats, and when it came to crimes against clergymen, to hatred towards the church. The analysis of the wider Croatian, Yugoslav, and even European context was completely absent because, in many European countries (such as France, for example), collaborationists were ruthlessly punished. Simultaneous with the Bleiburg myth in exile, the Jasenovac myth flourished in Yugoslavia. In postwar Yugoslavia, research on Jasenovac was adequately stimulated, and abundant documentation was collected. Quite a lot of valuable memoirs, and to some extent even professional research papers, have been published. However, the number of about 700,000 Jasenovac victims, seven to eight times exaggerated, was sacrosanct and under the protection of state authorities. It was not allowed to be touched, not even examined by expert examination, although, from the statistical point of view, something was obviously wrong.

Initially conceived merely as a matter of the war damage in Yugoslavia and related to its demands for reparations, this exaggerated number of Jasenovac victims eventually developed into an object of controversy that dangerously poisoned interethnic relations in the former Yugoslavia, and partly fueled the wars in the 1990s.[4] With the disintegration of Yugoslavia and the establishment of an independent Croatia, the Bleiburg myth moved from the emigration to Croatia. It also erupted indigenously from that part of the local people who, after forced silence, could hardly wait to speak freely about their Bleiburg-related trauma in public. The media became flooded with revelations and "discoveries" about the Bleiburg topic.

The state government and the Catholic Church became the main actors and patrons of the annual commemorations on the Bleiburg field, which served political propaganda much more than the deserved reverence for the Bleiburg victims. From the Bleiburg rostrum, with applause from the crowd, the defeated army, which had been fighting on the side of the greatest historical Evil for four years, suddenly became "the Croatian army on whose victims a new Croatia is growing."[5] Too few people in the prevailing nationalist intoxication immediately realized how much such metaphors tarnish the historical image of Croatia and endanger its future.[6] Jasenovac was not forgotten at that time, either, Jasenovac was not forgotten at that time, yet, an attempt was made to cover up or completely deny the genocidal character of the Jasenovac camps, which were allegedly just scenes of forced labor for punishing opponents of the then-Croatian state and its regime.

The Commission for the Identification of War and Postwar Victims of the Croatian Parliament, after its seven-years of activity, establishes in its summary Work Report in 1999 that only 2,238 people lost their lives in the Jasenovac camps during the Independent State of Croatia. In the same report, about 700 discovered cemeteries with victims of war and postwar killings are tabulated on 70 pages, for which "Partisans" or "FPRY authorities" (authorities of the Federal People's Republic of Yugoslavia) are marked as perpetrators 630 times, "Chetniks" are marked 65 times, "German army" four times, and only one time "Ustašas." In the late 1990s, this Report was the culmination of efforts to cover Jasenovac with the veil of Bleiburg.[7] Such tendencies subsided a decade later, only to gain new momentum in recent years, incomparable even to what was happening in the 1990s.[8]

To deny or cover up the truth about Jasenovac leads to the rehabilitation of the entire Ustaša movement, which causes discomfort in part of the Croatian public, and aversion to Croatia in the civilized world. The vast majority of those killed on the "Way of the Cross" and later in the detention camps were recruited soldiers who could not be blamed for war crimes, but among them was a unit called the Ustaša Defense Brigade (Croatian acronym: UOZ) which provided security and surveillance over all camps in the NDH, including Jasenovac. Its commander, Vjekoslav Maks Luburić, included the entire UOZ in the column of the NDH army on the retreat towards Austria. In some final battles, the UOZ was the forerunner of the entire column, so a considerable number of Jasenovac executioners and other war criminals found themselves on the field before Bleiburg. There were other units whose members had blood on their hands – for example, the Fifth Ustaša Coalition (partly derived from the infamous Black Legion), and the Poglavnik's Bodyguard Brigade

(Croatian acronym: PTS), which at the end of the war grew into the PTS Division, that is, the Bodyguard Division.[9]

Therefore, it should be concluded that none of the Jasenovac victims can be ascribed as a war criminal, but that some of the Bleiburg victims were Jasenovac war criminals. In other words, the cause-and-effect chronology must be considered – of course, Bleiburg did not influence Jasenovac in any way, because it happened when Jasenovac no longer existed. However, Jasenovac was undoubtedly one of the several causes of Bleiburg. If Jasenovac had not happened, Beliburg probably would have not happened either or it would have been much less cruel. While there are many more, several biographies of some Jasenovac criminals who ended their lives at Bleiburg can explain why this is so.

Miroslav Filipović-Majstorović (1915) was one of the four most responsible for the crimes in Jasenovac; one of, as the detainees called them, "Jasenovac's four Ms."[10] Apart from him, the four also included Vjekoslav Maks Luburić, Ljubo Miloš and Ivica Matković. Filipović graduated from the Franciscan high school in Visoko, and was ordained a priest in 1939, when he was given the name Tomislav.[11] He knew Latin and Greek, and probably both German and Italian. Even then, the Franciscan Province had problems with him: He was destined to go to the monastery in Kraljeva Sutjeska. For unknown reasons, he was soon transferred to Petrićevac near Banja Luka, but he went there only after repeated warnings from the Provincial Father. He immediately connected with Viktor Gutić, the organizer of the Ustaša movement in that area, and in 1940 Filipović joined the movement. After the proclamation of the Independent State of Croatia, he began to act as a self-proclaimed military chaplain. In January 1942 he was transferred from Banja Luka due to disobedience and "voluntary connection with the Ustašas," but turned a deaf ear. Between 6 and 9 February 1942, as a pastor of the Second Poglavnik's Bodyguard Battalion (Croatian acronym: PTB), he took part in the unit's attacks on the Serb villages of Drakulić, Motike, and Šargovac, north of Banja Luka, when a mass crime against civilians was committed. The Grand Prefect of the Great Parish Luka and Sana claims that 2,252 people were killed at the time, and the Provincial of Franciscan Province of Bosna Srebrena, Fr. Anđeo Katić, wrote in a letter in May 1942 to the Supreme Head of the Franciscan Order that, on that occasion the Ustašas killed "more than 1,600 Orthodox people." Witnesses claim that Filipović entered the school between the villages of Drakulić and Šargovac with several other Ustašas. He told a teacher who had known him from before to single out a Serbian child. Unsuspecting, the teacher chose "the beautiful and nicely dressed Radojka Glamočanin, the daughter of Đuro who was the richest host in the area, thinking that the child should recite something." Filipović "gently embraced and caressed her, then grabbed her and began tensely slaughtering her in front of the other children." The children began to "scream and jump frantically on the benches," and Filipović exclaimed: "This is me, in the name of God, baptizing degenerates and taking all the sins on my soul," and ordered the teachers to single out the Serbian children. He then left it to the other Ustašas to kill them. Shortly afterwards, he was arrested and placed in prison on the street Savska cesta in Zagreb, where, according to his own confession, he spent three and a half months. There are various versions of the reasons and circumstances of this arrest: Some claim that it happened at an Italian request, others, "at the German request," and still others say that "Muslims complained." It was even rumored that "Pavelić sentenced Filipović to death," and that "the next day his name appeared on posters for the shooting by the firing squad." But this was probably just Ustaša deception of the Allies, because they assured Filipović that, "even if he had to be extradited to the Germans or the Italians, they would cover him up and extradite somebody else."

After repeatedly ignoring instructions received from the Franciscan Province in Sarajevo, Filipović severed all formal ties with it on February 12. He was then suspended by the papal legate, Marcone, and was expelled from the Franciscan order in late April. The commissions of the Franciscan Province of Bosna Srebrena, which discussed the Filipović case, doubted whether he was just accompanying the Ustaša unit, or was actively participating in the massacre. They concluded that he should not have even accompanied them. Legate Marcone "presented him out before ecclesial fora as the originator of the massacre." For Ustašas, Miroslav Filipović was no ordinary prisoner on Savska cesta. He had a special status: On Easter 1942 he served mass and was taking confessions from detainees. He was visited by various Ustaša officials. His prison colleagues did not know why he was detained. They thought that "as an honest man he revolted, that as a Christian he protested against mass murders." Luburić allegedly sent him to Jasenovac on June 10 as a prisoner. But that was a farce, because Luburić's car came to pick up Filipović in prison – what kind of detainee was transferred to one of the camps in the car of the very commander of all the camps? Previously, Filipović received a new identity, allegedly given to him by Maks Luburić himself. Namely, in one conversation, Luburić confided in Filipović that everyone was "bothering" him because of Filipović and his alleged crimes, and that he (Filipović) was in fact "a master, so from now on he will be called Majstorović."[12] As soon as he arrived in Jasenovac, Miroslav Filipović–Majstorović was given the right to Ustaša food, he rode a horse, and one detainee even taught him to drive a car and a motorcycle. In just a few days, Majstorovic became a "free man" in Jasenovac, and when the Ustaša command received definitive confirmation that "specific abilities were hidden" in him, the charade over the alleged detainee-freeman status ended. The Ustaša command accepted him into its ranks and included him as an "officer" in the supervisory staff. He also immediately became an Ustaša captain, and Luburić, arriving in Jasenovac on June 27, appointed him commander in the Jasenovac III Ciglana camp. In October of the same year, he was transferred to Stara Gradiška, where he was appointed commander. He remained in Gradiška until March 1943, when he was transferred to Mostar and since then, until the spring of 1945, all his contact with Jasenovac ceased. On the one hand, everyone says that he was "extraordinarily sweet and kind, always smiling, childish–looking," that he takes great care of himself – "a priest's face, dressed in an elegant suit, with makeup and powdered, in a green hunting hat," that he "manicures himself, knows how to bow, has something feminine in his movements," yet, on the other hand, it was said that for a long time he was the main executor of mass slaughters in Gradina, and for that he would be specially dressed up. Usually in the evening he would put on a strange green raincoat, perform slaughter, and only in the morning of the second day, he would return all bloody.

Ljubo Miloš confirmed that the slaughter took place "mostly at night," and that Filipović–Majstorović "therefore almost always slept during the day and was incapable of any other work." Witnesses claim that Filipović "enjoyed slaughtering," and that he was "the immediate leader of a group of 12 to 14 Ustašas who killed with axes and mallets."

Ljubo Miloš later testified that Majstorović was "the immediate supervisor in the liquidation of the detainees who were newcomers." In 1945, Majstorović himself confided in investigator Vojdrag Berčić that he was trying to find a way to kill in the easiest and fastest way, especially children (in other words, he practiced the speed of slaughter – the hand movements). That is why at some point he was nicknamed "Fra Satan." In addition, some detainees testified that he also selected detainees to be taken to Gradina. At the trial, he himself claimed that he "witnessed the massacres but did not commit them," which, apparently, does not appear to be true. There are also many stories of his individual murders – for example,

> one summer day, during a detainee's midday break, he was sitting at a set table in front of the command and was having lunch. Suddenly, an Ustaša appeared in front of him and reported that a detainee had tried to escape, and Majstorović ordered him to be brought to him.

When the detainee arrived, Majstorović put down his fork and knife as peacefully as possible, took out a revolver, shot him, and when the poor victim collapsed in front of the table, he just said to the Ustaša: 'Call the gravediggers,' and continued eating.

On another occasion, "they brought in front of Majstorović a Serbian child of about 14 who tried to escape. Majstorović grabbed a large hammer without any interrogation, and used it to smash the child's skull in front of all of us." One witness describes how Filipović–Majstorović lined up a group of 10–12 Serbs, Partisans, took an old pot, saying

> he would now try to see how long they could last. He went from one to the other and would put a pot on their heads, and then hit them with a flat side of the pickaxe until he pushed the pot all the way down their faces.

If any of the detainees got up, he would start hitting him again. In the end, he took the dagger and killed them all by himself.

It is also claimed that Filipović–Majstorović personally killed 14 detainees under the alleged charge that they were asking their wives to bring weapons to the camp, when in fact two denunciators had found a detainee who wrote to his wife to bring him food, so they added a story about weapons and accused the whole group.

Witnesses describe (without much difference in details) how Filipović–Majstorović committed crimes that were, to say the least, monstrous not only in Jasenovac but also in Stara Gradiška: Majstorović watched the children with pleasure. He approached them, even patted them on the head. Ljubo Miloš and Ivica Matković joined the company. Fra Majstorović told the mothers that their children would be baptized at that moment. They deprived the mothers of their children, and the child carried by Fra Majstorović in their childlike innocence caressed the face of their murderer. The mothers, distraught, realized what was going to happen. They offer their lives seeking mercy for the little ones. These three children were put to the ground, while the third was thrown like a ball into the air, and Fra Majstorović, holding a dagger facing up, missed three times, while the fourth time, with a joke and laughter, the child remained on the dagger. The mothers threw themselves on the ground, pulling out their hair, and when they started shouting terribly, the Ustaša guards took them away and killed them. When all three children were so cruelly killed, the three two-legged beasts gave each other money, because they seemed to be betting on who would put the child on the dagger first.

There were rumors that Majstorović was in love with a "beautiful young Gypsy woman … it was said that he fell in love with her, but also that, according to the same story, she was liquidated together with Gypsy gravediggers, when Majstorović was already far from Jasenovac." It was also rumored that, along with other leading Ustašas in the camp, he also participated in the rapes and killings of young girls. Ilija Jakovljević deduced Majstorović's motives for the murder from "deeply ethical reasons." His motive for killing the Jews stemmed from the belief that they had "killed our dear Jesus." The motive for killing the Serbs was the alleged "gap between Eastern barbarism and Western culture," because Orthodoxy was a "plague to be destroyed by fire and sword." Majstorović was also an "ideologically charged man who knew that communism was a 'Jewish–Orthodox forgery of social justice,'" so he obviously drew from there an argument for the mass liquidation of communists. He did not need special motives to kill the Roma. In March 1943, Miroslav Filipović–Majstorović was transferred to Mostar, then to Zagreb, then to Lika and even later to Bosnia, but he occasionally visited Jasenovac. Towards the end of the war, in early April 1945, he came as a key figure in finding and destroying tombs, in an effort to cover up crimes. He appears to have been involved in the killing of the detainees again. After the collapse of the Independent State of Croatia, he withdrew to Austria. The British handed him over to the Yugoslav authorities who sentenced him to death in June 1945. During the investigation and trial in 1945, Majstorović, speaking of Ustaša crimes in the first months after the establishment of the Independent State of Croatia, claimed that they were the result of "paying back the Chetniks," because the Chetniks "were the first to burn and slaughter entire villages." He tried to attribute the responsibility for the mass liquidations in Jasenovac primarily to Luburić, and then to Ivica Matković, who "gave him personal orders for the liquidation of Serbs." Luburić allegedly told him "that Serbs must be ruthlessly exterminated." He presented himself as an obedient member of the Ustaša movement and as a "small child he did not look for reasons" for certain things. Describing his command of the camp, he claimed that he advocated "discipline, order and cleanliness," that he protected the inmates from Ustašas' "arbitrariness and beatings." He admitted that he "sometimes witnessed" mass executions, even "killing several people," but concluded by claiming that "the executions were carried out mainly by the detainees themselves."[13]

Ivica Matković (1913), attended high school in Šibenik and, after finishing textile school in the Czech Republic, he studied law. In the late 1930s, he presented himself as a "textile expert." In September 1941, he joined the Ustaša Defense and, as someone close to Luburić, was appointed superintendent of the General Department of the Jasenovac Camp Command with the rank of first lieutenant. At the beginning of 1942, he became Luburić's deputy or deputy commander of the Office of the Third Ustaša Surveillance Service (Croatian acronym: UNS). With the departure of Luburić from the position of Commander of the Office of the Third, Matković, together with Ljubo Miloš, took over the management of the Jasenovac camp, where he remained until the summer of 1943, when he was replaced by Marko Pavlović. "Matković himself used to carry out the liquidation of those who were singled out as incompetent, and sometimes he issued orders for that to be done," – these were Ljubo Miloš's accusations after the war. After the war, the former detainees confirmed Miloš's statement – meaning that Matković was the one who gave orders for liquidation. The detainees call the period of Matković's rule in Jasenovac a "shameful reign of terror," and him a "bestial criminal," a "hardened villain," a "nervous wreck," a "bloodthirsty," an "executioner," "known for atrocities." He is one of the few "most prominent executioners." In his memoirs, Đorđe Miliša paid more attention to Matković than to any other criminal in Jasenovac – he considered him an archetype of the bloodthirsty type, "an intellectual in the service of a dark and negative mind." Ciliga claims that Matković was "nervous, a bit abnormal." The third memoirist from Jasenovac, Milko Riffer, describes how Matković was so disgusting to him that he "dreamed of a rat with Matković's gray eyes and sharp black teeth. I flee from him into the unknown and wake up."

Riffer and Miliša considered Matković a key person who decided to abolish camp III C, and to sentence about 200 camp inmates to starvation. Other witnesses claim that Matković was co-responsible for burning the detainees in the so-called Pićilli's furnaces, that, "enjoying the torments of the victims who were imprisoned in the Bell Tower" and sentenced to death without food and water, he "walked before the tower and laughed." He is also credited with "most active participation in the great massacre on Christmas Day 1941" in Jasenovac III Ciglana, when, among other things, he killed the owner of a Pakrac restaurant Joca Divjak. Matković recognized him and asked, "'Do you know me?'; Divjak replied that he did not know him. "Well, do you remember when I came to the restaurant with some friends, and you did not want to give us chairs to sit on,' so he ordered Divjak to be tied up; then he knocked him to the ground with a butt in the back of his head." Then he turned him on his chest, he cut his coat and shirt with a dagger, and with one stroke of the dagger cut his left loin. A horrible scream, then a grunt, and – Matković held Divjak's heart in his hand. "This is how Matkovic takes his vengeance," he concluded. The detainees describe in great detail Matković's propensity for sadism during the performance, when he would leave the detainees for several hours "in uncertainty, enjoying their torments and fear whether they would be the ones selected for liquidation." Furthermore, as he had five detainees lined up in front of other detainees in the middle of winter for several stolen potatoes from the kitchen, he ordered them to "strip naked," and then "the Ustašas tied their hands behind their backs and hung them that way. In such a position they hung for an hour, their bodies turning blue. Then Matković had them untied, and then he shot them in the back of the head and gave a speech to the detainees, in which he threatened even heavier punishment if such a 'crime' was repeated." There are testimonies that he was one of those who "threw a 19-year-old girl naked on the ground, spread her legs and burned cigarettes on her genitals, into which they then shook off the ashes." Also, that, along with other leading Ustašas in the camp, he participated in the rapes and killings of young girls.

Unlike the monstrous behavior towards the detainees, Matković treated his mare completely differently – he took special care that she was well-groomed and fed and that she did not accidentally stay in foal. The delegation that visited Jasenovac in November 1942, led by Aleksandar Seitz, an ally and commissioner of the Main Ustaša Apartment, "congratulated Matković on his exemplary work." Seitz promised Matković "that he would nominate him for the decoration." The proposal was really sent, but it is not known whether Matković received the decoration. In the summer of 1943, Matković was withdrawn from Jasenovac to Zagreb, where he worked in the Ustaša Defense prison in Nova Ves. At the end of the war, then already in the rank of Ustaša lieutenant colonel, he was close to Chief Pavelić. He was involved in the assassination of the journalist and former head of the Ustaša University Staff Milivoj Karamarko (April 29, 1945). He then cooperated with Luburić, and when the withdrawal began on May 7, he was engaged in the transfer of Ustaša gold. He arrived in Austria in the following days. He was captured by the British and handed over to the Partisans. He allegedly did not want to remove his Ustaša military insignia (which others around him did en masse), so members of the Yugoslav Army executed him shortly after the surrender.[14]

Josip Mataija (often also referred to as Mataja in the sources) said Hadžija was a car mechanic before the war. First an ensign, then a lieutenant, and by the end of the war he was an Ustaša major. Since the establishment of the camp, he was based in Jasenovac. Mataija was Luburić's personal driver, at the same time the commander of the mechanic's workshop (the so-called *Quick Assembly*), therefore, obviously a person of Luburić's greatest confidence. He brought Vladko Maček to the camp, and he moved around the camp in the company of Miloš and Matković. At the end of 1941, on the orders of Ljubo Miloš, Mataija selected and liquidated 25 detainees, and soon after carried out Luburić's order that "all the sick, weak and incapable of working, 150 to 180 of them, be liquidated." In 1942, he commanded an Ustaša unit in attacks on Crkveni Bok and other Serb villages in the Sava Valley. Mataija was accused by several witnesses, including Ljubo Miloš, of personally participating in the mass executions. Miloš also claimed that in early 1942 Mataija had initiated that detainees should no longer be shot but killed with cold steel, which seems very likely because Mataija, as the bearer of Luburić's orders, was in a position to impose such a decision. At the beginning of May 1945, Mataija was commander of the "light-wing battalion" of the Ustaša Defense Brigade and withdrew to Austria. He was captured by the British and then returned to Slovenia. He allegedly did not want to take off his Ustaša military insignia (which others around him did en masse), so members of the Yugoslav Army executed him immediately after the surrender, just like Matković.[15]

Tihomir/Tiho Kordić, educated in Sarajevo, a lieutenant (who was an Ustaša lieutenant already in 1944), was a technician by profession, a commander of the work department in Stara Gradiška. He was one of a dozen well known Jasenovac criminals – the detainees remembered him as "dangerous." Many speak of him as an executor, and after the war investigators claimed that he "attended night operations," meaning he participated in the executions. His quick promotion was probably due to the fact that he was Luburić and Miloš's cousin. The detainees remember him for "smugly galloping on a black horse along the embankment," for being "elegantly dressed" in Ustaša uniform with "always ironed trousers." He always smelled of the elegant and famous *chypre* type of fragrance, so that the inmates could feel and "smell" it as he passed them by. In the fall of 1944, Kordić was transferred from the Jasenovac complex to Lepoglava. At the beginning of May 1945, he retreated towards Austria, commanding a "light-winged battalion" of Luburić's Defense. He was captured by the British and then returned to Slovenia, where he was captured and sentenced to death.[16]

Marko Pavlović (1900), before the war he was a captain in the Yugoslav army serving in Mostar. After the founding of the Independent State of Croatia, he took part in some Ustaša actions in the vicinity of Mostar. Following that, he joined the Home Guard. Since 1942, he was in the Ustaša army, working in the vicinity of Bosanska Dubica and on the forced settlement of the new population (after the "emigration" of Serbs). In the spring of 1943, he took command of the Ustaša Defense Brigade, based in Lipik, which was a combat unit. He was also in charge of Jasenovac, so Pavlović became the de facto commander of the Jasenovac camp. At the end of 1943, Ustaša leader Pavelić awarded him a high medal "for the courageous conduct and successful leadership of his units in the fight against the outlaws on Mount Kozara in 1942, on Grmeč, and near Bosanska Dubica in 1943." Shortly afterwards, he was promoted to colonel, and even a street in Bosanska Dubica was named after him. In April 1945, he was transferred and appointed as Vjekoslav Luburić's deputy. Luburić was the commander of the Ustaša Corps based in Sisak. He was known as a bloodthirsty, "executioner," and the one enforcing drastic punishments. "Pavlović's hand" was a synonym for terror in Jasenovac III Ciglana, in the period when it was objectively less than at the end of 1941 and during 1942, but Pavlović did not allow terror to be forgotten. He threw the entire camp into shackles after a number of detainees escaped, and about sixty people died from beatings. During the retreat in May 1945, he committed suicide somewhere in Slovenia.[17]

Marija/Maja Buždon–Slomić (1923), a housewife and worker in Zagreb at the time, became a member of the Ustaša movement in October 1942. She was assigned to the Stara Gradiška camp, where she soon became the commander of the women's section. She was the only female among senior Jasenovac officials whose signature is on a number of documents preserved in the archives. She was allegedly fascinated by Maks Luburić, to whom, after all, she owed her quick promotion. Witnesses listed her among the "butchers," claiming that she excelled in suffocating women. She was declared a "snake," "a leader of bloodsuckers and all evil in women and children." She is remembered as very cruel and violent. She punished detainees for even the smallest detail, either by "throwing them into solitary confinement or by whipping or beating them." Ilija Jakovljević describes that she "often appeared in front of the detainees with a revolver around her waist. A model of an Ustaša woman; she despised the detainees. Anyone who thought they could charm her by harmonious stature, sweet words, or a kind look was mistaken. She was strictly attached to her 'idea,' getting drunk and whoring only with the Ustašas. Maja cursed, beat, strangled, shot, and slaughtered. She preferred to do that to women detainees. She knew her job well. Maja admired herself; she was also admired by those of her kind: "Well done, Maja! You seem to have an Ustaša heart!" shouted one of the 'liquidators' when he saw how she shot a detainee easily." One witness claims to have seen Maja Buždon "order an exhausted detainee to get up, and when she could not get up due to weakness and illness, she strangled her with her own hands." Another witness said that she shot an old woman in front of her daughter for not handing her over to the camp administration a small tin watch which was a memory of her murdered son. The third one said that Maja Buždon, together with another Ustaša (Božica Obradović), while separating the children from their mothers, "threw one child that the mother did not give away into the well, and then beat the mother with a whip." Several witnesses describe how she came with the Ustaša Mirko Runjaš to the women's quarters, and "then they took 4–5 women to one room where they were slaughtering them."[18]

Marija's husband was Mirko Slišković-Slomić, a law student before the war. From November 1942 he was a deputy warden, then the head of the Administrative Department of Camp III Ciglana. As the person in charge, he was "up for the only task – killing." He probably met Marija Buždon in the camp. He married her at an unknown time. The couple stayed in Zagreb at the end of the war. According to some sources, it seems that they did not flee towards Bleiburg in May 1945, but were in Zagreb when the Partisan liberators arrived. They were arrested a few days later, on the street. According to another source, while trying to escape in a train, dressed as a farmer, Maja was recognized by a former detainee. At the end of the month, the Military Court of the Zagreb City Command sentenced the Slomićs to death.[19]

Dragutin Pudić – Paraliza (Paralysis, nickname), was a trade assistant in Slavonski Brod and in Zagreb, before the war. He was already then allegedly mentally ill and being treated. It is alleged that in the summer of 1941, Luburić took him directly from the hospital to Gospić, where he was appointed one of the commanders of the camps in Gospić and in Jadovno. By the end of the war, he had advanced to the rank of captain. One of those who in Jadovno called out the names of detainees every evening, or simply selected a group of detainees who were then taken out of the camp for liquidation, "he would throw them alive into the abyss." He spent some time in Slana (on the island of Pag), where he also participated in the liquidations. Because they liquidated the Jadovno detainees (thus disobeying the order to return them to Gospić), Pudić was arrested by Ustašas together with his boss Rubinić and his colleague Mihalović on September 13, 1941. in Jastrebarsko, but (unlike Rubinić who was tried later) Pudić and Mihalović were soon released. A few weeks later, he was already in Krapje, where "one night he ordered a 'performance' and ordered the detainees to head towards the gate. Suddenly, a machine gun fired into people. Pudić shouted that Serbs and Jews tried to flee." The witness claims that there were 150 killed. Later, in Camp III, Ciglana, Pudić "was catching the detainees" and took them to be liquidated; he was one of the "liquidators" or "butchers"; they even called him "the boss of mass killings." Ljubo Miloš claimed that Pudić was at the head of the "liquidation group," together with Majstorović. Miloš and other witnesses claim that he "led the liquidation of the Gypsies." There are numerous testimonies of his individual crimes. Probably Ustašas themselves, prone to morbid humor, gave him the nickname "Paralysis" because the victims were allegedly paralyzed with horror when they would see him approaching them armed. Those who met him claim that he had a "gaze of a lunatic." According to the testimony of Ljubo Miloš, Pudić was one of those who killed more often with a knife than with a gun. According to Miroslav Filipović–Majstorović, Pudić was "sick"; "he saw his persecutor in anyone who did not wear an Ustaša cap." And his behavior allegedly showed that he was "an abnormal type. He would walk around the camp in a blue work suit, with his hands in his pockets, in which he kept a revolver and a knife." According to the suggestions of his colleagues from Jasenovac, in June 1942 "he went for treatment." Majstorović claims that Pudić "was banned from returning to Jasenovac" since "because of some trifle he beat a Jew whom he [Majstorović] managed to defend." The detainees claimed that they were afraid of Ljubo Miloš and Matković, but that "panic would reach its peak" when they saw Pudić. Towards the end of the war, Pudić lived between Jasenovac and Zagreb: He served in Jasenovac, but practically at the same time he was arresting innocent people in Zagreb and was sending them to Jasenovac. Then he heard that his brother had joined the Partisans, so he ran to his brother's apartment and "threw his wife out into the street naked with a child, in the cold, at around midnight." Towards the end of the war, he was again in Jasenovac, where he burned corpses from mass graves and took part in the last executions of detainees. After the war, someone recognized him on a street in Zagreb. He was caught and sentenced to death.[20]

Ante Zrinušić was a bricklayer before the war. It seems that in Jasenovac III Ciglana he served from the founding of the camp, and from some point on as an Ustaša sergeant. He was the commander of the construction group. Witnesses ascribed him various characteristics – "perpetrator," "chief butcher," "best butcher," "known as the perpetrator of all the executions in Gradina," "one of the greatest butcherbirds." Numerous witnesses also cite specific crimes: in the spring of 1942, he was one of the leaders in the killing of detainees who were thrown into the so-called Pićilli's furnace. In August 1943, he managed the hanging of 15 Serbian peasants who were declared Partisans. Shortly afterwards, in one performance, he laid down on their backs five detainees who allegedly tried to escape, and then shot them in the head. In October, he led an Ustaša unit that slaughtered 25 inmates. That fall and winter, the group he commanded killed an unidentified number of detainees, allegedly taking them to work in the woods. And at the end of 1944, he was in a group that carried out mass liquidations in Granik. He was rumored to have, along with other leading Ustašas in the camp, participated in the rapes and killings of young girls. Dr. Arnold Schon, who worked as a detainee in the camp hospital, claims that Zrinušić was an alcoholic and that he was "in the Ustaša hospital three times in half a year for acute delirium." When Jasenovac was bombed at the end of March 1945, Zrinušić killed two detainees in order for them not to leave the building. In early April, he was in a group that burned corpses in Gradina and tried to erase the traces of the crime, while at the same time he was at the head of a group of Ustašas who killed about 30 detainees (possibly they were those who helped burn corpses and dig graves). He was seen throwing the bodies of detainees killed in the breakout the previous day into some water near the camp on the night of April 23. He was captured at the end of the war. At the end of May 1945, the Military Court of the Zagreb City Command sentenced him to death.[21]

Josip Šantić (1920) was a farmer before the war. After the establishment of the Independent State of Croatia, he joined the Ustaša organization.

In December 1941 he was promoted to sergeant major. After a short service in the area around Bihać, he was sent to Jasenovac, where he attended the NCO school. He was then transferred to Zagreb, and then to Lika and Kordun, where he took part in the fighting. He returned to Jasenovac in the spring/summer of 1943. During 1944, he led a group of Ustašas in and around Jasenovac. They killed 32 Roma – men, women and children, and then seven Jewish women. According to several witnesses, all of whom were former Ustašas, Šantić himself was also involved in those killings using a mallet or a stone. However, before or after these crimes, Šantić and five of his subordinates were detained in Jasenovac for about a month, because during an operation they "stole some pigs and transported them to Mlaka, thinking they were owned by Serbs," but since those pigs were owned by some Croats, even some Ustaša families, the owners sued them and so the thieves ended up in captivity. According to another witness, Šantić, "known as a robber and an outlaw," committed "some murders and was therefore imprisoned." However, when he served that short sentence, Šantić returned to his old position. After the war, Šantić was captured and convicted, but sentenced to prison. Probably neither the prosecutor nor the court knew about his crimes in Jasenovac. In 1955, Šantić was detained in a prison in Banja Luka. I was unable to establish why he was in prison, what happened to him after 1955, and whether he was tried at all for specific crimes in Jasenovac (it seems that he was not).[22]

Marko Pavlović committed suicide. Maja Buždon–Slomić, Mirko Slišković–Slomić, Pudić, Zrinušić, Šantić, Filipović–Majstorović were tried in court proceedings in which the outcome was known in advance, but due to the number and severity of the crimes proven to them, they undoubtedly did not deserve anything else. According to the norms of the legal profession at the time, they had a relatively fair trial.[23] It is possible that some witnesses were under pressure, it is possible that it was suggested to some witnesses what to say, but the numerous coincidences in the testimonies, in the description of specific situations, leave no doubt as to the guilt and responsibility of the convicts. To this, we should also add the fact that other witnesses (in memoirs, in later testimonies given in various parts of the world far from Zagreb where the trials took place) confirmed in principle and in detail what was established in the court hearings in 1945–1946. This was done, for example, by Ljubo Miloš. He was arrested and tried in 1947 and sentenced to death in 1948. Neither he nor the court had any reason then to confirm the results of the investigation or the court's verdict, completed two or three years earlier. After all, court records were not available to any of these later witnesses and memoirists. It is unclear whether Tihomir Kordić was tried or summarily executed. It seems that Ivica Matković and Josip Mataija were executed practically without a trial, but we can only speculate about that. As they were caught in uniform, as they had ranks on them, the members of the Yugoslav Army certainly established their identity. And if they connected them with Jasenovac, which was not difficult because their names were quite well known, the decision to liquidate them was easily made. At Bleiburg and the "Way of the Cross," captured and tried were also those whose responsibility and guilt is not directly related to the Jasenovac camp complex, if they were nevertheless connected to committing genocidal and war crimes and crimes against humanity during the NDH's four-year existence.

Pavelić himself, his interior minister Artuković, "Ustaša Himmler" Eugen Dido Kvaternik, as well as a number of ministers, officials and senior officers managed to hide in the postwar turmoil in Europe, and through illegal channels, they reached overseas countries, mostly Argentina, Paraguay and Australia, while some reached the United States and Spain.[24] The commander of the Dinara Chetnik Division, Duke Momčilo Đujić, also arrived in the United States. Of the 34 NDH ministers on the run, 21 died in exile, and 13 were repatriated and convicted. Their criminal responsibility can be linked to the term *Jasenovac* in the broadest sense of the word, as I defined it at the beginning of this text. Some of the perpetrators of the Jasenovac crimes were caught at Bleiburg and the "Way of the Cross," and were sanctioned then or later. Here I have described cases that had their epilogue, but many who were at the top of the command hierarchy, escaped. On the other hand, there were many innocent people who died there.[25] It is a war crime, that is, a crime against humanity. This crime can be partly explained by vengeful anger, as well as the desire to remove potential opponents of the new regime, but there is no justification for it.[26] From this unfortunate fact, new injustices and even new crimes arose. It is time for our generation to conclude this tragic chapter which burdens in various ways Croatia and its neighboring countries.

Notes

1 In detail, Slavko Goldstein and Ivo Goldstein, *Jasenovac i Bleiburg nisu isto* (Zagreb: Novi liber, 2011).
2 Ivo Goldstein, *Hrvatska 1918–2008* (Zagreb: Novi liber, 2008), pp. 350–381 and literature cited there; Milan Basta, *Rat je završen sedam dana kasnije* (Zagreb: Spektar, 1976); Petar Brajović, *Konačno oslobođenje* (Zagreb: Spektar, 1983), pp. 377; Vinko Nikolić (ed.) *Bleiburška tragedija hrvatskoga naroda* (Zagreb: Knjižnica Hrvatske revije, Agencija za marketing–Azinović, 1993), pp. 315–318; Vjekoslav Luburić, "Povlačenje hrvatske vojske prema Austriji," in John I. Prcela and Dražen Živić (eds.) *Hrvatski holokaust* (Zagreb: Hrvatsko društvo političkih zatvorenika, 2001), pp. 37–51; Ivo Rojnica, *Susreti i doživljaji*, vol. 1 (Zagreb: DoNeHa, 1994), pp. 262; very informative and balanced analysis, Jozo Tomasevich, *Rat i revolucija u Jugoslaviji, Okupacija i kolaboracija, 1941–1945* (Zagreb: EPH Novi Liber, 2010), pp. 848–858; Martina Grahek Ravančić, *Bleiburg i križni put 1945* (Zagreb: Hrvatski institut za povijest, 2009); see also a series of texts in: Nada Kisić-Kolanović, Mario Jareb and Katarina Špehnjak (eds.), *1945.–razdjelnica hrvatske povijesti* (Zagreb: Hrvatski institut za povijest, 2006) and in: Juraj Hrženjak (ed.), *Bleiburg i Križni put 1945* (Zagreb: Savez antifašističkih boraca i antifašista Republike Hrvatske, 2007).
3 In his book *Rat je završen sedam dana kasnije*, pp. 315–353, Basta was the first to write analytically and in detail about the events around Bleiburg in Yugoslavia. Yet, he only stated that he had seen columns going from Bleiburg towards the interior of the country (pp. 531). He did not deal with their fate.

4 Ivo Goldstein, "Jasenovac–Myth and Reality," in Emil Brix, Arnold Suppan and Elizabeth Vyslonzil (eds.) *Sudosteuropa. Traditionen als Macht* (Wien-Munchen: Oldenbourg Wissenschaftsverlag, 2007), pp. 97–111; Ivo Goldstein, *Hrvatska 1918–2008*, pp. 614, 621, 670, 777, 806.
5 Slavko Goldstein and Ivo Goldstein, *Jasenovac i Bleiburg nisu isto*, pp. 15.
6 Ivo Goldstein, *Hrvatska 1918–2008*, pp. 842–843.
7 A copy in the possession of the author.
8 Stipo Pilić, Blanka Matković, "Poslijeratni zarobljenički logor Jasenovac prema svjedočanstvima i novim arhivskim izvorima," Pilić, Stipo, and Blanka Matković "Poslijeratni zarobljenički logor Jasenovac prema svjedočanstvima i novima arhivskim izvorima." Radovi Zavoda za povijest HAZU u Zadru, 56 (2014), pp. 323–408; Vladimir Horvat, Blanka Matković, Stipo Pilić, Igor Vukić, *Jasenovački logori–istraživanja* (Zagreb: Društvo za istraživanje trostrukog logora Jasenovac, 2015).
9 Davor Marijan, *Ustaške vojne postrojbe 1941.–1945*, master's thesis (Zagreb, 2004).
10 HDA, fund 1561, SDS RSUP, 013.2.18., 30.
11 All sources used in writing the biography/psychological profile of Miroslav Filipović Majstorović are listed in note 12.
12 Majstorović is, in Croatian, a derivative from the noun "majstor" [master]; editors' remark.
13 Darko Stuparić (ed.) *Tko je tko u NDH* (Zagreb: Minerva, 1995), pp. 114–115. Đorđe (Jure) Miliša, *U mučilištu–paklu Jasenovac* (Zagreb: Naklada Pavičić, 1945/2011), pp. 72–73, 142, 167, 211, 257; Lazar Lukajić, "Fra Satana," in Zdravko Antonić and Janko Velimirović (eds.) *Jasenovac. Zbornik radova Četvrte međunarodne konferencije o Jasenovcu* (Kozarska Dubica, Banja Luka: Javna ustanova Spomen-područja Donja Gradina; Uružunje Jasenovac–Donja Gradina, 2007), pp. 235–254, loc. cit., pp. 242–243, 254; Egon Berger, *44 mjeseca u Jasenovcu* (Zagreb: Grafički zavod Hrvatske, 1966), pp. 64–65; Milko Riffer, *Grad mrtvih, Jasenovac 1943* (Zagreb: Naklada Pavičić, 1946/2011), pp. 8, 97, 133, 134; Ante Ciliga, *Jasenovac: ljudi pred licem smrti, Uspomene iz logora* (Zagreb: Naklada Pavičić, 2011), pp. 54, 93, 138; Cadik I. B. Danon, *Sasečeno stablo Danonovih, Sećanje na Jasenovac* (Beograd: S. Mašić, 2000), pp. 50–52; Milan Bulajić, *Ustaški zločini genocida i suđenje Andriji Artukoviću 1986. godine*, I–IV (Beograd: Rad, 1988–1989), loc. cit. t. II, at various locations; Nihad Halilbegović, *Bošnjaci u jasenovačkom logoru* (Sarajevo: Istraživačka publicistika. Vijeće Kongresa bošnjačkih intelektualaca, 2006), pp. 56; Radovan Trivunčić (ed.), *Neugasla sjećanja* (Jasenovac: Spomen područje Jasenovac, 1978), pp. 19; Dušan Sindik (ed.), *Sećanja Jevreja na logor Jasenovac* (Beograd: Savez jevrejskih opština Jugoslavije, 1972), pp. 43, 132, 134; *Borba* (Beograd) February 15, 1945; Velimir Blažević, *Aktualnosti trenutka. Studije i polemike* (Banja Luka, 2011); Antun Miletić, *Koncentracioni logor Jasenovac 1941–1945. Dokumenta knjiga I–III* (*Beograd: Narodna knjiga, 1986 and 1987*), book 2, pp. 1, 17, 24; book 2, pp. 726, 765, 877, 917, 985, 986, 991, 1014, 1015, 1018, 1020, 1024–1044, 1049, 1067, 1072, 1078–1080, 1088, 1089, 1098, 1099, 1120; book 3, 353, 434, 443, 456, 497, 500, 501, 508–509, 514, 515, 530–532, 543, 554, 560–561, 574, 713, 718; Dušan Lukač, *Banja Luka i okolica u ratu i revoluciji* (Banja Luka: Savez udruženja boraca NOR-a opštine, 1968), pp. 192–193; Nikola Nikolić, *Jasenovački logor smrti* (Sarajevo: Oslobođenje, 1977), pp. 252, 360–367; Ilija Jakovljević, *Konclogor na Savi* (Zagreb: Konzor, 1999), pp. 301–302, 318–319; Viktor Novak, *Magnum*

crimen, Pola vijeka klerikalizma u Hrvatskoj (Zagreb: Nakladni zavod Hrvatske, 1958), pp. 648, 649, 777, 871; Marko Ručnov, *Zašto Jasenovac* (Beograd: IKP Nikola Pašić, 2001), pp. 311–315; Ivo Goldstein and Slavko Goldstein, *Holokaust u Zagrebu* (Zagreb: Znanje, 2001), pp. 329, 340, 565, 587, 594.

14 Darko Stuparić (ed.) *Tko je tko u NDH*, pp. 261; Dušan Sindik (ed.) *Sećanja Jevreja*, pp. 200; Milko Riffer, *Grad mrtvih, Jasenovac 1943*, pp. 26, 32, 63, 83, 116, 120, 124; Đorđe (Jure) Miliša, *U mučilištu–paklu Jasenovac*, pp. 68–69; Ante Ciliga, *Jasenovac: ljudi pred licem smrti*, pp. 167; Milan Gavrić, *Otkosi smrti (sećanje na jasenovački logor istrebljenja)* (Beograd: Narodna armija Beograd, 1977), pp. 59; Drago Čolaković, *Kronika iz pakla* (Jasenovac: Spomen područje Jasenovac, 1971), pp. 65; Nikola Nikolić, *Jasenovački logor smrti*, pp. 70–74, 395–398; JUSP Jasenovac, "List of Victims," www.jusp-jasenovac.hr/Defa ult.aspx?sid=7618 (accessed August 19, 2019); Milan Bulajić, *Ustaški zločini genocida i suđenje Andriji Artukoviću 1986. godine*, pp. 167, 213, 220, 222; Dejan Motl and Đorđe Mihovilović, *Zaboravljeni–knjiga o posljednjim jasenovačkim logorašima* (Jasenovac–Zagreb: Spomen područje Jasenovac, 2015), pp. 719; Viktor Novak, *Magnum crimen, Pola vijeka klerikalizma u Hrvatskoj*, pp. 649; Antun Miletić, *Koncentracioni logor Jasenovac 1941–1945*, book 2–3, on various pages; Tomislav Sabljak and Ivo Smoljan (eds.), *Povlačenje 1945. Krivci i žrtve. Svjedočanstva o propasti NDH* (Zagreb: ZIB Mladost Omega, 2000), pp. 145, 148, 193; Ivo Goldstein and Slavko Goldstein, *Holokaust u Zagrebu*, pp. 315, 341, 587.

15 Dejan Motl and Đorđe Mihovilović, *Zaboravljeni–knjiga o posljednjim jasenovačkim logorašima*, pp. 629, 650; Antun Miletić, *Koncentracioni logor Jasenovac 1941–1945*, book 1–3, on various pages; Vladimir Dedijer, *Vatikan i Jasenovac, dokumenti* (Beograd: Rad, 1987), pp. 445–447, 449, 450; Dušan Sindik (ed.) *Sećanja Jevreja*, pp. 154–155, 200; Marko Ručnov, *Zašto Jasenovac*, pp. 453; Milan Bulajić, *Ustaški zločini genocida IV*, pp. 869; Tomislav Sabljak and Ivo Smoljan (eds.), *Povlačenje 1945. Krivci i žrtve. Svjedočanstva o propasti NDH*, pp. 193.

16 JUSP Jasenovac "List of Victims," www.jusp-jasenovac.hr/Default.aspx?sid=7618 (accessed August 19, 2019); Miletić, Jasenovac, book 1–3, on various pages; Milko Riffer, *Grad mrtvih, Jasenovac 1943*, pp. 8, 42, 57, 100, 122, 124, 125, 166; Nikola Nikolić, *Jasenovački logor smrti*, pp. 74, 368; Marko Ručnov, *Zašto Jasenovac*, pp. 387–388; Vladimir Dedijer, *Vatikan i Jasenovac, dokumenti*, pp. 654; Chypre is a combination of the scents of citrus, oakmoss and musk that served as a base for making various types of perfumes in the first half of the 20th century; Đorđe (Jure) Miliša, *U mučilištu–paklu Jasenovac*, pp. 212.

17 HDA, fund 487, Vjestnik MINORS, Z–2869, 164; Z–2871, 893; Z–2872, 1774; HDA, RSUP SRH SDS, 013.2.5., folder 4, pp. 15; Darko Stuparić (ed.) *Tko je tko u NDH*, pp. 314; Đorđe (Jure) Miliša, *U mučilištu–paklu Jasenovac*, pp. 239; Milko Riffer, *Grad mrtvih, Jasenovac 1943*, pp. 163; Marko Ručnov, *Zašto Jasenovac*, pp. 509–510; Antun Miletić, *Koncentracioni logor Jasenovac 1941–1945*, book 1–3, on various pages.

18 Vjesnik, Zagreb, May 29, 1945; Darko Stuparić (ed.) *Tko je tko u NDH*, pp. 62; Antun Miletić, *Koncentracioni logor Jasenovac 1941–1945*, book 1–3, in various months; Ilija Jakovljević, *Konclogor na Savi*, pp. 116; Marijana Amulić and Čedomil Huber (eds.) *Otpor u logoru Stara Gradiška (iz sjećanja bivših logoraša)* (Jasenovac: Spomen područje Jasenovac, 1980), pp. 100, 115, 121; Dušan Sindik (ed.) *Sećanja Jevreja*, pp. 41, 135, 166; Radovan Trivunčić (ed.), *Neugasla sjećanja*, pp. 13; Nikola Nikolić, *Jasenovački logor smrti*, pp. 96; Nihad Halilbegović,

Bošnjaci u jasenovačkom logoru, pp. 83, 98; Vladimir Dedijer, *Vatikan i Jasenovac, dokumenti*, pp. 355.
19 Zdravko Dizdar, Vladimir Geiger, Milan Pojić, Mate Rupić, *Partizanska i komunistička represija i zločini u Hrvatskoj 1944.–1946* (documents) (eds.) (Slavonski Brod: Hrvatski institut za povijest, 2005; Zagreb, 2009), pp. 406; Benedikta Zelić, *Nezavisna Država Hrvatska u mom sjećanju* (Split: Naklada Bošković, 2007), pp. 132; *Politika* (Beograd), May 30, 1945; Antun Miletić, *Koncentracioni logor Jasenovac 1941–1945*, book 1, pp. 17; book 2, pp. 1067; Đorđe (Jure) Miliša, *U mučilištu–paklu Jasenovac*, pp. 64; Bogdan Petković, *135 dana u logoru Jasenovac* (Banja Luka: Udruženje logoraša Drugog svjetskog rata, 2008), pp. 317; Marko Ručnov, *Zašto Jasenovac*, pp. 563–564.
20 Eti Neufeld, *Svjedočanstvo preživjelog* (*Novi Omanut*, 2000), pp. 42–43; Đorđe (Jure) Miliša, *U mučilištu–paklu Jasenovac*, pp. 230, 246, 308, 310; Milan Bulajić, *Ustaški zločini genocida*, II–III, various pages; Antun Miletić, *Koncentracioni logor Jasenovac 1941–1945*, book 1–3, various pages; Dušan Sindik (ed.) *Sećanja Jevreja*, pp, 170, 200; Dejan Motl and Đorđe Mihovilović, *Zaboravljeni–knjiga o posljednjim jasenovačkim logorašima*, pp. 461; Eti Neufeld, *Svjedočanstvo preživjelog*; Mira Kolar-Dimitrijević, "Sjećanja veterinara Zorka Goluba na trinaest dana boravka u logoru Jasenovac 1942. godine," *Časopis za suvremenu povijest*, vol. 15, no. 2 (1983), pp. 176; Nikola Nikolić, *Jasenovački logor smrti*, pp, 129, 265–269; Marko Ručnov, *Zašto Jasenovac*, pp. 531; Ivo Goldstein and Slavko Goldstein, *Holokaust u Zagrebu*, pp. 279, 281, 296, 297; Đuro Zatezalo, *Jadovno kompleks ustaških logora 1941*, vol. I–III (Beograd: Muzej žrtava genocida, 2007), pp. 191.
21 Antun Miletić, *Koncentracioni logor Jasenovac 1941–1945*, book 1–3, on various pages; Vladimir Dedijer, *Vatikan i Jasenovac, dokumenti*, pp, 396, 398; Marko Ručnov, *Zašto Jasenovac*, pp. 635; *Politika* (Beograd), May 30, 1945; Dejan Motl and Đorđe Mihovilović, *Zaboravljeni–knjiga o posljednjim jasenovačkim logorašima*, pp. 629, 631, 633; Dušan Sindik (ed.) *Sećanja Jevreja*, pp. 199; Nikola Nikolić, *Jasenovački logor smrti*, pp. 54, 281; Đorđe (Jure) Miliša, *U mučilištu–paklu Jasenovac*, pp. 64, 236, 243; Milko Riffer, *Grad mrtvih, Jasenovac 1943*, pp. 200; Ante Ciliga, *Jasenovac: ljudi pred licem smrti*, pp. 59, 164; Milan Bulajić, *Ustaški zločini genocida* II, pp. 216, 217, 223; IV, 869.
22 HDA, fund 487, Vjestnik MINORS, Z-2869, 624; HDA, fund 421, Public Prosecutor's Office of the People's Republic of Croatia, box 129, Pavelić-Artuković Indictment, 7a. Witness records, Ivan Grubišić, Alija Kapić, Josip Šantić.
23 Ivo Josipović, "Odgovornost za ratne zločine nakon II. svjetskog rata," in Juraj Hrženjak (ur.) *Bleiburg i Križni put 1945* (Zagreb: Savez antifašističkih boraca i antifašista Republike Hrvatske, 2007), pp. 38–41.
24 See in detail: Bogdan Krizman, *Pavelić u bjekstvu* (Zagreb: Globus, 1986), pp. 10 et seq.
25 Ivo Josipović, "Odgovornost za ratne zločine nakon II. svjetskog rata," speaks of the "selectivity" of justice and of the "conflict of some legal principles with morality."
26 Ivo Goldstein, "Značenje godine 1945. u hrvatskoj povijesti i osvetnički gnjev," in Ivo Goldstein *1945.–razdjelnica hrvatske povijesti* (Zagreb: Institut za povijest, 2006), pp. 59–73; also, Ivo Goldstein, "Historical Circumstances of Bleiburg and the Way of the Cross," in Juraj Hrženjak (ed.) *Bleiburg i Križni put 1945* (Zagreb: Savez antifašističkih boraca i antifašista Republike Hrvatske, 2007), pp. 31–38; Ivo Goldstein, *Hrvatska 1918–2008*, pp. 352 et seq.

Bibliography

Basta, Milan. *Rat je završen sedam dana kasnije*. Beograd: Spektar, 1976.
Berger, Egon. *44 mjeseca u Jasenovcu*. Zagreb: Grafički zavod Hrvatske, 1966.
Blažević, Velimir. *Aktualnosti trenutka. Studije i polemike*. Banja Luka, unpublished book, 2011.
Brajović, Petar. *Konačno oslobođenje*. Zagreb: Spektar, 1983.
Bulajić, Milan. *Ustaški zločini genocida i suđenje Andriji Artukoviću 1986. godine, I–IV*. Beograd: Rad, 1988–1989.
Ciliga, Ante. *Jasenovac: Ljudi pred licem smrti*. Zagreb: Naklada Pavičić, 2011.
Čolaković, Drago. *Kronika iz pakla*. Jasenovac: Spomen područje Jasenovac, 1971.
Dedijer, Vladimir. *Vatikan i Jasenovac*. Beograd: Rad, 1987.
Gavrić, Milan. *Otkosi smrti (sećanje na jasenovački logor istrebljenja)*. Beograd: Narodna armija Beograd, 1977.
Goldstein, Ivo. "Značenje godine 1945. u hrvatskoj povijesti i osvetnički gnjev," in Ivo Goldstein *1945. – razdjelnica hrvatske povijesti*. Zagreb: Institut za povijest, 2006, pp. 59–73.
———. "Povijesne okolnosti Bleiburga i Križnog puta," in Juraj Hrženjak (ed.) *Bleiburg i Križni put 1945*. Zagreb: Savez antifašističkih boraca i antifašista Republike Hrvatske, 2007, pp. 31–37.
———. "Jasenovac–Myth and Reality," in Emil Brix, Arnold Suppan and Elizabeth Vyslonzil (eds.) *Sudosteuropa. Traditionen als Macht*. Wien-Munchen: Oldenbourg Wissenschaftsverlag, 2007, pp. 97–111.
———. *Hrvatska 1918.–2008*. Zagreb: Novi liber, 2008.
———and Slavko Goldstein. *Holokaust u Zagrebu*. Zagreb: Znanje, 2001.
Goldstein, Slavko and Ivo Goldstein. *Jasenovac i Bleiburg nisu isto*. Zagreb: Novi liber, 2011.
Grahek Ravančić Martina. *Bleiburg i križni put 1945. Historiografija, publicistika i memoarska literatura*. Zagreb: Hrvatski institut za povijest, 2009; 2015.
Halilbegović, Nihad. *Bošnjaci u jasenovačkom logoru*. Sarajevo: Istraživačka publicistika. Vijeće Kongresa bošnjačkih intelektualaca, 2006.
Horvat, Vladimir, Igor Vukić, Stipe Pilić and Blanka Matković. *Jasenovački logori–istraživanja*. Zagreb: Društvo za istraživanje trostrukog logora Jasenovac, 2015.
Hrženjak, Juraj (ed.). *Bleiburg i Križni put 1945*. Zagreb: Savez antifašističkih boraca i antifašista Republike Hrvatske, 2007.
Jakovljević, Ilija. *Konclogor na Savi*. Zagreb: Konzor, 1999.
Josipović, Ivo. "Odgovornost za ratne zločine nakon II. svjetskog rata," in Juraj Hrženjak (ed.) *Bleiburg i Križni put 1945. Zbornik radova*. Zagreb: Savez antifašističkih boraca i antifašista Republike Hrvatske, 2007, pp. 38–41.
JUSP Jasenovac. "List of Victims," www.jusp-jasenovac.hr/Default.aspx?sid=7618. Accessed August 19, 2019.
Kisić-Kolanović, Nada, Mario Jareb and Katarina Špehnjak (eds.) *1945.- razdjelnica hrvatske povijesti*. Zagreb: Hrvatski institut za povijest, 2006.
Kolar-Dimitrijević, Mira. "Sjećanja veterinara Zorka Goluba na trinaest dana boravka u logoru Jasenovac 1942. godine," *Časopis za suvremenu povijest*, vol. 15, no. 2, 1983, pp. 155–176.
Krizman, Bogdan. *Pavelić u bjekstvu*. Zagreb: Globus, 1986.
Luburić, Vjekoslav. "Povlačenje hrvatske vojske prema Austriji," in John I. Prcela and Dražen Živić (eds.) *Hrvatski holocaust*. Zagreb: hrvatsko društvo političkih zatvorenika, 2001, pp. 37–51.

Lukač, Dušan. *Banja Luka i okolica u ratu i revoluciji.* Banja Luka: Savez udruženja boraca NOR-a opštine, 1968.
Marijan, Davor. *Ustaške vojne postrojbe 1941.–1945.* (master's thesis). Zagreb, 2004.
Miletić, Antun. *Koncentracioni logor Jasenovac 1941–1945. Dokumenta, I–III, Beograd, 1986. i 1987., IV.* Jagodina: Gambit, 2007.
Miliša, Đorđe (Jure). *U mučilištu–paklu: Jasenovac.* Zagreb: Naklada Pavičić 1945/2011.
Motl, Dejan and Đorđe Mihovilović. *Zaboravljeni–knjiga o posljednjim jasenovačkim logorašima.* Jasenovac–Zagreb: Spomen područje Jasenovac, 2015.
Neufeld, Eti. "Svjedočanstvo preživjelog," *Novi Omanut,* 2000, pp. 42–43.
Nikolić, Nikola. *Jasenovački logor.* Zagreb: Nakladni Zavod Hrvatske, 1948.
Nikolić, Vinko (ed.). *Bleiburška tragedija hrvatskoga naroda.* Zagreb: Knjižnica Hrvatske revije, Agencija za marketing–Azinović, 1993.
Novak, Viktor. *Magnum crimen, Pola vijeka klerikalizma u Hrvatskoj.* Zagreb: Nakladni zavod Hrvatske, 1958.
Pilić, Stipo, and Blanka Matković "Poslijeratni zarobljenički logor Jasenovac prema svjedočanstvima i novima arhivskim izvorima." *Radovi Zavoda za povijest HAZU u Zadru,* 56 (2014), pp. 323–408.
Prcela John I. and Živić Dražen (eds.) *Hrvatski holocaust.* Zagreb: Hrvatsko društvo političkih zatvorenika, 2001.
Riffer, Milko. *Grad mrtvih: Jasenovac 1943.* Zagreb: Naklada Pavičić, 1946/2011.
Rojnica, Ivo. *Susreti i doživljaji,* vol. 1. Zagreb: DoNeHa, 1994.
Ručnov, Marko. *Zašto Jasenovac.* Beograd: IKP Nikola Pašić, 2001.
Sindik, Dušan (ed.). *Sećanja Jevreja na logor Jasenovac.* Beograd: Savez jevrejskih opština Jugoslavije, 1972.
Stuparić, Darko (ed.). *Tko je tko u NDH.* Zagreb: Minerva: Zagreb, 1995.
Tomasevich, Jozo. *Rat i revolucija u Jugoslaviji, Okupacija i kolaboracija, 1941–1945.* Zagreb: EPH Novi Liber, 2010.
Trivunčić, Radovan. *Neugasla sjećanja.* Jasenovac: Spomen područje Jasenovac, 1978.
Zatezalo, Đuro. *Jadovno kompleks ustaških logora 1941,* vol. I– II. Beograd: žrtava genocida, 2007.
Zdravko, Dizdar, Vladimir Geiger, Milan Pojić and Mate Rupić (eds.). *Partizanska i komunistička represija i zločini u Hrvatskoj 1944.–1946. (dokumenti).* Slavonski Brod: Hrvatski institut za povijest, 2005; 2009.

Part II
Counting

5 Jasenovac and Bleiburg between Facts and Manipulations

Vladimir Geiger and Martina Grahek Ravančić

Introduction

The duration and intensity of the war on the territory of Croatia, namely in the Independent State of Croatia (NDH), and the presence of significant occupying forces of the German Reich, Italy, and Hungary, and the activities of the NDH Armed Forces, the Yugoslav Army in the Homeland and the People's Liberation Army as well as of the Yugoslav Army Partisan Detachments/Yugoslav Army, resulted in direct conflicts of the warring parties, which led to large human losses among both soldiers and the population. The irreconcilable ideologies and political and military interests of the opposing parties in the conflict and the civil war multiplied the human losses. Previous research on the demographic and actual losses of Yugoslavia and Croatia in World War II[1] provides insight into the approximate and possible number of victims and casualties.[2] There are no significant differences among researchers in determining the demographic and actual human losses of Yugoslavia and Croatia in World War II, but there are serious doubts about the number of casualties and victims according to national/ethnic, ideological, and military affiliation, as well as according to the place of the loss of life, and according to the perpetrator, that is, the cause of death. The question of the human losses of Yugoslavia and of Croatia in World War II became a first-class political question in the immediate postwar period of 1945, and has remained so to this day. Most of the discussions about the human losses of Yugoslavia and Croatia during World War II were not scientifically based and have a recognizable ideological/propaganda basis. Discussing the human losses of both Croatia and Yugoslavia in World War II and the post-war period is still an unrewarding task today. Namely, the human losses of Yugoslavia and Croatia in World War II – despite numerous estimates, calculations, and censuses[3] – constitute one of the most controversial research topics, and moreover, the most sensitive (daily) political topics. Especially regarding the Jasenovac camp and the Bleiburg case, there is a lot of literature,[4] which often mentions various unfounded, moreover fictional, events and numbers of victims and casualties, which has led to the creation of the "Jasenovac myth," on the one hand, and the "Bleiburg myth" on the other.

DOI: 10.4324/9781003326632-7

Jasenovac

In Yugoslavia after World War II, the number of victims and casualties was deliberately exaggerated, and their origin and structure were silenced and obscured, which facilitated the manipulation of statics for human losses. In 1946 the Federal People's Republic of Yugoslavia reported to the International Reparations Commission in Paris the number of 1.7 million human losses in World War II.[5] At the end of 1945, the State Commission for the Investigation of the Crimes of the Occupiers and Their Helpers of the National Committee for the Liberation of Yugoslavia (NKOJ) told the International Military Tribunal in Nuremberg that, by the end of 1943, at least 600,000 people had been killed in the Jasenovac camp, mostly Serbs, then Jews, Roma and Croats.[6] Thus, an unfounded assessment entered into international circulation and became a determinant for all subsequent exaggerations of the Jasenovac camp victims.[7] In 1946, the report of the National Commission for Determining the Crimes of the Occupiers and Their Helpers of the People's Republic of Croatia, entitled *Crimes in the Jasenovac Camp*, states that 500–600,000 people lost their lives in the camp.[8] The 1946 report of the National Commission for *Determining the Crimes of the Occupiers and Their Helpers* – made without documents and based on the statements of witnesses and the minutes of the three commissions that visited the Jasenovac camp on May 11 and 18, and June 18, 1945 and full of exaggerated, unbelievable, and even absurd allegations and claims – is the starting point on which the myth of the Jasenovac camp is based.[9] Thus, the Yugoslav encyclopedic allegations about the number of victims of the Jasenovac camp (and Stara Gradiška) mostly estimate 500,000 or 600,000.[10] However, the Yugoslav lists of human losses of World War II from 1944–1947, 1950, and 1964, as well as the later supplemented and revised lists of human losses of Yugoslavia and Croatia in the war do not confirm that hundreds of thousands or – as some have persistently stated or still state – more than a million people lost their lives in the NDH camps.[11] Even nowadays, Serbian historiography takes for granted the 1948 report of the National Commission on the Jasenovac camp – published several times since its inception – as well as many other hasty allegations and claims about the Jasenovac camp.[12]

According to all indicators, during World War II there were extremely large human losses including the tragic fate of Roma, Jews, and Serbs in the Independent State of Croatia. Namely, the NDH determined the attitude towards Jews and Roma primarily through racial laws, and Serbs were also exposed to various forms of discrimination, persecution, and violence. Those Croats and others who were declared enemies of the "new order" and who would violate the interests of the Croatian state were also under persecution and repressive measures. Repression and terror against all enemies and opponents of the NDH and the German Reich resulted, according to various and numerous indicators, in mass persecutions and arrests and large population losses and numerous individual and even mass killings, especially in forced-labor and camps. The testimonies and memories of the Jasenovac camp survivors about the number of Jasenovac detainees killed, many of which have been published on several occasions, differ when it comes to wide ranges of victims, individual cases as well as certain time periods, and are undoubtedly approximate and extremely unreliable.[13]

The first list of Yugoslavia's human losses in World War II was made by the State Commission for War Crimes, that is, the State Commission for Determining the Crimes of the Occupiers and Their Assistants, at the NKOJ (National Committee for the Liberation of Yugoslavia). In Croatia, the census was conducted from 1944 to 1947 by the National Commission for War Crimes, that is, the National Commission for Determining the Crimes of the Occupiers and Their Helpers. The second census of Yugoslav casualties in World War II was conducted in 1950, organized by the Association of People's Liberation War Veterans (in Croatian: SUBNOR) of Yugoslavia. In Croatia, the census was conducted by the Republic Board of the Croatian SUBNOR, Commission for collecting data on victims of the NOR (People's Liberation War). The third census of Yugoslav casualties in World War II, conducted in 1964 on the basis of a decision of the Government of the Socialist Federal Republic (SFR) of Yugoslavia, was conducted by the Commission for the Census of War Victims of the Federal Executive Council (SIV) of the Socialist Federal Republic of Yugoslavia; it was organized by the Federal Bureau of Statistics and the Republics' Institutes for Statistics for the purpose of obtaining a list of victims and casualties for negotiations with the Federal Republic of Germany, which was obliged by the peace treaty to pay Yugoslavia compensation for human losses and war devastation.[14]

According to the data of the most systematic Yugoslav census of human losses in World War II, that of the Commission for the Census of War Victims of the SIV of SFR Yugoslavia from 1964, 89,851 people lost their lives in all camps in Yugoslavia during the war. However, there were significant numbers of victims of the population of Yugoslavia and Croatia, both in the camps of the German Reich and in the camps of other occupying countries. Namely, according to the data of the Commission for the Census of War Victims of the SIV of SFR Yugoslavia from 1964, 24,752 people lost their lives in the camps in the German Reich, and 19,861 in the camps of other occupying countries. In all the camps where detainees from the territory of Yugoslavia were held, 134,464 people lost their lives during the war.[15] According to two reports from 1964, the highest number of victims lost their lives in Jasenovac camp. The 1964 report published by the Wartime Victims Census Commission of the Federal Executive Council, Socialist Federal Republic of Yugoslavia (Komisija za popis žrtava rata Saveznog izvršnog vijeća SFRJ), states the following number of victims: Jasenovac Camp (49,874), Gradina (128), Stara Gradiška Camp (9,587), which amounts to (59,589) of all victims. The *Individual Name List*, published by the same Commission for the Census of War Victims brings similar numbers, that is, 49,602 of victims in Jasenovac Camp, 9,586 in Stara

Gradiška Camp, which amount to 59,188 victims; among those victims were 33,944 Serbs, 6,546 Croats, and 1,471 Roma.[16]

However, as the work from 1964 of the Commission for the Census of War Victims of the SIV of SFR Yugoslavia did not provide the Yugoslav regime with the expected and desirable number of 1.7 Yugoslav casualties in World War II, but only half the number of casualties and victims, and an extremely smaller number of the Jasenovac camp victims from the official and public numbers (at least 500,000 to 600,000), it was concluded quite unconvincingly – citing everything that caused the failure of the census – that a number of omissions were made, and that the census was incomplete. Therefore, it was decided to put an embargo on the census.[17] The consequence was an extreme duplication in the human losses of Yugoslavia in World War II, especially the Serb victims in the Independent State of Croatia, and the victims of the Jasenovac camp. Although the 1964 census of Yugoslavia's human losses in World War II by the SFR Yugoslavia's SIV War Census Commission – organized by the Federal Bureau of Statistics and the Republic's Institute of Statistics – did not live up to expectations, it is difficult to accept that it was not conducted systematically.

The 1964 census, in addition to not showing human losses on the "enemy" side, is flawed primarily due to the effect of memory error or forgetfulness (memory effect), which could have been expected.[18] In 1964, the Commission for the Census of War Victims of the SIV of SFR Yugoslavia listed the human losses caused by the occupying forces and their associates. But sometimes those who lost their lives to the Western Allies and Partisans were also listed, and as a rule they were declared human losses incurred at another time and/or in another place and/or in another way. Therefore, among the alleged victims of the Jasenovac camp, we find people who actually died in forced labor in the German Reich camps, for example in Norway, died in Allied bombing, died as refugees, for example in El Shatt, then people killed by the German and Italian armies and Chetniks, as well as killed Partisans, even those who died as Home Guards and Ustašas. According to the 1964 data of the Commission for the Census of War Victims of the SIV of SFR Yugoslavia, allegations about persons who lost their lives in the NDH camps, primarily in Jasenovac and Stara Gradiška, are incomplete and not final; some persons have been reported two or more times, numerous victims were reported only numerically, and persons who passed through Jasenovac and Stara Gradiška camps were listed, whereas they lost their lives elsewhere.

Numerous victims of the Jasenovac camp were not stated nationally/ethnically, or their affiliation is incorrectly stated.[19] Of course, it is impossible to expect that the Yugoslav censuses of human losses of World War II from 1944–1947, 1950 and 1964 included all the casualties and victims intended to be enumerated, and that all the data collected were accurate. However, the similarity of the data collected in these specific lists of human losses leads to the conclusion that there should be a high degree of confidence in these lists, with possible and necessary corrections – which may not deviate significantly from the aggregate results (both at territorial and national/ethnic level) established by the above censuses.[20] The list of victims of the Jasenovac and Stara Gradiška camps – which according to the data of the Commission for the Census of War Victims of the SIV SFR Yugoslavia from 1964 was made or, better to say, *revised* in 1997 by the Museum of Genocide Victims and the Federal Statistical Office of the Federal Republic of Yugoslavia – provides data for 78,163 people, most of the victims being Serbs (47,123), then Jews (10,521), Croats (6,281), and Roma (5,836).[21] However, taking into account the unequivocal conclusion of the Commission in 1964 that the census included about 56 to 59 percent of people who should have been enumerated in the Museum of Genocide Victims, they estimate that between 122,300 and 130,100 people lost their lives in Jasenovac and Stara Gradiška.[22]

Based on the 1964 data of the Commission for the Census of War Victims, the amended and revised list of victims of the Jasenovac and Stara Gradiška camps, titled *The Nominal List of the Victims of the Jasenovac Concentration Camp 1941–1945*, made by the Jasenovac Memorial Site in 2007, provides data for 72,193 persons, of which 59,376 or 59,403 persons lost their lives in the Jasenovac camp, and 12,790 in the Stara Gradiška camp. According to the latter, the majority of victims were Serbs (40,251), followed by Roma (14,750), Jews (11,723) and Croats (3,563).[23] The latest amended and revised list of victims of the Jasenovac and Stara Gradiška camps, compiled by the Jasenovac Memorial Site in 2013, provides data for 83,145 persons who lost their lives in the Jasenovac and Stara Gradiška camps. According to that list, most victims are Serbs (47,627), followed by Roma (16,173), Jews (13,116) and Croats (4,255).[24] In his latest 'research', Antun Miletić, a persistent and longtime advocate of the thesis that at least 700,000 people lost their lives in the Jasenovac camp, summing up the current indicators of the partially supplemented and revised nominal 1964 census of the Commission for the Census of War Victims of SIV of SFR Yugoslavia, namely the census compiled by the Museum of Genocide Victims (Belgrade) and nominal and numerical indicators from numerous and different sources, easily concluded in 2010/2011 that at least 146,401 persons lost their lives in the Jasenovac camp (81,408 or 80,192 victims listed by names and 64,900 or 66,056 victims listed only by number), from which 98,252 or 97,972 Serbs, 26,268 or 26,535 Roma, 15,759 or 15,707 Jews and 3,637 or 3,668 Croats.[25]

Since 1992, the Commission for the Identification of War and Post-War Victims of the Republic of Croatia (RH) has been collecting data on the human losses of Croatia and Bosnia and Herzegovina in World War II and the postwar period. In the process of assembling the lists of human losses, the Commission primarily devoted its attention to Croats, meaning those who were not included in the previous lists of human losses in Croatia and Bosnia and Herzegovina in World War II, and others were listed systematically along the way. With such a selective approach and according to the report on its work from February 1992 to September 1999, the Commission listed a total of 261,415 casualties and victims, of which 153,700 were from Croatia and 99,228 from Bosnia and Herzegovina, mostly Croats, who lost their lives during World War II and in the postwar period. The Commission, by a biased division of human losses into desirable and undesirable, listed only 2,238 victims of the Jasenovac camp, and only 293 Jewish victims in Croatia in total,[26] explaining such an approach by the fact that there are several extensive lists of Jasenovac victims in the Jewish community in Zagreb and the Croatian State Archives (Croatian acronym: HDA) in Zagreb.[27] However, this was not true, despite all the barriers set up by the Commission because until then, the only systematic list of victims of the Jasenovac camp was the 1964 list of victims, subsequently published in 1992 and 1998;[28] and the lists of names of victims in Zagreb's Jewish community and the HDA in Zagreb (primarily those killed in Dotrščina, a park in Zagreb) are incomplete and unorganized. It is significant that the alarm in the Croatian and Serbian public was prompted by the figures of the Commission for primarily Jasenovac and Jewish victims, although the Commission, in its "Croatocentric" and selective approach and list also provides – besides mentioned categories of human losses in Croatia in World War II – negligible numbers of human losses of other national/ethnic groups other than Croats (79,318) and even Serbs (18,410): for example, Austrians/Germans (4 + 752), Roma (701), Hungarians (119) and Italians (65). The Commission for Determining War and Post–War Victims of the Republic of Croatia was abolished in 2002. The census of human losses in Croatia (and Bosnia and Herzegovina) in World War II and the postwar period – as was the case with previous such censuses from 1944–1947, 1950 and 1964 – was never completed.[29]

The lists of names of human losses of Yugoslavia, and Croatia in World War II, as well as the estimates of historians and the calculations of demographers, are often significantly different. There are also conflicting opinions on the reliability of the lists of names of victims and victims of Yugoslavia and Croatia in World War II – that is, on whether it is possible to determine the actual losses by individual identifications of victims. The warning of caution in the nominal lists of human losses in World War II and the postwar period, which were mostly based on testimonies and not documents, is the realization that many data providers could not, most frequently, know the circumstances, time and place of loss of life, sometimes not even its cause or who the perpetrator of the crime was. In addition to the necessary and inevitable additions and corrections of data in the nominal lists of human losses of both Yugoslavia and Croatia, in World War II, there were significant changes in the number and structure of casualties and victims, that is, transfer from one national/ethnic and ideological/military group to another, and even one place of loss of life to another place, which indicates possible manipulations. In short, the lists of names of the Jasenovac camp victims cannot be considered unequivocal and final. There are various estimates and calculations about the human losses of both Yugoslavia and Croatia in World War II, as well as about the victims of the Jasenovac camp and their national/ethnic structure. The most famous and most frequently cited estimates are by Vladimir Žerjavić, according to which about 83,000 people lost their lives in Jasenovac (Žerjavić's original estimates were 100,000), of which 45,000 to 52,000 were Serbs, 13,000 Jews, 10,000 Roma, 10,000 Croats, and 2,000 Muslims.[30] Some Croatian historians accept without verification Žerjavić's incorrect statement.[31] Bogoljub Kočović estimates/calculates that about 70,000 people lost their lives in the Jasenovac camp.[32] However, Kočović, as he himself emphasizes, never estimated the number of victims in the camp. Namely, Kočović only estimated the possible total number of Serb victims in the NDH camps, at 150,000 to 200,000.[33]

It is noticeable in Croatia that those to whom the numbers of names of victims of the Jasenovac camp seem too small state that up to 100,000 people lost their lives there.[34] Ivo and Slavko Goldstein have been the most persistent in promoting the number of 100,000 for many years.[35] Therefore, in Croatian anti-fascist circles, the number of 100,000 victims of the Jasenovac camp was accepted, although it was an estimate, originally Žerjavić's, without systematic research, and without confirmation in the sources, which the Goldsteins took over and kept repeating. In the Republic of Serbia and the Republika Srpska, where the megalomaniacal allegation still prevails, in most cases, of at least 700,000 Jasenovac camp victims, those who promote smaller and significantly diminishing numbers of Jasenovac victims are declared as those who minimize the tragedy of Serbian suffering and Ustaša genocide. The few Serbian historians and researchers who are not prone to excessive and unrealistic numbers of Jasenovac camp victims have been declared in Serbian nationalist circles to be "traitors of the Serb matter." There are unequivocal and clear indications that most Serbs lost their lives in the Independent State of Croatia during World War II. Proponents of the thesis that Croats are prone to genocide gladly ignore the fact that during World War II in the NDH, a very large number of Serbs died as members of the Partisan and Chetnik movement, that German and Italian occupation forces were responsible for the deaths of a large number of Serbs, and that there is a significant number of Serbs who lost their lives as collateral victims, in epidemics of infectious diseases, primarily typhus. However, according to the proponents of the thesis that Croats are prone to genocide, it follows that Serbs are only, or mostly, victims of the Ustašas, with special emphasis on the Jasenovac camp.[36] Estimates, calculations and censuses give different numbers on the actual losses of Serbs in the NDH during World War II.

Serbian nationalists are enormously increasing the estimates of Jasenovac camp victims, and Croatian nationalists are completely minimizing the number of Jasenovac victims. However, Serbian nationalist exaggerations about the number of Serb casualties and victims in the Independent State of Croatia, especially the victims in Jasenovac, and Croatian nationalist minimizations of those numbers are equally unpleasant. In estimating the number of Jasenovac camp victims, the Serbian side barricaded itself with 700,000 during the 1970s and 1980s. However, the number of victims at Jasenovac, stated at the time in Yugoslav historiography and journalism, showed a tendency to increase, especially among Serbian authors. Historians and demographers in Yugoslavia who tried to warn of the scientific unsustainability of official allegations about the numbers of victims in the NDH camps, primarily the Jasenovac victims (in Croatia, for example: Bruno Bušić, Ivan Jelić, Franjo Tuđman, Vladimir Žerjavić, Ljubo Boban[37]) experienced considerable inconveniences, and even fierce social accusations and condemnations.

Despite the evident indicators of all lists of Yugoslav casualties in World War II, the long and persistent campaign of proving hundreds of thousands killed in NDH camps, in which certain scientific, primarily historical, circles served as a 'transmission', the number of Jasenovac camp victims gradually escalated. After the Memorandum of the Serbian Academy of Sciences and Arts in 1986, it reached more than a million Serbs killed in Jasenovac alone. According to Radomir Bulatović's 'precise' calculation from 1990, 1,110,929 people, mostly Serbs, were killed in the Jasenovac camp.[38] The basis of Bulatović's ingenious calculation is anthropological research in the area of the Jasenovac camp. However, all conducted field inspections, aerial surveys, and anthropological research in the area of the Jasenovac, Gradina and Ciglana camps resulted in the discovery of a total of about 1,000 to a maximum of 1,500 human remains.[39] The works of Vladimir Dedijer,[40] Antun Miletić[41] and Srboljub Živanović[42] are unavoidable in the systematic spread of the "Jasenovac myth." A special role in preserving, upgrading and spreading the "Jasenovac myth" was played by the Serbian Museum of Genocide Victims, founded in 1992 under the direction of Milan Bulajić, one of the most persistent proponents of the anti-Serb orientation of the Catholic Church, of the proneness of Croats, that is, Croatian politics, to genocide, and to the assertion of hundreds of thousands of Jasenovac victims, mainly Serbs.[43] Serbian intellectual authorities and SANU (Serbian Academy of Sciences and Arts) academics Vasilije Krestić and Smilja Avramov[44] are unavoidable in promoting the thesis about the anti-Serbian orientation of the Catholic Church, the proneness of Croats and Croatian politics to genocide, and the hundreds of thousands of victims of the Jasenovac camp, mostly Serbs. A proponent of mystifications and blurring of facts about the human losses of Yugoslavia and Croatia, in World War II, virtual Jasenovac Research Institute, Brooklyn, New York, using data from the Commission for the Census of War Victims of SIV of SFR Yugoslavia from 1964, a total of 597,323 casualties and victims during World War II on the territory of Yugoslavia, on its website, persistently presented itself for years with a list of victims (*Victims List*) of the Jasenovac camp.[45] However, some confused users, even researchers in Croatia, did not realize that this was a 1964 census of the Commission for the Census of War Victims of the SIV of SFR Yugoslavia.[46] The myth of hundreds of thousands, or even more than a million, victims of the Jasenovac camp, mostly Serbs, collapsed in 1998 when the Bosniak Institute published a list of individual victims, titled *Jasenovac. Victims of War According to the Statistical Office of Yugoslavia*,[47] namely strictly kept data of the *Commission for the Census of War Victims* of the SIV of SFR Yugoslavia from 1964. Despite all speculations as to how the Bosniak Institute obtained the census that was under embargo, and contradictory reactions that followed the publication of *Jasenovac. Victims of War According to the Statistical Office of Yugoslavia*, many things became obvious and clear.[48] However, the megalomaniacal figure of 700,000 victims of the Jasenovac camp has remained to this very day.

Despite everything, it is ubiquitous and the only acceptable figure in certain Serbian circles. Longtime advocates of the "truth on Jasenovac" in the Republic of Serbia, Republika Srpska, Europe, the United States and elsewhere in the world, the International Commission for the Truth on Jasenovac, established in 2000, based in Banja Luka,[49] and its president, Srboljub Živanović, are most persistent in promoting insane allegations about the Jasenovac camp.[50] The Serbian nationalist "truth about Jasenovac," "confirmed" on May 25, 2011 by the *Declaration on the Genocide* of Serbs, Jews and Roma in World War II by the International Commission for the Truth on Jasenovac[51] is, to put it mildly, morbid:

> The International Commission for the Truth on Jasenovac (in which there are no members from the territory of the former Yugoslavia) determined that the Croatian state, together with the Roman Catholic Church, committed genocide against Orthodox Serbs, Jews and Roma in the period from 1941 to 1945. After terrible and horrific torture, they killed over 700,000 Serbs, 23,000 Jews and 80,000 Roma. Among the victims were 110,000 small children. The victims were killed with a sledgehammer, slaughtered, thrown into the red-hot hatch of Pacilli's furnace, soap was boiled from the victims, unborn children were taken from their mothers' wombs, children were impaled on bayonets, women's breasts were cut off, girls, young women and women were raped, Croats sold 'Serbian meat – 1 dinar per kilogram,' and so forth. It would take us a long way to list all the ways of torturing and killing the victims.[52]

It is noticeable that in order for the number of at least 700,000 victims of the Jasenovac camp to be convincing, and the description of the camp complete, old fabrications about "Serb slaughter" and "Ustaša competitions in slaughter," "Pacilli's furnace" ("the crematorium") and "the production of soap from human corpses,"[53] resurrected and circulated in Serbia but also elsewhere. Serbian nationalists and their like-minded people from abroad, gathered mostly in the *International Commission for the Truth on Jasenovac*, still consider revisionists all those, from Franjo Tuđman to Slavko Goldstein, who do not support the figure of 700,000 or at least 500,000 to 600,000, if not a million and more Jasenovac camp victims, as well as peculiar descriptions of the Jasenovac camp. Serbian politics, most of the Serbian media, and a significant part of Serbian historical and scientific circles have been persistently and uninterruptedly favoring them in public appearances to this day.[54]

However, in Croatia, numerous scientifically more or less well-founded, but also revisionist opponents of the genocide of Croats and the "Jasenovac myth" responded to Serbian old and old-new interpretations of crimes committed in the Independent State of Croatia, and especially about the victims of the Jasenovac camp. In 2010, an allegedly 'credible' and 'accurate' but unbased and difficult to prove number of detainees in the Jasenovac camp appeared in the Croatian public. Namely, Ilija Barbarić, a former Ustaša living in Brazil, claims that on May 1, 1945 he had in his hands the "registry books of the Jasenovac camp," and that all persons who passed through the camp from its founding to its dissolution were entered in the books. Barbarić claims that the books with the lists of detainees were "burned before we left Zagreb, on May 7, 1945." According to the "registration books," Barbarić claims, a total of 18,600 prisoners passed through Jasenovac, including those sent to the German Reich for forced labor.[55] This, in turn, is in contrast to the street and public wisdom of Croatian nationalists, according to which "documents from Jasenovac and lists of camp inmates are in Belgrade," that is, "Serbs are hiding documents from Jasenovac, or destroyed them because that is how they can continue to repeat fabrications."

According to both Croatian and Serbian nationalists, in everything that happened, the main, or one of the main, culprits is Josip Broz Tito and the Communist Party of Yugoslavia/Croatia. According to Croatian nationalists, such as Kazimir Katalinić,

> in the plans [of J. Broz] Tito and the [Communist] Party [of Yugoslavia] – that is, the UDBA (State Security Administration), in the trials in the immediate postwar period, as was the case with the commander of the Jasenovac camp Ljubo Miloš, the atrocities of Jasenovac were to be exaggerated not only to condemn the Ustaša regime, but also the Croatian state, and that it would ultimately lead to the conclusion that we do not deserve to have our own state.[56]

According to Serbian nationalists, such as Aleksandar S. Jovanović, the "Serb haters" J. Broz Tito and Ivan Krajačić Stevo are responsible for covering up and downplaying the Ustaša genocide in the Independent State of Croatia and the crimes in the Jasenovac camp. "The documentation that existed in the Independent State of Croatia, otherwise scarce, was destroyed, and what was left was finished off in Broz's Yugoslavia. In other words, everything that compromises the Yugoslav Communist Party and Croatia had to disappear."[57]

Sometimes statements and claims emerge and strongly inflame passions. Stjepan Razum spoke in 2012 for the revision of the prevailing – and for decades promoted – allegations about the extent of human losses during the Independent State of Croatia, and especially about the victims of Jasenovac. However, Razum had previously advocated in certain Croatian nationalist circles the only acceptable, but also difficult to prove and unlikely views that in the postwar period the Jasenovac camp "had a longer duration than the war camp. Immeasurably more people died in the post-war camp [Jasenovac] than in the war camp." In addition, Razum claims that Jasenovac was "a labor and transit camp during the NDH. No killings were carried [out]," and concludes without hesitation that "there is no evidence of mass killings in the Jasenovac camp," and that "most of the detainees were Croats themselves, opponents of the Ustaša regime," and that "the exact number of Jasenovac camp victims was lower than the lowest official communist estimate."[58] It is not an inconsiderable possibility that "the exact number of victims of the Jasenovac camp is lower than the lowest official communist estimate," but it is not clear based on which indicators Stjepan Razum claims that "the most numerous detainees were Croats themselves, those who were opponents of the Ustaša regime." Moreover, there is no credible evidence that the "postwar Jasenovac camp" lasted longer than the war camp (according to the Society for Research of the Triple Jasenovac Camp, the postwar Jasenovac camp operated until 1951),[59] nor are there indications that in Jasenovac, in the postwar period "an immeasurably larger number died than in the war camp." But Razum, the president of the Jasenovac Triple Camp Research Society, insists that "The Jasenovac victims' list (is) completely false and fictional. In Jasenovac, the NDH did not kill Serbs, but after the war Partisans and communists killed Croatian patriots [...]."[60] In 2014, an article by Stipe Pilić and Blanka Matković called "Post-war Jasenovac prison camp according to testimonies and new archival sources,"[61] received considerable attention, first in nationalist circles, in the Croatian press and on Internet portals, and then through bickering and elsewhere. This was followed by mostly intemperate attacks from the left and defenses from the right. However, despite all the efforts made to unite the previous knowledge about the postwar camp in Jasenovac and some new data, testimonies and some documents, this research, which is enviably self-promoted with the help of many "Croatian truth fighters," is not convincing, and we have not moved away from what was known and clear about the postwar camp in Jasenovac even before that point in time. In addition, the 'purification' of the nominal lists of victims of the Jasenovac camp, primarily the nominal lists of JUSP Jasenovac, Mladen Koić and Nikola Banić published in Zadar's *Hrvatski tjednik* (*Croatian Weekly*), with all the necessary and often justified warnings about incorrect entries, did not result in significant changes in the total number of Jasenovac camp victims.

As the question of the existence of the postwar Jasenovac camp in Croatia became inevitable, and undoubtedly timely for many, especially after the founding of the Jasenovac Triple Camp Research Society in 2015, various witnesses and alleged witnesses and researchers of the postwar Jasenovac camp appeared in the Croatian media. For example, in May 2017, Roman Leljak claimed in the newspaper *Glas Koncila* that according to a document from the military archives in Belgrade, but which he did not publish or make available, Josip Broz Tito ordered the closure of the Jasenovac camp on August 21, 1948.[62] The "truth" about the war and postwar Jasenovac camp was expertly compromised in 2016 by the Croatian film director, Jakov Sedlar, with the documentary *Jasenovac – The Truth*, using various unfounded allegations and claims, as well as undoubted forgeries. But the book by Đorđe Mihovilović,

Jasenovac 1945–1947: The Photomonograph, published in 2016, shows the situation in the area of the Jasenovac and Stara Gradiška camps in the immediate postwar period significantly differently from the way represented by the revisionist interpreters of Jasenovac history.[63]

In the predominantly nationalist Croatian press and on Internet portals, revisionist views and claims have become more frequent in recent years. The most direct and systematic are presented in the book by Mladen Ivezić, *Tito's Jasenovac*, and in the book by a group of authors – Vladimir Horvat, Igor Vukić, Stipe Pilić and Blanka Matković – *Jasenovac Camps*.[64] This was followed by a fierce response in the primarily anti-fascist, more precisely the left-wing press, but also in the, conditionally speaking, neutral press and on Internet portals, often unbalanced, as were most frequently unbalanced attempts to revise the prevailing allegations and claims. The most direct and systematic answers and counter-assertions with new and old-new data were presented in the book by Slavko Goldstein and Ivo Goldstein, *Jasenovac Tragedy, Mythomania, Truth*.[65] As was to be expected, each side, invoking truthfulness and a scientific approach, remained steadfast in its claims and position on the Jasenovac camp. There is no dialogue on the issue of the Jasenovac camp or, more precisely, the dialogue is full, to put it mildly, of an outpouring of contempt, and even undisguised hatred of the opposing parties towards those who think differently, calling each other pamphleteers and forgers.

Undoubtedly, the only correct determination of the facts about the Jasenovac camp, and about the number of detainees, especially about the number of victims, is possible only by checking and confirming all allegations and data. This in turn requires time, effort, and responsibility. All claims and allegations about the Jasenovac camp should have a credible confirmation, which is usually not the case. Much has been said and written by heart, both in the public and in the media, and even in historiography, without hesitation, both left and right lightly stated claims and allegations are repeated. The facts about the Jasenovac camp have been contaminated from the beginning, and we are witnessing contamination from various sides, which is difficult to see the end of.

Bleiburg

By the term *Bleiburg*, historiography refers to the events at the end of World War II on the Yugoslav (Slovenian) – Austrian border in May 1945, especially the events related to the final battles, that is, the activities of the Yugoslav Army (JA), which surrounded and captured military units of the German Reich and the NDH that were withdrawing in the direction of Celje–Slovenj Gradec–Dravograd–Bleiburg. Then, when the British extradited prisoners from Austria to the Yugoslav Army, an undetermined number of Croatian Home Guards and Ustašas, Slovenian Home Guards, Montenegrin and Serbian Chetniks, as well as civilians, were brutally executed near Dravograd,

Maribor, and Celje, and then in Kočevski Rog and some other Slovenian places, and in the so-called death marches, or the "Ways of the Cross" by which prisoners were returned to camps in Yugoslavia.

According to Yugoslav military historiography, in the final battles and earlier operations during the final offensive, the JA inflicted heavy losses on German and various "domestic" anti-communist forces, of over 100,000 dead and about 340,000 captured, meaning that just over 240,000 German and other soldiers managed to break into Austria. The Third Army (25,000 dead and over 100,000 captured) and the Fourth Army (25,664 dead and 52,260 captured), which operated on the wings of the battlefield, were the most effective in inflicting losses on the enemy. Of the approximately 340,000 captured, 221,287 were German soldiers, and about 120,000 were members of the NDH Armed Forces (Ustašas and Home Guards), Serbian and Montenegrin Chetniks, and others.[66] In a report to the JA commander in chief, Josip Broz Tito, the commander of the Third Army, Lieutenant General Kosta Nađ, emphasized that "domestic traitors, Chetniks and especially the Ustašas were dealt a decisive death blow, and thus prevented from escaping the deserved punishment for misdeeds and crimes committed these degenerates committed to our peoples."[67] It is difficult to determine how many people arrived at Bleiburg field. According to the diary of the 38th Irish Infantry Brigade, on the evening of May 14, 1945, a Croatian officer arrived at the command and informed that "two groups of the Croatian army were approaching British positions, each numbering about 100,000 men and accompanied by about 500,000 civilians."[68] Whether these figures are true indicators of the situation, remains an open question. Still, it seems hardly possible that so many people found themselves in retreat – especially by the very fact that they arrived in the Allied zone. Even more so, since the majority of people were arrested in the area of Slovenj Gradec–Dravograd–Bleiburg. In addition, a hitherto unidentified number were killed in fighting during the retreat.

All of the above carries a large number of unknowns and takes us away from the total. On May 17, 1945, the Cabinet of the Marshal of Yugoslavia informed the head of the British military delegation that Josip Broz Tito had received a dispatch from Field Marshal Harold Alexander, commander of the Allied forces in the Mediterranean, dated May 16, 1945, about the surrender of 200,000 "Yugoslavs" in Austria with the note "The aforementioned 200,000 will be taken over by the Headquarters of the Third Army, to which the necessary instructions had been issued."[69] After surrendering and capturing in the final battles and extradition at Bleiburg, columns of prisoners of war and civilians, accompanied by members of the JA, set out for an exhausting return through Slovenia, towards Croatia, and further to the prisoner of war camps.[70]

Numerous mass graves, primarily in Slovenia, testify to the unconditional and ruthless treatment of the prisoners.[71] So far, more than 500 mass graves of postwar liquidations have been found in Slovenia (at least 125 in which the victims are Croats), most of which are awaiting processing. The first steps were prompted by the construction of the Maribor bypass in 1999, when one part of the anti-tank trench in Tezno was excavated: 1,179 people were exhumed in a just 70-meters wide trench. In the soundings of the Commission of the Government of the Republic of Slovenia for the Regulation of Concealed Cemeteries in 2007, they established the existence of tombs at three different locations in a total length of approximately 950 m. The width of the buried trench is 3–4 m, and the remains lie at a depth of 1–1.5 m.[72] "Drilling was carried out for almost a thousand meters and everything was positive. Throughout the ditch, under one meter of the earth's surface, there is a layer of mortal remains one to one and a half meters high." According to estimates by the research group, it could be "the largest postwar execution site in Europe," in which about 15,000 to 20,000 victims were mostly Croats, members of the NDH armed forces.[73] This, so far the first concrete data, represents a big step forward and, despite the almost frightening figures, refutes the articles of Croatian daily newspapers that have written in recent years about "more than 40,000 people" killed in Tezno.[74]

On the other hand, he refutes the allegations of Ivan Fumić, a prominent member of the Alliance of Anti-Fascist Fighters and Anti-Fascists of Croatia, according to whom "1,500 Ustaša guards of Jasenovac and other camps were killed near Maribor."[75] It is estimated that in Kočevski Rog, one of the largest execution sites in Slovenia after World War II, tens of thousands of captured and extradited Slovenian Home Guards, Croatian Home Guards and Ustašas, Montenegrin and Serbian Chetniks were killed in the first days of June 1945. The executions were carried out under the command of the JA major, Simo Dubajić, and the direct perpetrators belonged to a selected company of the 11th Dalmatian Brigade of the 26th Division of the Fourth JA.[76] Quotations in the literature, historiography, journalism, and memoirs mention various figures that provoke numerous manipulations.[77] The latest field research of postwar cemeteries from May 1945 in Slovenia – for example in the mass graves of the Barbarin rov mine near Laško, conducted in March 2009,[78] as well as the discovery of new execution sites from May 1945 in Croatia – confirm the mass killings of prisoners of war as well as the ruthless and cruel manner in which executions were conducted. It is clear that the mass liquidations of prisoners could not have been committed by lone or even mass avengers imbued with hatred.

The Bleiburg case is not about the personal revenge of a drunken Simo Dubajić, officer of the 11th Dalmatian Brigade of the 26th Dalmatian Division JA, in charge of mass liquidations of prisoners, or hundreds or thousands of such lunatics.[79] Mass liquidations cannot be an excess. In the communist movement in the period of Stalinism, and such was the Yugoslav communist movement led by Josip Broz Tito during World War II and in the immediate postwar period, "there are no (mis)deeds especially when they are mass, without proper directive."[80] And what the orders about the treatment of a captured enemy were like is shown by a number of examples.

The instructions of the Third Section of the Department for the Protection of the People (OZNA) of the First Army to the subordinate divisional plenipotentiaries of the OZNA from May 6, 1945, when the JA units were preparing for the battle for Zagreb, clearly show the treatment of prisoners:

> [A]ll prisoners and other persons who are captured by the brigades and sent to the division, need to be taken into a procedure and cleansed. This does not mean that the brigades should send all the prisoners to you, but clean them on the spot, and what is left, what is collected after that, which brigades will not have time to clean due to their military tasks, let them send to you. [...] The attitude towards captured officers and prisoners is valid according to previous instructions. Officers clean everything, unless you get orders from OZNA or the party that someone should not be liquidated. In general, you should be energetic and ruthless in cleaning.[81]

Particularly significant is the cruel treatment of captured enemy soldiers, the wounded and the sick, who were extrajudicially executed.[82] Documents of the JA units unequivocally confirm the mass executions of prisoners. For example, according to the book of dispatches of the 15th Majevica Brigade sent to the headquarters of the 17th Division, upon arrival in Maribor on May 20, 1945, the 17th Division began to carry out its task defined, obviously, by a clear directive.

> The brigade arrived on the twentieth at 6 o'clock. We are affiliated with the OZNA. The task of our brigade is the liquidation of Chetniks and Ustašas, of whom there are two and a half thousand. [...] We continued shooting today. The brigade is located in the City. [...] We are in the same room. Throughout the day, we did the same as yesterday (liquidation).[83]

Zdenko Zavadlav, the OZNA deputy chief for the Maribor area who was in charge of organizing the liquidation of the prisoners, describing where and how the liquidations were carried out in May 1945, mentions the "transports" and "serial shootings by a firing squad" of prisoners carried out by the OZNA and the Yugoslav National Defense Corps. He also states that the order to execute the prisoners came "from the top," because "the enemy should be killed without trial" while "the revolution is still going on."[84]

The events along the "Way of the Cross" and in numerous (passing) camps speak in favor of that. Upon entry, the prisoners were mostly sorted and searched. In the camp's daily routine, many interrogations followed. Accommodation and meals in the camps did not comply with the regulations laid down in the provisions of the Geneva Conventions. Due to poor hygienic conditions, lack of food and exhaustion of prisoners, various diseases often appeared and spread in the camps. Liquidations were also carried out in the camps, but some specific figures are difficult to establish given that new prisoners arrived in the camps almost daily. Documentation that would fill some of the gaps in determining the numbers of those killed is very rare and provides only some information.[85]

Although there is a large amount of historical, journalistic, and memoir literature on the events of May 1945 and those that followed, research to date has not resulted in an exact or even accurate number of those killed in these liquidations. Namely, the historical and journalistic literature on this problem is based mainly on the memories of the participants in Bleiburg and the "Way of the Cross." Memories are presented on various occasions, they are charged with emotions and traumas, and are unreliable and completely unsubstantiated when it comes to total numbers. Of course, memoirs and testimonies are invaluable when it comes to testifying about individual cases or groups, and in describing the atmosphere and the like. In the numerous literature on Bleiburg and the "Way of the Cross," which gives various estimates and allegations, the number of casualties ranges from about 50,000 thousand to, especially among Croatian and Serbian emigrant authors, usually 200,000, 250,000, but also half a million, and also to an incredible number of more than a million killed and executed, captured Ustašas, Home Guards, and civilians of the Independent State of Croatia, as well as Slovenian Home Guards and Serbian and Montenegrin Chetniks. According to generally accepted estimates in historiography, the total losses related to the Bleiburg case could amount to at least about 70,000 to 80,000, and the losses of Croats to at least about 50,000 to 55,000. In addition, when talking and writing about the victims of Bleiburg and the "Way of the Cross" in Croatia, estimates are often vague. A large number of authors cite approximate estimates, citing "tens of thousands of people."[86]

The nominal lists of those who lost their lives at Bleiburg and the "Way of the Cross" are unsystematic and incomplete. Nominal data on the human losses of Croats, but also of others, during and especially at the end of the war and in the immediate postwar period are provided primarily via numerous lists of victims and in similar publications, which list victims from different parts of Croatia and Bosnia and Herzegovina. With all the incompleteness and errors, it is difficult to dispute the allegations stated on the victim lists about the dead, killed, and those who died as a result of injuries and illnesses (estimations range from thousands to tens of thousands of victims), especially on the "Way of the Cross" and in postwar prisoner of war, convict and internment camps. Zdravko Dizdar, referring to numerous victim lists, states that the Croatian victims of Bleiburg and the "Way of the Cross" exceed 50,000, and then that the victims' "personal identification" determined about 62,000 postwar Croatian human losses, mostly Bleiburg and the "Way of the Cross." These figures, although statistically possible, are clearly just rough figures, as it is not clarified which victim lists and similar publications were considered, how many human losses are reported on each list, and whether and how the data was checked and revised.[87] However, in numerous victim lists for Croatia and Bosnia and Herzegovina, as far as can be determined by systematic insight, only a little more than 5,000 people who lost their lives at

Bleiburg and on the "Way of the Cross" are listed by name.[88] The most comprehensive list of the Commission for the Identification of War and Post–War Victims of the Republic of Croatia, in its report on its work from February 1992 to September 1999, shows that 13,300 people lost their lives at Bleiburg and on the "Way of the Cross."[89]

The Croatian media, as well as the public, sometimes mentioned significantly higher numbers of human losses in Bleiburg and the "Way of the Cross," which were allegedly listed by the Commission for the Identification of War and Post-War Victims of the Republic of Croatia. This is obviously a list of names (database) of the Commission, which for unknown reasons was not submitted to the Croatian State Archive (HDA) in Zagreb. Although this list was supplemented until the abolition of the Commission in 2002, the list is still unorganized, and even full of misinformation. However, although questionable and disorderly, the data of the Commission, submitted to the HDA, are also unavoidable because they provide a quantity of useful information about people who lost their lives during World War II and in the immediate postwar period.

According to Vladimir Žerjavić, at Bleiburg and the "Way of the Cross" most of the lives lost were Croats (45,000) and 4,000 Muslims, that is, 45,000 to 55,000 Croats and Muslims, then 8,000 to 10,000 Slovenes, and about 2,000 Serbs and Montenegrins.[90] Based on various data, Žerjavić concludes that the total number of captured Croats could be 93,600. The highest number of deaths is related to the events on the "Way of the Cross," where it is estimated that 26,500 soldiers and 6,800 civilians were killed.[91] Although there are a number of works dealing with the number of victims of Bleiburg and the "Way of the Cross," historiography most often cites, apparently in the absence of more convincing data, Žerjavić's estimate that about 55,000 to 67,000 people lost their lives in Bleiburg and the "Way of the Cross," not counting the Germans. However, most historians, pointing to some other estimates and recent Slovenian research, think that Žerjavić's estimates are still too low. Namely, the latest research on archives and execution sites or mass graves in Slovenia suggests that the final figures of actual losses related to the Bleiburg case could be higher than the above calculations or, apparently, that the figures of actual losses of some national groups, primarily Slovenes and Montenegrins, could be significantly larger than the above calculations. According to some earlier statistical calculations, for example by Kazimir Katalinić, the actual losses of Croats (including Muslims) related to Bleiburg and the "Way of the Cross" are much higher – a minimum of 85,000, probably 135,500 and a maximum of 198,500 people.[92] According to a recent systematic comparison of estimates, calculations and lists of human losses caused by Partisans and communists in Yugoslavia during World War II and in the postwar period, by Michael Portmann, about 80,000 prisoners of war (Croats, Bosniaks, Serbs, Montenegrins, Slovenes, Germans, mostly soldiers, but also civilians)[93] lost their lives at Bleiburg and the "Way of the Cross." The inconsistency in the presentation of human losses related to Bleiburg and the

"Way of the Cross" is also present in Croatian encyclopedic citings, in which the death toll ranges from 200,000 Croats killed and about 12,000 Slovenes, 6,000 Montenegrins, 3,000 Serbs and about 60,000 Germans to about 250,000 Croatian civilians, especially women, children and prisoners of war, members of defeated Croatian units, or a general estimate of "tens of thousands of victims."[94] But most often, when the total number of victims of Bleiburg and the "Way of the Cross" is mentioned, as the Croatian encyclopedia states, "different estimates are still given today."[95]

Therefore, there remains a space used for ideological and national needs. Despite the frequently cited orders in the literature of the commander in chief of the People's Liberation Army and Partisan's Detachments of the Yugoslavia/Yugoslav Army and the general secretary of the Communist Party of Yugoslavia, Josip Broz Tito, on the treatment of prisoners of war, especially the order of May 14, 1945, to take "the most energetic measures to prevent the killing of prisoners of war and detainees by units, individual organs and individuals,"[96] numerous events and documents confirm that the killing of prisoners of war during, at the end of and immediately after World War II was common and unpunished. Although the dispatch of Josip Broz Tito, dated 14 May 1945, is disputed by some, holding that it was a later forgery,[97] Josip Broz Tito was, or should have been, informed in good time about the number of prisoners of war. Numerous events and documents show that there was an obvious difference between what was prescribed and what was done. Josip Broz Tito's orders were most likely only for "public" and "external" use.

The atmosphere and developments of that time left a lot of freedom and space to individuals in command positions, certainly not without the knowledge of the highest military and political figures and institutions, in order to deal with many opponents and dissidents of the new system. Josip Broz Tito, the Marshal of Yugoslavia, in his speech held in Ljubljana on May 27, 1945, which had a wider impact with its publication in Borba on May 28, 1945, unequivocally pointed out what had happened:

> As for these traitors who found themselves within our country, in every nation in particular – it is a thing of the past. The hand of justice, the hand of vengeance of our people has already reached the vast majority of them, and only a small part managed to escape under the wing of patrons outside our country.[98]

Milovan Đilas thinks that there was no written order for the mass executions of prisoners in May 1945:

> According to the structure and hierarchy – such a thing could not be done by anyone without the approval of the top. Even before that, an atmosphere of revenge and reckoning was created. The Central Committee did not decide that. [...] We never mentioned it either in the Central Committee or among ourselves. I once mentioned in an unrelated conversation [...]

that we exaggerated then, because there were also those who fled only for ideological reasons. Tito responded, immediately, as if he had long ago made a final, if not comforting, conclusion: You end it once and for all![99]

Some Croatian historians, such as Ivo Goldstein, seek to create a "framework" for understanding "revenge."[100] Goldstein seeks to portray the mass executions of prisoners in Slovenia in May 1945 as "programmed selective killing accompanied by occasional individual outbursts."[101] Since the late 1990s, Ivo Goldstein has published numerous articles in the Croatian press, and he has also written about Bleiburg and the "Way of the Cross" in several of his books, the most important of which, published in 2011 and co-authored with Slavko Goldstein, titled *Jasenovac and Bleiburg Are Not the Same*.[102] Significantly, when Goldstein mentions the total estimates of human losses at Bleiburg and on the "Way of the Cross," he states that according to Žerjavić's estimates (which is the only source he refers to in all his accounts) there are a total of 55,000, although Žerjavić's works clearly show that the figure refers to 55,000 Croats. It should not be forgotten, Žerjavić adds to that the losses of the Slovenes, about 8,000 to 10,000, and about 2,000 Serbian and Montenegrin Chetniks, which ultimately amounts to, not counting the German soldiers, about 70,000. But there is no mention of this in any of Goldstein's syntheses. With Goldstein, in addition to dubious interpretations, the figures are particularly controversial. Goldstein states that "scrupulous" research shows that there were between 100,000 and 150,000 people in the retreating column, "probably about 134,000." The first figures mentioned can be considered possible, but it is not known on what estimates this last figure is based, and it can only be concluded that it is arbitrary.[103] According to Ivo Goldstein, there was, especially on the "Way of the Cross," frequent arbitrariness, revenge, and even robbery. There were relatively few calls for responsibility for arbitrary Partisan outbursts and the killing of prisoners, and there was almost no severe punishment; "it is said that several Partisans were shot for arbitrary outbursts, but no documents have been found about it."[104] When it comes to Goldstein, and interpreters with similar explanations, such claims are symptomatic.

Josip Jurčević in his book *Bleiburg. The Yugoslav Post–War Crimes Against Croats*,[105] which despite its title has the least to do with Bleiburg and the "Way of the Cross," show only a very superficial picture of the May 1945 events, fitting into long, complex unfounded Croatian views, insufficiently documented and hastily argued. By the way, it is clear to anyone familiar with the subject that Jurčević chose the supertitle "Bleiburg" primarily for "commercial," and only then for some other reasons. Jurčević's book, *Hidden Executioners and Cemeteries of Yugoslav Communist Crimes*, remained on the same track: It is full of inaccurate data, and is in fact a compilation without checking of what the Parliamentary Commission for Determining War and Post–War Victims of the Republic of Croatia, the Government Commission of the Republic of Slovenia and the State Commission for the Secret Graves of

Those Killed After September 12, 1944 in Serbia.[106] Some Croatian historians, such as Mladen Ivezić and Josip Jurčević, advocate the old Croatian emigrant thesis that only Croats, or mostly Croats, were killed in Bleiburg, and that a "genocide" of Croats took place in May 1945, that is, they superficially and schematically present everything as the hatred of Croatia.[107] Such attitudes are still present today, and even almost prevalent, in a large part of the Croatian people. Although it can be accepted that most of the victims were Croats, we must not forget the fact that many Germans, Slovenes, Serbs, Montenegrins, Bosniaks and others, soldiers and civilians, were among those captured and then killed. On the other hand, the key theses of some individuals and "anti-fascist" groups in Croatia are that, in the Bleiburg and immediate events of the murder of prisoners there were "excesses," that is, most of those killed were criminals, and that Josip Broz Tito bears no responsibility for those events. Mass killings of prisoners on the "Way of the Cross" are minimized and justified. Approaching the Partisan movement and communist ideology hagiographically, they offer us their view of World War II and issues of Partisan and communist repression or, as they prefer to call it, "confrontation with the enemies of the people," declaring such a view "scientific," and other approaches "revisionism," "fascism" and "Ustašism."[108]

According to the 1929 *Geneva Convention Relative to the Treatment of Prisoners of War*, which was in force at the time of the events discussed here, and which had to be adhered to by members of the People's Liberation Army and Partisan's Detachments of Yugoslavia/Yugoslav Army, enemy disarmed by force or voluntarily is no longer an enemy but a prisoner of war, and as such must be spared; a prisoner of war no longer falls under the authority of the soldier or unit that captured him, but of the state to whose army that soldier or unit belongs to; to kill a disarmed opponent in war is not allowed and constitutes a crime, and any abuse means cowardice and barbarism.[109] In Croatia, individuals persistently advocate the old thesis that enemy soldiers captured until May 9, 1945 were prisoners of war, and that those captured from May 9 to 15, 1945, could not be considered prisoners of war because they were "captured as armed rebels against an internationally recognized state, the Democratic Federal Yugoslavia." According to such views, "they are outlaws or terrorists" to whom "the rules of the law of war cannot be applied, because the war ended on May 9, [1945]."[110] By doing so, they obviously want to reduce the gravity of the Bleiburg case. When persons and groups captured in the period after 9 May 1945 were not considered prisoners of war, but "rebels," "outlaws" or "terrorists," which is not confirmed by international conventions on the law of war, such persons and groups should be spared out-of-court liquidations and should have the right to regular court proceedings, especially since they are in the power of an "internationally recognized state."[111] The Alliance of Anti-Fascist Fighters and Anti-Fascists of Croatia published the conference proceedings titled *Bleiburg and The Way of the Cross 1945*, which brings together papers from the scientific conference of the same name held in 2006 in Zagreb.[112] Although, as the editor in chief Juraj Hrženjak states, the proceedings is based on "objective truth," its publication did not move away from what was already known about postwar events; on the contrary! Only a few articles published in the proceedings move away from the already known, and the vast majority was written "according to expectations and needs."[113]

However, the Alliance of Anti-Fascist Fighters and Anti-Fascists of Croatia, persisting in one-dimensional views and interpretations of past events, held in 2017 a "scientific conference" on Bleiburg and the "Way of the Cross," attended by "historians, lawyers and journalists," including publicly known and prominent individuals like: Ivan Fumić, Drago Pilsel, Anto Nobilo, and Milan Gorjanc, representing themselves as "experts" on Bleiburg and the May 1945 events. At the conference, it was said that, "Anti-fascists must be ready for dialogue and, unlike right-wingers, insist on respecting other people's victims and condemning their crimes," and that "each side must confess its sins and respect the truths about its crimes and other people's victims." What kind of readiness is in question? There were picturesque presentations at the conference, which besides a mostly ancient anti-fascist depiction of the actions and crimes of the defeated side, only along the way with manneristic and strange explanations, mention questionable events and actions of the victors towards the defeated at the end of the war and in the immediate postwar period.[114] We do not know if this is the true meaning of looking at the past, because if we continue to condemn only some crimes under the guise of "objective truth" (in this case crimes committed during the Ustaša regime), and on the other hand apologetically absolutely amnesty any human rights violations, even undoubted crimes, invoking the "positive achievements of anti-fascism," we will not go far in that dead race.

The process of retribution, "cleansing," in the immediate postwar period of 1945, also took place in Western Europe, but it was mostly carried out by judicial and administrative measures. Part of these liquidations in Western Europe were revenge, which occurred sporadically in the first days of the liberation of individual countries. The basis of denazification in a democratic Europe was that proceedings must be based on law and regular court proceedings and that revenge must be avoided and prevented by all means. In the Soviet Union and Yugoslavia, the process was significantly different, as it was only partially carried out by judicial and administrative measures, but on different foundations of courts and administration, and mass killings immediately after the war were organized and carried out by the state rather than vengeful individuals or groups. In Soviet-dominated states that carried out a "socialist revolution," the content was vastly different, and it depended more and more on the principles of the system being established than on guilt itself.[115]

The issue of Bleiburg is one of the most complicated topics, not only in Croatian historiography, and at the same time full of emotional charge which, despite numerous memoirs, publicity and even historiographical literature, makes it much more difficult to judge. Historiography is undoubtedly faced with a series of open questions and counter-questions. The winners, creating a mythical picture of history, ascribed to themselves the role of Good, and to the defeated the role of Evil. Historiography has yet to make well-founded answers about these events. It can be assumed that these answers will not be pleasant for many.

It is difficult to disagree with the opinion of Mihael Sobolevski, that on the issue of Jasenovac and Bleiburg "the research of human losses was very often out of reality and left to the individual and collective imagination. Extreme situations have been created on the basis of extreme traumas."[116] The emphasis on suffering throughout history, as a key part of the ideas that Croats and Serbs have about their past, was largely determined by the myth of suffering, which sometimes takes a caricatured form. Such views have not changed to this day, moreover, Croatian and Serbian historiography and especially historical journalism, full of insufficient knowledge and catastrophic interpretations, not only preserve the old one-dimensional and pathetic views but also encourage them. Due to the lack of systematic research, but also many unfounded, or even false allegations and claims, many still make arbitrary estimates, increasing or decreasing certain categories of human losses in Croatia and Yugoslavia in World War II and the postwar period. Increasing or decreasing, and even keeping silent, the number of certain categories of human losses, besides the ignorance of the facts, usually results from personal, national or political reasons, because the victims are "ours" and the perpetrators are "theirs," or the victims are "theirs," and the perpetrators "ours."

Proponents of both the left and right worldviews in Croatia continue, despite their declarative statements condemning every crime, to remain silent and belittle any research that does not support their desired picture of the past. At the same time, events and facts that have become public and unquestionable, try to minimize and present their inherent explanations. It is noticeable that the Croatian media are mostly the transmission of such efforts. The ubiquitous discourse on the human losses of Yugoslavia, and Croatia, in World War II and the postwar period, in the relation between fascists and anti-fascists is distinctly political and not scientific. In addition, there is actually no scientific dialogue on human losses in World War II and the postwar period in Croatia. In Croatia, the phrase about the need to leave the past to historians is constantly repeated. Moreover, according to some opinions, politicians should, of course, be stage managers to historians on how and what to write, and even on human losses in World War II and the postwar period. The question is to what extent today's Croatian society and the individual, quite obsessed with "distress mania," are able to face the past, that is, how much they are consciously prevented from doing so by politics. Mostly the same individuals, both from the "left" and from the "right," the scientists who are "general practitioners" and experts on every controversial issue and for every occasion, with the support of the media, lobotomize us with their mannerist views of the human losses of Yugoslavia and Croatia, and the casualties and victims both Croats and Serbs, but also others in World War II and the postwar period. Both compete in one-dimensional interpretations, selective and tendentious views of human losses in World War II and the postwar period, disregarding the indicators obtained by research. Simply put, it is most often a question of who and/or which side invents and lies more, more persistently and convincingly.

In addition, in the daily political skirmishes between the "left" and the "right," the human losses of Croatia and Yugoslavia in World War II and the postwar period were mainly reduced to Jasenovac and Bleiburg, that is, human losses caused by Ustašas and Partisans. However, the issue of human losses in Croatia and Yugoslavia is much more complex and layered, both in terms of casualties and victims, and in terms of those who caused human losses. In determining the number and names of human losses, of both soldiers and civilians, killed, murdered, victims of war and missing persons, it is not possible to approach on the basis of improvisations, but on the basis of certain real indicators, in order to obtain the most approximate data on the number and the names of the victims. The issue of human losses is for many reasons one of the most complicated research topics to be questioned and supplemented. However, in the research of human losses in Croatia and Yugoslavia, in World War II and the postwar period, the problem is most often not only the lack of sources and credible indicators, but also "good will" and "common sense" to properly address certain issues. In researching the human losses, it is inevitable to face the past. So far, we have mostly not shown the readiness and ability to think like that.

Table 5.1 Fatalities in the Jasenovac and Stara Gradiška camps according to different estimates, computations and lists

	Jasenovac	Stara Gradiška	total
estimate of the State Commission for Investigation of the Crimes of the Occupiers and Their Collaborators of the People's Liberation Committee of Yugoslavia in 1945	600 000	-	600 000
estimate of the Territorial Commission for Investigation of the Crimes of the Occupiers and Their Collaborators in 1946/1947	500 000 to 600 000		500 000 to 600 000
Lexicographical Institute Encyclopaedia, 1958/1959	500,000 to 600,000 350 000	-	500 000 to 600 000 350 000
individual name list of the Wartime Victims Census Commission of the Federal Executive Council, Socialist Federal Republic of Yugoslavia, 1964	49 602	9 586	59 188
Military Encyclopaedia, 1967 and Encyclopaedia of Yugoslavia, 1971	600 000	75 000	675 000

(*continued*)

Table 5.1 Cont.

	Jasenovac	Stara Gradiška	total
estimate Milan Bulajić, 1988	700 000	-	700 000
estimate Franjo Tuđman, 1989	30 000 to 40 000	-	30 000 to 40 000
computation Radomir Bulatović, 1990	1 110 929	-	1 110 929
computation/estimate Vladimir Žerjavić, 1992	85 000	-	85 000
name list and computation/estimate Museum of Genocide Victims, 1997/2007	78 163 122 300 to 130 100	-	78 163 122 300 to 130 100
name list Commission on Establishment of Wartime and Post-war Victims of the Republic of Croatia, 1999	2 238	-	2 238
name list Jasenovac Memorial Zone, 2007/2013	59 403 83 145	12 79 -	72 193 83 145
name list and estimate Antun Miletić, 2010/2011	146 401 146 248	- -	146 401 146 248
estimate Srboljub Živanović, 2008/2012 and International Commission for the Truth about Jasenovac, 2011	700 000	-	700 000
estimate Slavko Goldstein and Ivo Goldstein, 2011/2016	80 000 to 100 000	-	80 000 to 100 000

Table 5.2 Fatalities on Bleiburg and the "Way of the Cross," 1945, according to different estimates, computations and lists

estimate Ivo Bogdan, 1963 Vinko Nikolić, 1976/1993	ca. 200 000	200,000 Croats and 12,000 Slovenes
estimate Danijel Crljen, 1966	500 000	mainly Croats
estimate Borivoje M. Karapandžić, 1970/1990	250 000	
calculation Kazimir Katalinić, 1988/1995	minimum 85 000 probably 135 500 maximum 198 500	Croats and Muslims
calculation Vladimir Žerjavić, 1992/1997	ca. 70 000	45,000 to 55,000 Croats and Muslims 8,000 to 10,000 Slovenes ca. 2,000 Serbs and Montenegrins
name list Commission on Establishment of Wartime and Post-war Victims of the Republic of Croatia, 1992–1999	13 300	mainly Croats
estimate Zdravko Dizdar, 2005	over 50 000 ca. 62 000	Croats
estimate Michael Portmann, 2004/2007	ca. 80 000	Croats, Bosniaks, Serbs, Montenegrins, Slovenes, and Germans
estimate Ivo Goldstein, 2008/2011	ca. 55 000	Croats, Bosniaks, Serbs, Montenegrins, Slovenes, and Germans

Notes

1 Demographic losses include those killed, murdered, and deceased during the war, falling birth rates due to the war ,and the migration balance. Actual losses, on the other hand, include those killed, murdered, and deceased during the war.
2 Victims include primarily civilians killed, murdered, and deceased as a result of the war, but also soldier prisoners of war who were killed or who died. The casualties are primarily soldiers killed in the war.
3 Estimates include allegations, more or less substantiated, about the number of human losses, both for certain periods, and for certain areas, and for certain categories of casualties and/or victims. Calculations are mathematical-statistical calculations, more or less well-founded, on the number of human losses, both for certain periods, and for certain areas, and for certain categories of casualties and/or victims. Censuses are lists of names of casualities and/or victims, more or less well-founded, both for certain periods, and for certain areas, and for certain categories of human losses.
4 Cf. Jovan Mirković, *Objavljeni izvori i literatura o jasenovačkim logorima* (Banja Luka–Beograd: Muzej žrtava genocida, 2000); Martina Grahek Ravančić, *Bleiburg i križni put 1945. Historiografija, publicistika i memoarska literatura* (Zagreb: Hrvatski institut za povijest, 2009; Zagreb: Hrvatski institut za povijest, 2015).
5 Cf. *Ljudske i materijalne žrtve Jugoslavije u ratnom naporu 1941–1945*, Beograd, 1947.
6 *Izveštaj Jugoslovenske Državne komisije za utvrđivanje zločina okupatora i njihovih pomagača Međunaro nom vojnom sudu u Nürnbergu*, Beograd, 1947, pp. 35.
7 Cf. Gunnar Heinsohn, *Lexikon der Völkermorde* (Reinbeck bei Hamburg: Rowohlt, 1999), pp. 193–194; 227–228 and the literature cited therein.
8 Cf. *Zločini u logoru Jasenovac* (Zagreb, 1946, Jasenovac, 1977, Jasenovac, 1980, Banja Luka, 2000), pp. 38.
9 Vladimir Geiger, "Brojidbeni pokazatelji o žrtvama logora Jasenovac, 1941.–1945. (procjene, izračuni, popisi)," *Časopis za suvremenu povijest*, 45, no. 2 (2013), pp. 213 or Vladimir Geiger, "Numerical indicators of the victims of the Jasenovac camp, 1941–1945 (estimates, calculations, lists),"*Review of Croatian History* 9, no. 1 (2013), pp. 153–154. Cf. Josip Jurčević, *Nastanak jasenovačkog mita. Problemi proučavanja žrtava Drugog svjetskog rata na području Hrvatske* (Zagreb: Hrvatski studiji Sveučilišta u Zagrebu, 1998), pp. 34–42.; Mladen Ivezić, *Jasenovac. Brojke* (Zagreb: Samizdat, 2003), pp. 29–36; Vladimir Mrkoci and Vladimir Horvat, *Ogoljela laž logora Jasenovac* (Zagreb: Naklada E. Čić, 2008), pp. 19.
10 Cf. for example: *Enciklopedija Leksikografskog zavoda*, s.v. "Jasenovac," (Zagreb: LZMK, 1958), pp. 648–649; *Vojna enciklopedija*, no. 8, s.v. "Ustaše," (Begorad, Zagreb: Grafički zavod Hrvatske, 1967), pp. 321; *Enciklopedija Jugoslavije*, no. 8, s.v. "Ustaše," (Zagreb: LZMK, 1971), pp. 444.
11 Cf. Vladimir Geiger, "Ljudski gubici Hrvatske u Drugom svjetskom ratu koje su prouzročili 'okupatori i njihovi pomagači'. Brojidbeni pokazatelji (procjene, izračuni, popisi),"*Časopis za suvremenu povijest* 43, no. 3 (2011), pp. 717–725, 729; Vladimir Geiger, "Brojidbeni pokazatelji o ljudskim gubicima Hrvatske u Drugom svjetskom ratu i poraću," in Zorislav Lukić (ed.) *Represija i zločini komunističkog režima u Hrvatskoj* (Zagreb: Matica hrvatska, 2012), pp. 64.
12 Cf. for example Mira Radojević, "Jasenovac, logor smrti (1941–2016)" / "Jasenovac, death concentration camp (1941–2016)," in Vasilije Đ. Krestić and Mira Radojević, *Jasenovac* (Beograd: SANU, 2017), pp. 79–91.

13 Cf. Dušan Nikodijević, "Prilog utvrđivanju broja žrtava sistema logora Jasenovac 1941.godine," in *Godišnjak za istraživanje genocida* 8 (Beograd– Kragujevac: Muzej žrtava genocida, 2016), pp. 169–213; Dušan Nikodijević, "Brojevi žrtava u koncentracionom logoru Jasenovac 1942.godine prema iskazima preživelih svedoka," in *Godišnjak za istraživanje genocida 9* (Beograd– Kragujevac: Muzej žrtava genocida, 2017), pp. 95–117 and the sources and literature cited therein.
14 Cf. Vladimir Geiger, "Ljudski gubici Hrvatske u Drugom svjetskom ratu koje su prouzročili 'okupatori i njihovi pomagači'. Brojidbeni pokazatelji (procjene, izračuni, popisi)," pp. 702–709; Vladimir Geiger, "Brojidbeni pokazatelji o ljudskim gubicima Hrvatske u Drugom svjetskom ratu i poraću," pp. 64 and the sources and literature cited therein.
15 Cf. *Žrtve rata 1941–1945. godine. Rezultati popisa* (Beograd, 1966; Beograd, 1992), pp. 47–55; Mihael Sobolevski, "Prešućena istina–žrtve rata na području bivše Jugoslavije 1941.–1945.prema popisu iz 1964.godine," *Časopis za suvremenu povijest*, vol. 25, no. 2–3 (1993), pp. 96–101; Vladimir Geiger, "Ljudski gubici Hrvatske u Drugom svjetskom ratu koje su prouzročili 'okupatori i njihovi pomagači'. Brojidbeni pokazatelji (procjene, izračuni, popisi)," pp. 716, 719.
16 Cf. *Žrtve rata 1941–1945. godine. Rezultati popisa* (Beograd, 1966; Beograd, 1992), pp. 47; *Spisak žrtava rata 1941–1945. Ustaški logor Jasenovac* (Beograd, 1992); Meho Visočak and Bejdo Sobica (eds.) *Jasenovac. Žrtve rata prema podacima Statističkog zavoda Jugoslavije* (Zürich–Sarajevo: Bošnjački institut: 1998). Cf. Davor Kovačić, "Jasenovac–žrtve rata prema podacima Statističkog zavoda Jugoslavije, Sarajevo–Zürich, 1998., 1171. str.," *Časopis za suvremenu povijest* 32 no. 1 (2000) 222–223. [overview]; Vladimir Geiger, "Brojidbeni pokazatelji o žrtvama logora Jasenovac, 1941.–1945. (procjene, izračuni, popisi)," pp. 216. or Vladimir Geiger, "Numerical indicators of the victims of the Jasenovac camp, 1941–1945 (estimates, calculations, lists)," pp. 156–157.
17 Cf. *Žrtve rata 1941–1945. godine. Rezultati popisa, VII-XV*, 5–7.; Vladimir Žerjavić, *Opsesije i megalomanije oko Jasenovca i Bleiburga. Gubici stanovništva Jugoslavije u drugom svjetskom ratu* (Zagreb: Globus, 1992), pp. 36; Vladimir Žerjavić, *Population losses in Yugoslavia 1941–1945* (Zagreb: Dom i svijet, Hrvatski institut za povijest, 1997), pp. 68; Srđan Bogosavljević, "Drugi svetski rat–žrtve. Jugoslavija," *Dijalog povjesničara–istoričara 4* (Zagreb: Friedrich Naumann Stiftung, 2001), pp. 499–500; Vladimir Geiger, "Ljudski gubici Hrvatske u Drugom svjetskom ratu koje su prouzročili 'okupatori i njihovi pomagači'," pp. 707.
18 Srđan Bogosavljević, "Drugi svetski rat–žrtve. Jugoslavija," 497–499; Vladimir Geiger, "Ljudski gubici Hrvatske u Drugom svjetskom ratu koje su prouzročili 'okupatori i njihovi pomagači'," pp. 708.
19 Mihael Sobolevski, "Prešućena istina–žrtve rata na području bivše Jugoslavije 1941.–1945. Prema popisu iz 1964. godine," pp. 89, 91, 111; Davor Kovačić, "Jasenovac–žrtve rata prema podacima Statističkog zavoda Jugoslavije, Sarajevo–Zürich: Bošnjački instiut, 1998., 1171 str.," pp. 220–222.; Vladimir Geiger, "Brojidbeni pokazatelji o žrtvama logoraJasenovac, 1941.–1945. (procjene, izračuni, popisi)," pp. 218 or Vladimir Geiger, "Numerical indicators of the victims of the Jasenovac camp, 1941–1945 (estimates, calculations, lists)," pp. 159 and the literature cited therein.
20 Mihael Sobolevski, "Prešućena istina–žrtve rata na području bivše Jugoslavije 1941.–1945. prema popisu iz 1964. godine," pp. 89; Vladmir Geiger, "Ljudski

gubici Hrvatske u Drugom svjetskom ratu koje su prouzročili 'okupatori i njihovi pomagači'," pp. 709 and the literature cited therein.
21 Cf. *Jasenovac. Koncentracioni logor 1941–1945. Spisak ustaških žrtava identifikovanih do 30. X 1997.*, I–III (Beograd, 1997) or *Jasenovac. Concentration camp 1941–1945. List of victims of Ustašas identified up to 30. X 1997.*, I–III (Beograd, 1997).
22 Dragan Cvetković, "Jasenovac u sistemu stradanja civila u NDH–kvantitativna analiza (ili, ponovo o brojevima)," in: *Jasenovac. Zbornik radova Četvrte međunarodne konferencije o Jasenovcu*, ed. Zdravko Antonić and Janko Velimirović (Kozarska Dubica, Banja Luka: Javna ustanova Spomen-područja Donja Gradina; Uruženje Jasenovac–Donja Gradina, 2007), pp. 7; Dragan Cvetković, "Stradanje civila Nezavisne Države Hrvatske u logoru Jasenovac," *Tokovi istorije*, no. 4 (2007), pp. 160.
23 Cf. Jelka Smreka and Đorđe Mihovilović (eds.). *Poimenični popis žrtava koncentracijskog logora Jasenovac 1941.–1945.*, ed. (Jasenovac: Spomen područje Jasenovac, 2007).
24 Cf. www.jusp-jasenovac.hr (accessed December 11, 2020).
25 Cf. Antun Miletić, *NDH–Koncentracioni logor Jasenovac 1941–1945* (Beograd: Dokumenta, 2010), pp. 123; Antun Miletić, *Ubijeni u koncentracionom logoru Jasenovac 1941–1945 / The Assassinated in the Jasenovac Concentration Camp 1941–1945* (Jagodina: Gambit, 2011), pp. 27.
26 Cf. *Izvješće o radu Komisije za utvrđivanje ratnih i poratnih žrtava od osnutka (11. veljače 1992.) do rujna 1999. godine* (Zagreb, 1999), pp. 15–16, 19–20. Cf. Vladimir Geiger, "Brojidbeni pokazatelji o ljudskim gubicima Hrvatske u Drugom svjetskom ratu i poraću," pp. 56–58.
27 Vladimir Geiger, "Brojidbeni pokazatelji o žrtvama logora Jasenovac, 1941.–1945. (procjene, izračuni, popisi)," pp. 219 or Vladimir Geiger, "Numerical indicators of the victims of the Jasenovac camp, 1941–1945 (estimates, calculations, lists)," pp. 161 and the literature cited therein.
28 Cf. *Spisak žrtava rata 1941–1945. Ustaški logor Jasenovac* (Beograd, 1992); Meho Visočak and Bejdo Sobica (eds.) *Jasenovac. Žrtve rata prema podacima Statističkog zavoda Jugoslavije* (Zürich–Sarajevo: Bošnjački institut, 1998).
29 Cf. *Izvješće o radu Komisije za utvrđivanje ratnih i poratnih žrtava*, 16; Vladimir Geiger, "Brojidbeni pokazatelji o žrtvama logora Jasenovac, 1941.–1945. (procjene, izračuni, popisi)," 220 or Vladimir Geiger, "Numerical indicators of the victims of the Jasenovac camp, 1941–1945 (estimates, calculations, lists)," pp. 161–162 and the literature cited therein.
30 Vladimir Žerjavić, *Opsesije i megalomanije oko Jasenovca i Bleiburga*, pp. 69, 72; Vladimir Žerjavić, *Population losses in Yugoslavia 1941–1945*, pp. 89, 92.
31 Vladimir Žerjavić, *Opsesije i megalomanije oko Jasenovca i Bleiburga*, pp. 74; Vladimir Žerjavić, *Population losses in Yugoslavia 1941–1945*, pp. 93.
32 Cf. for example: Nataša Mataušić, *Jasenovac 1941.–1945. Logor smrti i radni logor* (Jasenovac: Javna ustanova Spomen područje Jasenovac; Zagreb: Jesenski i Turk, 2003), pp. 123; Filip Škiljan, *Politički zatvorenici u logorima Jasenovac i Stara Gradiška*, Jasenovac: Javna ustanova Spomen područje Jasenovac, 2009), pp. 204; Filip Škiljan, "Logorski sustav Jasenovac–kontroverze," u: Sabrina P. Ramet (ed.) *Nezavisna Država Hrvatska 1941.–1945* (Zagreb: Alinea, 2009), pp. 125.
33 Cf. Bogoljub Kočović, *Žrtve Drugog svetskog rata u Jugoslaviji* (Sarajevo: Svjetlost, 1990: XVI; Beograd, 2005: XVI); Bogoljub Kočović, *Nauka, nacionalizam*

i propaganda (Između gubitaka i žrtava Drugoga svetskog rata u Jugoslaviji) (Paris: Editions du Titre, 1999), pp. 87–88, 147–148. Nataša Mataušić, *Jasenovac 1941.–1945. Logor smrti i radni logor*, 120–122; Mišo Deverić and Ivan Fumić, *Hrvatska u logorima 1941.–1945.* (Zagreb: Savez antifašističkih boraca i antifašista Republike Hrvatske, 2008), pp. 126.

34 Ibid (German or kindred blood).

35 Cf. Slavko Goldstein and Ivo Goldstein, *Jasenovac i Bleiburg nisu isto* (Zagreb: Novi liber, 2011); Slavko Goldstein, co-author Ivo Goldstein, *Jasenovac. Tragika, mitomanija, istina* (Zagreb: Fraktura, 2016).

36 Dragan Cvetković, "Stradanje civila Nezavisne Države Hrvatske u logoru Jasenovac," pp. 154; Vladimir Geiger, "Brojidbeni pokazatelji o ljudskim gubicima Hrvatske u Drugom svjetskom ratu i poraću," pp. 72–73.

37 Cf. Bruno Bušić, "Žrtve rata," *Hrvatski književni list* 15 (1969), pp. 2–3; *Enciklopedija hrvatske povijesti i kulture*, s.v. "Koncentracioni logori," (Zagreb: Školska knjiga, 1980), pp. 304–305; Ljubo Boban, *Kontroverze iz povijesti Jugoslavije 2* (Zagreb: Školska knjiga/Stvarnost, 1989), pp. 315–431; Ljubo Boban, *Kontroverze iz povijesti Jugoslavije 3* (Zagreb: Školska knjiga/Stvarnost, 1990), pp. 275–342; Franjo Tuđman, *Bespuća povijesne zbiljnosti. Rasprava o povijesti i filozofiji zlosilja* (Zagreb: Hrvatska sveučilišna naknada, 1989); Vladimir Žerjavić, *Gubici stanovništva Jugoslavije u drugom svjetskom ratu* (Zagreb: Jugoslavensko viktimološko društvo, 1989).

38 Cf. Radomir Bulatović, *Koncentracioni logor Jasenovac, s posebnim osvrtom na Donju Gradinu. Istorijsko-sociološka i antropološka studija* (Sarajevo: Svjetlost, 1990).

39 Vladimir Geiger, "Brojidbeni pokazatelji o žrtvama logora Jasenovac, 1941.–1945. (procjene, izračuni, popisi)," pp. 219 or Vladimir Geiger, "Numerical indicators of the victims of the Jasenovac camp, 1941–1945 (estimates, calculations, lists)," pp. 163–164 and the literature cited therein.

40 Cf. for example: Vladimir Dedijer, *Vatikan i Jasenovac* (Beograd: Rad, 1987); Vladimir Dedijer, *Jasenovac. Das jugoslawische Auschwitz und der Vatikan* (Freiburg im Breisgau: Ahriman–Verl., 1987); Vladimir Dedijer, *The Yugoslav Auschwitz and the Vatican. The Croatian Massacre of the Serbs During World War II* (Buffalo, NY: Prometheus Books, 1992); Vladimir Dedijer and Antun Miletić, *Protiv zaborava i tabua (Jasenovac 1941–1991)* (Sarajevo: Prerges, 1991).

41 Cf. for example: Antun Miletić, Koncentracioni logor Jasenovac 1941–1945. Dokumenta knjiga I–III (Beograd: Narodna knjiga, 1986 and 1987), Koncentracioni logor Jasenovac 1941–1945. Dokumenta knjiga IV (Jagodina, 2007); Antun Miletić, Ustaška fabrika smrti 1941–1945, Beograd: Vojnoizdavački i novinski centar, 1988; Vladimir Dedijer, Antun Miletić, Protiv zaborava i tabua (Jasenovac 1941–1991) (Sarajevo: Udruženje za istraživanje genocida i ratnih zločina, 1991); Antun Miletić, NDH–Koncentracioni logor Jasenovac 1941–1945., Beograd, 2010.; Antun Miletić, Ubijeni u koncentracionom logoru Jasenovac 1941–1945. / The Assassinated in the Jasenovac Concentration Camp 1941–1945., Jagodina, 2011.

42 Cf. Srboljub Živanović, *Jasenovac. Odabrani radovi, članci, intervjui, govori i diskusije* (Beograd–London, 2008; Beograd: Pešić i sinovi, 2012; Beograd: Pešić i sinovi, 2017); Srboljub Živanović, *Jasenovac 2* (Beograd: Pešić i sinovi, 2017).

43 Cf. for example: Milan Bulajić, *Ustaški zločini genocida i suđenje Andriji Artukoviću 1986. godine, I–IV* (Beograd: Rad, 1988–1989); *"Jasenovački mit"*

Franje Tuđmana–Genocid nad Srbima, Jevrejima i Ciganima (Beograd: Stručna knjiga, 1994) or Milan Bulajić, *Tudjman's "Jasenovac Myth." Genocide against Serbs, Jews and Gypsies* (Beograd: Stručna knjiga 1994); Milan Bulajić, *Jasenovac. Ustaški logor smrti. "Srpski mit?" Hrvatski ustaški logori genocida nad Srbima, Jevrejima i Ciganima* (Beograd: Stručna knjiga, 1999); Milan Bulajić, *Jasenovac na sudu. Suđenje D. Šakiću (Jasenovac–sistem ustaških logora genocida, balkanski Aušvic)* (Beograd: Muzej žrtava genocida, 2001) or Milan Bulajić, *Jasenovac. Balkan Auschwitz. System of Croatian Nazi-Ustasha Genocide Camps for Serbs, Jews and Gypsies* (Beograd: Muzej žrtava genocida, 2001).

44 Cf. for example: Smilja Avramov (ed.) "Jasenovac. A Collection of Papers, Banja Luka, May 24 and 25, 2011," *The Fifth International Conference on the System of Concentration Camps and Execution Stations of the Croatian State for the Extermination of Serbs, Jews and Roma in the Second World War*. Kozarska Dubica–Banja Luka, 2011; Kosta Čavoški, Avramov, Smilja and Vasilije Krestić (eds.), "*Deklaracija o genocidu Nezavisne Države Hrvatske nad Srbima, Jevrejima i Romima tokom Drugog svjetskog rata," Peta međunarodna konferencija o Jasenovcu, 24–25. maj 2011. Banja Luka* / "Declaration on the genocide committed against the Serbs, Jews and Roma by the Independent State of Croatia during the Second World War," *The Fifth International Conference on Jasenovac, May 24–25, 2011 Banja Luka*. Banja Luka: Jasenovac-Donja Gradina, 2011; Vasilije Đ. Krestić, "O genocidnosti Hrvatske politike" / "On the genocidal nature of Croatian politics," u: Vasilije Đ. Krestić, Mira Radojević, *Jasenovac* (Beograd: SANU, 2017), pp. 13–48.

45 Vladimir Geiger, "Ljudski gubici Hrvatske u Drugom svjetskom ratu koje su prouzročili 'okupatori i njihovi pomagači'," pp. 72; Vladimir Geiger, "Brojidbeni pokazatelji o žrtvama logora Jasenovac, 1941.–1945. (procjene, izračuni, popisi)," pp. 223 or Vladimir Geiger, "Numerical indicators of the victims of the Jasenovac camp, 1941–1945 (estimates, calculations, lists)," pp. 165. Cf. www.jasenovac.org. In recent years, many have referred to the list from the mentioned website, but the list was removed several months ago for unknown reasons, i.e. access to the list is currently unavailable.

46 Cf. for example: Josip Kljaković–Šantić, *Jasenovac – enigma holokausta* (Zagreb: Tkanica, 2016).

47 Meho Visočak and Bejdo Sobica (eds.) *Jasenovac. Žrtve rata prema podacima Statističkog zavoda Jugoslavije* (Zürich–Sarajevo: Bošnjački institut, 1998).

48 Cf. Bogoljub Kočović, *Nauka, nacionalizam i propaganda (Između gubitaka i žrtava Drugoga svetskog rata u Jugoslaviji)*, 143–144; Davor Kovačić, "Jasenovac – žrtve rata prema podacima Statističkog zavoda Jugoslavije, Sarajevo–Zürich: Bošnjački institut, 1998, 1171 str.," 2192–24; Vladimir Geiger, "Brojidbeni pokazatelji o žrtvama logora Jasenovac, 1941.–1945. (procjene, izračuni, popisi)," pp. 223 or Vladimir Geiger, "Numerical indicators of the victims of the Jasenovac camp, 1941–1945 (estimates, calculations, lists)," pp. 165 and and the literature cited therein.

49 Cf. http://sr.wikipedia.org/sr-el/Међународна_комисија_за_утврђивање_истине_о_Јасеновцу (accessed 12 May 2017).

50 Cf. Vladimir Geiger, "Sumanuti i bolesni navodi i tvrdnje Međunarodne komisije za utvrđivanje istine o Jasenovcu (The International Commission for the Truth on Jasenovac)," *Politički zatvorenik*, 23 no. 253 (2013), pp. 13–17.

51 Cf. Kosta Čavoški, Smilja Avramov, Vasilije Krestić (eds.), "*Deklaracija o genocidu Nezavisne Države Hrvatske nad Srbima, Jevrejima i Romima tokom Drugog svjetskog rata.*"
52 Cf. www.objektivno1.rs/region-gradovi/cacak/3070/tribina-dveri-u-cacku-istina-o-jasenovcu.html (accessed 15 February 2016).
53 Cf. for example: Srboljub Živanović, *Jasenovac. Odabrani radovi, članci, intervjui, govori i diskusij*; Srboljub Živanović, *Jasenovac 2*; Jaša Almuli, *Jevreji i Srbi u Jasenovcu* (Beograd: Službeni glasnik, 2009); Lea Maestro, *Logor Đakovo / Djakovo Camp* (Sarajevo: Jevrejska opština Sarajevo–La Benevolencija, 2013); Aleksandar S. Jovanović, *Beg iz jasenovačkog pakla* (Beograd: Muzej žrtava genocida, 2014).
54 Vladimir Geiger, "Brojidbeni pokazatelji o žrtvama logora Jasenovac, 1941.– 1945. (procjene, izračuni, popisi)," pp. 223– 234 or Vladimir Geiger, "Numerical indicators of the victims of the Jasenovac camp, 1941–1945 (estimates, calculations, lists)," pp. 177–178 and the literature cited therein.
55 Ilija Barbarić, *Nezavisna Država Hrvatska bilo je pravo ime* (Split: Biblioteka Svjedočanstva, 2010), pp. 100.
56 Kazimir Katalinić, *Od poraza do pobjede. Povijest hrvatske političke emigracije 1945.–1990.*, *Svezak I. 1945.–1959.* (Zagreb: Naklada Trpimir, 2017), pp. 69.
57 Aleksandar S. Jovanović, *Beg iz jasenovačkog pakla*, pp. 165–166.
58 Cf. Andrea Červinec, "Interview. Dr. Stjepan Razum, historian and archivist: It is time to overthrow the Greater Serbia myth of Jasenovac. There is no evidence for mass Ustaša crimes in Jasenovac, but there is evidence for partisan crimes!," *Hrvatski list* (Zadar), no. 411, August 8, 2012, 28–35. Cf. for example Ivica Marijačić, "Interview. Dr. Stjepan Razum. In Jasenovac, the partisans planted their cruel and mass crimes on the Ustašas–we historians will prove it!" *Hrvatski tjednik* (Zadar), no. 501, May 1, 2014, 30–33; Stjepan Razum, "Jasenovac, the biggest historical lie that is becoming more and more transparent day by day," *Hrvatski tjednik* (Zadar), no. 559, June 15, 2015, pp. 18–25.
59 Cf. Vladimir Horvat, "Tri jasenovačka logora," in: Vladimir Horvat, Igor Vukić, Stipo Pilić and Blanka Matković (eds.), *Jasenovački logori–istraživanja* (Zagreb: Društvo za istraživanje trostrukog logora Jasenovac, 2015), pp. 11–54.
60 Cf. Stjepan Razum, "Logor Jasenovac kao sredstvo trajne komunističke indoktrinacije," Hrvatski tjednik (Zadar), no. 581, November 12, 2015, pp. 18–20.
61 Cf. Stipo Pilić and Blanka Matković, "Poslijeratni zarobljenički logor Jasenovac prema svjedočanstvima i novim arhivskim izvorima," Radovi Zavoda za povijesne znanosti HAZU u Zadru, no. 56 (2014), pp. 323–408. Published under the same title as a chapter in the book: Vladimir Horvat, Igor Vukić, Stipo Pilić and Blanka Matković, *Jasenovački logori–istraživanja*, pp. 145–235.
62 Cf. Tomislav Vuković, "Interview. Roman Leljak on the post-war camp in Jasenovac. Tito ordered the Jasenovac camp to be closed on August 21, 1948," Glas Koncila (Zagreb), no. 1 (2220), January 8, 2017, pp. 6–7.
63 Đorđe Mihovilović, *Jasenovac 1945.–1947. Fotomonografija* (Jasenovac: Javna ustanova Spomen–područje Jasenovac, 2016).
64 Mladen Ivezić, *Titov Jasenovac* (Zagreb, 2014); Vladimir Horvat, Igor Vukić, Stipo Pilić and Blanka Matković, *Jasenovački logori–istraživanja*.
65 Slavko Goldstein, co–author Ivo Goldstein, *Jasenovac. Tragika, mitomanija, istina*.
66 Mladenko Colić, *Pregled operacija na jugoslovenskom ratištu* (Beograd: Vojnoistorijski institut, 1988), pp. 401.

67 Jovo Popović, *Druže Tito rat je završen 15. maja 16,00 na Dravi Kosta Nađ* (Beograd: Četvrti jul, 1985), pp. 196.
68 Jerome Jareb and Ivo Omrčanin, "The end of the Croatian Army at Bleiburg Austria in May 1945 according to English Military Documents," *Journal of Croatian Studies* 18–19, no. 51 (1977–1978); Cf. Anthony Cowgill, Thomas Brimelow, Christopher Booker, *The Repatriations from Austria in 1945. The Report of an Inquiry* (London: Sinclair-Stevenson, 1990), pp. 23; Anthony Cowgill, Thomas Brimelow and Christopher Booker, *The Repatriations from Austria in 1945. Cowgill Inquiry. The documentary evidence reproduced in full from British, American, German and Yugoslav sources* (London: Sinclair-Stevenson, 1990), pp. KP 93. These headlines are better known to the public as the "Cowgill Report."
69 Martina Grahek Ravančić, *Bleiburg i križni put 1945. Historiografija, publicistika i memoarska literatura* (Zagreb: Hrvatski institut za povijest, 2009; Zagreb: Hrvatski institut za povijest, 2015), pp. 145–146 and the sources and literature cited therein.
70 Martina Grahek Ravančić, "V kolonah po štirje skozi Slovenijo," *Prispevki za novejšo zgodovino* 48, no. 2 (2008), pp. 95–116; Martina Grahek Ravančić, *Bleiburg i križni put 1945. Historiografija, publicistika i memoarska literatura* (2009), pp. 203–316; (2015), pp. 203–326 and the sources and literature cited therein.
71 Cf. Mitja Ferenc, *Prikrito in očem zakrito. Prikrita grobišča 60 let po koncu druge svetovne vojne* (Celje: Muzej novejše zgodovine, 2005); Mitja Ferenc and Želimir Kužatko, *Prikrivena grobišta Hrvata u Republici Sloveniji / Prikrita grobišča Hrvatov v Republiki Sloveniji / Hidden Croatian Mass Graves in the Republic of Slovenia* (Zagreb: Počasni bleiburški vod/Burlimgame: Damir Radoš, 2007); Jože Dežman (ed.) *Poročilo Komisije Vlade Republike Slovenije za reševanje vprašanj prikritih grobišč 2005–2008* (Ljubljana: Družina, 2008/2009). or Jože Dežman (ed.) *Prikrita grobišča. Izvješće komisije Vlade Republike Slovenije za rješavanje pitanja skrivenih grobišta 2005–2008* (Sarajevo: Hrvatsko katoličko dobrotvorno društvo, 2010); Jože Dežman (ed.) *Resnica in sočutje. Poročilo Komisije Vlade RS za reševanje vprašanj prikritih grobišč 2009–2011. Prispevki k črni knjigi titoizm* (Ljubljana: Družina, 2012).
72 Cf. Mitja Ferenc and Želimir Kužatko, *Prikrivena grobišta Hrvata u Republici Sloveniji / Prikrita grobišča Hrvatov v Republiki Sloveniji / Hidden Croatian Mass Graves in the Republic of Slovenia*, pp. 40, 42, 126–129; Mitja Ferenc, "Tezno–največe prikriveno grobište u Sloveniji. O istraživanju grobišta u prototenkovskom rovu u Teznom (Maribor)," *Časopis za suvremenu povijest*, vol. 44, no. 3 (2012), pp. 539–569.
73 Cf. The Way of the Cross. The Slovenes suspect that the core of the Croatian army was buried in the tank trench. Tezno–the largest tomb of Croats," *Večernji list* (TN: a daily) (Zagreb), August 10, 2007, 4; Ivica RADOŠ, "Mass grave near Maribor confirmed by checks. Tezno: Investigation of the grave of 20,000 NDH soldiers," *Jutarnji list* (TN: a daily) (Zagreb), August 10, 2007, 2; Ivica RADOŠ, "Interview. Jože Dežman, The president of the Slovenian Commission for Resolving the Issue of Concealed Cemeteries. We have at least two Srebrenicas in Tezno," *Jutarnji list* (Zagreb), September 24, 2007, pp. 8–9.
74 Cf. for example: "Apart from Tezno, the Špitalić canyon near Slovenske Konjice is the largest tomb of Croats in Slovenia," *Večernji list* (Zagreb), July 29, 1999, pp. 15.
75 www.hkv.hr/vijesti/jugo-ostavtina/822-fumi-o-bleiburgu.html (accessed February 23, 2018).

76 Cf. Simo Š. Dubajić, I do not regret killing 30,000 Croats!" *Globus* (TN: a weekly) (Zagreb), no. 217, February 3, 1995, pp. 46–47, 49; Simo Š. Dubajić, "Kočevski rog," *Ljetopis Srpskog kulturnog društva "Prosvjeta,"* vol. 11 (2006), pp. 89–168; Simo Š. Dubajić, *Život, greh i kajanje. Ispovedna autobiografska hronika. Knjiga I. Od Kistanja do Kočevskog Roga* (Beograd: Vesti, 2006), pp. 278–394. Cf. Borivoje M. Karapandžić, *Kočevje. Tito's Bloodiest Crime* (Cleveland, 1965, Cleveland, 1970) or Borivoje M. Karapandžić, *Kočevje. Titov najkrvaviji zločin* (Cleveland, 1959, Beograd: Knjižnica Obradović Bgd., 1990); Ivo Žajedela, *Kočevski Rog* (Maribor: Založba za alternativno teorijo, 1990).

77 Cf. Martina Grahek Ravančić, *Bleiburg i križni put 1945. Historiografija, publicistika i memoarska literatura* (2009), pp. 250–254; (2015), pp. 255–259 and the literature cited therein.

78 Cf. Jože Dežman, *Hudo zlo iz hudih jam / Terrible evil from Caves of Evil* (Ljubljana: Družina, 2009); Roman Leljak, *Huda Jama* (Radenci: Društvo Huda Jama; 2010); Mitja Ferenc, Mehmedalija Alić, Pavel Jamnik, *Huda jama. Skrito za enajstimi pregradami* (Ljubljana: Družina, 2011); Mitja Ferenc, *Huda Jama (Grave pit). Coal mine mass massacre (May, June 1945)* (Ljubljana: Znanstvena založba Filozofske fakultete, 2013); Roman Leljak, *Huda Jama* (Radenci/Zagreb: Društvo Huda jama, 2015) and sources and literature cited therein.

79 Mladen Ivezić, *Titova umjetnost mržnje* (Zagreb: Samizdat, 2001), pp. 303.

80 Ivo Banac, "Antifascism is not an independent idea," *Jutarnji list* (Zagreb), February 16, 2008, pp. 38.

81 Vladimir Geiger, *Josip Broz Tito i ratni zločini. Bleiburg i folksdojčeri* (Zagreb: Hrvatski institut za povijest, 2013), pp. 12 and sources and literature cited therein.

82 Cf. for example: Želimir Žanko and Nikola Šolić (eds.) *Jazovka* (Zagreb: Vjesnik, 1990); Srećko Božičević, *Jame (kao) grobnice* (Zagreb: Azur journal, 1991); Lovro Šturm (ed.) *Brez milosti. Ranjeni, invalidni in bolni povojni ujetniki na Slovenskem* (Ljubljana: Nova revija, 2000); Milan Marušić, *Žrtve komunističkih zlodjela u Zagrebu svibanj 1945. i sljemenskim stratištima bolnica Brestovac i Gračani* (Zagreb: Hrvatsko žrtvoslovno društvo, 2001); Blanka Matković, "Odvođenja i likvidacije ranjenih pripadnika Hrvatskih oružanih snaga (HOS) iz zagrebačkih bolnica u svibnju i lipnju 1945.kroz arhivsko gradivo Državnog arhiva u Zagrebu," *Arhivski vjesnik* 54 (2011), pp. 179–214 and sources and literature cited therein.

83 Zdravko Dizdar, Vladimir Geiger, Milan Pojić, Mate Rupić, *Partizanska i komunistička represija i zločini u Hrvatskoj 1944.–1946.* (documents) (eds.) (Slavonski Brod: Hrvatski institut za povijest, 2005; Zagreb, 2009), pp. 130; Martina Grahek Ravančić, *Bleiburg i križni put 1945. Historiografija, publicistika i memoarska literatura* (2009), pp. 218; (2015), pp. 220.

84 Zdenko Zavadlav, *Iz dnevniških zapiskov mariborskega oznovca (Izbrani listi). 1. del: Leto 1945* (Maribor: Založba za alternativno teorijo, 1990), pp. 91–93; Mladen Genc, "Shocking Confession of Zdenko Zavadlav (79), former Deputy Chief of OZNA for the Maribor area, about the mass liquidations of Croats in 1945 in Slovenia. We were ordered to kill!" *Jutarnji list* ("Panorama") (Zagreb), May 25, 2003, 12–13; Zdenko Zavadlav, *Pozna spoved. Iz dnevnika slovenskega oznovca* (Celovec: Mohorjeva, 2010), pp. 17–27, 124–128.

85 Martina Grahek Ravančić, *Bleiburg i križni put 1945. Historiografija, publicistika i memoarska literatura* (2009), pp. 203–316; (2015), pp. 203–325 and the sources and literature cited therein.

86 Cf. Martina Grahek Ravančić, "Controversies about the Croatian victims at Bleiburg and in 'Death marches'," *Review of Croatian History* 2, no. 1 (2006), pp. 851–868; Martina Grahek Ravančić, "Razmišljanja o broju pogubljenih na Bleiburgu i križnom putu," *Časopis za suvremenu povijest* 40, no. 3 (2008), pp. 851–868; Martina Grahek Ravančić, Bleiburg i križni put 1945. Historiografija, publicistika i memoarska literatura (2009), pp. 317–333; (2015), pp. 327–343 and the sources and literature cited therein.
87 Zdravko Dizdar, "Stradanja Hrvata u II. svjetskom ratu i neposredno nakon njega," in: Vicko Kapitanović (ed.) *Crkva i društvo uz Jadran. Vrela i rezultati istraživanja* (Split: Katolički bogoslovni fakultet, Sveučilište u Splitu, 2001), pp.179; Zdravko Dizdar, "Prilog istraživanju problema Bleiburga i križnih putova (u povodu 60. obljetnice)," *Senjski zbornik* 32, no. 1 (2005), pp.188.
88 Cf. Martina Grahek Ravančić, "Razmišljanja o broju pogubljenih na Bleiburgu i križnom putu," 866; Martina Grahek Ravančić, Bleiburg i križni put 1945. Historiografija, publicistika i memoarska literatura (2009), pp. 326–328; (2015), pp. 336–338.
89 Cf. *Izvješće o radu Komisije za utvrđivanje ratnih i poratnih žrtava od osnutka (11. veljače 1992.) do rujna 1999. godine*, pp. 20.
90 Vladimir Žerjavić, Opsesije i megalomanije oko Jasenovca i Bleiburga. Gubici stanovništva Jugoslavije u drugom svjetskom ratu, 74; Vladmir Žerjavić, Population losses in Yugoslavia 1941–1945, pp. 94–97.
91 Vladimir Žerjavić, "Žrtve oko Bleiburga i na križnom putu," in: Jozo Marević (ed.) *U Bleiburgu iskra* (Zagreb: Vidokrug, 1993).
92 Kazimir Katalinić, "Hrvatske i srpske žrtve 1941.–1945.," *Republika Hrvatska* 38, no. 160 (1988), pp. 15–63; Kazimir Katalinić, "Broj bleiburških žrtava," in: Jozo Marević (ed.) *50 godina Bleiburga* (Zagreb: Croatiaprojekt, 1995), pp. 49–61.
93 Cf. Michael Portmann, "Comunist Retaliation and Persecution on Yugoslav Territory during and after WWII (1943–1950)," *Tokovi istorije* no. 1–2 (2004), pp. 45–74; Michael Portmann, *Kommunistische Abrechnung mit Kriegsverbrechern, Kollaborateuren, "Volksfeinden" und "Verrätern" in Jugoslawien während des Zweiten Weltkriegs und unmittelbar danach (1943–1950)* (Wien: GRIN Publishing, 2007).
94 Cf. Vinko Nikolić, "Bleiburg," in: *Hrvatski leksikon, vol. I (A–K)* (Zagreb: Naklada Leksikon d.o.o., 1996), pp. 110; "Križni put," in: *Hrvatski leksikon, I. sv. A–K*, 649; "Križni put," in: *Hrvatski opći leksikon* (Zagreb: LZMK, 1996), pp. 507; *Hrvatska enciklopedija*, vol. 2 Be–Da, "Bleiburg," (Zagreb: LZMK, 2000), pp. 175.
95 *Hrvatska enciklopedija, vol. 2 Be–Da*, s.v. "Bleiburg," pp. 175.
96 Josip Broz Tito, *Sabrana djela*, Tom dvadeset osmi, *1. maj–6. jul 1945.* (Beograd, 1988), pp. 43.
97 Milovan Đilas, *Revolucionarni rat* (Beograd: Književne novine, 1990), pp. 433.
98 Josip Broz Tito, *Sabrana djela*, Tom dvadeset osmi, *1. maj–6. jul 1945.*, 78; Josip Broz Tito, *Jugoslavenska revolucija i socijalizam*, Prvi svezak (Zagreb: Globus, 1982), pp. 313.
99 Milovan Đilas, *Revolucionarni rat*, pp. 433.
100 His opinion is: "The revenge that culminated in May 1945 was not unreasonable. It was motivated by a crime that began in April 1941." He also raises the question as to "whether this revenge, that is, whether the punishment, received by individuals and entire groups, was appropriate." Ivo Goldstein, "Povijesne okolnosti Bleiburga i Križnog puta," in: Juraj Hrženjak (ed.) *Bleiburg i Križni*

put 1945 (Zagreb: Savez antifašističkih boraca i antifašista Republike Hrvatske 2007), pp. 32–33.
101 Ivo Goldstein, *Hrvatska 1918–2008* (Zagreb: Novi liber, 2008), pp. 364. Cf. Ivo Goldstein, "Kriteriji za selekciju i masovne likvidacije," *Jutarnji list* (Zagreb), November 22, 2008, pp. 80.
102 The Goldsteins declare their account of the events of May 1945 (which has the same basis in all their works, only occasionally the data, given the scope of the content, is expanded or shortened) as being "so far the only one that gives such a concise historiographical overview[,...] an overview based on careful research and an objective historiographical approach, without one-sided politicizing of interpretations." Cf. Slavko Goldstein and Ivo Goldstein, *Jasenovac i Bleiburg nisu isto*, pp. 109.
103 Likewise, when talking about the number of casualties on the Bleiburg field, for which we really do not have any reliable estimates, Goldstein without any hesitation states that "27 Ustašas" were killed there. Cf. Ivo Goldstein, *Hrvatska 1918.–2008*; Ivo Goldstein, *Povijest Hrvatske 1945.–2011*. 1st volume (Split: EPH Media, 2011); Slavko Goldstein i Ivo Goldstein, *Jasenovac i Bleiburg nisu isto*.
104 Ivo Goldstein, *Hrvatska 1918–2008.*, pp. 365; Ivo Goldstein, "Kriteriji za selekciju i masovne likvidacije," pp. 81.
105 Josip Jurčević, *Bleiburg. Jugoslavenski poratni zločini nad Hrvatima* (Zagreb: Dokumentacijsko informacijsko središte 2005).
106 Cf. Josip Jurčević, *Prikrivena stratišta i grobišta jugoslavenskih komunističkih zločina* (Zagreb: Dokumentacijsko informacijsko središte, 2012).
107 Cf. for example: Mladen Ivezić, *Genocid nad Hrvatima zapovijeda Tito* (Zagreb: Samizdat, 1999); Josip Jurčević, *Bleiburg. Jugoslavenski poratni zločini nad Hrvatima*.
108 Cf. for example: Juraj Hrženjak (ed.) *Bleiburg i Križni put 1945*. (Zagreb: Savez antifašističkih boraca i antifašista Republike Hrvatske, 2007); Tomislav Badovinac (ed.) *Titovo doba. Hrvatska prije, za vrijeme i poslije* (Zagreb: Savez društava Josip Broz Tito, 2008).
109 Cf. Jovica Patrnogić, *Priručnik za međunarodno ratno pravo. Zakoni i običaji za rat na kopnu i u vazduhu* (Beograd: Vojnoizdavački zavod JNA, 1956), 76; Boško Petković, *Međunarodne konvencije o ratnom pravu* (Zagreb: Sveučilišna tiskara, 1992), pp. 398–424.
110 Cf. for example: Slavko Komar, "Iz rasprave na okruglom stolu," in: Juraj Hrženjak (ed.) *Bleiburg i Križni put 1945.*, pp. 97.
111 Cf. Mirjan Damaška, "Po onodobnom međunarodnom pravu, neosporna je Titova odgovornost za zločine 1945." [Intervju: Jadranka Jureško-Kero], in: Zvonimir Despot, *Tito. Tajne vladara. Najnoviji prilozi za biografiju Josipa Broza, Večernji list* (2009), pp. 468–469.
112 Cf. Juraj Hrženjak, *Bleiburg i Križni put 1945*.
113 Cf. Vladimir Geiger, "O zborniku Bleiburg i Križni put Saveza antifašističkih boraca i antifašista Republike Hrvatske, Zagreb, 2007," *Časopis za suvremenu povijest* 39, no. 3 (2007), pp. 809–827; Vladimir Geiger, *Josip Broz Tito i ratni zločini. Bleiburg i folksdojčeri*, pp. 83–98.
114 Cf. www.portalnovosti.com/nobilo-danasnja-hrvatska-ne-moze-biti-sljednica-kvislinske-ndh (accessed October 10, 2017).
115 Jerca Vodušek Starič, "Kako se čistila Jugoslavija?" *Gordogan, II* 21, no. 4–5 (48–49) (2004), pp. 37.
116 Mihael Sobolevski, "Između Jasenovca i Bleiburga," *Erasmvs* 4 (1993), pp. 44.

Bibliography

Almuli, Jaša. *Jevreji i Srbi u Jasenovcu*. Beograd: Službeni glasnik, 2009.
Avramov, Smilja (ed.). "Jasenovac. Zbornik radova, Banja Luka, 24. i 25. maj 2011. godine" / *Peta Međunarodna konferencija o sistemu koncentracionih logora i stratišta hrvatske države za istrebljenje Srba, Jevreja i Roma u Drugom svjetskom ratu*. Kozarska Dubica–Banja Luka, 2011.
Tomislav Badovinac (ed.). *Titovo doba. Hrvatska prije, za vrijeme i poslije*. Zagreb: Savez društava Josip Broz Tito, 2008.
Banac, Ivo. "Antifašizam nije samostojeća ideja," *Jutarnji list*, February 16, 2008.
Barbarić, Ilija. *Nezavisna Država Hrvatska bilo je pravo ime*. Split: Biblioteka Svjedočanstva, 2010.
Boban, Ljubo. *Kontroverze iz povijesti Jugoslavije, 2*. Zagreb: Školska knjiga, Stvarnost, 1989.
———. *Kontroverze iz povijesti Jugoslavije, 3*. Zagreb: Školska knjiga, Stvarnost, 1990.
Bogosavljević, Srđan. "Drugi svetski rat–žrtve. Jugoslavija," *Dijalog povjesničara-istoričara*, vol. 4, 2001, pp. 487–507.
Božičević, Srećko. *Jame (kao) grobnice*. Zagreb: Azur Journal, 1991.
Broz, Josip Tito. *Jugoslavenska revolucija i socijalizam*, vol. 1. Zagreb: Globus, 1982.
Broz, Josip Tito. *Sabrana djela, Tom dvadeset osmi, 1. maj–6. jul 1945*. Beograd: Komunist, 1988.
Bulajić, Milan. *Ustaški zločini genocida i suđenje Andriji Artukoviću 1986. godine, I–IV*. Beograd: Rad, 1988–1989.
———. *"Jasenovački mit" Franje Tuđmana – Genocid nad Srbima, Jevrejima i Ciganima*. Beograd, 1994.
———. *Tudjman's "Jasenovac Myth." Genocide against Serbs, Jews and Gypsies*. Beograd: Stručna knjiga, 1994.
———. *Jasenovac. Ustaški Slogor smrti. "Srpski mit?" Hrvatski ustaški logori genocida nad Srbima, Jevrejima i Ciganima*. Beograd: Stručna knjiga, 1999.
———. *Jasenovac na sudu. Suđenje D. Šakiću (Jasenovac–sistem ustaških logora genocida, balkanski Aušvic)*. Beograd: Muzej žrtava genocida, 2001.
———. *Jasenovac. Balkan Auschwitz. System of Croatian Nazi-Ustasha Genocide Camps for Serbs, Jews and Gypsies*. Beograd: Muzej žrtava genocida, 2001.
Bulatović, Radomir. *Koncentracioni logor Jasenovac, s posebnim osvrtom na Donju Gradinu. Istorijsko-sociološka i antropološka studija*. Sarajevo: Svjetlost, 1990.
Bušić, Bruno. "Žrtve rata," *Hrvatski književni list*, vol. 15, 1969, pp. 2–3.
Čavoški, Kosta, Avramov, Smilja and Krestić Vasilije. "Deklaracija o genocidu Nezavisne Države Hrvatske nad Srbima, Jevrejima i Romima tokom Drugog svjetskog rata," *Peta međunarodna konferencija o Jasenovcu, 24–25. maj 2011. Banja Luka* / "Declaration on the genocide committed against the Serbs, Jews and Roma by the Independent State of Croatia during the Second World War," *The Fifth International Conference on Jasenovac, May 24–25, 2011 Banja Luka*. Banja Luka: Jasenovac-Donja Gradina, 2011.
Colić, Mladenko. *Pregled operacija na jugoslovenskom ratištu*. Beograd: Vojnoistorijski institut, 1988.
Cowgill, Anthony, Brimelow, Thomas and Booker, Christopher. *The Repatriations from Austria in 1945. Cowgill Inquiry. The documentary evidence reproduced in full from British, American, German and Yugoslav sources*. London: Sinclair-Stevenson, 1990.

―――, Brimelow, Thomas and Booker. Christopher. *The Repatriations from Austria in 1945. The Report of an Inquiry*. London: Sinclair-Stevenson, 1990.

Cvetković, Dragan. "Stradanje civila Nezavisne Države Hrvatske u logoru Jasenovac," *Tokovi istorije*, no. 4, 2007, pp. 153–168.

Cvetković, Dragan. "Jasenovac u sistemu stradanja civila u NDH–kvantitativna analiza (ili, ponovo o brojevima)," in: Zdravko Antonić and Janko Velimirović (eds.) *Jasenovac. Zbornik radova Četvrte međunarodne konferencije o Jasenovcu*. Kozarska Dubica, Banja Luka: Javna ustanova Spomen-područja Donja Gradina; Uruženje Jasenovac–Donja Gradina, 2007, pp. 69–82.

Červinec, Andrea. "Intervju. Dr. Stjepan Razum, povjesničar i arhivist: Vrijeme je da srušimo velikosrpski mit o Jasenovcu. Nema dokaza za masovne ustaške zločine u Jasenovcu, ali ima za partizanske!" [interviewed by Andrea Černivec], *Hrvatski List* (Zadar), no. 411, August 9, 2012, pp. 28–35.

Damaška, Mirjan. "Po onodobnom međunarodnom pravu, neosporna je Titova odgovornost za zločine 1945." [Intervju: Jadranka Jureško-Kero], in: Zvonimir Despot, *Tito. Tajne vladara. Najnoviji prilozi za biografiju Josipa Broza*. Zagreb: *Večernji list*, 2009, pp. 467–471.

Dedijer, Vladimir. *Vatikan i Jasenovac*. Beograd: Rad, 1987.

―――. *Jasenovac. Das jugoslawische Auschwitz und der Vatikan*. Freiburg im Breisgau: Ahriman-Verl., 1987.

―――. *The Yugoslav Auschwitz and the Vatican. The Croatian Massacre of the Serbs During World War II*. Buffalo, NY: Prometheus Books, 1992.

――― and Antun Miletić. *Protiv zaborava i tabua (Jasenovac 1941–1991)*. Sarajevo: Udruženje za istraživanje genocida i ratnih zločina, 1991.

Deverić, Mišo and Ivan Fumić. *Hrvatska u logorima 1941.–1945*. Zagreb: Savez antifašističkih boraca i antifašista Republike Hrvatske, 2008.

Dežman, Jože (ed.). *Poročilo Komisije Vlade Republike Slovenije za reševanje vprašanj prikritih grobišč 2005–2008*. Ljubljana: Družina, 2008; 2009.

―――. *Hudo zlo iz hudih jam / Terrible evil from Caves of Evil*. Ljubljana: Družnina, 2009.

――― (ed.). *Prikrita grobišča. Izvješće komisije Vlade Republike Slovenije za rješavanje pitanja skrivenih grobišta 2005.–2008*. Sarajevo: Hrvatsko katoličko dobrotvorno društvo, 2010.

――― (ed.). *Resnica in sočutje. Poročilo Komisije Vlade RS za reševanje vprašanj prikritih grobišč 2009–2011. Prispevki k črni knjigi titoizma*. Ljubljana: Dužina, 2012.

Dizdar, Zdravko. "Prilog istraživanju problema Bleiburga i križnih putova (u povodu 60. obljetnice)," *Senjski zbornik*, vol. 32, 2005, pp. 117–196.

―――. "Stradanja Hrvata u II. svjetskom ratu i neposredno nakon njega," in: Vicko Kapitanović (ed.) *Crkva i društvo uz Jadran. Vrela i rezultati istraživanja*. Split: Katolički bogoslovni fakultet, Sveučilište u Splitu, 2001, pp. 129–186.

Dubajić, Simo. "Ne kajem se što sam ubio 30.000 Hrvata!" *Globus*, no. 217, February 3 1995, pp. 46–47, 49.

―――. "Kočevski rog," *Ljetopis Srpskog kulturnog društva "Prosvjeta,"* vol. 11, 2006, pp. 89–168.

―――. *Život, greh i kajanje. Ispovedna autobiografska hronika. Knjiga I. Od Kistanja do Kočevskog Roga*. Beograd: Vesti, 2006.

Đilas, Milovan. *Revolucionarni rat*. Beograd: Književne novine, 1990.

Ferenc, Mitja. *Prikrito in očem zakrito. Prikrita grobišča 60 let po koncu druge svetovne vojne*. Celje: Muzej novješe zgodovine, 2005.

———. "Tezno–najveće prikriveno grobište u Sloveniji. O istraživanju grobišta u protutenkovskom rovu u Teznom (Maribor)," *Časopis za suvremenu povijest*, vol. 44, no. 3, 2012, pp. 539–569.

———. *Huda Jama (Grave pit). Coal mine mass massacre (May, June 1945)*. Ljubljana: Znanstvena založba Filozofske fakultete, 2013.

———, and Kužatko, Želimir. *Prikrivena grobišta Hrvata u Republici Sloveniji / Prikrita grobišča Hrvatov v Republiki Sloveniji / Hidden Croatian Mass Graves in the Republic of Slovenia*. Zagreb: Počasni bleiburški vod/Burlimgame: Damir Radoš, 2007.

———, Mehmedalija Alić and Pavel Jamnik. *Huda jama. Skrito za enajstimi pregradami*. Ljubljana: Družina, 2011.

Geiger, Vladimir. "O zborniku Bleiburg i Križni put Saveza antifašističkih boraca i antifašista Republike Hrvatske, Zagreb, 2007." *Časopis za suvremenu povijest*, vol. 39, no. 3, 2007, pp. 809–827.

———. "Ljudski gubici Hrvatske u Drugom svjetskom ratu koje su prouzročili 'okupatori i njihovi pomagači'. Brojidbeni pokazatelji (procjene, izračuni, popisi)," *Časopis za suvremenu povijest*, vol. 53, no. 3, 2011, pp. 699–749.

———. "Brojidbeni pokazatelji o ljudskim gubicima Hrvatske u Drugom svjetskom ratu i poraću," in: Zorislav Lukić (ed.) *Represija i zločini komunističkog režima u Hrvatskoj*. Zagreb: Matica hrvatska, 2012, pp. 51–90.

———. "Brojidbeni pokazatelji o žrtvama logora Jasenovac, 1941.–1945. (procjene, izračuni, popisi)," *Časopis za suvremenu povijest*, vol. 55, no. 2, 2013, pp. 211–242.

———. "Numerical indicators of the victims of the Jasenovac camp, 1941–1945 (estimates, calculations, lists)," *Review of Croatian History*, vol. 9, no. 1, 2013, pp. 151–187.

———. "Sumanuti i bolesni navodi i tvrdnje Međunarodne komisije za utvrđivanje istine o Jasenovcu (The International Commission for the Truth on Jasenovac)," *Politički zatvorenik*, vol. 23, no. 253, 2013, pp. 13–17.

———. *Josip Broz Tito i ratni zločini. Bleiburg i folksdojčeri*. Zagreb: Hrvatski institut za povijest, 2013.

Genc, Mladen. "Šokantna ispovijest Zdenka Zavadlava (79), bivšeg zamjenika načelnika OZN-e za područje Maribora, o masovnim likvidacijama Hrvata 1945. u Sloveniji. Naređeno nam je da ubijamo!" *Jutarnji list ("Panorama")*, May 25, 2003, pp. 12–13.

Goldstein, Ivo. "Povijesne okolnosti Bleiburga i Križnog puta," in: Juraj Hrženjak (ed.) *Bleiburg i Križni put 1945*. Zagreb: Savez antifašističkih boraca i antifašista Republike Hrvatske, 2007, pp. 31–37.

———. "Kriteriji za selekciju i masovne likvidacije," *Jutarnji list*, November 22, 2008, pp. 81.

———. *Hrvatska 1918.–2008*. Zagreb: Novi liber, 2008.

———. *Povijest Hrvatske 1945.–2011., vol 1*. Split: EPH Media, 2011.

Goldstein, Slavko and Ivo Goldstein. *Jasenovac i Bleiburg nisu isto*. Zagreb: Novi liber, 2011.

——— and Ivo Goldstein. *Jasenovac. Tragika, mitomanija, istina*. Zagreb: Fraktura, 2016.

Grahek Ravančić, Martina. "Controversies about the Croatian victims at Bleiburg and in 'Death marches'." *Review of Croatian History*, vol. 2, no. 1, 2006, pp. 27–46.

———. "Razmišljanja o broju pogubljenih na Bleiburgu i križnom putu," *Časopis za suvremenu povijest*, vol. 40, no. 3 (2008), pp. 851–868.

———. "V kolonah po štirje skozi Slovenijo," *Prispevki za novejšo zgodovino*, vol. 48, no. 2. 2008, pp. 95–116.

———. *Bleiburg i križni put 1945. Historiografija, publicistika i memoarska literatura*. Zagreb: Hrvatski institut za povijest, 2009; 2015.

Heinsohn, Gunnar. *Lexikon der Völkermorde*. Reinbeck bei Hamburg: Rowohlt, 1999.

Horvat, Vladimir. "Tri jasenovačka logora," in: Vladimir Horvat, Igor Vukić, Stipo Pilić and Blanka Matković (eds.) *Jasenovački logori–istraživanja*. Zagreb: Društvo za istraživanje trostrukog logora Jasenovac, 2015, pp. 11–44.

———, Igor Vukić, Stipe Pilić and Blanka Matković. *Jasenovački logori–istraživanja*. Zagreb: Društvo za istraživanje trostrukog logora Jasenovac, 2015.

Hrženjak, Juraj (ed.). *Bleiburg i Križni put 1945*. Zagreb: Savez antifašističkih boraca i antifašista Republike Hrvatske, 2007.

Ivezić, Mladen. *Genocid nad Hrvatima zapovijeda Tito*. Zagreb: Samizdat, 1999.

———. *Titova umjetnost mržnje*. Zagreb: Samizdat, 2001.

———. *Jasenovac. Brojke*. Zagreb: Samizdat, 2003.

———. *Titov Jasenovac*. Zagreb: Samizdat, 2014.

Izveštaj Jugoslovenske Državne komisije za utvrđivanje zločina okupatora i njihovih pomagača Međunarodnom vojnom sudu u Nürnbergu. Beograd, 1947.

Izvješće o radu Komisije za utvrđivanje ratnih i poratnih žrtava od osnutka (11. veljače 1992.) do rujna 1999. godine. Zagreb, 1999.

Jareb, Jerome and Ivo Omrčanin. "The end of the Croatian Army at Bleiburg Austria in May 1945 according to English Military Documents," *Journal of Croatian Studies*, vol. 18–19, no (1977–1978), pp. 115–182.

Jasenovac. Concentration camp 1941–1945. List of victims of ustashas identified up to 30. X 1997., I–III. Beograd, 1997.

Jasenovac. Koncentracioni logor 1941–1945. Spisak ustaških žrtava identifikovanih do 30. X 1997., I–III. Beograd, 1997.

Jazovka, eds. Želimir Žanko i Nikola Šolić, Zagreb, 1990.

Jovanović, Aleksandar S. *Beg iz jasenovačkog pakla*. Beograd: Muzej žrtava genocida, 2014.

Jurčević, Josip. *Nastanak jasenovačkog mita. Problemi proučavanja žrtava Drugog svjetskog rata na području Hrvatske*. Zagreb: Hrvatski studiji Sveučilišta u Zagrebu, 1998.

———. *Bleiburg. Jugoslavenski poratni zločini nad Hrvatima*. Zagreb: Dokumentacijsko informacijsko središte, 2005.

———. *Prikrivena stratišta i grobišta jugoslavenskih komunističkih zločina*. Zagreb: Dokumentacijsko informacijsko središte, 2012.

Karapandžić, Borivoje M. *Kočevje. Tito's Bloodiest Crime*. Cleveland, 1965. / Cleveland, 1970.

———. *Kočevje. Titov najkrvaviji zločin*. Cleveland, 1959. /Beograd: Knjižnica Obradović, 1990.

Katalinić, Kazimir. "Hrvatske i srpske žrtve 1941.–1945.," *Republika Hrvatska*, vol. 39, no. 160, 1988, pp. 15–63.

———. "Broj bleiburških žrtava," in: Jozo Maraević (ed.) *50 godina Bleiburga*. Zagreb: Croatiaprojekt, 1995, pp. 49–61.

———. *Od poraza do pobjede. Povijest hrvatske političke emigracije 1945.–1990., Svezak I. 1945.–1959*. Zagreb: Naklada Trpimir, 2017.

Kljaković-Šantić, Josip. *Jasenovac–enigma holokausta.* Zagreb: Tkanica, 2016.
Kočović, Bogoljub. *Nauka, nacionalizam i propaganda (Između gubitaka i žrtava Drugoga svetskog rata u Jugoslaviji).* Paris: Editions du Titre, 1999.
———. *Žrtve Drugog svetskog rata u Jugoslaviji.* Sarajevo: Svjetlost, 1990/ Beograd, 2005.
Komar, Slavko. "Iz rasprave na okruglom stolu" (Slavko Komar), in: Juraj Hrženjak (ed.) *Bleiburg i Križni put 1945. Zbornik radova.* Zagreb: Savez antifašističkih boraca i antifašista Republike Hrvatske, 2007, pp. 96–97.
Kovačić, Davor. "Jasenovac – žrtve rata prema podacima Statističkog zavoda Jugoslavije, Sarajevo–Zürich, 1998., 1171 str.," *Časopis za suvremenu povijest*, vol. 32, no. 1 (2000), pp. 219–224.
Krestić, Vasilije Đ., "O genocidnosti Hrvatske politike" / "On the genocidal nature of Croatian politics," in: Vasilije Đ. Krestić and Mira Radojević *Jasenovac.* Beograd: SANU, 2017, pp. 13–48.
"Križni put." In: *Hrvatski leksikon, I. sv. A-K.* Zagreb: Naklada Leksikon d.o.o., 1996, pp. 649.
"Križni put." In: *Hrvatski opći leksikon.* Zagreb: LZMK, 1996, pp. 507.
"Križni put." In: Slovenci sumnjaju da je u tenkovskom rovu pokopana jezgra hrvatske vojske. Tezno–najveća grobnica Hrvata," *Večernji list.* Zagreb, August 10, 2007, pp. 4.
Leljak, Roman. *Huda Jama.* Radenci: Društvo Huda Jama, 2010.
———. *Huda Jama.* Radenci–Zagreb: Društvo Huda Jama, 2015.
Ljudske i materijalne žrtve Jugoslavije u ratnom naporu 1941–1945. Beograd, 1947.
Maestro, Lea. *Logor Đakovo / Djakovo Camp.* Sarajevo: Jevrejska opština Sarajevo–La Benevolencija, 2013.
Marijačić, Ivica. "Intervju. Dr. Stjepan Razum. U Jasenovcu partizani su svoje okrutne i masovne zločine podmetnuli ustašama–mi povjesničari to ćemo i dokazati!" *Hrvatski tjednik* (Zadar), no. 501, May 1, 2014, pp. 30–33.
Marušić, Milan. *Žrtve komunističkih zlodjela u Zagrebu svibanj 1945. i sljemenskim stratištima bolnica Brestovac i Gračani.* Zagreb: Hrvatsko žrtvoslovno društvo, 2001.
Mataušić, Nataša. *Jasenovac 1941.-1945. Logor smrti i radni logor.* Jasenovac: Javna ustanova Spomen područje Jasenovac; Zagreb: Jesenski i Turk, 2003.
Matković, Blanka. "Odvođenja i likvidacije ranjenih pripadnika Hrvatskih oružanih snaga (HOS) iz zagrebačkih bolnica u svibnju i lipnju 1945. kroz arhivsko gradivo Državnog arhiva u Zagrebu," *Arhivski vjesnik*, vol. 54 (2011), pp. 179–214.
Mihovilović, Đorđe. *Jasenovac 1945.–1947. Fotomonografija.* Jasenovac: Javna ustanova Spomen-područje Jasenovac, 2016.
Miletić, Antun. *Ustaška fabrika smrti 1941–1945.* Beograd: Vojnoizdavački i novinski centar, 1988.
———. *Koncentracioni logor Jasenovac 1941–1945. Dokumenta, I–III, Beograd, 1986. i 1987., IV.* Jagodina: Gambit, 2007.
———. *NDH–Koncentracioni logor Jasenovac 1941–1945.* Beograd: Dokumenta, 2010.
———. *Ubijeni u koncentracionom logoru Jasenovac 1941–1945. / The Assassinated in the Jasenovac Concentration Camp 1941–1945.* Jagodina, 2011.
Mirković, Jovan. *Objavljeni izvori i literatura o jasenovačkim logorima.* Banja Luka–Beograd: Objavljeni izvori i literatura o jasenovačkim, 2000.
Mrkoci, Vladimir and Horvat Vladimir. *Ogoljela laž logora Jasenovac.* Zagreb: Naklada E. Čić., 2008.

Nikodijević, Dušan. "Prilog utvrđivanju broja žrtava sistema logora Jasenovac 1941. godine," in: *Godišnjak za istraživanje genocide 8*. Beograd–Kragujevac: Muzej žrtava genocida, 2016, pp. 169–213.

———. "Brojevi žrtava u koncentracionom logoru Jasenovac 1942. godine prema iskazima preživelih svedoka," in: *Godišnjak za istraživanje genocide 9*. Beograd–Kragujevac: Muzej žrtava genocida, 2017, pp. 95–117.

Nikolić, Vinko. "Bleiburg," in: *Hrvatski leksikon, I. sv. A–K*. Zagreb: Naklada Leksikon d.o.o, 1996, pp. 110.

"Osim Teznog kanjon Špitalić kod Slovenskih Konjica najveća je grobnica Hrvata u Sloveniji," *Večernji list* (Zagreb), July 29, 1999, pp. 15.

Partizanska i komunistička represija i zločini u Hrvatskoj 1944.–1946. (documents). Zdravko Dizdar, Vladimir Geiger, Milan Pojić and Mate Rupić (eds.). Slavonski Brod: Hrvatski institut za povijest, 2005; 2009.

Patrnogić, Jovica. *Priručnik za međunarodno ratno pravo. Zakoni i običaji za rat na kopnu i u vazduhu*, Beograd: Vojnoizdavački zavod JNA, 1956.

Petković, Boško. *Međunarodne konvencije o ratnom pravu*. Zagreb: Sveučilišna tiskara, 1992.

Pilić, Stipo and Blanka Matković. "Poslijeratni zarobljenički logor Jasenovac prema svjedočanstvima i novim arhivskim izvorima," *Radovi Zavoda za povijesne znanosti HAZU u Zadru*, no. 56. 2014, pp. 323–408.

———. "Poslijeratni zarobljenički logor Jasenovac prema svjedočanstvima i novim arhivskim izvorima," in: Vladimir Horvat, Igor Vukić, Stipo Pilić and Blanka Matković (eds.) *Jasenovački logori–istraživanja*. Zagreb: Društvo za istraživanje trostrukog logora Jasenovac, 2015, pp. 145–235.

Popović, Jovo. *Druže Tito rat je završen 15. maja 16,00 na Dravi Kosta Nađ*. Beograd: Četvrti jul, 1985.

Portmann, Michael. "Communist Retaliation and Persecution on Yugoslav Territory during and after WWII (1943–1950)," *Tokovi istorije*, no. 1–2. 2004, pp. 42–74.

———. *Kommunistische Abrechnung mit Kriegsverbrechern, Kollaborateuren, "Volksfeinden" und "Verrätern" in Jugoslawien während des Zweiten Weltkriegs und unmittelbar danach (1943–1950)*. Wien: GRIN Publishing, 2007.

Radojević, Mira. "Jasenovac, logor smrti (1941–2016)"/ "Jasenovac, death concentration camp (1941–2016)," in: Vasilije Đ. Krestić and Mira Radojević *Jasenovac*. Beograd: SANU, 2017, pp. 49–93.

Radoš, Ivica. "Intervju. Jože Dežman, Predsjednik slovenske Komisije za rješavanje pitanja prikrivenih grobišta. U Teznom imamo bar dvije Srebrenice," *Jutarnji list*, Zagreb, September 24 2007, pp. 8–9.

———. "Provjerama potvrđena masovna grobnica nedaleko Maribora. Tezno: Istraga groba 20.000 vojnika NDH," *Jutarnji list*, Zagreb, August 10, 2007, pp. 2.

Razum, Stjepan. "Jasenovac, najveća povijesna laž koja iz dana u dan postaje sve prozirnija," Hrvatski tjednik, Zadar, br. 559, 11. VI. 2015., 18–25.

———. "Logor Jasenovac kao sredstvo trajne komunističke indoktrinacije," *Hrvatski tjednik*, Zadar, no. 581, September 12, 2015, pp. 18–20.

Škiljan, Filip. "Logorski sustav Jasenovac–kontroverze," in: *Nezavisna Država Hrvatska 1941.–1945*. Sabrina P. Ramet (ed.) *Zbornik radova*. Zagreb, 2009, pp. 117–130.

———. *Politički zatvorenici u logorima Jasenovac i Stara Gradiška*. Zagreb: Javna ustanova Spomen područje Jasenovac, 2009.

Smreka, Jelka and Đorđe Mihovilović (eds.). *Poimenični popis žrtava koncentracijskog logora Jasenovac 1941.–1945*. Jasenovac: Spomen područje Jasenovac, 2007.
Sobolevski, Mihael. "Između Jasenovca i Bleiburga," *Erasmvs*, no. 4, 1993, pp. 42–47.
———. "Prešućena istina–žrtve rata na području bivše Jugoslavije 1941.–1945. prema popisu iz 1964. godine," *Časopis za suvremenu povijest*, vol. 25, no. 2–3, 1993: 87–114.
Spisak žrtava rata 1941–1945. Ustaški logor Jasenovac. Beograd, 1992.
Šturm, Lovro (ed.). *Brez milosti. Ranjeni, invalidni in bolni povojni ujetniki na Slovenskem*. Ljubljana: Nova revija, 2000.
Tuđman, Franjo. *Bespuća povijesne zbiljnosti. Rasprava o povijesti i filozofiji zlosilja*. Zagreb: Hrvatska sveučilišna naklada, 1989.
Visočak, Meho and Sobica Bejdo. *Jasenovac. Žrtve rata prema podacima Statističkog zavoda Jugoslavije*. Zürich–Sarajevo: Bošnjački institut, 1998.
Vodušek Starič, Jerca. "Kako se čistila Jugoslavija?" *Gordogan*, vol. 21, no. 4–5/48–49, 2004, pp. 36–49.
Vuković, Tomislav. "Intervju. Roman Leljak o poslijeratnom logoru u Jasenovcu. Tito je naredio 21. kolovoza 1948. da se zatvori jasenovački logor," *Glas Koncila* (Zagreb), no. 1. 2220, January 8, 2017, pp. 6–7.
Žajdela, Ivo. *Kočevski Rog*. Maribor: Založba za alternativno teorijo, 1990.
Zavadlav, Zdenko. *Iz dnevniških zapiskov mariborskega oznovca (Izbrani listi). 1. del: Leto 1945*. Maribor: Založba za alternativno teorijo, 1990.
Zavadlav, Zdenko. *Pozna spoved. Iz dnevnika slovenskega oznovca*. Celovec: Mohorjeva, 2010.
Zločini u logoru Jasenovac. Zagreb, 1946., Jasenovac, 1977, Jasenovac, 1980, Banja Luka, 2000.
Žerjavić, Vladimir. *Gubici stanovništva Jugoslavije u Drugom svjetskom ratu*. Zagreb: Jugoslavensko viktimološko društvo, 1989.
———. *Opsesije i megalomanije oko Jasenovca i Bleiburga. Gubici stanovništva Jugoslavije u drugom svjetskom ratu*. Zagreb: Globus, 1992.
———. "Žrtve oko Bleiburga i na križnom putu," in: Jozo Marević (ed.) *U Bleiburgu iskra*. Zagreb: Vidokrug, 1993, pp. 75–89.
———. *Population losses in Yugoslavia 1941–1945*. Zagreb: Dom i svijet, Hrvatski institut za povijest, 1997.
Živanović, Srboljub. *Jasenovac. Odabrani radovi, članci, intervjui, govori i diskusije*. Beograd–London, 2008; Beograd: Pešić i sinovi, 2012; Beograd: Pešić i sinovi, 2017.
Živanović, Srboljub. *Jasenovac 2*. Beograd: Pešić i sinovi, 2017.
Žrtve rata 1941–1945. godine. Rezultati popisa. Beograd, 1966, Beograd, 1992.
www.jasenovac.org (Jasenovac Research Institute). Accessed October 27, 2017.
www.jusp-jasenovac.hr (JU Spomen područje Jasenovac). Accessed February 20, 2018.
www.objektivno1.rs/region-gradovi/cacak/3070/tribina-dveri-u-cacku-istina-o-jasenovcu.html (Tribina Dveri u Čačku: "Istina o Jasenovcu"). Accessed Februrary 15, 2016.
www.portalnovosti.com/nobilo-danasnja-hrvatska-ne-moze-biti-sljednica-kvislinske-ndh (Nobilo: Današnja Hrvatska ne može biti sljednica kvislinške NDH). Accessed October 10, 2017.
www.hkv.hr/vijesti/jugo-ostavtina/822-fumi-o-bleiburgu.html (Fumić o Bleiburgu). Accessed February 23, 2018.
sr.wikipedia.org/sr-l/Међународна_комисија_за_утврђивање_истине_о_Јасеновцу. Accessed February 20, 2018

6 Jasenovac Concentration Camp and Its Role in the Destruction of the NDH People

Calculation of the Possible Number of Victims Based on the Partially Revised 1964 Census

Dragan Cvetković

Yugoslav historiography, as well as the historiographies of the successor states, did not neglect the topic of the suffering of the civilian population in the concentration camps during World War II, which was a significant segment of the total human losses.[1] Most of the works are dedicated to the Jasenovac camp, which was the largest and most known camp in Southeast Europe, but the quantity of published works was not accompanied by quality.[2] All the works, nonetheless, influenced the creation of the notion about the camp, which often did not match the reality. Somehow, other camps in historiography remained in Jasenovac's shadow, and a much smaller number of works were dedicated to them. The suffering in the concentration camps, primarily in Jasenovac, was often written about within other topics which, to a greater or lesser extent, referred to the suffering of the population. Overall, estimates of total losses and estimates of casualties in Jasenovac and other camps have varied and changed over the years. So far the number of victims has remained an open issue that is still debated, both in professional circles and the general public.[3] The long-standing ideological notion of World War II, which unilaterally viewed everything through the context of the socialist revolution and its glorification, did not have a positive effect on determining the number of casualties. Although the victims of war, primarily those who participated in the Partisan movement, were said to be the foundation on which the state rested, and were considered a pledge for the existence and survival of the state and the system, socialist Yugoslavia never made a complete list of victims of World War II.[4] Due to the lack of approximately accurate data, space had been opened for various speculations, victim appropriations, manipulations, both scientific and political – as well as for the creation of new myths. In 1964, the state tried to conduct a census of victims on the territory of Yugoslavia. Burdened by the ideology, the implementation started for the wrong reasons, and the methodology of making the census was deficient.[5] The 1964 census of "Victims of War 1941–1945" established that 597,323 people died on the

DOI: 10.4324/9781003326632-8

territory of Yugoslavia,[6] of which 134,464 died in internment (22.51%). The Census Commission determined that there were a number of omissions in the preparation of the census, and concluded that it covered 56–59 percent of the total number of those who should have been included therein.[7] Since the list of casualties was primarily made to collect war damages from Germany,[8] and the number of war casualties was far below the expected, and hitherto valid, number of 1.7 million, it was decided to ban the use of the census. All material was handed over to the Archives of Yugoslavia for safekeeping. The ban lasted for almost thirty years, until 1992. The loss of time reduced the possibility of determining the true number of victims due to the biological disappearance of witnesses, thus significantly complicating the initiated revision of the census.[9]

In addition to the main question of how many people died in Jasenovac, a significant issue for researchers is, as the census results show, the internal structure of the victims in the camp and their relations with the total losses of civilians from the territory of the Independent State of Croatia (NDH). Although incomplete, and with all the limitations that it carries as such,[10] the list of "Victims of War 1941–1945" is, according to the data at its disposal, very indicative because it provides the possibility of analysis on a very representative sample. Experience to date with the presentation of the achieved results of the census revision shows that they were mostly wrongly (or perhaps intentionally) considered final, and as such were presented in the historiographical literature and media. Based on the results achieved in the audit of the comprehensiveness of the census, an estimate of the number of victims was made, and all analyses were made on the basis of the estimated number of victims.[11] The paper comparatively analyzes the ethnicity of the killed civilians from the territory of the Independent State of Croatia, determines the years of their suffering, determines the circumstances of their suffering with a focus on losses in concentration camps, presents the number of victims in Jasenovac concentration camp, and considers its role in destroying people on the territory in question.

In 1941, the military collapse of the Kingdom of Yugoslavia in the brief "April War" led to the disintegration of the state, which was divided into eight parts of various sizes and demographic potential, and with different legal statuses. According to the 1931 census, the territory given to the newly formed NDH included 5,559,420 inhabitants, which was 39.90 percent of the population of the former Yugoslavia.[12] The national structure of the population[13] found in the newly formed state was extremely heterogeneous, consisting of 47.58 percent Croats, 13.00 percent Muslims (treated as Croats of other faiths), 32.02 percent Serbs, 2.63 percent Germans, 1.23 percent of Hungarians, 0.66 percent of Slovenes, 0.57 percent of Jews and 2.31 percent of other and unknown nationalities,[14] which include Roma (about 0.50 percent of the population).[15] All antagonisms, all oppositions, contrasts and divisions, national, political, ideological, religious, cultural, and economic that existed

140 *Dragan Cvetković*

in the prewar society in that territory, gained their extreme dimensions in the war and, to some extent, participated in creating preconditions for mass suffering, with the undeniable influence of external factors that were permanently realized in the field.

Civil Losses in the Independent State of Croatia – Quantitative Analysis

The suffering of the civilian population was very pronounced in the extremely complex and layered total war fought on the territory of the Independent State of Croatia, in which several warring parties of different political, ideological, national, religious, and economic inclinations and aspirations took part. The killed civilians from the territory of the Independent State of Croatia (between 499,000 and 530,000) represented 73.39 percent of the total World War II losses of Yugoslav civilians.[16]

The losses suffered by civilians from the territory of the NDH were nominally 2.76 times higher than the losses in the rest of the country but, given the representation of the NDH population in the total population of Yugoslavia (39.90%), they were 4.20 times higher in real terms. Two-thirds of all civilian casualties (65.56%) of the NDH lost their lives in the first two years of the war.

Nominal suffering in 1942 was one-third higher (1.32 times) than in the first year of the war, but given the effective duration of the war in each year, the casualties were realistically 1.11 times higher. The next period of the war led to a decrease in civilian casualties, so it was 2.45 times less in 1943 than in the previous year. The death rate in the last year of the war,[17] due to the

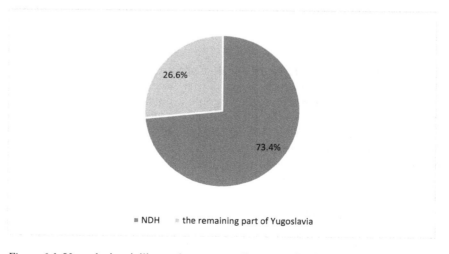

Figure 6.1 Yugoslavia, civilians – losses according to territorial affiliation.

Destruction of the NDH People 141

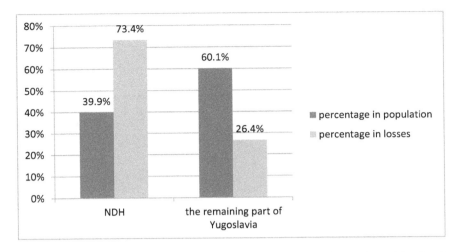

Figure 6.2 Yugoslavia, civilians – participation in the population and participation in losses according to territorial affiliation.

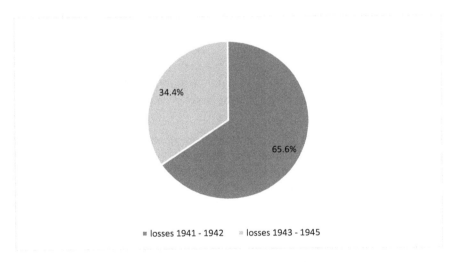

Figure 6.3 NDH, civilians – the dynamic of suffering.

fighting for the liberation of these areas and increased terror of the NDH regime, was 1.29 times higher than in 1944. The implementation of genocide and the Holocaust as its most extreme form, over a part of the population, by the Ustaša regime and the German occupiers, and the mass commission of war crimes by most warring parties, led to disproportionate suffering of civilians of different nationalities.

142 *Dragan Cvetković*

Table 6.1 NDH, civilians – the dynamic of losses over years

NDH, civilians	Total	Losses in Jasenovac	%	At other locations	%
Total	499.000–530.000	122.279–130.120	24.53	376.721–399.880	75.47

Calculation based on database "Žrtve rata 1941–1945"

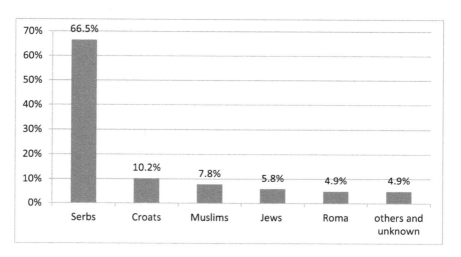

Figure 6.4 NDH, civilians – percentage in the loss of civilians according to nationality.

Among the killed NDH civilians there were 66.48 percent Serbs (331,735 to 352,344), 10.20 percent Croats (50,898 to 54,060), 7.77 percent Muslims (38,772 to 41,181), 5.83 percent Jews (29,092 to 30,899), 4.86 percent of Roma (24,251 to 25,758), 1.26 percent of other nationalities (6,287 to 6,678), and 3.60 percent of unidentified nationalities (17,964 to 19,080).[18] The losses suffered by different nationalities were not in line with their representation in the NDH population.

Declared an undesirable element in the newly formed state, exposed to pogrom since the first day of the war, Serbs accounted for two-thirds of the civilian population's losses, which was twice as much (2.07 times) as their representation in the NDH population. Based on racial laws, with the intention of completely destroying them, Jews and Roma were the biggest victims of the war and their losses were 10.23 and 9.72 times higher than the representation in the population. On the other hand, the civilian losses of the Croat and Muslim people were 4.66 and 1.67 times less, respectively, than the participation of these national groups in the NDH population. Considering the representation in the population, the losses of the Serb civilian population

Table 6.2 NDH, civilians – percentage in the population and percentage in the loss of civilians according to nationality

NDH, civilians Nationality	percentage in the NDH population	percentage among civilian victims
Croats	47.58	10.2
Serbs	32.02	66.48
Muslims	13	7.77
Jews	0.57	5.83
Roma	0.5	4.86
Others/Unidentified	6.33	4.86

Source: 1931 Census, AMŽG, "Žrtve rata 1941–1945" database

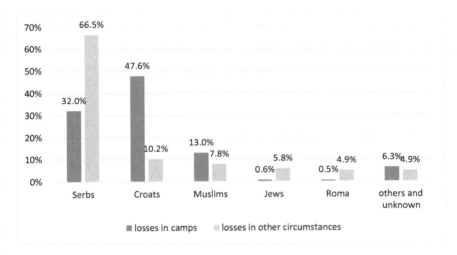

Figure 6.5 NDH – national structure of population and the civilian losses according to nationality.

in the Independent State of Croatia were 9.64 times more numerous than the Croats, and 3.48 times more than the Muslim civilian losses, while the losses of Muslim civilians were 2.79 times higher than the Croats. The losses of Jews and Roma, who were decimated in the Holocaust, were realistically many times greater than the losses of all other nationalities.[19] Therefore, the dynamics of losses suffered, as well as the participation in the civilian casualties was not equal among all nationalities in the NDH during the war.

The terror against the Serb population began immediately after the establishment of the Independent State of Croatia and was carried out with undiminished dynamics of killings in the first two years of the war.[20] As a result, more than two-thirds (68.45%) of the killed Serb population, lost their lives in that period. Until the last year of the war, Serbs accounted

Table 6.3 NDH, civilians – national structure of losses according to the year of losses

NDH–Civilians	Total	1941	%	1942	%	1943	%	1944	%	1945	%
Serbs	331.735–352.344	99.056–105.210	29.86	128.016–135.969	38.59	55.002–58.419	16,58	37.453–39.780	11.29	12.208–12.966	3.68
%	66,48	74,96	//	65,65	//	69,14	//	60,18	//	40,57	//
Croats	50.898–54.060	3.288–3.492	6.46	8.877–9.428	17,44	11.248–11.947	22,1	16.791–17.834	32.99	10.689–11.353	21
%	10,2	2,49	//	4,55	//	14,15	//	26,99	//	35.52	//
Muslims	38.772–41.181	10.042–10.666	25.9	12.581–13.363	32,45	9.158–9.727	23,62	4.474–4.752	11.54	2.512–2.668	6.48
%	7,77	7,6	//	6,45	//	11,52	//	7,19	//	8.35	//
Jews	29.092–30.899	8.460–8.985	29.08	16.102–17.102	55,35	1.303–1.384	4,48	707–751	2.43	2.519–2.676	8.66
%	5,83	6,4	//	8,25	//	1,63	//	1,14	//	8.37	//
Roma	24.251–25.758	2.830–3.006	11.67	18.889–20.063	77,89	427–453	1,76	2.003–2.128	8.26	102–108	0.42
%	4,86	2,14	//	9,68	//	0,54	//	3,22	//	0.34	//
Others and unknown	24.251–25.758	8.459–8.984	34.88	10.547–11.202	43,49	2.398–2.547	9,89	790–840	3.26	2.056–2.185	8.48
%	4,86	6,4	//	5,41	//	3,01	//	1,27	//	6.84	//
Total	499.000–530.000	132.135–140.344	26.48	195.009–207.124	39.08	79.541–84.482	15.94	62.225–66.091	12.47	30.090–31.959	6.03

Calculation based on data base "Žrtve rata 1941–1945"

Destruction of the NDH People 145

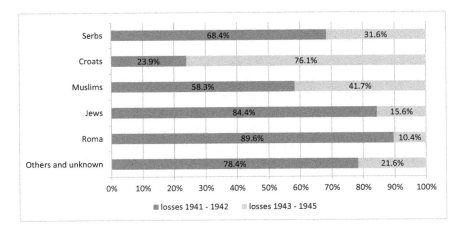

Figure 6.6 NDH, civilians – the dynamic of losses over years.

for the absolute majority of losses, making up more than three quarters in the first and two thirds in the second year of the war. In the last year of the war, they represented the largest group of civilians killed with two-fifths of losses. Excluded from society by racial laws, affected by the Holocaust, Jews and Roma were mostly killed in the first two years of the war (85.04% and 89.56%, respectively). The first two years of the war were the most devastating for Muslims as well. They suffered 58.35 percent of civilian casualties in that period. Their largest share in civilian casualties was in 1943, when it was almost as high as their national representation in the NDH population. The Croatian population had a steady increase in civilian casualties during the war, with half (53.99%) losing their lives in the last two years of the war and with the death rate in the last year of the war being 1.70 times higher than the previous year. During the last two years of the war, Croats accounted for a quarter and a third of civilian casualties. Serbs accounted for most of the civilian casualties throughout the war with a share that was permanently above their representation in the population – 2.39 times at the beginning, and 1.39 times at the end. In 1942, Jews and Roma were also represented in losses many times above their share of the population throughout the war, a maximum of 14.47 and 19.36 times, respectively. Participation in the losses of Muslim and Croat civilians throughout the war was constantly less than their participation in the NDH population. Considering the representation in the population of the Independent State of Croatia, the losses of Serbs at the beginning and end of the war were 44.55 and 1.69 times higher in real terms than the loss of Croat civilians, and 4.01 and 1.97 times higher than the losses of Muslim civilians, so in relation to the loss of Croats, the loss of Muslims was, in real terms, 11.17 times higher in 1941, and 1.16 times lower in 1945.

Circumstances of the Suffering of Civilians of the Independent State of Croatia – the Role of Concentration Camps in Their Destruction

In the war fought on the territory of the Independent State of Croatia, civilians lost their lives in various circumstances,[21] among which the casualties in the concentration camps accounted for more than a third of their total losses, and represented the second group in number, behind the victims of direct terror. The percentage of camp victims in total casualties differs among nationalities. Same is the case for victims who died under different circumstances. The loss of life in the camps was predominant among Jews and Roma, while the majority of Serb, Croat, and Muslim victims lost their lives in mass or individual crimes throughout the NDH; mostly in the places where they lived or in their immediate vicinity.

The loss of life in the concentration camp was a circumstance of suffering that included almost all the killed Jews and Roma, a third of the killed Serbs, a quarter of Croats, a twentieth of the loss of Muslims, and half of members of other and unidentified nationalities. The share of victims in the camps among Jews and Roma was 2.99 and 2.94 times higher than the share of Serbs killed in these circumstances, 3.82 or 3.77 times higher than among Croats and 20.04 and 19.75 times higher than among killed Muslims, while the share of Serb casualties in the concentration camp was 1.28 times higher than the share of Croats, and 6.71 times higher than the share of Muslims. The share of Croats killed in these circumstances was 5.24 times higher than the share of Muslims.

Table 6.4 Circumstances of suffering according to nationality

NDH, civilians - the circumstances of suffering	Total	Losses in camps	%	in other circumstances	%
Serbs	331.735–352.344	105.338–111.881	31.75	226.397–240.463	68.25
%	66.48	57,93	//	71.38	//
Croats	50.898–54.060	12.619–13.403	24,79	38.279–40.657	75,21
%	10.2	6.94	//	12.07	//
Muslims	38.772–41.181	1.836–1.950	4,73	36.936–39.231	95,27
%	7.77	1.01	//	11.64	//
Jews	29.092–30.899	27.584–29.298	94.82	1.508–1.601	5.18
%	5.83	15.17	//	0.47	//
Roma	24.251–25.758	22.657–24.064	93.43	1.594–1.694	6.57
%	4.86	12.46	//	0.5	//
Others/unknown	24.251–25.758	11.783–12.515	48.59	12.468–13.243	51.41
%	4.86	6.48	//	3.93	//
Total	499.000–530.000	181.836–193.132	36.44	317.164–336.868	63.56

Calculation based on the database "Žrtve rata 1941–1945"

Destruction of the NDH People 147

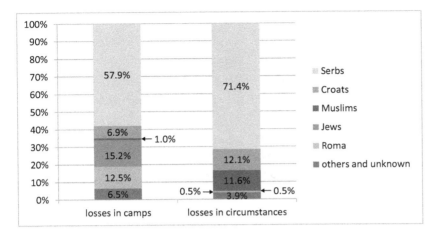

Figure 6.7 NDH, civilians – national structure according to circumstances of death.

Among the losses in the camps, Serbs accounted for the largest share of casualties, with almost three-fifths of the total losses. Their participation among the camp victims was 1.23 times lower than the share of Serbs among NDH civilians who died in other circumstances. In the second group, Serbs accounted for three-quarters of all losses. Having suffered mainly in the camps, Jews and Roma accounted for one-sixth and one-eighth of the total losses in the camps, respectively, while their participation in the number of casualties who died in other circumstances was negligible (it was 32.28 and 24.92 times lower in comparison to the camp victims). The representation of Croats and Muslims among the victims who died in other circumstances was 1.74, meaning 11.52 times higher than the share of Croats and Muslims who died in the camps.

Role of Jasenovac in Destruction of Civilians from NDH and Its Position among Other Concentration Camps

Jasenovac camp, or the camp system, was the largest concentration camp in Southeast Europe and, in terms of losses, certainly the largest camp in Europe not organized by Nazi Germany. From its founding at the end of August 1941 until the close of the war, Jasenovac was the primary place for the killing of civilians in the Independent State of Croatia. A quarter of all NDH civilians were killed in it.

One third of the killed civilians from the Independent State of Croatia lost their lives in one of the concentration camps inside or outside the Independent State of Croatia. Among all these camps, according to the number of killed civilians, Jasenovac took the leading place.

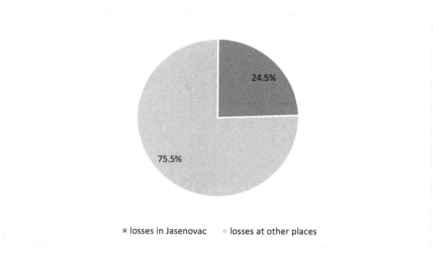

Figure 6.8 NDH, civilians – the participation of Jasenovac in total losses.

Table 6.5 NDH, civilians – the participation of Jasenovac in total losses

NDH, civilians	Total	Losses in Jasenovac	%	At other locations	%
Total	499.000–530.000	122.279–130.120	24.53	376.721–399.880	75.47

Calculation based on the database "Žrtve rata 1941–1945"

Jasenovac accounts for two-thirds of all NDH civilians killed in the camps, taking into account all the camps – whether organized by the NDH or not, whether on the territory of the NDH or outside. The extent of the crime committed in the Jasenovac camp clearly defined it as an extermination camp.

The Jasenovac camp existed almost throughout the war, but its participation in the destruction of civilians from the territory of the Independent State of Croatia was not constant, just as the dynamics of losses suffered inside and outside the camp were not equal.

The role of Jasenovac in the destruction of NDH civilians was constantly changing during the war. During the four months of the camp's existence in the first year of the war, one-eighth of all civilians killed that year lost their lives there.[22] Already in 1942, the participation of the Jasenovac camp in the destruction of civilians reached its peak, increasing its participation in their destruction 3.50 times compared to the previous year, thus reaching two-fifths of the total losses. Jasenovac had the smallest share in the destruction of civilians in the central year of the war, 1943, when one-twelfth of all civilian losses that year was killed there, which was five times less than in the

Destruction of the NDH People 149

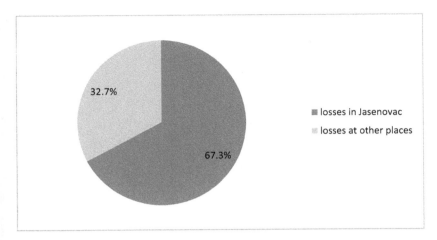

Figure 6.9 NDH, civilians – the participation of Jasenovac in total losses.

Table 6.6 NDH, civilians – the participation of Jasenovac in losses suffered at concentration camps

NDH–Civilians	Losses at camps	Losses in Jasenovac	%	Other and unknown camps	%
Total	181.836–193.132	122.279–130.120	67.31	59.557–63.012	32.69

Calculation based on the database "Žrtve rata 1941–1945"

previous year. In the last two years of the war, Jasenovac's participation in the destruction of civilians increased to one-sixth, actually one-fifth of the losses suffered, respectively, which was 2.06 and 2.25 times higher than in the middle of the war, but it was still 2.43 or 2.22 times less than the share in 1942.

The first two years of the war were the most 'productive' period of the camp's existence. During that period, four-fifths of all camp victims were killed in Jasenovac (80.89%). In the second year of the war, the nominal loss was 5.16 times higher than in 1941, but the death rate in 1942, given the periods of camps' existence in those years, was realistically 1.72 times higher. The casualties in the camp in the central year of the war were 12.28 times less than in the previous one; the suffering in the last years of the war increased 1.63 times in 1944, while the mortality rate in the last year of the war was 1.41 times higher than in the previous one.[23] The share in the losses of the victims in 1941 at Jasenovac, considering the periods of suffering in the first year of the war, was equal to the losses outside of the camp. During the culmination of civilian casualties in 1942, both inside and outside the camp, the share of casualties in Jasenovac was 2.28 times higher than the share of casualties

Table 6.7 NDH, civilians – the role of Jasenovac in the destruction of civilians according to the year of suffering

NDH, civilians	Total	1941	%	1942	%	1943	%	1944	%	1945	%
Losses at Jasenovac	122.279–130.120	16.043–17.072	13.12	82.868–88.182	67.77	6.750–7.183	5.52	10.895–11.594	8.91	5.723–6.090	4.68
%	24.53	12.16	//	42.54	//	8.5	//	17.52	//	19.14	//
In other places	376.721–399.880	116.092–123.272	30.82	112.141–118.942	29.75	72.791–77.299	19.33	51.330–54.497	13.63	24.367–25.869	6.47
%	75.47	87.84	//	57.46	//	91.5	//	82.47	//	80.96	//
Total	499.000–530.000	132.135–140.344	26.48	195.009–207.124	39.08	79.541–84.482	15.94	62.225–66.091	12.47	30.090–31.959	6.03

Calculation based on the database "Žrtve rata 1941–1945"

Destruction of the NDH People 151

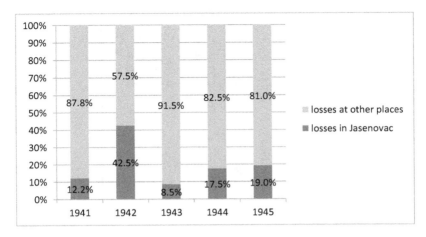

Figure 6.10 NDH, civilians – the participation of Jasenovac in total losses according to the year of suffering.

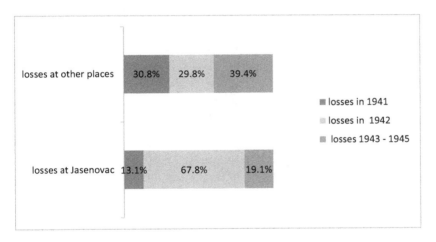

Figure 6.11 NDH, civilians – the dynamics of losses in Jasenovac and according to the year of suffering.

outside the camp. In the last three years of the war, the share of casualties at Jasenovac (19.11%) was 2.06 times lower than the share of losses outside the camp (39.43%). NDH civilians who lost their lives in one of the concentration camps, whether they were founded by the NDH or not, and whether they were on its territory or not, died throughout the war, with the largest loss of four-fifths (78.31%) of total victims in the first two years of the war.

The role of Jasenovac in the destruction of the part of the NDH population who lost their lives in one of the concentration camps varied during the

152 *Dragan Cvetković*

Table 6.8 NDH, civilians – the role of Jasenovac in the destruction of civilians in concentration camps according to the year of death

NDH civilians–camps	Total	1941	%	1942	%	1943	%	1944	%	1945	%
Jasenovac	122.279–130.120	16.043–17.072	13.12	82.868–88.182	67.77	6.750–7.183	5.52	10.895–11.594	8.91	5.723–6.090	4.68
%	67.31	42.64	//	79.2	//	52.18	//	75.25	//	47.73	//
Others and unknown	59.557–63.012	21.615–22.926	36.34	21.869–23.062	36.66	6.197–6.568	10.41	3.597–3.799	6.04	6.278–6.657	10.55
%	32.69	57.36	//	20.8	//	47.81	//	24.75	//	52.26	//
Total	181.836–193.132	37.658–39.998	20.71	104.737–111.244	57.6	12.947–13.751	7.12	14.492–15.393	7.97	12.001–12.747	6.6

Calculation based on the database "Victims of War 1941–1945"

Destruction of the NDH People 153

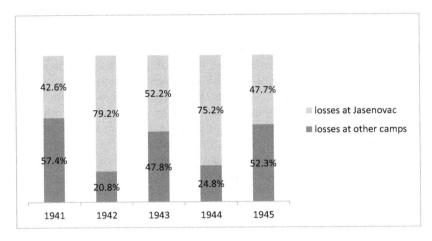

Figure 6.12 NDH, civilians – the participation of Jasenovac in the losses suffered at concentration camps.

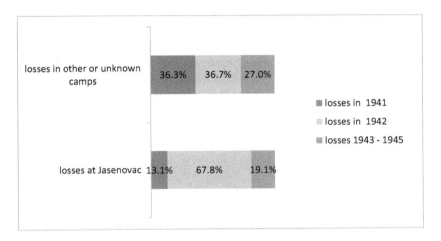

Figure 6.13 NDH, civilians – the dynamics of losses in camps.

war, but the differences existed both in its participation in the losses, and in the dynamics of suffering.

The smallest share in the losses of the victims under these circumstances was in the first year of the war, when the victims from Jasenovac accounted for two-fifths of the losses.[24] Already In the following year, the representation in losses doubled (1.86 times higher), reaching its maximum of four-fifths of the losses killed in the camps. In the next three years of the war, in which the total suffering in the camps was less, the role of Jasenovac varied between half and three quarters of the losses.[25]

In the mass camp deaths during the first two years of the war, the share of casualties in Jasenovac (80.89%) was 1.11 times higher than in other and unknown concentration camps (73.00%). In the last three years of the war, the number of casualties at Jasenovac was 1.41 times smaller than the number of casualties in other known and unknown camps. Within the period of the greatest suffering, the share of casualties in other known and unknown camps in 1941 was 2.77 times higher than at Jasenovac, while in the following year the share of casualties at Jasenovac was 1.85 times higher than in other camps. The last year of the war brought increased casualties in all camps, with the death rate in Jasenovac being 1.41 times higher than in the previous year, while in other known and unknown camps it was 4.66 times higher, which was 3.30 times more than at Jasenovac.

National Structure of the Victims of the Jasenovac Concentration Camp

The clearly defined intention of the Ustaša movement to eliminate individual nations from the population of the Independent State of Croatia, in part or in whole, determined the national structure of the losses of the concentration camp in Jasenovac. Three-fifths of the total losses at Jasenovac were represented by Serbs, one-sixth by Roma, one-seventh by Jews, and one-twentieth by Croats, with a minor share in the losses of Muslims and members of other and unknown nationalities. Nominally, the loss suffered by Serbs in the camp was 4.30 and 4.07 times greater than the loss of Jews and Roma, and 12.83 and 56.74 times greater than the loss of Croats and Muslims. The loss of Jews and Roma was 2.98 and 3.15 times greater than the loss of Croats, and 13.21 and 13.96 times greater than the loss of Muslims, while the loss suffered by Croats was 4.42 times greater than the loss of Muslims.

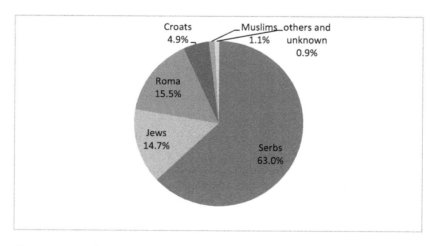

Figure 6.14 National structure of victims in Jasenovac camps.

Table 6.9 Camp Jasenovac – national structure of losses

NDH–Jasenovac	Total	Serbs	%	Jews	%	Roma	%	Croats	%	Muslims	%	Others and unknown	%
Total	122.279–130.120	77.011–81.950	62.98	17.926–19.076	14.66	18.916–20.129	15.47	6.004–6.389	4.91	1.357–1.444	1.11	1.064–1.132	0.87

Calculation based on the database "Victims of War 1941–1945"

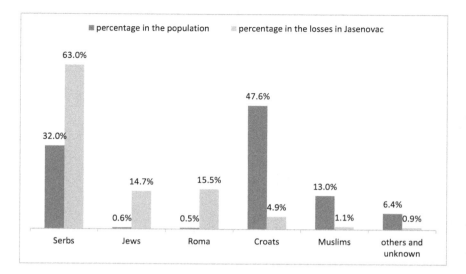

Figure 6.15 NDH, civilians – percentage in the population and percentage in the losses in the Jasenovac camp.

The pre-determined intention to destroy certain peoples in the NDH completely or in a significant part was most noticeable in the example of the Jasenovac camp. Such an aspiration led to the fact that the national structure of the victims in Jasenovac was not in line with the representation of nationalities in the population, and their real losses were not equal.

Jews and Roma were the largest victims of the camp in terms of their participation in the population of 0.57 and 0.50 percent, respectively. Therefore, the participation of Jews among the victims in the camp was 25.72 times higher than their participation in the NDH population, and the participation of the Roma was 30.94 times higher than their share in the overall population. Also, the representation of Serbs in the losses of the camp was twice as high (1.97 times) as their share in the population of the Independent State of Croatia (32.02%). On the other hand, the participation of Croats and Muslims among the victims in the Jasenovac camp was 9.69 and 11.71 times less than their representation in the population (47.58 and 13.00%, respectively). Thus, the loss suffered by Jews and Roma[26] was actually 13.09 and 15.73 times greater than the loss of Serbs, 248.75 and 299.75 times greater than the loss of Croats, and 301.96 and 392.96 times greater than the loss of Muslims. As the most numerous among the victims in the camp, Serbs suffered losses that were numerically 18.99 and 23.06 times higher than the losses of Croats and Muslims, while the loss of Croats was 1.21 times higher than the loss of Muslims.

Table 6.10 NDH, civilians – the role of Jasenovac in the destruction of civilians according to ethnicity

NDH, civilians	Total	Victims at Jasenovac	%	At other places	%
Serbs	331.735–352.344	77.011–81.950	23.24	254.724–270.394	76.75
%	66.48	62.98	//	67.62	//
Croats	50.898–54.060	6004–6.389	11.81	44.894–47.671	88.19
%	10.2	4.91	//	11.92	//
Muslims	38.772–41.181	1.357–1.444	3.5	37.415–39.737	96.5
%	7.77	1.11	//	9.93	//
Jews	29.092–30.899	17.926–19.076	61.68	11.166–11.823	38.32
%	5.83	14.66	//	2.96	//
Roma	24.251–25.758	18.916–20.129	78.08	5.335–5.629	21.92
%	4.86	15.47	//	1.42	//
Others/unknown	24.251–25.758	1.064–1.132	4.39	23.187–24.626	95.61
%	4.86	0.87	//	6.15	//
Total	499.000–530.000	122.279–130.120	24.53	376.721–399.880	75.47

Calculation based on the database "Victims of War 1941–1945"

During the 44 months' existence of the Jasenovac camp, a quarter of the killed NDH civilians lost their lives in it, and the losses were suffered by members of all nationalities from that territory. The role of the camp in the destruction of individual nationalities was not equal, and there were differences in the share of casualties in the camp in the total losses of individual nationalities as well as differences in the terms of participation of individual nationalities in the losses in the camp to the total losses of civilians of the same nationality, and also differences in comparison to the losses suffered in other places.

For Jews and Roma who were determined for annihilation by racial laws, Jasenovac was a central place of suffering. Four-fifths of the Roma victims and three-fifths of the Jewish victims of the Independent State of Croatia lost their lives there. The mass terror carried out against the Serbian people in the Independent State of Croatia had all the characteristics of the crime of genocide, whether it was carried out institutionally in camps and prisons or was a matter of either mass or individual crimes. Jasenovac had a prominent place in the implementation of these crimes, considering that a quarter of all Serb civilian victims from the Independent State of Croatia

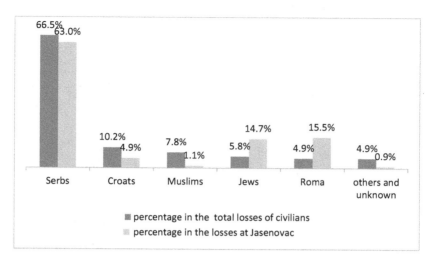

Figure 6.16 NDH, civilians – national structure of total casualties and casualties at Jasenovac camp.

lost their lives in it, which made it the primary place of their suffering. One-eighth of the killed civilians of Croatian nationality – the thirtieth part of the civilians of Muslim nationality, and the twenty-third part of the killed members of other and unknown nationalities – lost their lives in Jasenovac. The share of Jews and Roma victims in Jasenovac in the total losses of these nationalities was 2.65 and 3.36 times higher than the share of Serbs, 5.22 and 6.61 times higher than the share of Croats and 17.62 and 22.31 times higher than the share of Muslims. The share of Serbs killed in Jasenovac was 1.97 and 6.64 times higher than the share of losses of Croats and Muslims, while the share of Croats was 3.37 times higher than the share of killed Muslims.

The representation of certain nationalities in the losses at the Jasenovac camp was not always in line with the share in the total losses, as well as with the representation in the losses at other places. The smallest differences existed among Serbs as the nation most numerous in losses, with a share of two-thirds, both in the total number of civilians killed as well as the number of civilians killed outside Jasenovac. Their share among the victims at Jasenovac (of three-fifths of losses) was slightly lower (1.05 or 1.07 times) than the previous number. Among other nationalities, two groups stand out. The first consists of Jews and Roma, whose shares in losses in Jasenovac were 2.51 and 3.18 times higher than their share in total losses, and 4.95 and 10.89 times higher than the share in losses elsewhere. The second group consists of other nationalities: Croats whose representation in the Jasenovac victims was 2.08 times lower than in the total loss of civilians, or 2.43 times less than among

Destruction of the NDH People 159

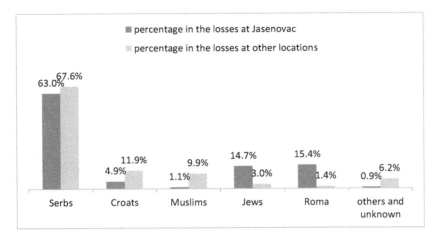

Figure 6.17 NDH, civilians – national structure according to the location of suffering.

civilians killed elsewhere; Muslims with 7.00 and 8.94 times lower participation and members of other and unknown nationalities among which the participation in the victims at Jasenovac was 5.58 times less than in the total losses of civilians and 7.07 times less than in the suffering outside Jasenovac.

During the war members of all nations from the territory of the NDH lost their lives in concentration camps founded by the NDH, Nazi Germany and, to a lesser extent, fascist Italy and the Jasenovac camp took leading places in their destruction.[27] During the existence of the Jasenovac camp, two-thirds of the NDH civilians killed in one of the concentration camps lost their lives in it, whether they were founded by the NDH or not, and whether they were on its territory or not. The role of camps in the destruction of individual nationalities was not equal, and there were differences, both in the share of victims at Jasenovac in the losses of individual nationalities in concentration camps and in the ratio of participation of individual nationalities in losses at Jasenovac to losses of civilians killed in the camps overall, and also in relation to losses suffered in other known or unknown camps.

For most of the NDH peoples who lost their lives in concentration camps, Jasenovac was the primary place of suffering. Four-fifths of all Roma[28] killed in the camps, three-quarters of Serbs and Muslims, two-thirds of Jews, just under half of the Croats, and a ninth of the members of other known and unknown nationalities,[29] ended their lives there. The share of Roma victims in Jasenovac in the losses of this nationality suffered in one of the concentration camps was 1.13 times higher than the share of Serbs and Muslims, 1.28 times higher than the share of Jews, and 1.75 times higher than the share of Croats. The share of Serbs and Muslims killed in Jasenovac was 1.12 and 1.14 times higher than the share of Jews and 1.54 and 1.55 times higher than the share

Table 6.11 NDH, civilians – the role of Jasenovac in the destruction of civilians in concentration camps according to ethnicity

NDH–Civilians	Losses at camps	Losses at Jasenovac	%	Other and unknown camps	%
Serbs	105.338–111.881	77.011–81.950	73.18	28.327–29.931	26.82
%	57.93	62.98	//	47.56	//
Jews	27.584–29.298	17.926–19.076	65.05	9.658–10.222	34.95
%	15.17	14.66	//	16.22	//
Roma	22.657–24.064	18.916–20.129	83.57	3.741–3.935	16.43
%	12.46	15.47	//	6.28	//
Croats	12.619–13.403	6004–6.389	47.62	6.615–7.014	52.37
%	6.94	4.91	//	11.11	//
Muslims	1.836–1.950	1.357–1.444	73.98	479–493	26.02
%	1.01	1.11	//	0.8	//
Others/unknown	11.783–12.515	1.064–1.132	9.04	10.719–11.383	90.96
%	6.48	0.87	//	18	//
Total	181.836–193.132	122.279-130.120	67.31	59.557–63.012	32.69

Calculation based on the database "Victims of War 1941–1945"

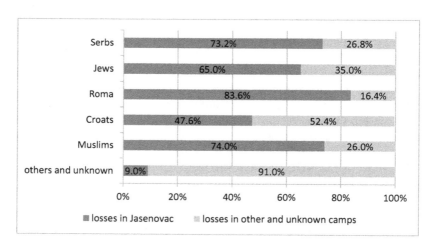

Figure 6.18 NDH, civilians – the participation of Jasenovac in the losses suffered at concentration camps according to nationality.

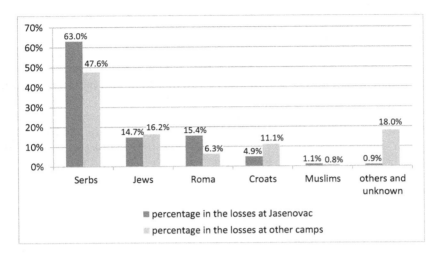

Figure 6.19 NDH, civilians – participation in the losses at concentration camps according to nationality.

of Croats, while the share of losses of Jews killed was 1.37 times higher than the share of Croats.

The participation of certain nationalities in the suffering at the Jasenovac camp was not always in line with their representation in the total losses in the concentration camps, nor with the participation in the losses suffered in other known and unknown concentration camps. According to the shares in the losses, two groups stand out. The first consisted of Serbs, Roma and Muslims, whose share in the losses in Jasenovac was 1.09 and 1.24 and 1.10 times higher, respectively, than the representation in the total losses in the concentration camps overall. It was also 1.32, 2.46, and 1.39, respectively, times greater than the share of losses in other known and unknown camps. The second group consisted of Jews, whose representation in Jasenovac victims was slightly lower (1.03 times) than in the total loss of civilians in concentration camps overall, or 1.11 times lower than in civilians killed in other and unknown camps, Croats with 1.41, that is, 2.26 times lower participation and members of other known and unknown nationalities – the share of their victims in Jasenovac was 7.45 times less than losses in concentration camps overall and 20.69 times less than in the suffering in other known and unknown camps.

Different Role of Jasenovac in the Destruction of Certain Nationalities during the War, in the Concentration Camp Itself and in the Total Losses

Different reasons why members of certain nations were imprisoned in the Jasenovac camp also caused different periods of their deaths. Differences in the losses suffered existed in the time span in which they lost their lives in the camp, as well as in the representation of certain nationalities in the losses during the years of the camp's existence.

The dynamics of suffering at Jasenovac was not the same for all nationalities. The first two years of the war (i.e., the first 16 months of the camp's existence) were disastrous for almost all Roma, Jews, and members of other known and unknown nationalities, who died in it (92.88% and 88.23% and 86.24%, respectively), as well as for four-fifths of the Serbs who died in Jasenovac concentration camp (79.97%). On the other hand, half of Croats (48.59%) and Muslims (53.32%) lost their lives in the last two years of the war. The share of losses of Roma, Jews and Serbs killed in the first two years of the war was 2.17 and 2.06 and 1.87 times higher, respectively, than the share of Croats killed in the same period, and 2.76 and 2.62 and 2.38 times higher, respectively than the share in the losses of the Muslims. On the other hand, the shares in the losses of Croats and Muslims killed in the last two years of the camp's existence were 3.50 and 3.84 times higher than the share of Serbs, 7.13 and 7.83 times higher than the share of Jews, and 9.27 and 10.17, respectively, times higher than the share of Roma victims in the same period. The Ustaša regime's tendency to deal with undesirable elements within the "state-building" people caused that, in the small loss of Croats and Muslims at the beginning of the camp's existence, the casualties in the first year were 1.43 and 1.46 times higher in real terms than in 1942. For those peoples that the NDH determined to be destroyed, the second year of the camp's existence was the most disastrous. The loss suffered in 1942 was 2.68 times higher in real terms than in the previous year, that is, 2.96 times higher among the killed Serbs and Roma, and 1.41 times higher among the Jews. The death rate of Croats in the last year of the war at Jasenovac, given the period of the camp's existence, was 4.59 times higher than in the previous year. The loss among Jews was 4.48 times higher. It was also 2.53 times higher among Muslims. Among Serbs, it was equal, while among Roma it was 6.60 times smaller.

Throughout the war, Serbs were the most numerous victims of the camp, with a share of losses that never fell below half of the casualties, with the highest representation of three quarters in 1944, which was 1.32 and 1.13 times higher than in the first two years of war and 1.45 times greater than in the last year of the war. Their share of losses in the camp was permanently above their representation in the population, 1.70 times in the first year, 1.99 times in 1942, 2.25 times in 1944, and 1.55 times in the last year of the war. Jews accounted for a quarter of the losses in the first year of the war, and a seventh for the following year, which was 41.53 and 25.44 times more represented in the losses than their share of the population. Their share in the losses in the first year of the camp's existence was 5.21 times higher than in the penultimate year of the war. With the share of one-seventh and one-fifth of all losses in the first two years of the Jasenovac camp, the share of Roma casualties was 28.56 or 36.84 times higher than their representation in the NDH population. Their

Table 6.12 Jasenovac camp – national structure according to the year of suffering

Jasenovac	Total	1941	%	1942	6.4 pt%	1943	%	1944	%	1945	%
Serbs	77.011–81.950	8.763–9.326	11.38	52.822–56.209	68.59	4.728–5.032	6.14	7.855–8.359	10.2	2.842–3.024	3.69
%	62.98	54.62	//	63.75	//	70.06	//	72.1	//	49.66	//
Jews	17.926–19.076	3.798–4.042	21.19	12.017–12.788	67.04	889–946	4.96	495–526	2.76	726–773	4.05
%	14.66	23.67	//	14.5	//	13.18	//	4.54	//	12.68	//
Roma	18.916–20.129	2.291–2.438	12.11	15.278–16.258	80.77	357–380	1.89	950–1.010	5.02	42–44	0.22
%	15.47	14.28	//	18.42	//	5.31	//	8.72	//	0.73	//
Croats	6004–6.389	828–882	13.8	1.739–1.850	28.96	519–553	8.65	1.160–1.235	19.33	1.757–1.869	29.26
%	4.91	5.16	//	2.1	//	7.7	//	10.65	//	30.71	//
Muslims	1.357–1.444	149–159	11	307–326	22.61	177–187	13.07	394–420	29.07	329–350	24.25
%	1.11	0.93	//	0.37	//	2.6	//	3.62	//	5.75	//
others and unknown	1.064–1.132	213–226	20	704–750	66.24	78–83	7.31	41–44	3.89	27–29	2.55
%	0.87	1.32	//	0.85	//	1.15	//	0.38	//	0.47	//
Total	122.279–130.120	16.043–17.072	13.12	82.868–88.182	67.77	6.750–7.183	5.52	10.895–11.594	8.91	5.723–6.090	4.68

Calculation based on the database "Victims of War 1941–1945"

164 *Dragan Cvetković*

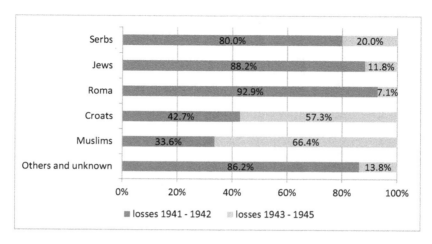

Figure 6.20 NDH, Jasenovac – the dynamic of losses according to nationality.

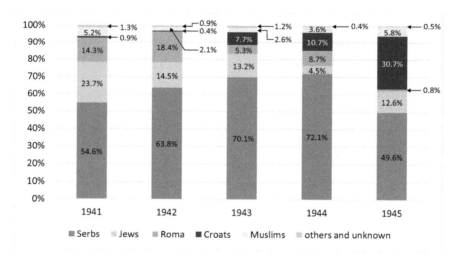

Figure 6.21 NDH, Jasenovac – national structure according to the year of suffering.

share in losses in the last year of the war was 25.23 times less than in 1942, but still above their representation in the population (1,46 times). Croats and Muslims killed in the camp had a permanent increase in their share of losses since the second year of the war, but their participation never reached their representation in the NDH population. From the minor share in losses in the first years of the camp's existence, which in 1942 was 22.66 or 35.13 times less than their representation in the population, the representation of Croats and

Muslims in losses in the last year of the war reached one-third, and that is the seventeenth part of all casualties (1.55 or 2.26 times less than the share in the population). That nevertheless was an increase of 14.62 and 15.54 times in losses, compared to the second year of the camp.

The role of the Jasenovac camp in the suffering of certain nationalities was not equal during the war. There were differences both in the participation of the camps in their suffering in certain periods of the war, and in the dynamics of the losses suffered inside and outside the camp.

Losses of Serbs

Marked as the main enemies of the newly established state, Serbs were killed in and outside concentration camps. According to the share in the total losses of Serb civilians, Jasenovac was the primary place of their extermination, but its role in their destruction changed during the war.

Jasenovac had a key place in the planned elimination of a part of the Serbian people in the Independent State of Croatia, but its role in their destruction varied. In the first year of the war, the eleventh part of the killed civilians of Serbian nationality lost their lives at the camp, while the far larger part of them died outside this camp.[30] In the following year, two-fifths of the losses suffered by Serb civilians in that year were killed in Jasenovac, which was an increase of 4.67 times in the participation in the destruction of civilians compared to the previous year. The development of war events in the Independent State of Croatia and the organizing of the Serbian population for their defense, contributed to a decrease in casualties, so Jasenovac's participation in the destruction of civilians was smaller – one twelfth of the losses suffered, which was 4.80 times less than in the previous year. In the generally less suffering of Serb civilians in the last two years of the war, Jasenovac participated with a fifth or a quarter of the losses suffered. During the entire war, Serb civilians suffered more in mass or individual crimes outside Jasenovac, 10.30 times in 1941,[31] 1.42 times in the following year, 10.63 times in 1943, and 3.76 and 3.29 times in the last two years of war.

The dynamics of the losses suffered by Serbs in Jasenovac and beyond was not the same. Together, they had a significantly higher loss in the first two years of the war, 79.97 percent at Jasenovac and 64.96 percent in casualties elsewhere, which was 3.99 that is 1.85 times higher than the loss of Serb civilians in the latter period.[32] Within the losses suffered in the first two years of the war, in which the Serbs suffered the greatest losses, there were differences in the dynamics of suffering. Nominally, in the first year of the war, the share of casualties outside Jasenovac was 3.11 times higher than in the camp, but given the periods of suffering inside and outside the camp,[33] the loss in the camp was really 1.38 times lower. On the other hand, the share of losses during 1942 in the camp was 2.32 times higher than the share of losses outside it. In the next two years of the war, the share in the losses of Serb

Table 6.13 NDH civilians, Serbs – the role of Jasenovac in destruction according to the year of suffering

NDH Civilians Serbs	Total	1941	%	1942	%	1943	%	1944	%	1945	%
Killed at Jasenovac	77.011–81.950	8.763–9.326	11.38	52.822–56.209	68.59	4.728–5.032	6.14	7.855–8.359	10.2	2.842–3.024	3.69
%	23.24	8.85	//	41.3	//	8.6	//	20.99	//	23.3	//
At other locations	254.724–270.394	90.293–95.884	35.45	75.194–79.760	29.51	50.274–53.387	19.74	29.598–31.421	11.62	9.366–9.942	3.68
%	76.75	91.15	//	58.69	//	91.39	//	79.01	//	76.7	//
Total	331.735–352.344	99.056–105.210	29.86	128.016–135.969	38.59	55.002–58.419	16.58	37.453–39.780	11.29	12.208–12.966	3.68

Calculation based on the database "Victims of War 1941–1945"

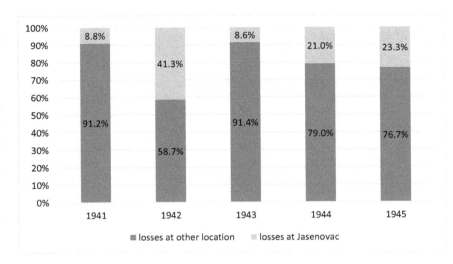

Figure 6.22 NDH, civilians, Serbs – the participation of victims at Jasenovac in total losses according to the year.

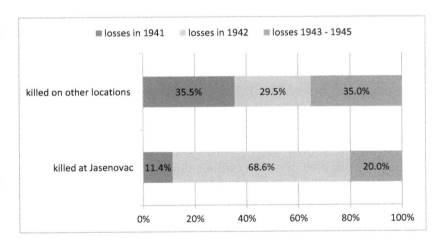

Figure 6.23 NDH civilians, Serbs – the dynamic of suffering according to the location.

civilians killed outside Jasenovac was 1.92 times higher than at Jasenovac, so that the suffering in the last year of the war was even.

Jewish and Roma Losses

For the Ustasha regime, the Jasenovac concentration camp was a central place for the annihilation of Jews and Roma from the Independent State of Croatia.

The role of Jasenovac in the extermination of these two nations varied during the war, both in its participation in their extermination during the war, and in the different dynamics of the destruction of these peoples during the war.

Since its formation, Jasenovac has become the central place of the Holocaust in the Independent State of Croatia. In the first year of its existence, more than two-fifths of the Jews killed that year lost their lives there.[34] Jasenovac participation in the extermination of Jews reached its maximum in 1942, when three-quarters of those killed in that year lost their lives in Jasenovac, which was 1.66 times higher than in the previous year. In the next two years, two thirds of Jewish victims lost their lives there which was slightly lower participation than in the previous year (1.09 and 1.07 times, respectively). In the last year of the war, more than a quarter of the Jewish victims lost their lives in Jasenovac, which was 2.43 times less than in the previous year. Nominally lower suffering of Jews in Jasenovac than in other places during the first year of the war was actually 1.84 times higher in real terms, when accounted for the period of the camp's existence in 1941. The trend continued in the following years – Jewish losses were 2.95 times higher in 1942, 2.15 and 2.34 times higher in the next two years, until the last year of the war when the loss suffered in Jasenovac was 2.46 times smaller than in other places.[35]

Determined for annihilation by racial laws, the Jews of the Independent State of Croatia suffered the greatest losses everywhere in the first two years of the war; 88.23 percent of those killed in Jasenovac and 78.28 percent of those killed elsewhere lost their lives in the first two years. In the first year of the war, Jewish losses in Jasenovac, given the period of the camp's existence, were realistically 1.14 times higher than in other places. In 1942, the number was 1.83 times higher, which points out that Jasenovac was the primary place of their destruction and played a central role in the Holocaust carried out in this territory. During the last three years of the war, the share of losses of Jews killed in Jasenovac (11.75%) was 1.85 times lower than the share of losses suffered in other places (21.70), with the share of losses in Jasenovac being slightly higher during 1943 and 1944, and 3.98 times smaller in the last year.[36]

For the Roma, Jasenovac was the primary place of suffering in the Independent State of Croatia from the beginning of the war. Of all Roma killed during the first three years of the war, four-fifths lost their lives at the Jasenovac camp.[37] Only in the last two years of the war, in which the suffering of the Roma was significantly lower, the role of Jasenovac in their extermination decreased. Jasenovac in that period accounted for the half of the losses suffered which, in 1944, was 1.76 times less than in the previous period.

The racial laws according to which the Roma were sentenced to annihilation effectively also determined their dynamics of suffering, so that 92.88 percent of the victims at the Jasenovac camp lost their lives in the first two years of the war. Moreover, 77.63 percent of those who lost their lives elsewhere were killed in the same period. The second year was the most devastating for members of the Roma nationality with the death rate in Jasenovac, which was

Table 6.14 NDH, civilians, Jews – the role of Jasenovac in destruction according to the year of suffering

NDH civilians–Jews	Total	1941	%	1942	%	1943	%	1944	%	1945	%
Killed at Jasenovac	17.926–19.076	3.798–4.042	21.19	12.017–12.788	67.04	889–946	4.96	495–526	2.76	726–773	4.05
%	61.68	44.94	//	74.71	//	68.29	//	70.03	//	28.86	//
At other locations	11.166–11.823	4.662–4.943	41.79	4.085–4.314	36.49	414–438	3.7	212–225	1.89	1.793–1.903	16.11
%	38.32	55.06	//	25.29	//	31.71	//	29.97	//	71.14	//
Total	29.092–30.899	8.460–8.985	29.08	16.102–17.102	55.35	1.303–1.384	4.48	707–751	2.43	2.519–2.676	8.66

Calculation based on the database "Victims of War 1941–1945"

170 *Dragan Cvetković*

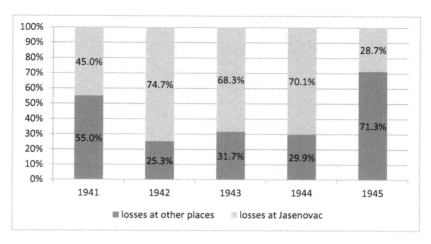

Figure 6.24 NDH, civilians, Jews – the participation of losses at Jasenovac in the total losses according to the year of suffering.

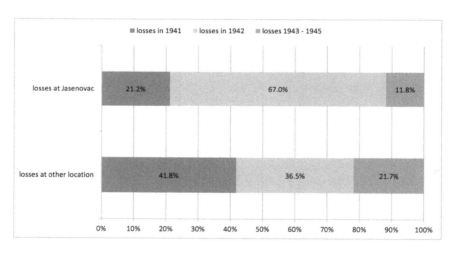

Figure 6.25 NDH, civilians, Jews – dynamics of suffering according to the location.

2.22 times higher than in the previous year, while the number of victims outside Jasenovac was 5.36 times higher.[38] In the generally minor suffering of the Roma during the last three years of the war, it stands out that one-fifth of all Roma victims lost their lives outside Jasenovac in 1944.

Croatian and Muslim Losses

For the Ustasha regime, the Jasenovac concentration camp was a central place for confrontation with anti-fascists and political opponents among

Table 6.15 NDH, civilians, Jews – the role of Jasenovac in destruction according to the year of suffering

NDH civilians–Roma	Total	1941	%	1942	%	1943	%	1944	%	1945	%
Losses at Jasenovac	18.916–20.129	2.291–2.438	12.11	15.278–16.258	80.77	357–380	1.89	950–1.010	5.02	42–44	0.22
%	78.07	81.03	//	80.96	//	83.75	//	47.45	//	48.53	//
At other locations	5.335–5.629	539–568	10.08	3.611–3.805	67.55	70–73	1.28	1.053–1.118	19.24	60–64	0.96
%	21.92	18.97	//	19.04	//	16.25	//	52.55	//	51.47	//
Total	24.251–25.758	2.830–3.006	11.67	18.889–20.063	77.89	427–453	1.76	2.003–2.128	8.26	102–108	0.42

Calculation based on the database "Victims of War 1941–1945"

172 *Dragan Cvetković*

Figure 6.26 NDH, civilians, Roma – the participation of losses at Jasenovac in total losses according to the year.

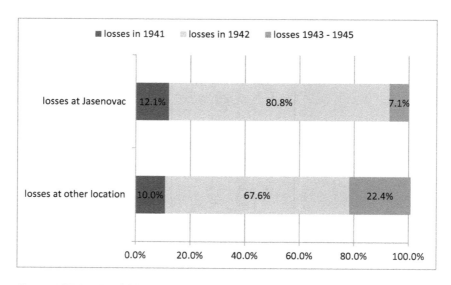

Figure 6.27 NDH, civilians, Roma – dynamics of losses according to the location.

Croats and Muslims. The role of Jasenovac in their elimination varied during the war.

As part of the NDH regime's confrontation with political enemies in the first two years of the war, in the generally small number of Croats killed in that period, the loss suffered at Jasenovac represented a quarter or a fifth of all killed civilians of this nationality.[39] In the next two years of the war, the loss of Croatian civilians at Jasenovac was small (4.24 times smaller in 1943 than in the previous year). In the last year of the war, it reached one-sixth of all the Croatian civilian losses. The share of losses in Jasenovac in the first two years of the war was twice as high as among those killed outside the camp[40] and, also in the last year of the war, the loss suffered was 1.47 times higher, making Jasenovac a central place for confrontation with NDH political opponents from among the Croatian people.

The generally small number of Muslim losses in Jasenovac was particularly pronounced in the first three years of the war, and in 1944 the loss suffered in the camp represented one-eleventh of the civilians killed (a 4.57 times greater share in losses than in the previous year), and one-eighth of the losses in the last year of the war. The share of casualties in Jasenovac in the last two years of the war was 3.18 times higher than among those killed outside the camp.

Conclusion

In this extremely complex and layered war fought on the territory of the Independent State of Croatia, in which several warring parties participated, the suffering of the civilian population was very pronounced. The killed civilians from the territory of the Independent State of Croatia (between 499,000 and 530,000) represented 73.39 percent of the total losses of Yugoslav civilians. The implementation of genocide and the Holocaust, as its most extreme form, over the part of the population by the Ustaša regime and the German and Italian occupiers, in addition to the mass commission of war crimes by most warring parties, led to disproportionate suffering of civilians of different nationalities. Among the killed civilians of the Independent State of Croatia, there were 66.48 percent Serbs, 10.20 percent Croats, 7.77 percent Muslims, 5.83 percent Jews, 4.86 percent Roma, 1.26 percent of other nationalities, and 3.60 percent of unidentified nationalities. The losses suffered by different nationalities were not in line with their representation in the NDH population, so the losses of Serbs were twice as high (2.07 times) as their representation in the NDH population. Jews and Roma, determined for total extermination under racial laws, were the principal victims of the war as their losses were 10.23, which is 9.72 times greater than their presentation in the population. On the other hand, the civilian losses of the Croat and Muslim peoples were 4.66 and 1.67 times smaller, respectively, than the participation of these national groups in the NDH population.

The Jasenovac concentration camp, or the system of camps, which lasted from the end of August 1941 to the end of April 1945, with 122,279–130,120 killed in it, was the largest concentration camp in Southeast Europe and, in terms of losses, certainly the largest camp in Europe not organized by Nazi Germany. During the 44 months of the camp's existence, a quarter of all civilian casualties (24.53%) of the NDH lost their lives there, that is, two-thirds of all civilians from the NDH who died any of the camps (67.31%), whether organized by the NDH or not, and regardless of whether they were

Table 6.16 NDH, civilians, Croats—the role of Jasenovac in destruction according to the year of suffering

NDH civilians–Croats	Total	1941	%	1942	%	1943	%	1944	%	1945	%
Losses at Jasenovac	6004–6.389	828–882	13.8	1.739–1.850	28.96	519–553	8.65	1.160–1.235	19.33	1.757–1.869	29.26
%	11.81	25.22	//	19.61	//	4.62	//	6.92	//	16.45	//
At other locations	44.894–47.671	2.460–2.610	5.48	7.138–7.578	15.9	10.729–11.394	23.9	15.631–16.599	34.82	8.932–9.484	19.89
%	88.19	74.78	//	80.39	//	95.38	//	93.08	//	83.55	//
Total	50.898–54.060	3.288–3.492	6.46	8.877–9.428	17.44	11.248–11.947	22.1	16.791–17.834	32.99	10.689–11.353	21

Calculation based on the database "Victims of War 1941–1945"

Destruction of the NDH People 175

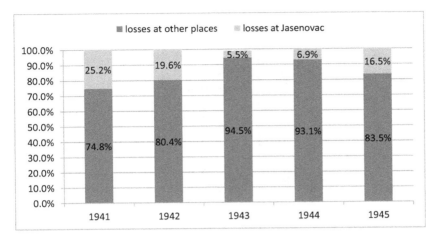

Figure 6.28 NDH, civilians, Croats – the participation of losses at Jasenovac in total losses according to the year.

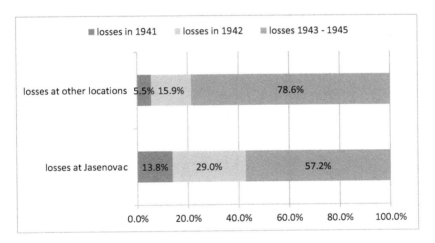

Figure 6.29 NDH, civilians, Croats – dynamics of losses according to the location.

on the territory of the NDH or not. The extent of the crime committed in the Jasenovac Camp clearly defined it as an extermination camp.

The reasons for the formation of the Jasenovac camp as primarily a place for the elimination of "undesirable" peoples in the NDH, in part or in full, and then for confrontation with political and ideological opponents among Croats and Muslims, caused differences in losses suffered by the nationalities. Three-fifths of the total losses in Jasenovac were represented by Serbs (62.98%), one sixth by Roma (15.47%), one seventh by Jews (14.66%), one

Table 6.17 NDH, civilians, Muslims–the role of Jasenovac in extermination according to the year of suffering

NDH civilians– Muslims	Total	1941	%	1942	%	1943	%	1944	%	1945	%
Losses at Jasenovac	1.357–1.444	149–159	11	307–326	22.61	177–187	13.07	394–420	29.07	329–350	24.25
%	3.5	1.49	//	2.44	//	1.93	//	8.82	//	13.11	//
In other places	37.415–39.737	9.893–10.507	26.44	12.348–12.978	32.83	8.981–9.540	24	4.080–4.332	10.9	2.183–2.318	5.83
%	96.5	98.51	//	97.56	//	98.07	//	91.18	//	86.89	//
Total	38.772–41.181	10.042–10.666	25.9	12.581–13.363	32.45	9.158–9.727	23.62	4.474–4.752	11.54	2.512–2.668	6.48

Calculation based on the database "Victims of War 1941–1945"

Destruction of the NDH People 177

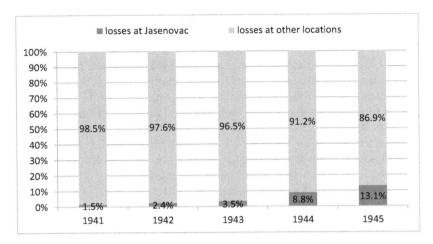

Figure 6.30 NDH, civilians, Muslimans – the participation of losses in Jasenovac in the total losses according to the year.

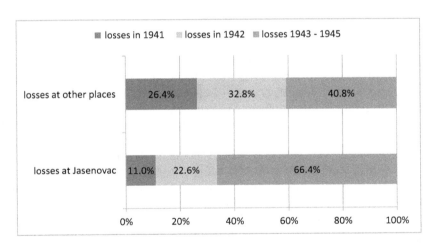

Figure 6.31 NDH, civilians, Muslims – dynamics of losses according to the location.

twentieth by Croats (4.91%), with a minimal share in the losses of Muslims (1.11%), and members of other and unknown nationalities (0.87%). The first 16 months of the camp's existence were fatal for almost all Roma (92.88%), Jews (88.23%) and members of other known and unknown nationalities (88.24%), as well as for four-fifths of Serbs killed in it (79.97%). On the other hand, half of the Croats (48.59%) and Muslims (53.32%) lost their lives in the last two years of the war.

Throughout the war, Serbs represented the most numerous victims of the camp, with a share in the losses that never fell below half of the casualties. Their share of losses in the camp was permanently above their representation in the population – 1.70 times in the first year (54.62%), 1.99 times in 1942 (63.75%), 2.25 times in 1944 year (72.10%) and 1.55 times in the last year of the war (49.66%).

Jews accounted for a quarter of losses in the first year of the war (23.67%), and a seventh in the following year (14.50%), which was 41.53 and 25.44 times more represented in losses than their share of the population. Their share in losses in the first year of the camp's existence was 5.21 times higher than in the penultimate year of the war (4.54%). With one-seventh (14.28%) and one-fifth (18.42%) of losses in the first two years, the share of Roma in losses was 28.56 or 85.71 times higher than their representation in the NDH population, so that their share in losses in the last year of the war (0.73%) was 25.23 times less than in 1942.

From the minor participation of Croats and Muslims in the losses in the first years of the camp's existence, which in 1942 (2.10 and 0.37%, respectively) were 22.66 and 35.13 times less than their representation in the population, their share in losses in the last year of the war reached a third (30.71%) or a seventeenth part (5.75%) of losses (1.55 or 2.26 times less than participation in the population), which was an increase in participation in losses of 14.62 and 15.54 times compared to the second year of the camp's existence.

The role of Jasenovac in the destruction of the people in the Independent State of Croatia was not the same for everyone. For Jews and Roma, Jasenovac was a central place of suffering in which four-fifths of Roma victims (78.08%), and three-fifths of Jewish victims (61.68%), lost their lives. Jasenovac had a prominent place in the commission of crimes against Serbs, given that a quarter (23.24%) of all Serb civilians killed in the NDH lost their lives, making it the primary site of their suffering. The magnitude of the crime has turned it into a paradigm of the total suffering of Serbs in the NDH. One–eighth of the killed civilians of Croatian nationality (11.81%), the thirtieth part of the civilians of Muslim nationality (3.50%), and the twenty–third part of the killed members of other known and unknown nationalities (4.39%) lost their lives in Jasenovac.

With its character, number of victims and brutality and the monstrosity of the committed crimes, Jasenovac certainly represents a paradigm of genocide and holocaust committed on the territory of the NDH, but that does not mean that it should fall into the trap of generalization that leads to neglect of losses elsewhere in the NDH and abroad.

Notes

1 The general Yugoslav project "Yugoslavs in Fascist Prisons, Prison and Concentration Camps, and Resistance Movements of Other Countries in the Second World War," started in 1982, was to fully address this topic. Quoted according to: Milan Koljanin, *Nemački logor na beogradskom Sajmištu 1941–1944* (Beograd: Institut za savremenu istoriju, 1992), pp. 5.

2 On the extensive opus of works on Jasenovac (but also on other camps in the Independent State of Croatia) until 2000, see: Jovan Mirković, *Objavljeni izvori i literatura o jasenovačkim logorima* (Banja Luka-Beograd: Muzej žrtava genocida, 2000); later: Nataša Mataušić, *Jasenovac 1941.–1945., Logor smrti i radni logor* (Jasenovac-Zagreb: Spomen područje Jasenovac, 2003); Davor Kovačić, "Iskapanja na prostoru koncentracijskog logora Stara Gradiška neposredno poslije završetka Drugog svijetskog rata i procjene broja žrtava," *Srinia Slavonica*, no. 3 (2003), pp. 500–520; Slavko Odić and Slavko Komarica, *Zašto Jasenovac nije oslobođen* (Beograd, 2005); Tea Benčić Rimay (ed.) *Spomen-područje Jasenovac* (Jasenovac: Spomen područje Jasenovac, 2006); Nihad Halilbegović, *Bošnjaci u jasenovačkom logoru* (Sarajevo: Istraživačka publicistika. Vijeće Kongresa bošnjačkih intelektualaca, 2006); Antun Miletić, *Koncentracioni logor Jasenovac*, book 4 (Jagodina: Gambit, 2007); Zdravko Antonić and Janko Velimirović (eds.) *Jasenovac. Zbornik radova Četvrte međunarodne konferencije o Jasenovcu*. Kozarska Dubica, Banja Luka: Javna ustanova Spomen-područja Donja Gradina; Uruženje Jasenovac–Donja Gradina, 2007; Srboljub Živanović, *Jasenovac, odabrani radovi, članci, intervijui, govori i diskusije*, in Todor Bjelkić (ed.) (Beograd–London: Pešić i sinovi, 2008); Vladimir Markoci and Vladimir Horvat, *Ogoljela laž logora Jasenovac* (Zagreb: Naklada E. Čić, 2008); Mario Kevo, "Posjet poslanika Međunarodnog odbora Crvenog križa logorima Jasenovac i Stara Gradiška u ljeto 1944," *Časopis za suvremenu povjest*, vol. 40, no. 2 (2008), pp. 547–585; Jaša Almuli, *Jevreji i Srbi u Jasenovcu* (Beograd: Službeni glasnik, 2009); Dejan Motl and Đorđe Mihovilović, *Zaboravljeni–knjiga o posljednjim jasenovačkim logorašima* (Jasenovac–Zagreb: Spomen područje Jasenovac, 2015); Vladimir Horvat, Igor Vukić, Stipo Pilić, Blanka Matković, *Jasenovački logori–istraživanja* (Zagreb: Društvo za istraživanje trostrukog logora Jasenovac, 2015); Slavko Goldstein and Ivo Goldstein, *Jasenovac. Tragika, mitomanija, istina* (Zagreb: Fraktura, 2016); Vasilije Krestić and Mira Radojević, *Jasenovac* (Belgrade: SANU, 2017); Josip Pečarić and Stjepan Razum, *Razotkrivena jasenovačka laž* (Zagreb: Društvo za istraživanje trostrukog logora Jasenovac, 2018); Ivo Goldstein, *Jasenovac*, Zagreb–Jasenovac: Fraktura i JUSP Jasenovac, 2018; Andriana Benčić and Stipe Odak and Danijela Lučić (ed.), *Jasenovac Manipulacije, kontroverze i povjesni revizionizam* (Jasenovac: JUSP Jasenovac, 2018); Igor Vukić, *Radni logor Jasenovac* (Zagreb: Naklada Pavičić, 2018); Ivo Goldstein, *Jasenovac* (Novi Sad: Akademska knjiga, 2019 (amended chapter According to the apocalyptic end – On the number of victims / Prema apokaliptičnom kraju – O broju žrtava, 772–797). On the number of victims in Jasenovac camp, see: Vladimir Geiger, "Brojidbeni pokazatelji o žrtvama logora Jasenovac, 1941.–1945. (procjene, izračuni, popisi)," *Časopis za suvremenu povjest*, vol. 55, no. 2 (2013), pp. 211–242; Igor Graovac and Dragan Cvetković, *Ljudski gubici Hrvatske1941.–1945. godine: pitanja, primjeri, rezultati* (Zagreb: Hrvatski institut za povijest, 2005), pp. 72–75, 97; Tea Benčić Rimay (ed.) *Jasenovac, žrtva je pojedinac–Poimenični popis žrtava koncetracijskog logora Jasenovac 1941.–1945.* (Jasenovac: Spomen područje Jasenovac, 2007); Dragan Cvetković, "Stradanje civila Nezavisne Države Hrvatske u logoru Jasenovac," *Tokovi istorije*, no. 4 (2007), pp. 153–168; Antun Miletić, *Ubijeni u koncentracionom logoru Jasenovac 1941–1945* (Jagodina: Gambit, 2011); Dušan Nikodijević, "Prilog utvrđivanju broja žrtava sistema logora Jasenovac 1941. godine," *Godišnjak za istraživanje genocida*, no. 8 (2016), pp. 169–213; Dušan Nikodijević, "Brojevi žrtava u koncentracijskom logoru Jasenovac 1942. godine prema iskazima preželih svjedoka, *Godišnjak za istraživanje*

genocida, no. 9 (2017), pp. 95–117; Dragan Cvetković, "Geostatistička analiza ljudskih gubitaka u koncentracionom logoru Jasenovac," *Istorija 20. veka*, 1/2019, 93–120; Душан Никодијевић, Јасеновац између броја и жртве. Прилог проучавању броја жртава у систему концентрационог логора Јасеновац (Belgrade: Музеј жртава геноцида, 2019).

3 More in Vladimir Geiger, "Ljudski gubici Hrvatske u Drugom svjetskom ratu koje su prouzročili 'okupatori i njihovi pomagači' Brojdbeni pokazatelji (procjene, izračuni, popisi)," *Časopis za suvremenu povijest*, vol. 43, no. 3 (2011), pp. 699–749; Vladimir Geiger, "Brojidbeni pokazatelji o žrtvama logora Jasenovac, 1941.–1945."

4 The first attempt to enumerate war victims was made by the *State Commission for Determining the Crimes of the Occupiers and Their Helpers* in 1946, but the census was unsuccessful due to omissions and non-cooperation among the Land Commissions, and included only 505,182 people, which was considered insufficient, so it needed to be repeated and that was not done. See: Miodrag Zečević and Jovan Popović, *Dokumenti iz istorije Jugoslavije, Državna komisija za utvrđivanje zločina okupatora i njihovih pomagača iz drugog svetskog rata*, book 1 (Beograd: Arhiv Jugoslavije, 1996), pp. 42. In 1950, the *Alliance of the Associations of the Former Fighters of the People's Liberation War in Serbia* (SUBNOR)made lists by municipalities (individual data were never published; there are aggregate data for Croatia). They also madelists of survivors of the *National Liberation War* and participated with other researchers in the preparation and publication of local monographs with lists of fallen fighters and "the victims of fascist terror." The *Red Cross* also collected data on casualties. Jewish communities collected data for their compatriots killed in the Holocaust.

5 For more information on the list of "Žrtve rata," see: Dragan Cvetković, "*Gubici pripadnika partizanskog pokreta sa teritorije Jugoslavije 1941–1945*," doctoral dissertation (University of Belgrade, Faculty of Philosophy, Department of History, 2016), pp. 6–10.

6 The census was made for the then territory of Yugoslavia, meaning that they also included those who died and were from the territories annexed after the Second World War. By deducting the number of casualties from the territories annexed to Yugoslavia after 1945, the number of casualties from the territories of the Kingdom of Yugoslavia is 580,981. See: *Žrtve rata 1941–1945 (rezultati popisa)* (Beograd: Savezni zavod za statistiku, 1966), pp. 27–39.

7 *Žrtve rata*, op.cit., pp. 5–23. The census commission calculated that the census should include 1,016,000 to 1,066,000 victims. The estimation of the suffered losses was performed in the *Federal Bureau of Statistics* with the expert cooperation of Dr. Dušan Breznik, director of the *Center for Demographic Research*. The number that was to be included in the census did not include an estimated 50,000 Quislings, as well as an estimated 40,000 Roma and Jews for whom there was no one to provide data, which shows that a total of between 1,106,000 and 1,156,000 individuals died in the war in Yugoslavia, meaning that the census covered between 51.7 and 54% of the actual victims from Yugoslavia. Recent demographic surveys, as well as the analysis of the results of this census, suggest that the starting point in the surveys should be an estimate of the number of casualties ranging between 1,070,000 and 1,120,000 people, which shows that the census covers 53.3–55.8% of the victims. The estimated number for the territory of the Kingdom of Yugoslavia is between 1,042,000 and 1,092,000 in total. These numbers do not include the victims of the communist reprisals after May 15, 1945, a significant part of which, of course, lost their lives, and that was a consequence of their involvement in the war.

8   More on war damage and reparation negotiations: Zoran Janjetović, *Od Auschwitza do Brijuna, Pitanje odštete žrtava nacizma u jugoslovensko-zapadnonjemačkim odnosima* (Zagreb: Hrvatski institut za povijest, 2007).

9   In 1995, using a variety of archives, literature and survey forms, the *Federal Institute for Statistics* (in Croatian: *Savez za statistiku*, acronym: SZS), with the assistance of the *Museum of Genocide Victims* (MGV), began to revise the census, identify new individuals and verify existing census data by comparing them with data from other sources. The idea is to include in the audit all persons who lived in the territory of Yugoslavia, regardless of national, religious, ethnic, political, and military affiliation, thus correcting the basic methodological error of not listing "collaborators." Such a poor methodological approach of the enumerators in 1964 led to the entire national group of Germans being declared "collaborators" and not enumerated (the few enumerated Germans, mostly killed as Partisans, were classified under other nationalities). A similar thing happened, although on a much smaller scale, with some other national groups. Corrections are also aimed at identifying the perpetrators of crimes or those responsible for the deaths, which was not done in 1964 (although the censuses are full of data on perpetrators of crimes), at determining the number of Roma who were not specifically enumerated, but were mostly registered as other or unknown nationalities, or on the other hand, as was the case in the territory of the Independent State of Croatia, as Croats, and to a lesser extent as Serbs or Muslims. Then, this was also done in order to eliminate inaccuracies in the data, which all leads to data variability. Therefore, the data presented related to these categories should be taken with a grain of salt. The audit was carried out intermittently in the SZS until 1999, and since 2003 it has been carried out in the MGV, in accordance with the personnel, material and technical possibilities of the Museum. So far, the audit for the territory of Yugoslavia has determined the number of 657,290 victims, which is an increase of 10.04% (59,967 people). (Arhiv Jugoslavije u Beogradu: fond 179, "Popis Žrtve rata 1941–1945" iz 1964. godine; Archives of the *Museum of Genocide Victims*/ Arhiv Muzeja žrtava genocida (hereinafter AMŽG), Fund of Victims of War 1941–1945).

10 The lists of names of human losses of the Second World War and the postwar period were mostly made on the basis of testimonies (survivors, relatives, friends ...), and less often by the use of documents. This raises the question of the reliability of the obtained data, and they should be approached critically when it comes to the circumstances, time and place of the suffering, and the allegations about the perpetrator of the crime. One of the tasks of census revision is to check this data by comparing it with knowledge from other sources, and to verify or reject it.

11 All relationships between the observed parameters, expressed as a percentage (%) represent their real relationship in the revised census, and based on them, calculations were made. The possibility of calculation error is ± 0.15% and is a consequence of the accepted round numbers of total losses in Yugoslavia, i.e. NDH, which served as the starting point of the calculation, and the rounding of numbers (given that these are victims), as well as data crossings.

12 The calculation for the population of the Independent State of Croatia was made on the basis of the 1931 census. (*Definitivni rezultati popisa stanovništva od 31.3.1931. godine knjiga I; Prisutno stanovništvo, broj kuća i domaćinstava*, Beograd, 1937). According to the 1942 Census Report, the territory included 5,657,085 inhabitants based on the 1931 census, but it also included some territories that belonged to

Hungary and Italy. See: Fikreta Jelić-Butić, *Ustaše i NDH* (Zagreb: Sveučilišna naklada Liber, 1977), pp. 105–106.
13 The calculation of nationality was made on the basis of the same census (*Definitivni rezultati popisa stanovništva od 31. marta.1931. godine, knjiga II, Prisutno stanovništvo prema veroispovesti*, Beograd, 1938), then the publication *Demografska statistika, Stanovništvo predratne Jugoslavije po veroispovesti i maternjem jeziku po popisu od 31–III–1931. god., pregled po srezovima*, Beograd, 1945; *Demografska statistika, Stanovništvo po veroispovesti i maternjem jeziku po popisu od 31-III-1931. god., Hrvatska, pregled po opštinama*, Beograd, 1945; *Demografska statistika, Stanovništvo po veroispovesti i maternjem jeziku po popisu od 31-III-1931 godine, Bosna i Hercegovina, Pregled po opštinama*, Beograd, 1945; *Demografska statistika, Stanovništvo po veroispovesti i maternjem jeziku po popisu od 31-III-1931 godine, Srbija sa Vojvodinom i Kosovom–Metohijom, Pregled po opštinama*, Beograd, 1945; Bogoljub Kočović, *Žrtve drugog svetskog rata u Jugoslaviji* (London: Veritas Foundation Press, 1985); Vladimir Žerjavić, *Gubici stanovništva Jugoslavije u drugom svjetskom ratu* (Zagreb: Jugoslavensko viktimološko društvo, 1989).
14 According to the 1931 census, 1,780,457 Serbs, 2,644,462 Croats, 722,663 Muslims, 31,469 Jews, 146,019 Germans, 68,628 Hungarians, 37,000 Slovenes, and 128,724 other and unknown nationalities lived on the territory where the NDH was later formed. According to the estimates of the German Ministry of Foreign Affairs from May 1941, there were 6,285,000 inhabitants in the Independent State of Croatia, of whom 52.51% were Croats (3,300,000), 30.63% Serbs (1,925,000), and 11.14%. Muslims (700,000), 2.39% Germans (150,000), 1.19% Hungarians (75,000), 0.59% Jews (38,000), 0.48% Slovenes (30,000) and 1.03% Czechs and Slovaks (65,000) and 40,000 Jews. The authors from the Independent State of Croatia established a population of 6,439,331 inhabitants, of which 4,868,831 were Croats, 1,250,000 Serbs, 170,500 Germans, 69,000 Hungarians, 37,000 Slovenes, 44,000 Czechs and Slovaks. See: Fikreta Jelić-Butić, *Ustaše i NDH*, pp. 106.
15 An approximate number of 30,000 Roma in the Independent State of Croatia was taken as the basis for the calculations in the further work. Demographic research based on the census of linguistic affiliation showed that there were about 21,000 Roma living in that territory, although there was certainly a part that did not declare their nationality, or was assimilated enough to speak another language (mostly Croatian and less Serbian, which raises the question of their national identity), and they often opted for it in the same way. (Bogoljub Kočović, *Žrtve drugog svetskog rata u Jugoslaviji*, pp. 173–176; Vladimir Žerjavić, *Gubici stanovništva Jugoslavije u drugom svjetskom ratu*, pp. 36–45); The results gained so far in the number of Roma identified during the census revision, the current coverage of potential victims and the disproportionate share of children under 14 among those identified show that the total number of Roma victims is higher than the demographers estimated as the total number of Roma in the territory.
16 Based on the achieved results of the partially revised census "Victims of the War 1941–1945," the estimated number of civilians killed from the territory of the Kingdom of Yugoslavia is between 680,000 and 722,000. Dragan Cvetković, "Stradanje stanovništva NDH u logorima–numeričko određenje," u: *Logori, zatvori i prisilni rad u Hrvatskoj / Jugoslaviji 1941–1945* in Vladimir Geiger, Martina

Grahek Ravančić and Marica Karakaš Obradov (ed.) *Logori, zatvori i prisilni rad u Hrvatskoj / Jugoslaviji 1941.–1945*. (Zagreb: Hrvatski institut za povijest, 2010), pp. 45.

17 There is a real possibility that the number of victims in the last year of the war was lower, given that for some victims during the census "Žrtve rata 1941–1945" due to the lack of accurate information about the year of death, the last year of the war was reported as the year of death.

18 Preliminary analyzes conducted for the group of "Others/Unidentified" show that it is among them mostly Roma and Serbs, but for now there are no valid sources that confirm these assumptions.

19 More in Dragan Cvetković, "Holokaust u NDH–numeričko određenje," *Istorija 20. veka*, vol. 1 (2011), pp. 163–182.

20 The real mortality rate of Serb civilians in the first year of the war was slightly higher (1.03 times) than in the following year, only to decrease 2.33 times in 1943.

21 Of the civilian casualties in the NDH, almost half (47.31%) lost their lives in direct terror, more than a third (36.44%) in camps, and another 2.70% in prisons, 4.72% lost their lives in fighting and bombing, and 11.53% died in other circumstances (deportation, exile, forced labor …). The circumstances of the civilian casualties were not the same for all national groups. More than half (55.82%) of Serbs lost their lives in direct terror, and 56.55% of Muslims and 41.17% of Croats died in the same way. One third of Serbs (31.75%) and one quarter (24.79%) of Croats died in the camps (another 5.98% lost their lives in prisons), with 4.72% of Muslims, 94.82% of Jews, 93.43% of Roma, and half of the others and unknown nationalities, while 16.92% of Croats, 10.46% of Muslims and 3.04% of Serbs lost their lives as civilians during the fighting and bombing. Of all NDH civilian casualties in direct terror, Serbs accounted for 80.10%, Muslims 9.38%, Croats 8.78%, while of those killed in concentration camps Serbs represented 57.93%, Jews 15.17%, Roma 12.46%, Croats 6.94%, Muslims 1.01% and members of other and unknown nationalities 6.48%. Serbs represented 43.67% of NDH civilians killed in fighting and bombing, Croats 36.14%, Muslims 17.39% and others and unknown 2.80%.

22 The suffering of civilians outside Jasenovac in 1941 was 7.22 times greater, but, given the fact that the camp existed for only four months, and that civilians suffered losses since the beginning of the war, the loss suffered in Jasenovac was realistically 3.21 times smaller.

23 There is a real possibility that the number of victims at the camp in the last year of the war was lower, as for some victims during the census "Victims of War 1941–1945" due to lack of accurate information about the year of death, the last year of the war was reported as the year of death, meaning the last year of the camp's existence.

24 The Gospić group of camps (Gospić, Jadovno, Pag) played an extremely important role in the destruction of the population of the Independent State of Croatia during the first year of the war, as 40.18% of the victims in the 1941 camps lost their lives there. Thus, given the periods of the camps' existence in 1941, the death rate in the Gospić group of camps was 1.25 times higher than in Jasenovac in that year. For more information on the number of victims in the Gospić group of camps, and the national structure of losses, see Dragan Cvetković, "Stradanje stanovništva NDH u logorima…," pp. 53.

25 Among the civilians in the Independent State of Croatia who lost their lives in concentration camps, since 1942 German camps had a significant share in the losses no matter whether they were on the territory of Yugoslavia or elsewhere
26 Considering the representation in the population of the Independent State of Croatia, the loss of Roma in Jasenovac was realistically one fifth higher (1.20 times) than the loss of Jews.
27 For more details, see Dragan Cvetković, "Stradanje stanovništva NDH u logorima...," pp. 41–57.
28 The share of Roma victims in Jasenovac is probably higher because most of the members of this nationality who died outside Jasenovac lost their lives in an unknown camp.
29 Among members of other and unknown nationalities, a significant part of the victims were stated to have died in an unknown camp, so there is a high possibility that they lost their lives at Jasenovac. It especially refers to persons for whom there are indications that they are Roma.
30 A significant part of the Serb civilians killed in 1941 (13.32% of the total losses and 14.62% of the killed outside Jasenovac) lost their lives in the Gospić group of camps (Gospić, Jadovno, Pag). Thus, the loss of Serbs in the Gospić group of camps was 1.50 times higher than in Jasenovac, but, given the periods of existence of these camps in 1941, the death rate in the Gospić group of camps was twice as high. A comparison of the role in the total losses of Serb civilians shows that in the Jasenovac group of camps (23.24% of losses) 5.87 times more people died than in the Gospic group of camps (3.96%), but, given the periods of existence of these camps during the war, the mortality rate of Serb civilians in the Gospić group of camps was 2.50 times higher in real terms.
31 Considering the period of the camp's existence in 1941 and the period of suffering of Serb civilians since the beginning of the war, the loss suffered in Jasenovac was realistically 4.58 times smaller.
32 Considering the periods of casualties in the first two years of the war, the shares in losses in the first two years of the war were 7.11 times higher in real terms among the losses in Jasenovac, and 2.51 times higher among the losses in other places.
33 The camp did not operate during the whole year.
34 A significant part of the killed civilians of Jewish nationality in 1941 (21.77% of the total losses or 39.61% of the losses outside Jasenovac) lost their lives in the Gospić group of camps (Gospić, Jadovno, Pag). Thus, the loss of Jews in the Gospić group of camps was twice less (2.06 times) than in Jasenovac, but, given the periods of existence of these camps in 1941, the death rate in the Gospić group of camps was in real terms 1.65 times lower.
35 Most of the Jews killed in 1945 lost their lives in German camps. It is probable that some of the victims in the camps of the Third Reich lost their lives earlier, but due to the lack of accurate data, the last year of the war was reported as the year of death.
36 The mortality rate of Jews killed outside the Jasenovac Camp in 1945 was realistically 22.73 times higher than in the previous year, while at Jasenovac it was 3.91 times higher.
37 The loss of Roma in Jasenovac in 1941, given the time of the camp's existence, was 9.61 times higher in real terms than the loss in other places during that year.

38 Among the Roma killed in other places during 1942, most were reported killed in an unknown camp, so there is a high possibility that they were also victims of the Jasenovac camp.
39 Among the Croats killed in Jasenovac during the first two years of the war were people who, according to the etymology of the name, can be said to have been Jews, but were reported or registered as Croats of the Roman Catholic faith in the "Victims of War 1941–1945" list. It is possible that these are converts that the Ustaša movement did not recognize as such on the basis of racial laws.
40 The loss of Croats in Jasenovac in 1941, given the time of the camp's existence, was in real terms 5.67 times greater than the loss in other places during that year.

Bibliography

Unpublished Sources

Arhiv Jugoslavije u Beogradu: fSond 179, "Popis Žrtve rata 1941–1945." Beograd, 1964.
Arhiv Muzeja žrtava genocida u Beogradu: fond "Žrtve rata 1941–1945." Baza podataka "Žrtve rata 1941–1945."

Published Sources

Almuli, Jaša. *Jevreji i Srbi u Jasenovcu*. Beograd: Službeni glasnik, 2009.
Antonić, Zdravko and Velimirović Janko (eds.). *Jasenovac. Zbornik radova Četvrte međunarodne konferencije o Jasenovcu*. Kozarska Dubica, Banja Luka: Javna ustanova Spomen-područja Donja Gradina; Uruženje Jasenovac–Donja Gradina, 2007.
Benčić Rimay, Tea (ed.). *Spomen područje Jasenovac–katalog–monografija*. Jasenovac: Spomen područje Jasenovac, 2006.
Cvetković, Dragan. "Stradanje civila Nezavisne Države Hrvatske u logoru Jasenovac," *Tokovi istorije*, vol. 4, 2007, pp. 153–168.
———. "Stradanje stanovništva NDH u logorima–numeričko određenje" in Vladimir Geiger, Martina Grahek Ravančić and Marica Karakaš Obradov (eds.) *Logori, zatvori i prisilni rad u Hrvatskoj / Jugoslaviji 1941.–1945., 1945–1951*. Zagreb, 2010, pp. 41–57.
———. "Holokaust u NDH–numeričko određenje," *Istorija 20. veka*, vol. I, 2011, pp. 163–182.
———. "Gubici pripadnika partizanskog pokreta sa teritorije Jugoslavije 1941–1945." (Doctoral dissertation) University of Belgrade, Faculty of Philosophy, Department of History, 2016, pp. 6–10.
———. "Jasenovac–u ili o brojevima bez konačnog broja," *Novi magazin*, no. 209, April, 30 2015, pp. 36–38. www.novimagazin.rs/vesti/jasenovac--u-ili-o-brojevima-bez-konacnog-broja (accessed January 10, 2018).
Definitivni rezultati popisa stanovništva od 31.3. 1931. godine knjiga I; Prisutno stanovništvo, broj kuća i domaćinstava. Beograd, 1937.
Definitivni rezultati popisa stanovništva od 31. marta. 1931.godine, knjiga II, Prisutno stanovništvo prema veroispovesti. Beograd, 1938.
Demografska statistika, Stanovništvo predratne Jugoslavije po veroispovesti i maternjem jeziku po popisu od 31–III–1931. god., pregled po srezovima. Beograd, 1945.

Demografska statistika, Stanovništvo po veroispovesti i maternjem jeziku po popisu od 31–III–1931. god., Hrvatska, pregled po opštinama. Beograd, 1945.

Demografska statistika, Stanovništvo po veroispovesti i maternjem jeziku po popisu od 31–III–1931. godine, Bosna i Hercegovina, Pregled po opštinama. Beograd, 1945.

Demografska statistika, Stanovništvo po veroispovesti i maternjem jeziku po popisu od 31–III–1931. godine, Srbija sa Vojvodinom i Kosovom–Metohijom, Pregled po opštinama. Beograd, 1945.

Geiger, Vladimir. "Ljudski gubici Hrvatske u Drugom svjetskom ratu koje su prouzročili 'okupatori i njihovi pomagači' Brojdbeni pokazatelji (procjene, izračuni, popisi)," *Časopis za suvremenu povijest*, br. 3, 2011, pp. 699–749.

———. "Brojidbeni pokazatelji o žrtvama logora Jasenovac, 1941.–1945. (procjene, izračuni, popisi)," *Časopis za suvremenu povijest*, vol. 45, no. 2. 2013, pp. 211–242.

Graovac, Igor and Dragan Cvetković. *Ljudski gubici Hrvatske 1941.–1945. godine: pitanja, primjeri, rezultati.* Zagreb: Hrvatski institut za povijest, 2005.

Goldstein, Slavko and Goldstein Ivo. *Jasenovac–tragika, mitomanija, istina.* Zagreb: Fraktura, 2016.

Halilbegović, Nihad. *Bošnjaci u jasenovačkom logoru.* Sarajevo: Istraživačka publicistika. Vijeće Kongresa bošnjačkih intelektualaca, 2006.

Horvat, Vladimir, Igor Vukić, Stipo Pilić and Blanka Matković. *Jasenovački logori-istraživanja*: Zagreb: Društvo za istraživanje trostrukog logora Jasenovac, 2015.

Kevo, Mario. "Posjet poslanika Međunarodnog odbora Crvenog križa logorima Jasenovac i Stara Gradiška u ljeto 1944," *Časopis za suvremenu povijest*, vol. 2 (2008), pp. 547–585.

Kočović, Bogoljub. *Žrtve drugog svetskog rata u Jugoslaviji.* London, 1985.

Koljanin, Milan. *Nemački logor na beogradskom Sajmištu 1941–1944.* Beograd: Institut za savremenu istoriju, 1992.

Krestić, Vasilije and Radojević, Mira. *Jasenovac.* SANU, Beograd, 2017.

Kovačić, Davor. "Iskapanja na prostoru koncentracijskog logora Stara Gradiška neposredno poslije završetka Drugog svijetskog rata i procjene broja žrtava," *Srinia Slavonica*, vol. 3, no. 1 (2003), pp. 500–520.

Markoci, Vladimir and Vladimir Horvat. *Ogoljela laž logora Jasenovac.* Zagreb: Naklada E. Čić, 2008.

Mataušić, Nataša. *Jasenovac 1941.–1945., Logor smrti i radni logor.* Jasenovac-Zagreb: Spomen područje Jasenovac, 2003.

Mihovilović Đorđe and Jelka Smreka. *Jasenovac, žrtva je pojedinac–Poimenični popis žrtava koncetracijskog logora Jasenovac 1941.-1945.*, in: Tea Benčić Rimay (ed.) *Spomen područje Jasenovac–katalog-monografija.* Jasenovac: Spomen područje Jasenovac, 2006, pp. 218–226.

Miletić, Antun. Koncentracioni logor Jasenovac, knjiga IV, Jagodina, 2007.

———. *Ubijeni u koncentracionom logoru Jasenovac 1941–1945.* Jagodina: Gambit, 2011.

Mirković, Jovan. *Objavljeni izvori i literatura o jasenovačkim logorima*, B. Luka-Beograd: Muzej žrtava genocida, 2000.

Motl, Dejan and Đorđe Mihovilović. *Zaboravljeni Knjiga o posljednjim jasenovačkim logorašima.* Jasenovac–Zagreb: Spomen područje Jasenovac, 2015.

Nikodijević, Dušan. "Prilog utvrđivanju broja žrtava sistema logora Jasenovac 1941. godine," *Godišnjak za istraživanje genocida*, vol. 8, 2016, pp. 169–213.

———. "Brojevi žrtava u koncentracijskom logoru Jasenovac 1942. godine prema iskazima preželih svjedoka," *Godišnjak za istraživanje genocida*, vol. 9, 2017, pp. 95–117.

Odić, Slavko and Komarica, Slavko. *Zašto Jasenovac nije oslobođen*. Beograd, 2005.
Zečević, Miodrag and Jovan Popović. *Dokumenti iz istorije Jugoslavije, Državna komisija za utvrđivanje zločina okupatora i njihovih pomagača iz drugog svetskog rata*, book I. Beograd: Arhiv Jugoslavije, 1996.
Žerjavić, Vladimir. *Gubici stanovništva Jugoslavije u drugom svjetskom ratu*. Zagreb: Jugoslavensko viktimološko društvo, 1989.
Živanović, Srboljub. *Jasenovac, odabrani radovi, članci, intervijui, govori i diskusije*, in Todor Bjelkić (ed.), Beograd–London: Pešić i sinovi, 2008.
Žrtve rata 1941–1945 (rezultati popisa). Savezni zavod za statistiku. Beograd, 1966, reprint Beograd, 1992.

7 Forgotten Victims of World War II

The Suffering of Roma in the Independent State of Croatia, 1941–1945

Danijel Vojak

Introduction

The history of the Roma population in Croatian lands underwent periods of tolerance and coexistence alternating with periods of strong antigypsyism[1] when the authorities attempted forcible assimilation. This chapter will analyse the World War II period, when the Ustaša state authorities attempted to eliminate what was called the "Gypsy problem" by genocidal extermination measures. Because of the lack of systematic research about this suffering, there are several questions that need to be addressed first. One is the attitude of the non-Roma population towards the Roma and towards the Ustaša policy of extermination directed at them. Furthermore, it is necessary to place this suffering in the broader context of the Ustaša racist policy of creating a "pure Croatian space." The analysis will also include the matters of saving the "White Gypsies" (a sedentary Muslim Roma population in Bosna and Herzegovina) and of the Roma resistance against the repressive policies of the Ustaša government. Finally, the question of determining the number of Roma victims in Croatia will be addressed.

On Academic Research on the Suffering of Roma in World War II in Croatian and Other (Especially European) Historiographies

Over the past ten years and more I have often emphasised the term "forgotten holocaust" in my academic writing in order to point out as directly as possible that research on the suffering of Roma in World War II is still an insufficiently explored area in the historiography of many European countries, including Croatia. This marginal academic interest can be traced to a lack of interest by the general public and its political representatives for the understanding of this suffering. It is important to bear in mind that the Roma communities themselves were still politically and economically marginalised after World War II, disconnected, with no central home country to promote their rights or dedicated academic and cultural institutions to initiate and carry out academic research. The marginalisation of Roma victims was especially evident

DOI: 10.4324/9781003326632-9

in this context.² A further lack of understanding of the extent of the Roma suffering was noticeable on the judiciary level: There was no compensation – material, or of any other kind – for the Roma victims and their descendants. Moreover, after the war most European countries, such as West Germany, refused to acknowledge the Roma suffering as a consequence of the Nazi racial extermination policy; they insisted the persecution of Roma should be examined in a criminal context. In simple words, Roma were said to have been targeted more because of "criminal" charges than because of their race-based social exclusion. It was only in the beginning of the 1980s that, by political acknowledgement by the German state authorities, the decades-long process of building awareness in the German general public started, leading up to 2012 when German chancellor Angela Merkel, together with Roma survivors, unveiled a monument to Roma and Sinti victims in the centre of Berlin.³ In recent years an increasing number of European countries has been commemorating the suffering of Roma on the 2nd of August. The date refers to August 2, 1944, and the Nazi mass killing of several thousand Roma in the Auschwitz concentration camp.⁴ In Croatia, since 2012, an annual commemoration to honour Roma victims killed in Croatia and throughout Europe is held in the cemetery in the village of Uštice, part of Jasenovac Memorial Area.⁵

Bearing in mind the marginal interest of most European governments in the Roma suffering in World War II, it is important to note that it corresponded to a marginal academic (historiographic) interest. In 2015, Ilsen About and Anna Abakunova published a bibliographic review of published works about the suffering of the Roma in World War II for the International Holocaust Remembrance Alliance. The authors noted a lack of interest by the academic community for research about the suffering of Roma in World War II. For example, it was only 20 years after the end of World War II that the first synthesis on this subject was written: *Die Zigeuner im nationalsozialistischen Staat* by German scholar Hans-Joachim Döringy, published in Hamburg in 1964. The lack of academic interest was still evident between 1960 and 1970, when only about fifty works on the suffering of the Roma were published. From the 1980s to the present day more syntheses dedicated to this subject have been published. Notably, there is *Rassenutopie und Genozid. Die nationalsozialistische Lösung der Zigeunerfrage* by German historian Michael Zimmermann, published in Hamburg in 1996. A significant step in understanding the subject was made by the three-volume work *The Gypsies during the Second World War*, published by *Centre de recherches tsiganes* and *University of Hertfordshire Press* from 1999 to 2006, which analysed the suffering of the Roma in most European countries. Numerous authors collaborated on this work: Giovanna Boursier, Reimar Gilsenbach, Marie-Christine Hubert, Michelle Kelso, Elena Marushiakova, Vesselin Popov, Ctibor Nečas, Erika Thurner, Michael Zimmermann, Herbert Heuss, Henriette Asseo, Frank Sparing and others.⁶ Gunter Lewy's *The Nazi Persecution of the Gypsies* (1999) is one of the attempts at a synthesis of the Roma suffering in World War II, but some authors stated that it has caused controversies, both in academic and in wider circles. In 2007 Michael Zimmermann published his extensive work *Zwischen Erziehung und Vernichtung. Zigeunerpolitik und Zigeunerforschung im Europa des 20. Jahrhunderts* in Stuttgart. It is important to note the contribution and encouragement by historians whose subject was the suffering of Jews in the same war, such as Gilad Margalit.[7] Croatian historiography showed even less interest in the research of the suffering of the Roma in World War II than other European historiographies. After the end of World War II Roma victims were only briefly mentioned in the context of victims of fascism in general, especially in monographies dedicated to a certain area ravaged by the war and in written memoirs. To name some examples, Milko Riffer, Nikola Nikolić, and Ilija Jakovljević published memoirs of their detainment in the Jasenovac camp, including descriptions of the suffering of the Roma in the camp.[8] But the first academic papers about the suffering of Roma in the Independent State of Croatia were published by Narcisa Lengel-Krizman and Slavica Hrečkovski in the mid-eighties, when the Zagreb scholarly journal *Naše teme* published a themed issue on the suffering of Roma on the territory of certain Yugoslavian republics. In 2003, Narcisa Lengel-Krizman published her book *Genocid nad Romima: Jasenovac 1942*, in which she analysed the suffering of the Roma population in Jasenovac concentration camp in 1942, when the largest number of them were deported, with a list of names of Roma victims of the concentration camp at the end.[9] There is also my own work dealing with the World War I, interbellum, and World War II periods (published in collaboration with Bibijana Papo and Alen Tahiri).[10]

A Short History of Roma in Croatian Territories Prior to World War II

In order to place the social position of the Roma population in the Independent State of Croatia into a historical context, it is necessary to look back at the previous period. In brief, from their arrival in Croatian territories in the 14th century, the periods in which the government tried to assimilate them repressively outnumbered the periods of peaceful coexistence with the non-Roma population.[11] Like the rest of the population, after World War I the Croatian Roma became a part of the new Yugoslavian state union. Despite the fact that demographic data from the period is not sufficiently reliable because of bad methodology and frequent ethnic mimicry, it still shows that the number of Roma in the Kingdom of Yugoslavia before World War II was larger than 70,000, and that around 15,000 lived in Croatian territories (the Banovina of Croatia[12]). In interbellum Croatia most of them lived in the eastern parts of Slavonia, Syrmia, and Baranja; their religious affiliation was mostly Roman Catholic, they tended to be younger in age, and were almost entirely illiterate.[13] The policy of the Yugoslavian state authorities towards the Roma did not differ much from the policies of the previous governments: There were many unsuccessful attempts at repressive assimilation and forced sedentarisation.[14] Most of the Roma lived in rural areas, and the minority that lived in urban areas was, from the end of the 1920s, subjected to expulsion in order to "prevent Roma criminality."[15] In this period both the Yugoslavian central authorities and the individual Banovina authorities, especially those in the Sava Banovina and later in the Banovina of Croatia, strived to prevent the Roma nomadic way of life and to force sedentarisation. Even though there was public demand for the passing of a special law, especially in the period of the Banovina of Croatia, no such law was passed. Instead, the authorities used legislation from the Austro-Hungarian state supplemented with *ad hoc* orders.[16] The socio-economic marginalisation of Roma in this period is evident in the lack of any kind of institutional organising in order to improve their position in Croatian society. This passivity most likely stemmed from the pressure of the authorities that had been going on for centuries to assimilate and colonise them, and also from the lack of unity among the Roma themselves. The most usual occupations for Roma in interbellum Croatia were the processing of wood and metal, agriculture, trading in horses, collecting secondary raw materials (such as scrap iron), begging, and entertainment (as musicians and animal tamers in circuses).[17] A small number of Roma in the Sava Banovina managed to receive land for agriculture as part of the state agricultural policy. In spite of this, Roma living in this area were still perceived as burglars, frauds, spreaders of disease, abductors of children, and idlers. This perception was often (over)emphasised by the newspapers, especially in cases when a Roma person committed burglary or fraud, or in other cases of breaking the law; consequently, there were frequent cases of violence against the Roma by the rest of the population.[18]

The World War II period left devastating consequences in Roma communities in many European countries. Even before the war, the German state had a leading role in 'innovative' measures against what they called "the Gypsy menace." Notably, in 1899 a special unit of police was established, the Gypsy informative service (Ger. *Zigeuenernachrichtendienst* or *Zigeunerzentrale*) within the Munich police. A few years later a card index was established within this unit with personal data on several thousand Roma and Sinti individuals, in order to limit their movement.[19] Since the beginning of the 20th century German authorities attempted to assimilate the Roma through various repressive regulations in order to "racially cleanse" German society from all criminal and "racially inferior" elements.[20] When the National Socialists came to power in Germany in 1933, they inherited this model of repression and assimilation in their treatment of Roma and developed it further in accordance with their racial and eugenic theories. It was in this context that the National Socialist "project" of *Endlösung* ("the final solution") was created, suggesting measures such as euthanasia and forcible sterilisation of Roma in order to protect the racial purity of the German (and other) people.[21] The National Socialist model of the treatment of Roma was based on racial laws, and it started with eugenic measures such as sterilisation, limitation of movement, and concentration of the Roma in camps. The basis for these measures was a racial theory that saw Roma as parasites and "half-breeds" of several nations or races (Ger. *Mischvolk*). Racial theoreticians such as Robert Ritter created a classification of the Roma, dividing them into seven racial categories. Ritter's classification claimed that the *Reinrassiger Zigeuner* ("purebred Gypsies") were a small part of the Gypsies as a whole, which was harmless to the racial purity off the German people, but that most of the Roma were racially impure due to mixing with other races (Ger. *Mischlinge*). Because of this, most of the Roma were defined as *Zigeunermischlinge* ("gypsy half-breeds") and as part of the "work-shy" (Ger. *Asoziale*), and considered to be social parasites with a biological predisposition for crime. Ritter himself suggested that they should be imprisoned in camps and sterilised.[22] Based on these racial policies, and to fight the "gypsy plague," the Nazi government passed orders such as the "Decree on Combating the Gypsy Menace," passed by SS commander Heinrich Himmler in late 1938. Among other things, it prohibited entry to foreign Roma and demanded their expulsion; it ordered the registration of all Roma in order to define their racial status, and limited the issuing of permits for travelling tradesmen and for staying in border areas.[23] Since the beginning of World War II, the National Socialist treatment of the Roma included measures such as deportation to concentration camps, where they were tortured, used as a work force, and killed.[24] The result of this policy was genocide against the Roma, referred to by the Roma themselves by the name *Porajmos* ("cutting up," "fragmentation," "destruction") or, increasingly, by the name *Samudaripen* ("complete destruction/mass killing"), both terms with a meaning similar to the term *holocaust*.[25]

The Beginning of Roma Suffering in NDH: Racial Laws

World War II reached Croatian territories in April 1941 as a short armed conflict between the Axis powers, led by Germany, and the army of the Kingdom of Yugoslavia. After the capitulation of the Kingdom of Yugoslavia, the Independent State of Croatia (henceforth: NDH) was established. The profascist Ustaša movement led by Ante Pavelić took power in the new state with the help and support of the Axis powers; only states affiliated with this military–political alliance recognised it. The state was divided into a German and an Italian occupation zone, each with its own military and political influence. It should be pointed out that the Ustaša regime governed in a dictatorial and authoritative way and carried out policies in accordance with the racial laws they passed. A part of the Croatian population started an organised resistance, forming a Partisan (anti-fascist) movement led by the Communists.[26]

Ustaša political and ideological thought on shaping the newly founded state excluded members of minority groups, such as Jews, Serbs, and Roma, singling them out as unfit for life in the new state.[27] An example of such thought was published by an anonymous author in the Varaždin magazine *Hrvatsko jedinstvo* ("Croatian Unity") in the beginning of May 1941, which lists these three ethnic groups as the main "social and political problems" faced by the new government. Serbs are described as "dangerous and deadly vipers," Jews as "parasites," and Roma as those who should be "removed" from Croatian society because

> a people with healthy vital juices, with young and fresh forces – needs to shake off all such unsuitable parasites. Our present demands this of us, our future, our peace and our freedom; concern for our future Croat generations demands this of us. All ulcers need to be cut out from the national body. The operation will be difficult, but the national body, once its fever is over, will once again be young, fresh and energetic[; ...] we believe that in this way, everything that stands against our Croatian people in word or deed will be removed. There is no room for traitors in a free, Ustaša Croatia![28]

The Ustaša authorities did not wait long before attempting to solve "the Gypsy problem." This task was made easier by the already-existing prejudice against the Roma, which led to them being presented as "parasites" in the new Ustaša Croatia. Based on this, the Ustaša authorities began their persecution of the Roma soon after gaining power. In order to isolate the Roma population legally and socially, racial laws were passed by the end of April 1941: the *Statutory Provision on Race*, the *Statutory Provision on Citizenship*, and the *Statutory Provision on the Protection of the Aryan Blood and Honour of the Croatian People* with a clearly laid out racial classification of Roma in article 4.[29] These laws are noticeably influenced by the 1935 Nuremberg Laws, especially in their definition of Aryan ancestry.[30] It is also interesting to note the similarities in racial classification between the Ustaša government and the German government in Serbia.[31] One of the implementing acts of the *Statutory Provision on Race* was the use of a document called a *Statement on Racial Affiliation*, accompanied by *Instructions for writing a Statement on Racial Affiliation*.[32] The *Instructions* give additional explanations needed to fill out the form: "Besides Jews, non-Aryans are first of all Gypsies, and also Tatars, Kalmyks, Armenians, Persians, Arabs, Malayans and Blacks."[33]

In addition to these racial laws, the Roma were discriminated against by other laws passed in NDH. They were forbidden to work in civil service or to apply for such positions (e.g., on the railway), and if an individual of Aryan ancestry wanted to marry a Roma individual, they needed to obtain a special permit from the Ministry for Internal Affairs.[34]

The Colonisation and Registration of Roma

Soon after the legal basis for the persecution of Roma was established, the state authorities moved on to the next step: Creating a registry of Roma in order to determine their exact number in every location. It is important to note that the state authorities were not able to determine the precise number of Roma because the start of World War II prevented the population census planned for 1941, so they were forced to use data from the 1931 census.[35]

At the same time, the Institute for Colonisation of NDH ("Institut za kolonizaciju")[36] initiated the creation of a registry of Roma due to pressure from the local authorities in Križevci. In 1937, the district and town authorities in Križevci had sent a petition to what was then the Sava Banovina authorities about the necessity of solving the "Gypsy problem," suggesting that a special law on Roma should be passed (the "Law on Colonising and Civilising the Nomadic Gypsy Tribe").[37] In the background of this petition were accusations by the local authorities about Roma criminality and the spreading of cattle disease, which caused violent confrontations, such as in the case from January 1936, when villagers from Sela (in the vicinity of Križevci) banished the Roma and burned all their property.[38] Based on this initiative, the Sava Banovina authorities polled the local governments, asking them whether they supported the "colonisation of Roma" and how much they would be willing to contribute to its funding. A considerable number of local governments responded to this "poll," expressing clear support, but not many were willing to contribute significantly to the funding of this project, which is why it was eventually abandoned.[39] Similar complaints and petitions continued during the Banovina of Croatia period, when town representatives in Križevci made an appeal to collect money from townspeople and villagers for the "colonisation of Gypsies."[40] In spite of numerous attempts by the district and town authorities in Križevci, what they saw as the "Gypsy problem" remained unsolved. A good example is an official petition signed by nineteen inhabitants of Sveti Ivan Žabno on June 3, 1941 and addressed to the city council of Križevci. In the petition, Roma are accused of potential spreading of disease (anthrax) because they had consumed the carcass of a cow that died naturally, and of criminality. The petitioners demanded the "removal" of the Roma and the confiscation of their property.[41] This initiative was passed on to the Ministry for Internal Affairs of NDH, and in mid-June 1941. The Ministry sent the Institute for Colonisation an inquiry about "Gypsy colonization."[42] On July 1, 1941 the Institute replied, stating that the biggest problem in the colonisation of Roma is the unreliability of statistical data on their number:

> statistical data collected by the 1921, 1931 and 1941 censuses show a very small number of gypsies because the numbers were concealed to achieve a desirable ratio of ethnicities, so the Gypsies would declare themselves according to religion or native language as either Catholic, Muslim or Eastern Orthodox, while a certain number of Gypsies declared the Gypsy language as their native language. As officials from the Institute for Statistics have themselves declared, this data cannot be considered as correct because the number of declared Gypsies is smaller than the real number; an example is Sarajevo, where statistic data gives a number of

only 2, while in reality Sarajevo has an entire so-called Gypsy *mahala* [neighbourhood] with a considerably large number of Gypsies. The data for Bosnia and Herzegovina is particularly incorrect. According to the stated facts, the statistic data, published as well as unpublished, available to the State Institute for Statistics is insufficient and practically unusable, both for devising a plan for the colonisation of Gypsies and for its implementation.[43]

Because of these difficulties in determining the real number of Roma, the Institute suggested that the Roma should, following article 4 of the Statutory provision on Race, report to their municipalities to be registered as soon as possible, and that these registries should be sent to the district authorities in charge and to the Ministry for Internal Affairs. The district authorities were also asked to suggest possibilities, ways and locations for a "full colonisation of the Roma." At the end of this letter it is suggested that

[T]he Institute for Colonisation suggests the aforementioned method of collecting data on the Gypsies via the recipient, because a general order by the Ministry for Internal Affairs would lead to correct data being collected far more quickly, and it would temporarily obscure the purpose of the collecting.[44]

This quote is significant because it suggests that the Institute for Colonisation aimed to obscure the real reason for making a registry of all the Roma: Preparing for their complete colonisation. In this political context, on July 3, 1941, the NDH Ministry for Internal Affairs passed a decree on registration of the Roma, stating that it was a "first step in actions to be taken against the Gypsies."[45] The decree demanded that municipal authorities, aided by police forces, should make a registry by the end of July, listing the name and surname, sex, occupation and way of life (sedentary or nomadic) of every Roma individual on their territory. Notably, data about their religion was not requested. Of special interest in this decree is the expulsion of foreign Roma, which calls back to similar decrees on Roma passed in Croatian territories from the 16th century onwards.[46] In order to facilitate the implementation of the decree, some local authorities published a call (or order) for the registration of Roma in the media. As an example, the police directorate in Sarajevo gave this order on July 3, 1941:

[U]nder threat of severe punishment, all Serbian Gypsies residing in the city of Sarajevo, regardless of sex and occupation, are called to register within two days in Room 12 of the Police Directorate. An elder (head) of a household may only register his own family members. They may not register men or women living alone; these are under obligation to register in person. Anyone who does not heed this order will be severely punished and condemned to forced labour... .[47]

Two weeks later, the police directorate in Zagreb published a "notice," saying,

> by decree No. 13542 Pr. M.U.P.-1941 of the Ministry for Internal Affairs from July 3, 1941 all Gypsies of both sexes, including children, residing permanently or temporarily on the territory of the city of Zagreb, regardless of their occupation, must be registered. To this end, all Gypsies who reside on the territory of the city of Zagreb are called to turn in for registration at the Police Directorate in Zagreb, Gjorgjićeva Street no. 4, the upper floor, room 12 on July 22 and 23 this year, from 16 to 19.[48]

The registration of Roma on the territory of NDH was carried out in the summer of 1941; some contemporaries saw it as "the beginning of the open abuse of Gypsies."[49] Regrettably, according to available sources, not all of the local registries of Roma made in NDH survived to this day; among the surviving are the registries made in the municipalities of Ludbreg, Križovljan-Cestica, Jalžabet, Bartolovac, Berek, Podravske Sesvete, Erdevik, Banja Luka and the Krapina district.[50] The registries show that most of the Roma lived sedentary lifestyles – as evident in the Roma registries from Jalžabet and Bartolovec – while a smaller number still lived as nomads. For some Roma the listed occupation was begging; others were listed as tradesmen, day labourers or trough-makers.

The registries available reveal that the Ustaša authorities were provided with key data on the Roma population in their respective areas, especially data concerning their number and lifestyle (sedentary or nomadic) and their economic status. These data were meant to be used, first of all, for the colonisation of Roma. The Institute listed the benefits of the colonisation of Roma in July 1941 as,

> 1. Gypsies cause the spread of infectuous diseases in people and cattle alike, because of their vagrant way of life and their ways of earning such as begging, playing music, tinkering, mending, trading in horses, poultry, eggs and the like, and because of the bad hygiene of their living conditions, as well as their consumption of carcasses of poultry and animals that died naturally, whose diseases they often spread intentionally in order to obtain them [the carcasses].
> 2. In this way our villages and towns, especially the tourist locations, would be free of begging, threats to personal safety and the safety of property, lesser or larger cases of theft of cattle and cattle feed, poultry etc., fraud, fights and other lesser or larger misdemeanours.
> 3. The forced colonisation of Gypsies would free land that is now usurped by the gypsies, largely village pastures, but also pastures belonging to village communities, forest enclaves and land belonging to private owners, which the Gypsies have usurped in order to build their primitive homes.[51]

The Ministry for Internal Affairs was to forward the collected data to the Institute with suggestions "on the possibility, method and location for complete colonisation of the Gypsies." In addition to this, the Institute suggested that travel permits should be denied, in effect banning the Roma from moving until a "further decree" is passed; in other words, they wished to have complete control over the position of the Roma until specific plans were made on what should be done with them.[52] Any further activities of the Institute in preparations for the colonisation of Roma in NDH, or for its implementation, are not known; the logical conclusion is that the idea of colonisation was abandoned, probably because the NDH authorities were not sufficiently prepared to implement it due to increasingly difficult war-related circumstances.

Mass Killings of Roma

There is no known document or programme by the Ustaša authorities ordering mass liquidations of Roma, but there are known cases of this happening. The first known case of a mass liquidation of Roma happened on July 29, 1941, when 15 Roma were killed in Ivanić Jarak near Karlovac.[53] On the last day of July 1941, Ustaša forces on the territory of Donja Bučica (in the Glina district) killed 19 Serbs, 11 Roma, and 3 Croats.[54] At the end of December 1941 and the beginning of January 1942, 74 Roma from the villages of Desno Sredičko, Štipan and Lasinje were killed in Rakov Potok, and 105 Roma were killed in Banski Kovačevac (in the Vrginmost district). On the same day, 24 Roma from the Pištac and Glavica settlements near the village of Skakavac were killed, and on January 6, 1942, Ustaša authorities killed 41 Roma from Popović village in the forest Domaći Lug.[55] Mass killings of Roma continued until the end of the war, as shown by the killing of 30 Roma from Jezerane (in the Brinje area) and of 11 Roma from Lučko Cerje and Sveti Rok (in the Gračac district) in mid-July 1944.[56] When the Ustaša took power in the wider Grubišno Polje area, they started persecuting the Roma inhabitants living in Stalovice: Their hair was cut off, and they were in fear that the Ustaša would "destroy" them, similarly to what the German allies were known to have done.[57] It should also be noted the Italian authorities helped NDH authorities in the imprisonment of Roma. An example of this was a group of 7 Roma from the Hudorović family (Dreženica), who were "caught" by the Italian authorities in early June 1942, and surrendered to the NDH authorities in Ogulin, where they were soon killed.[58] According to the sources available, these mass killings of Roma in and prior to the first half of 1942 were not systematic, and there was no specific command or instruction by NDH military or civilian authorities that they should be carried out. In these cases, the Roma were probably collateral victims, most likely of conflicts between the NDH authorities and the growing Partisan movement, but this does not diminish the extent of their suffering.

Deportations of Roma

The next phase had a key role in the persecution of Roma in NDH: in the spring of 1942, the Ustaša government ordered that the Roma should be deported to Jasenovac concentration camp, where most of them were eventually killed. The sources available show that there were some deportations of Roma to the Jasenovac camp before May 1942, but it was then that the deportations became systematic and included the whole territory of NDH. During 1941 and up until May 1942 deportations of Roma to Jasenovac camp were sporadic and unsystematic, as shown by the examples of Roma deported from Slavonski Brod, Virovitica, Vrginmost, Križevci, and Duga Resa.[59] The period of systematic deportations began with a circular by the Ministry for Internal Affairs and a decree by the Ustaša Surveillance Service supported by the Directorate for Public Order and Security, from May 19, 1942, with the following order:

> [F]ollowing a verbal notice by the Directorate for Public Order and Security, county police authorities are ordered to collect all Gypsies from all districts and to surrender them to the district authorities, who will treat them in accordance with received orders.[60]

We might ask ourselves about the circumstances that brought about the passing of this decree. Some authors point out the influence of the Nazi authorities, who were behind similar deportations in Romania and Bulgaria.[61] It has been suggested that NDH authorities were waiting for more favourable weather, which would allow them to better organise the deportations of Roma, but this thesis has not been substantiated.[62] Other scholars state that NDH authorities only started deporting Roma in the late spring of 1942, after certain deportations of the Serb and Jewish population, because the latter were considered a priority over the deportations of Roma.[63] In this context, some claim that the deportations of Roma were a consequence of deportations of the Serb population, which led to a "radicalisation of treatment" of other minority groups by the NDH authorities.[64] Most of these theses are hypotheses, but they are not extensively supported by the available sources.

On the basis of this decree, mass arrests and detainment of Roma began. Newspapers reported that the "Gypsy problem" was being solved by the use of their work force in camps.[65] NDH authorities must have been aware of potential problems in carrying out the deportations of Roma to the Jasenovac camp, such as their potential resistance. For this reason they deceived the Roma, trying to convince them they were being detained in order to colonise land taken from Serbs and Montenegrins forced out of Kosovo, or moved to other parts of the state (such as Bosnia or the central parts of NDH) or to a "Gypsy state."[66] Some of the Roma were told by Ustaša authorities that they were being deported in order to return to their homeland of Romania, and others that they would be taken to Slovenia (Celje) as a labour force.[67]

This was the beginning of deportations of the Roma to the Jasenovac camp. Sources reveal that the Zagreb police deported 69 Roma to Jasenovac on May 28, 1942; the next day, Roma from Ladimirevci (in the Valpovo district) were deported, followed by Roma from Petrijevci (also in the Valpovo district). That same year, in early June, around 400 Roma were deported to Jasenovac by the Zemun police, and 127 Roma by the Ogulin authorities. On June 6, 1942, the Županja authorities reported that around 2,000 Roma had been gathered and deported to Jasenovac.[68] Three days later, the NDH authorities deported 39 Roma from the village of Šeketino Brdo (in the Duga Resa district).[69] On July 9, 1942, 29 Roma from Tušilovićki Cerovac (in the Vojnić district) were deported to Jasenovac.[70] There are also records of deportations of Roma from Vukovar (1,136 adults and 469 children), Vinkovci (1,154 Roma), Đakovo, Orahovica, Našice, Podravska Slatina, Daruvar, Virovitica (33 Roma were taken from the village of Budanice on August 8 1941,[71] and the inhabitants of the Roma village of Kapetanovo Selo near Suhopolje were taken away in early September 1942[72]), Grubišno Polje, Slavonska Požega, Brod na savi (Slavonski Brod), Nova Gradiška, Novska, Irig, Hrvatski Karlovci (Sremski Karlovci), Grabovci, Jamena, Slatina and Ogulin.[73] Deportations of Roma continued after the summer of 1942. On October 15, 1942, NDH authorities deported 10 Roma from Slakovci (near Novi Jankovci) to Jasenovac.[74] The next year, the same authorities deported a group of 35 Roma from Gudinci (in the Županja area) to the Jasenovac camp.[75]

Expropriation of Roma Property

The difficult economic standing of most Roma from the prewar period continued and worsened during World War II. The aforementioned ban on Roma movement, associated with their registration in the summer of 1941, made it impossible for them to trade (e.g., in horses, pigs, poultry) or work in crafts (such as blacksmithing, making wooden household objects or troughs).[76] Still, some Roma owned houses, land, fields and other valuable property both in rural and in urban areas of NDH. An example of the Ustaša taking over Roma property after they had been deported was recorded in the Marijanci and Čađavica municipality (in the Donji Miholjac district). Archival documents reveal that the Colonisation Bureau in Osijek (a part of the Fifth Department for Nationalised Property, under the Treasury) made an inventory of Roma property after the people were deported to the Jasenovac camp, and then sold it to the local population in public auctions.[77] Some Roma real estate was given to "poor homeless residents" for "temporary use," or used to provide housing for doctors – an example is a decree by the municipal authorities in Čađavica.[78] The Colonisation Bureau in Osijek took over the land of 63 Roma families displaced from this area, which shows that the Roma property was significant in amount and value.[79] Similar cases of expropriation of Roma property occurred in the Karlovac area, where the city authorities took over the property of Roma deported from the villages of Pokuplje, Brdo and

Velika Jelsa and sold it at a public auction. It is interesting to note that before the auction the authorities decided that priority in buying would be given to "poor peasants with large families who do not have the necessary land."[80] In addition to this, the same city authorities allowed for the lease of Roma property in their jurisdiction area. Among the individuals who applied for the lease of Roma property was Stjepan Mikšić from Turanj, who pointed out that he was a poor reserve sergeant in the army, with an unemployed wife and two children.[81] From 18 to 20 September 1942, an auction of "Gypsy items" was held in the Vinkovci area. The items sold were mostly household objects (beds, tables and chairs, bedding, dishcloths, curtains), and lists were made of buyers and of the prices paid.[82] As we can see, the Ustaša authorities sought to profit from the property of the deported Roma, and by doing this to finance their anti-Gypsy policy of extermination.

Roma in the Jasenovac Camp

Unlike other prisoners, the Roma deported to camps were not listed individually, but as part of a "train carriage." Roma were forced to the camp not only in trains but also by foot, in long marches. On their arrival at the camp, their personal belongings were taken (plundered) from them. Some of the non-Roma survivors, such as Zorko Golub and Daniel Kovačević, mention that a considerable amount of gold coins, money, jewellery, musical instruments, horses and other belongings were taken from the Roma.[83] Upon arrival at the Jasenovac camp, the Roma would be divided into two groups: The infirm, the sick and the women and children would be placed into group "3b," and the "stronger and more resilient" Roma into group "3c."[84] In the Jasenovac camp system, the Roma were held in the northeast part of the camp, which was built on swampy terrain prone to flooding, which made it difficult for the Partisans to reach and liberate it. The camp area was around 30 m x 60 m in size (around 400 meters according to some estimates), wire-fenced and guarded. This part of the camp was named Camp III C (C for "ciganski," meaning *gypsy*).[85] Commander Vjekoslav Luburić planned to make it into a labour camp and a camp for executions of the prisoners. The Ustaša authorities used it as a place to leave seriously ill prisoners.

Other Roma were, at first, settled in the village of Uštica in the houses of displaced Serbs, but because of their large number, a part was moved into the village of Gradina across the Sava, the place of the largest mass liquidations.[86] Some of the Roma were, for a short while, placed in the part of the Jasenovac camp called "Brickworks," according to the testimony of Vladimir Čerkez, who states that when he entered Brickworks in the autumn of 1941 he found a large group of Roma "by the name of Parapatić" who were "in rags, terrified, thin, starved."[87] Some of the Roma were put up tents or supports with roofs within the Jasenovac camp, but many others were left with no protection of any kind. The Roma prisoners were given worse food than the others. Their number would vary between several hundred and several thousand. According to witnesses, there was not enough room to sleep in their part of the camp, so the prisoners would "suffocate in a seated position." After the Roma prisoners were exhausted by starvation, mass liquidations followed. In addition to this, some of the Roma inmates were forced to sing and entertain the Ustaša guards.[88] In July 1942, camp commander Vjekoslav Luburić was recorded as ordering that a special orchestra should be formed out of a group of Roma musicians in order to entertain the camp authorities and prisoners on Sundays. Other witnesses claim this was a group of 30 Roma from Zemun, who had been working as musicians for a hotel before the war.[89] Some of the Roma were used as a work force for building a nearby embankment, a task that was considered by some prisoners to be the most strenuous in the camp, but like the others, they were killed soon afterwards.[90] This is how Zorko Golub remembered the life of Roma in the Jasenovac camp:

> After the meal you lie down for a while on the ground next to 3 C. Inside are the Gypsies, those who work on the embankment, and inmates in detention. It's an open space, they sleep on the ground, when the sun is scorching they sweat, when it rains they spend the night in rain and mud. And they work on the Sava embankment all day: you push a cart full of soil, and if you stagger – a buttstroke on the head and they push you with a stick into some hole or into the Sava. They eat only once a day, that smelly bean soup. Not a single one lasts longer than ten days.[91]

The testimonies of other surviving inmates are similar. The Roma are said to have been the most vulnerable among the inmates, because, "if you kill a Gypsy, you have done a useful thing, as if you've squashed a bedbug with your fingernail."[92]

Witness testimonies and official reports after World War II often mention that NDH authorities "spared" a group of around a hundred Roma from Lika, who were given village houses to live in, received good food and "drank themselves into oblivion." According to other witnesses these were "Gypsies from Lika" ("free Gypsies") who, with some other prisoners, formed "group D" used by the camp authorities to kill and bury other prisoners and to build embankments and walls around the camp. The camp authorities had them all killed in early 1945.[93] The majority of Jasenovac survivors testify that most of the Roma prisoners were killed within a few months. One of the witnesses to the Jasenovac crimes, Jovan Živković, observed,

> when it comes to genocide, the Gypsies were a priority and not a single one of them survived. Those who could not work were killed immediately, they never stood a chance. Jews and Serbs in the rest of the camp at least had a chance of sorts. The Gypsies had no chance.[94]

The "White Gypsies" – Rescuing a Part of the Roma Population

During World War II, a part of the Croatian–Muslim Society, together with Islamic religious authorities, organised to protect a part of the NDH Roma population. According to some sources, an important part in the protection of this group of Roma was played by the Zagreb Croatian–Muslim Society, which intervened on May 19, 1941.[95] Still, most authors agree that the protection was initiated by representatives of Muslim societal elites and Islamic religious authorities in Bosnia and Herzegovina. The registration of Roma in Tešanj in July 1941 provoked a reaction in part of the Muslim population, who condemned this action done by the Ustaša authorities. A special commission was formed with the task of writing an expert study in order to protect the Muslim Roma population, who were at the time referred to as "White Gypsies." Leading Muslim intellectuals, such as Derviš M. Korkut, Hamdija Kreševljaković, Mehmed Handžić, and Muhamed Kantardžić, were appointed to this commission. The commission soon presented their study to the NDH authorities, claiming that the "White Gypsies" should be considered a part of the Muslim population, completely "assimilated," "Croatised," and Aryan. They cited scholarly work by Leopold Glück on the anthropology of Roma in Bosnia and Herzegovina from the late 19th century as an argument in favour of their thesis. The NDH authorities accepted this study, and in late August they ordered that the registration of the "White Gypsies" should be cancelled.[96] The study also attempted – unsuccessfully – to protect the Eastern Orthodox Roma, citing the scholarly work of Teodor Filipescu and claiming that these Roma were of Romanian origin and that their killing could cause problems in the relations between NDH and Romania.[97]

This concession by the Ustaša is sometimes interpreted as evidence of their fear of a "rebellion" of Muslims in Bosnia and Herzegovina.[98] However, the NDH authorities temporarily 'forgot' their own decree and, in addition to the mass deportations of Roma, after May 19, 1942, they started to deport the "White Gypsies" from Bosnia and Herzegovina, especially those from Travnik.[99] A week later, 27 distinguished Muslims from Zenica wrote a special resolution emphasising the need to protect the White Gypsies as a part of the Muslim community.[100] In addition to this, the resolution demanded that the previous decree on the protection of "White Gypsies" from late August 1941 be regarded, and for the already deported Roma to be released from the camp.[101] The resolution was forwarded to the Ulema Mejlis of the Islamic religious community in Sarajevo, who consulted the office of the Reis–ul–Ulema and then appealed to the central authorities in Zagreb. On May 29, 1942, the Ministry for Internal Affairs responded by cancelling further deportations of "White Gypsies," noting that these were Muslim Roma, defined as Aryans. This decision saved the lives of a substantial number of Muslim Roma. Following the decree by the Ministry for Internal Affairs, county authorities soon proclaimed that deportations should only include nomadic Roma "without no permanent residence, occupation and property," and that "Muslim White

Gypsies" should not be included in the deportations.[102] Understandably, other Roma tried to exploit this policy of the NDH authorities by converting to Islam. The Sarajevo authorities sought to prevent this. There is a recorded case of Roma in the Karlovac area starting to wear fezzes and civil suits; the Ustaša Surveillance Service issued a warning on June 9, 1942, that such cases should be prevented.[103]

This leads to the question of how many Roma were saved after the issuing of the order that deportations should be cancelled. Some say that the NDH authorities did not obey the decree to spare the "White Gypsies," but deported them to the Jasenovac camp and killed them just like the others. It has also been stated that only those "White Gypsies" who managed to bribe the local NDH authorities were spared from deportations and from further suffering.[104] This is supported by the case of the Roma from Janja and Bijeljina, who saved themselves by bribing the Ustaša authorities with gold.[105]

Roma and the Partisan Movement

The participation of Roma in Yugoslav Partisan units is one of many issues from that period that demand more comprehensive scholarly research. Roma joined Partisan movements on the territories of many European countries: In Serbia, Italy, France, Slovakia, Montenegro, Bulgaria, Macedonia, Greece, and Albania.[106] Scholars researching the involvement of ethnic minorities in the Yugoslavian Partisan movement do not mention the Roma; the Hungarian minority is mentioned most of all as being involved in Partisan units, the Slovakian and German minority are also common, while the Roma are given only a passing mention.[107] Roma resisted collaboration with the Ustaša authorities, as the example of Grubišno Polje demonstrates: it is stated that throughout the war, not a single Roma ever joined the Ustaša.[108] But sources show that some Roma actively participated in the Partisan movement. Some see their involvement in the movement as a reaction to Ustaša violence, especially in mid-1942, during the mass deportations of Roma to the Jasenovac camp.[109] The best example is the aforementioned case of four Roma from Bobota, the only ones who managed to avoid deportation to the Jasenovac camp in the summer of 1942, who joined the Partisan movement soon afterwards. There is also the example of a Roma man called Mile Radosavljević, who avoided the deportation of Roma from Vrbanja because he was working in the forest; he and his family then joined the Partisans.[110] A woman called Danica Nikolić managed to avoid the deportation of her fellow Roma from the village of Negoslavci (in the Vukovar area), and afterwards joined the Partisan movement.[111] Some of the Roma who managed to escape from the Jasenovac camp joined the Partisan movement, too: among others, Josip–Joka Nikolić from the village of Predavac (in the Čazma area), Janko Gomen from Novoselac, Milan Radosavljević from Novi Jankovci (in the Vinkovci area), Štefan Nikolić from Zagreb, and so forth.[112] In mid-July 1942, three "local" Roma Home Guard soldiers escaped from the Jezerane barracks to join the Partisans, bringing with them six guns and some "enemy mail." It is interesting to note that Roma had been collaborating with the Partisans from the beginning of the year.[113] In late July 1942, at his hearing before the NDH authorities, Josip Babić from Gornja Garešnica reported that an increasing number of Roma were joining the Partisan movement. Babić had been captured by the Partisans in mid-May 1942 near Podravska Slatina and held captive; he escaped two months later. At his hearing before the NDH authorities he mentioned that he had noticed Roma joining the Partisan movement "lately," and he had been told they "had come from the camp."[114] Some have pointed out that the NDH authorities may have started to deport the Roma because of fear that they might cooperate with the Partisan movement, as demonstrated in the case of deportations of Roma from the Zemun area in mid-1942.[115] In this context we should mention a proposition by the local authorities in Derventa from May 1943, which lists the Roma's disloyalty to NDH and inclination to help "the Partisans and Chetniks" as reasons to "remove" them from the area into camps.[116]

An especially interesting case was the creation of the first "Gypsy Partisan unit" in the vicinity of Daruvar. In July 1942 the Partisans came across a few Roma families, around 40 people in all, in the forest between Kreštelovac and Goveđe Polje (in the Daruvar area), who had escaped there in fear of Ustaša deportations.[117] An interesting case of a clash between Partisans and a group of Roma accused of stealing happened in the Sesvete area. In June 1941 it was reported that "some robbers" had appeared in the villages of Cerje, Šašinovec, Popovec and Soblinec, taking money and food from people allegedly in the name of Partisans, beating up and terrorising people. The local population blamed the Partisans for this, which lead to the Partisans reacting and investigating these events. The culprits were soon identified as some Roma who lived in the Cerje area, or Roma from Farkaševac, who had been with the Partisans in Moslavina and deserted, along with a few local inhabitants. The Partisans caught the accused Roma, along with two non-Roma, organised a trial in the woods behind the church in the village of Cerje, sentenced them to death and shot them.[118] This was, in short, a case of Roma who had been Partisan deserters and who were robbing locals while presenting themselves as Partisans.

Roma Victims: The Numbers

The number of Roma victims is one of the central questions that need to be addressed in order to understand the extent of their suffering in NDH. Moreover, there have been more than a few attempts in Croatian public life to manipulate the number of Roma victims in order to prove certain revisionist viewpoints on this matter.[119] For this reason, it is important to address the problem of the number of Roma victims in NDH in some detail. To start with, it needs to be said that it is impossible to establish the exact number of Roma killed in Jasenovac concentration camp and in other parts of NDH.

The reasons for this lie in several aspects of the problem. The first aspect is the lack of relevant documents recorded by the NDH authorities as the ones responsible for the persecution of Roma in World War II. These documents do not exist because, as some suggest, the Ustaša authorities destroyed them, and/or because they never even created them, counting the Roma only as a number of "train carriages" arriving in the camp. This aspect of anonymity of the Roma victims only emphasises the extent of their suffering. Still, we must not forget that some documents do exist, such as the ones recorded by the "occupiers": Documents by the Hungarian and Italian authorities on "occupied" Croatian territories. Documents recorded by German authorities are exceptionally important for research on this subject as well.[120] Even though there are no known Ustaša documents on the Roma from the Jasenovac camp itself, there are surviving documents from the registration of Roma organised in the summer of 1941, albeit only for around twenty communities in NDH. There are also some documents referring to deportations of Roma to the Jasenovac camp, mostly from the period from May 1942 to the end of the year, but they are not known in their entirety. A step towards a systematic approach to this subject was the publishing of the "List of Individual Victims of Jasenovac Concentration Camp" by Public Institution Jasenovac Memorial Area, although we have to keep in mind that, according to the authors, this list "is not definitive or complete, but offers the option to add to the data and to correct mistakes if any are found."[121]

In spite of criticism of this list of names, referring above all to the methods of collecting (and verifying) data, it offers a framework for determining the scale of suffering of individual groups of victims, including the Roma. Regrettably, inexpert criticism of this list led certain 'scholars' to tendentious conclusions, such as that there were no Roma victims in the Jasenovac camp at all.[122]

The second aspect of the impossibility of determining the exact number of Roma victims is the impossibility of determining the exact number of Roma who had been living in NDH. The greatest problem is caused by the fact that the 1941 census was not held because of the outbreak of World War II, leaving scholars with no choice but to use data from the previous census, held in 1931. In doing this, data on the number of Roma from the Sava Banovina and the Littoral Banovina can be added together, and then the numbers from other areas (today's Bosnia and Herzegovina, then the Vrbas Banovina and the Drina Banovina). Based on data from the 1931 census, the number of Roma living on the NDH territory can be estimated to around 15,000. But how can we determine the number of Roma in 1941, when NDH was established? This is exceptionally difficult, because demographers and other experts are faced with the problem of methodological deficiencies in the way not only the 1931 census, but also the previous ones – in 1921, 1910, 1900 and so forth – were conducted. There is, for instance, the issue of registering nomadic Roma, and the issue of ethnic mimicry among the Roma – the hiding of one's own ethnic identity because of fear of discrimination by the societal majority.[123] It is interesting to note that experts from the Statistics Department were analysing this issue during World War II – the calculations preserved in their archival records, available in the Croatian National Archives, confirm this.[124]

The third aspect of this issue is the lack of systematic scholarly research on this subject. Even though the sets of documents mentioned above are significant, partially preserved, and available to researchers, not much has been done to analyse them. We must bear in mind that it was only with the modest, but significant, scholarly work by Slavica Hrečkovski and Narcisa Lengel-Krizman in the 1980s, over 40 years after the suffering of the Roma, that this subject appeared on the Croatian historiographic horizon. The reason for this is a lack of systematic scholarly research. The lack of this research reflects a certain lack of interest in Croatian historiography for this subject. Most notably, there is a lack of scholarly contributions about the suffering of Roma on a local level, which is a reflection of insufficient research of this topic in local archives. However, a source we can use to determine the numbers of Roma victims in World War II are witness testimonies given before the Land Commission for Investigation of War Crimes of the Occupiers and Their Collaborators of Croatia, and before the equivalent Commission for Bosnia and Herzegovina. Furthermore, some scholars use victims' lists that were made at several points after World War II. Another significant source are the written records from the hearings and trials of those who held certain positions in state and local governments in NDH and, hence, also took part in the persecution of Roma.[125] Without analysing in more detail the advantages and disadvantages of the use of these sources, it has to be pointed out that they cannot build a complete picture of Roma suffering.

The issue of Roma victims in NDH was, in most cases, necessarily tied to the issue of the Roma killed in the Jasenovac camp. Employees of Jasenovac Memorial Area Public Institution have compiled the "List of Individual Victims of Jasenovac Concentration Camp 1941–1945" including Roma victims of the camp, and available on the institution's website is a victims' database, which can be searched according to several parameters (name and surname, year of birth, place and municipality of birth).[126]

The extent of the suffering of the Roma population in World War II in Croatia is best illustrated by the fact that the prewar censuses recorded around 15,000 (Roma) (1931), and the first postwar census, in 1948, recorded only 405 in Croatia and 442 in Bosnia and Herzegovina. It is evident that the Roma population on the territory of NDH was practically annihilated, even though these "official data" should always be taken with great caution due to methodological and other issues (such as "ethnic mimicry" by the Roma).[127] It was only in the last, 2011 census, that the registered number of Roma came close to the number from 1931, a fact that demonstrates that it took 80 years for the Roma population in Croatia to "regenerate demographically."[128]

These are the reasons for the significant differences in the "estimates" of the number of Roma killed in NDH. According to data from the List of Individual Victims of Jasenovac Concentration Camp, compiled by Jasenovac

Memorial Area employees, there are 16,173 registered Roma victims.[129] Based on her research of available archival documents and relevant sources, Narcisa Lengel-Krizman gives a number of 8,570 Roma victims (including around 3,000 unidentified individuals), most of them from the territories of the present-day Vukovar-Syrmia and Osijek_Baranja counties.[130] In his work on victims of the Jasenovac camp, Antun Miletić gave the numbers as 19,532 Roma victims from the territory of the present-day Republic of Croatia, and 4,126 Roma from the territory of today's Bosnia and Herzegovina.[131] Other scholars offer different numbers of Roma victims in NDH. Milan Bulajić mentions 40,000 Roma killed in NDH, Rajko Đurić between 40,000 and 60,000, Manachem Shelah and Dennis Reinhartz 26,000, Ferdo Čulinović 30,000, Jozo Tomašević 20,000 and Ivo Goldstein 15,000.[132] In addition to this, there is the opinion in a part of Croatian historiography that the extent of Roma suffering in NDH is being exaggerated, especially when speaking about the victims of the Jasenovac camp.[133]

Dennis Reinhartz wrote in one of his works that the territory of NDH was "proportionally" the place of the greatest genocide against the Roma population in World War II.[134] I believe that it is not possible to determine the actual number of Roma killed in NDH, and that we need to focus on a systematic analysis of existing documents and on searching for new sources instead. Considering that over 70 years have passed since the end of World War II, time is running out for recording testimonies by Roma survivors and by non-Roma who have witnessed their suffering.

Conclusion

In the history of Roma in Croatian territories up to the present day, the periods of persecution and repressive anti-gypsy policies of assimilation outnumbered the periods of peaceful coexistence and mutual tolerance. Negative perceptions of the Roma by the governments as well as by the population of many European countries, including Croatia, were based on prejudice and "othering." The pinnacle of Roma persecution on Croatian territories happened during World War II, when the Ustaša authorities declared the Roma to be among the enemies of the newly founded Independent State of Croatia. In a sense, the Ustaša authorities had a convenient period to "solve" this issue because there was no immediate opposition to their policy of extermination of the Roma. The Ustaša authorities saw the Roma as "parasites" or "sores" that needed to be removed as soon as possible from the Croatian racially pure organism. It did not take long for the systematic persecution of the Roma in NDH to begin: A few weeks after coming into power, the Ustaša authorities passed racial laws which made the Roma social outcasts. The next step was the registration of the Roma in July 1941 in order to determine the real demographics of the Roma population and to create a foundation for the solution of what they saw as the "Gypsy issue." The Ustaša authorities briefly considered the colonisation of the Roma in certain areas, but they soon abandoned this idea, largely because it was difficult to carry out due to the war. Instead, a little more than a year after coming into power, the Ustaša authorities decided on mass deportations of Roma from all parts of the country to the Jasenovac camp. As the organised deportations were carried out, the authorities deceived the Roma that they were being taken to areas where they would be able to live and work in peace. Instead, their final destination was the Jasenovac camp, where the majority of Roma were brought from the end of May 1942 to the end of the summer of the same year. In the camp the Roma were tortured, and large numbers of them were killed. A part of the Roma managed to avoid the deportations, especially the sedentary Muslim Roma in Bosnia and Herzegovina (the "White Roma"), who were saved due to interventions by some Muslim intellectuals supported by the Islamic religious community. When World War II ended in May 1945, the drastic effect the war had on the Roma community in Croatia became clear. The genocidal policy of the Ustaša almost completely destroyed the prewar Roma community, and it would take over sixty years for the community to compensate for the demographic losses. The postwar policy of marginalisation of the suffering of the Roma in NDH was similar to the treatment this topic received in most European countries, which led to the epithet, "the forgotten holocaust." This work is a scholarly contribution to the fight against the repression of this subject and to a better understanding of the history of the suffering of the Roma minority in Croatian territories.

Notes

1 Antigypsyism is defined as a special form of racism, determined by historical and geographical factors in specific communities, often manifested through violence, hate speech, exploitation, discrimination, segregation, dehumanisation, stigmatisation, abuse, ethnic mimicry (concealment of one's own ethnic identity) negative (stereotypical) discourse and an unfavourable standing in political, scientific, public and civic society for the Roma. In addition to this, the term is similar to "anti-Semitism." The word Antigypsyism was first used in the Soviet Union in the 1920s, but its current definition was shaped in scientific discussions in the 1970s and 1980s, forming the basis for the final definition given by Valeriu Nicolae Ciolan, a Roma activist from Romania, in 2006. This term is not as widely known and used in academic discourse as it is in contemporary public and political discourse. In this context we can point out the activities of the European Parliament, which used the term "Antigypsyism" for the first time in April 2005, describing it in one of its resolutions as equal to Anti-Semitism. In the same year and the years that followed other European Union institutions started using the term: *Antigypsyism – a Reference Paper (version June 2017)*, http://antigypsyism.eu/wp-content/uploads/2017/07/Antigypsyism-reference-paper-16.06.2017.pdf (accessed November 8, 2017); Valeriu Nicolae Ciolan, *The Role of Diplomacy in Achieving Representation and Participation for the Roma; dissertation Faculty of Arts University of Malta, 2006*, pp. 22–32, www.diplomacy.edu/sites/default/files/23082010104317%20Nicolae%20(Library).pdf (accessed October 15, 2017); The Support Team to the Special Representative of the Secretary General for Roma Issues, *Dosta! oslobodimo se*

predrasuda–upoznajmo Rome! (Strasbourg, 2011), pp. 23–24; *Council of Europe Descriptive Glossary of terms relating to Roma issues*, http://a.cs.coe.int/team20/cah rom/documents/Glossary%20Roma%20EN%20version%2018%20May%202012. pdf (accessed November 15, 2017.); The International Holocaust Remembrance Alliance (IHRA) in October 2020 had adopted non-legally binding working definition of Antigypsyism as "a manifestation of individual expressions and acts as well as institutional policies and practices of marginalization, exclusion, physical violence, devaluation of Roma cultures and lifestyles, and hate speech directed at Roma as well as other individuals and groups perceived, stigmatized, or persecuted during the Nazi era, and still today, as 'Gypsies.' This leads to the treatment of Roma as an alleged alien group and associates them with a series of pejorative stereotypes and distorted images that represent a specific form of racism," *About the IHRA working definition of antigypsyism/anti-Roma discrimination*, www.holoc austremembrance.com/resources/working-definitions-charters/working-definition-antigypsyism-anti-roma-discrimination (accessed September 9, 2021).

2 Anton Weiss-Wendt, "Introduction," in *The Nazi Genocide of the Roma*, ed Anton Weiss-Wendt (New York-Oxford: Beghahn, 2013), pp. 1–26; Becky Taylor, *Another Darkness, Another Dawn: A History of Gypsies, Roma and Travellers* (London: Reaktion Books, 2014), pp. 187–192.

3 Nadine Blumer, "Disentangling the Hierarchy of Victimhood. Commemorating Sinti and Roma and Jews in Germany's National Narrative," in: Anton Weiss-Wendt (ed.) *The Nazi Genocide of the Roma* (New York-Oxford: Berghahn, 2013), pp. 1–26.

4 Danijel Vojak, "Međunarodni dan sjećanja na romske žrtve holokausta Jasenovac, 2. kolovoza 2012.," *Povijest u nastavi*, vol. 10, no. 20 (2), 2014, pp. 247–250.

5 Ibid.

6 The first volume was translated and published in Croatia by Ibis grafika in 2006 with the title Od 'rasne znanosti' do logora, and the second (*U sjeni svastike*) and third volume (*Završno poglavlje*) were translated by the same publisher in 2009.

7 Yaron Matras, "Gilad Margalit, 1959–2014," *Romani Studies*, vol. 26, no. 2, pp. 211–212.

8 Milko Riffer, *Grad mrtvih: Jasenovac 1943* (Zagreb: Naklada Pavičić, 2011); Nikola Nikolić, *Jasenovački logor* (Zagreb: Nakladni zavod Hrvatske, 1948); Ilija Jakovljević, *Konclogor na Savi* (Zagreb: Konzor, 1999)

9 Narcisa Lengel-Krizman, *Genocid nad Romima: Jasenovac 1942* (Jasenovac: Javna ustanova Spomen područje Jasenovac, 2003.)

10 See: Danijel Vojak, "Izbor iz bibliografije radova o stradanju Roma u Nezavisnoj Državi Hrvatskoj," in: Danijel Vojak, Bibijana Papo, Alen Tahiri (eds.) *Stradanje Roma u Nezavisnoj Državi Hrvatskoj, 1941.–1945* (Zagreb: Institut društvenih znanosti Ivo Pilar /Romsko nacionalno vijeće, 2015), pp. 353–369.

11 For more on the history of Roma in Croatian territories from their arrival in the 14th century to World War I, see: Danijel Vojak, *U predvečerje rata: Romi u Hrvatskoj 1918.–1941* (Zagreb: Romsko nacionalno vijeće/ Udruga za promicanje obrazovanja Roma u Republici Hrvatskoj Kali Sara, 2013), pp. 9–39; Danijel Vojak, *Romi u Prvome svjetskom ratu u Hrvatskoj 1914.–1918.* (Zagreb: Romsko nacionalno vijeće, 2015).

12 The Banovina of Croatia (Banovina Hrvatska) was one of the autonomous provinces in the Kingdom of Yugoslavia. It was established 1939 and in these area had lived the majority of the Croatian population in Yugoslavia.

13 Vojak, *U predvečerje rata*, pp. 66–89; Danijel Vojak, "Romi u popisima stanovništva iz 1921. i 1931. na području Hrvatske," *Migracijske i etničke teme*, vol. 20, no. 4, 2004, pp. 447–476.
14 Vojak, *U predvečerje rata*, pp. 66–89; Vojak, "Romi u popisima stanovništva iz 1921. i 1931," pp. 447–476.
15 "Hapšenje cigana," *Riječ Međimurja* (Čakovec), November 1, 1931, pp. 3; "Progon cigana s gradskog područja," *Obzor* (Zagreb), July 28, 1930, pp. 3; "Pokušaj civiliziranja cigana," *Jutarnji list* (Zagreb), June 5, 1938, 14; "Koloniziranje cigana," *Jutarnji list* (Zagreb), March 21, 1939, pp. 13.
16 Zoran Janjatović, *Deca careva, pastočard kraljeva: Nacionalne manjine u Jugoslaviji 1918–1941* (Beograd: Institut za noviju istoriju Srbije, 2005), pp. 17; Mihael Sobolevski, "Nacionalne manjine u Kraljevini Jugoslaviji," in: Hans-Georg Fleck and Igor Graovac (eds.) *Dijalog povjesničara-istoričara*, vol. 2 (Zagreb: Zaklada Friedrich Naumann, 2000), pp. 395; Ljubomir Maštrović, "Kako bi cigani postali radiše?," *Dom* (Zagreb), May 8, 1929, pp. 5.
17 Vojak, "Romi u popisima stanovništva," pp. 447–476.
18 Mihovil (Miškina) Pavlek, "K agrarnoj reformi ili–što ćemo s ciganima?," *Razgovor* I/1920, no. 2–3, pp. 37–38; Ivan Zatluka, "Ciganski problem," *Podravske novine* (Koprivnica), September 3,1938, pp. 2; Vojak, "Romi u popisima stanovništva," pp. 187–200.
19 Angus Fraser, *The Gypsies* (Oxford: Wiley-Blackwell, 1995), pp. 251–252; Gilad Margalit, *Germany and its Gypsyies: a Post–Auschwitz Ordeal* (Madison: University of Wisconsin Press, 2002), pp. 30–31; Guenter Lewy, *The Nazi Persecution on the Gypsies* (Oxford: Oxford Universuty Press, 2000), pp. 5.
20 Lewy, *The Nazi Persecution*, pp. 24–25.
21 On the German model of the persecution of Roma, see: Michael Zimmermann, "Intent, Failure of Plans, and Escalation: Nazi Persecution of the Gypsies in Germany and Austria, 1933–1942," in: *Roma and Sinti: Under-Studied Victims of Nazism*, ed. Paul A. Shapiro, Robert M. Ehrenreich (Washington: United States Holocaust Memorial Museum, Center for Advanced Holocaust Studies, 2002), pp. 9–21; Herbert Heuss, "Njemačka politika Cigana 1870.–1945," in: *Romi u Drugom svjetskom ratu: Od 'rasne znanosti' do logora*, ed. Karola Fings, Herbert Heuss, Frank Sparing, vol. 1 (Zagreb: Ibis grafika, 2006), pp. 1–67; Frank Sparing, "'Ciganski logori': nastanak, karakter i značenje logora kao sredstva progona Sinta i Roma u doba nacionalsocijalizma," in: *Romi u Drugom svjetskom ratu: Od 'rasne znanosti' do logora*, pp. 27–67.
22 Heuss, "Njemačka politika," pp. 18–19; Sparing, "Ciganski logori," pp. 51; Lewy, *The Nazi Persecution*, pp. 43–49, 102–106; Margalit, *Germany*, pp. 34–38.
23 Heuss, "Njemačka politika," pp. 15; Fraser, *The Gypsies*, pp. 257–260; J. K. Peukert Detlev, *Inside Nazi Germany: Conformity, Opposition and Racism in Everyday Life* (London: Batsford, 1987), pp. 211–216.
24 For more on the suffering of Roma in Nazi Germany, see: Karola Fings, "Romi i Sinti u koncentracijskim logorima," in: *Romi u Drugom svjetskom ratu: Od 'rasne znanosti' do logora*, vol. 1, ed. Karola Fings, Herbert Heuss, Frank Sparing (Zagreb: Ibis grafika, 2006) pp. 69–114.; Reimar Gilsenbach, "Pregledna kronologija progona Cigana pod nacionalsocijalizmom (1933.–1945.), in: *Romi u Drugom svjetskom ratu: U sjeni svastike*, vol. 2, ed. Donald Kenrick (Zagreb: Ibis grafika, 2009), pp. 201–222; Myriam Novitch, "Genocid nad Romima u nacističkom režimu," *Europski glasnik*, XVII/2012, no. 17, pp. 829–833.

25 The term Holocaust is, in this context, used for the Nazi genocide against Jews, Roma, and others. Some scholars use the term Holocaust for mass terror and genocide against certain ethnic groups. Besides, some Romologists such as Ian Hancock emphasise the necessity to use the term Porraimos (tearing apart, devouring, rape), but other scholars criticise this term as "ethically and linguistically incorrect" because it primarily refers to sexual violence and is not a part of the "historic memory" of the Roma. Other scholars use the Romani term *Samudaripen* (complete destruction/murder), while German scholars use *Zigeunermord* as an analogous term to *Judenmord*. In Croatia the term *Porraimos* was used for the suffering of Roma in World War II at first; it was used in the ceremonies held on August 2 in Jasenovac to commemorate the International day of Roma victims of Porajmos/the Holocaust, in memory of August 2, 1944 when around 3,000 Roma were killed in Auschwitz. In 2016, the term Porajmos in the name of this commemoration was replaced with *Samudaripen*, in accordance with guidelines given by the International Romani Union in August 2016. Donald Kenrick, "Holocaust," in: *Historical Dictionary of the Gypsies (Romanies)* (Lanham-Toronto-Plymouth, 2007), pp. 109–113; Donald Kenrick, "Porraimos," in: *Historical Dictionary of the Gypsies* (Lanham-Toronto-Plymouth, 2007), pp. 203; Weiss-Wendt, "Introduction," pp. 23–24; Ian Hancock, *We are the Romani People* (Hatfield, 2012), pp. 34; Elena Marushiakova, Vesselin Popov, "Holocaust, Porrajmos, 'Samudaripen … Tworzenienowej mitologii narodowej," *Studia Romologica,* III/ 2010, pp. 75–94; "Zaključci sa sastanka Međunarodne romske unije (URU), Riga, Latvija," in Andrea Šimek and Veljko Kajtazi (eds.) *Svjetski dan romskog jezika 03–05/11/2016* (Zagreb: Udruga za promicanje obrazovanja Roma u Republici Hrvatskoj "Kali Sara"), pp. 86.
26 Dragutin Pavličević, *Povijest Hrvatske* (Zagreb: Naklada Pavičić, 2007), pp. 399–461; Ivo Goldstein, *Hrvatska 1918–2008* (Zagreb: Znanje, 2008), pp. 205–349.
27 *Zločini na jugoslovenskim prostorima u Prvom i Drugom svetskom ratu: Zbornik Dokumenata*, vol. 1: *Zločini Nezavisne Države Hrvatske 1941.–1945* (Beograd: Vojnoistorijski institut, 1993), pp. xxxiii.
28 "Tri socijalno–politička problema," *Hrvatsko jedinstvo* (Varaždin), May 3, 1941, pp. 1.
29 Narcisa Lengel-Krizman, "Prilog proučavanju terora u tzv. NDH: Sudbina Roma 1941–1945," *Časopis za suvremenu povijest*, vol. 18, no. 1 (1986), pp. 30–32; Pavao Matijević, "Rasna pripadnost," *Glasnik biskupija bosanske i srijemske* (Đakovo), April 15 1942, pp. 52–53.
30 Mark Biondich, "Persecution of Roma–Sinti in Croatia, 1941–1945," in: Paul A. Shapiro and Robert M. Ehrenreich (eds.) *Roma and Sinti: Under-Studied Victims of Nazism* (Washington, DC: United States Holocaust Memorial Museum, Center for Advanced Holocaust Studies, 2002), pp. 34.
31 Fikreta Jelić–Butić, *Ustaše i Nezavisna Država Hrvatska* (Zagreb: Liber, 1978), pp. 179.
32 HR–DAV–25, box 16, 1941, no. 9774/41.
33 Ibid.
34 Danijel Vojak, Bibijana Papo, Alen Tahiri, "Dokumenti," in: *Stradanje Roma u Nezavisnoj Državi Hrvatskoj 1941.–1945*. (Zagreb: Institut društvenih znanosti Ivo Pilar / Romsko nacionalno vijeće, 2015), pp. 82–85.
35 It is interesting to note that demographic estimates of the number of Roma in NDH based on the 1931 census can be found in the State Institute for Statistics

archives, available at the Croatian State Archives: HR–HDA–367, vol. 81–82, box. 63.

36 The Institute for Colonization ("Zavod za kolonizaciju") was an independent state institution established on May 5, 1941 by a law decree. The Institute was responsible for redistributing land, relocating people, and overseeing the state's agrarian reforms. In this context and further in the article, "colonization" refers primarily to resettling groups of people from one area to another. However, this was largely a pretext for creating Roma registries, which were subsequently used to prosecute and exterminate them.

37 HR–HDA–246, box 79, no. 9972–III–6–1937; "Križevčani žele riješiti pitanje cigana." *Jutarnji list*, September 16, 1937, pp. 12.

38 "Navala seljaka na ciganske šatore," *Jutarnji list*, January 15, 1936, pp. 13.

39 HR–HDA–246, box. 79, no. 9972–III–6–1937; for more on this topic, see: Danijel Vojak, "Anketa o kolonizaciji cigana ili pokušaj koloniziranja Roma u Savskoj banovini," *Časopis za suvremenu povijest*, XLVII/2016, no. 2, pp. 431–458.

40 "Koloniziranje cigana," *Jutarnji list*, March 21, 1939, pp. 13.

41 HR–HDA–246, box 79, no. 5186, 1941.

42 For more on this topic, see: Danijel Vojak, "Počeci progona Roma u Nezavisnoj Državi Hrvatskoj ili o inicijativi Križevaca o potrebi 'odstranjenja' Roma," in: *Zbornik radova: Druga međunarodna konferencija Holokaust nad Jevrejima, Romima i Srbima u Drugom svetskom ratu*, ed. Vojislav Vučinović (Beograd: Beopress, 2015), pp. 43–51.

43 HR–HDA–246, box 79, no. 1179/1941.

44 Ibid.

45 HR–DAZG–1050, box 25, no. 4066; Slavica Hrečkovski, "Progoni i deportacije slavonskih Roma u koncentracioni logor Jasenovac," in: *Okrugli stol 21. travnja 1984.*, ed. Dobrila Borović (Jasenovac: Spomen područje Jasenovac, 1985), pp. 35.

46 HR–DAZG–1050, box 25, no. 4066; Milan Bulajić, *Ustaški zločini genocida i suđenje Andriji Artukoviću 1986. godine*, book 2 (Beograd: Rad, 1988), pp. 83–84; Lengel- Krizman, *Genocid nad Romima*, pp. 35.

47 Žak Finci, "O kontroli i ograničenju kretanja stanovništva," in: *Sarajevo u revoluciji, vol. 2: Komunistička partija Jugoslavije u pripremama i organizaciji ustanka*, ed. Nisim Albahari (Sarajevo: Istorijski arhiv, 1977), pp. 195; Mehmed Džinić, "Vraća–Stratište nepokorenih i nepobijeđenih," in: *Sarajevo u revoluciji, vol. 4: U borbi do punog oslobođenja (novembar 1943–april 1945)*, ed. Nisim Albahari (Sarajevo: Istorijski arhiv, 1981), pp. 642.

48 *Građa za povijest Narodnooslobodilačke borbe u Sjeverozapadnoj Hrvatskoj 1941.–1945.,br. 1 (ožujak–prosinac 1941.)* (Zagreb: Savjet za izdavanje "Građe za povijest NOP-a i socijalističke revolucije u sjeverozapadnoj Hrvatskoj 1941-1945," 1981), pp. 72; for more on this topic, see: "Cigani s područja Zagreba moraju se prijaviti," *Hrvatski narod* (Zagreb), July 19, 1941, pp. 7; "Zigeuner müssen sich polizeilich melden," *Deutsche Zeitung in Kroatien* (Agram/Zagreb), July 19,1941, pp. 4.

49 Emil Ivan, *Nepokorena mladost (SKOJ u prvim godinama ustanka)* (Zagreb: Lykos, 1961), pp. 120.

50 HR–HDA–255, box 10, no. 15 / no. 114 / no. 24/ no. 71; HR–DABJ–21, no. Br. E1–I, 12; HR–DABJ–20, box 7, no. E 3–1 i, 14 / no. E 3–1 i, 14; HR–HDA–223, box 28, no. bb. /41; ARSBL–74, box, no. 661/41; HR–HDA–255, box 10, no. 8.

51 HR–HDA–246, box 79, no. 1179/1941.

52 Ibid.

53 Narcisa Lengel-Krizman, *Genocid nad Romima*, pp. 40.
54 Ljuban Đurić, Banijski partizanski odredi: 41–45 (Beograd: Vojnoizdavački i novinski centar, 1988), pp. 42.
55 Adam Dupalo, *Banija i Sisak u NOP–u 1941: događaji, svjedočanstva, dokumenti* (Zagreb: Savez antifašističkih boraca i antifašista Republike Hrvatske, 2014), pp. 71, 218–219, 262; Dušan Baić, *Kotar Vrginmost u NO borbi: 1941–1945* (Vrginmost: Općinski odbor Saveza boraca NOR-a Vrginmost, 1980), pp. 262, 445–446, 597–599, 857; Božo Vukobratović, "Teror i zločini fašističkih okupatora i njihovih pomagača na Kordunu 1941.," in: *Simpozij o Petrovoj gori: u povodu 25–godišnjice III zasjedanja ZAVNOH-a, Topusko, 10.–13. studenog 1969.*, ed. Dušan Čalić (Zagreb: Jugoslavenska akademija znanosti i umjetnosti, 1972), pp. 360; Bogdanka Romčević, "Žrtve fašističkog terora i rata s područja kotara Vojnić 1941.–1945.," in: *Kotar Vojnić u narodnooslobodilačkom ratu i socijalističkoj revoluciji*, ed. Đuro Zatezalo (Karlovac: Historijski arhiv, 1989), pp. 1276–1279; Narcisa Lengel-Krizman, *Genocid nad Romima*, pp. 40–41.
56 Milan Bukvić, *Otočac i Brinje u NOB 1941.–1945*. (Otočac: Savez udruženja boraca NOR-a općine, 1971), pp. 38; Milica Banda "Ljudski gubici na području kotara Gračac tokom NOR-a." in: *Kotar Gračac u narodnooslobodilačkom ratu 1941.–1945.*, ed. Đuro Zatezalo, book 1 (Karlovac: Historijski arhiv u Karlovcu, 1984), pp. 997.
57 Milan Bastašić, *Bilogora i Grubišno Polje 1941–1991*. (Banja Luka-Beograd: Udruženje bivših logoraša Drugog svjetskog rata i njihovih potomaka u Republici Srpskoj, 2009), pp. 103.
58 Milica Banda, "Ljudski gubici na području općine Drežnica od 1941. do 1945. godine," in: *Partizanska Drežnica*, ed. Đuro Zatezalo. (Karlovac: Historijski arhiv u Karlovcu, 1982), pp. 882.
59 Slavica. Hrečkovski, *Slavonski Brod u NOB i socijalističkoj revoluciji 1941–1945* (Slavonski Brod: Historijski institut Slavonije I Baranje, 1982), pp. 381, 386–387, 397, 399.
60 VARS, NDH K148aI F4 D29; Vladimir Dedijer, *Vatikan i Jasenovac: dokumenti* (Beograd: Rad, 1987), pp. 302–303; Narcisa Lengel-Krizman, *Genocid nad Romima*, pp. 41–42.
61 Narcisa Lengel–Krizman, *Genocid nad Romima*, pp. 42; Mark Biondich, "Persecution of Roma," pp. 36, 43–44.
62 Narcisa Lengel–Krizman "Genocid nad Romima–Jasenovac 1942." in: Tea Benčić Rimay (ed.) *Spomen–područje Jasenovac* (Jasenovac: Javna ustanova Spomen–područje Jasenovac, 2006), pp. 162.
63 Mark Biondich, "Persecution of Roma," pp. 35–36.
64 Alexander Korb, "Ustaša Mass Violence Against Gypsies in Croatia, 1941–1942" in: Anton Weiss–Wendt (ed.) *The Nazi Genocide of the Roma: Reassessment and Commemoration* (New York and Oxford: Berghahn, 2013), pp. 72–95.
65 "Koprivnica," *Deutsche Zeitung in Kroatien* (Agram/Zagreb), June 18, 1942, pp. 10; "Krizevci," *Deutsche Zeitung in Kroatien* (Agram/Zagreb), June 12, 1942, pp. 8; "Hrvatska se sela čiste od cigana," *Nova Hrvatska* (Zagreb), June 3, 1942, pp. 8.; "Hrvatska rješava pitanje Cigana," *Hrvatski narod* (Zagreb), June 14, 1942, pp. 4.
66 Narcisa Lengel–Krizman, *Genocid nad Romima*, pp. 43–44; Mark Biondich, "Persecution of Roma," pp. 36, 44; Hrečkovski, "Progoni i deportacije," pp. 36; Luka Šteković, *Romi u virovitičkom kraju* (Beograd: Radnička štampa, 1998), pp. 38, 42.

67 Vinko Juzbašić, "Bošnjački Cigani," in: Stjepan Bogutovac, Ivan Ćosić–Bukvin, Vinko Juzbašić, Stjepan Tomislav Krčelić (eds.) *Priče iz spačvanske šume* (Gunja: Castrum Alšan, 2001), pp. 101–102; Veljko Bulajić, *Ustaški zločini*, pp. 98–99.
68 Mark Biondich, "Persecution of Roma," pp. 36; Mihael Sobolevski, "Konzultirati dopunske izvore," *Naše teme*, vol. 30, no. 9 (1986), pp. 1285; Đuro Šovagović, Josip Cvetković, *Valpovština u revoluciji (Kronika revolucionarnih zbivanja 1918–1945)* (Valpovo: Općinski komitet saveza komunista Valpovo, 1970), pp. 101, 104.
69 Dragutin Ljubić, Josip Lulik, Emil Ludviger, "Općina Duga Resa u okupaciji i NOB-i 1941–1945. godine," in Đuro Zatezalo (ed.) *Duga Resa: radovi iz dalje prošlosti NOB-e i socijalističke izgradnje* (Karlovac: Historijski arhiv, 1986), pp. 412.
70 Bogdanka Romčević, "Žrtve fašističkog terora i rata s područja kotara Vojnić 1941.–1945.," in: Đuro Zatezalo (ed.) *Kotar Vojnić u narodnooslobodilačkom ratu i socijalističkoj revoluciji* (Karlovac: Historijski arhiv, 1989), pp. 1257–1259.
71 Luka Šteković, *Romi u virovitičkom kraju*, pp. 18.
72 Ibid., pp. 36.
73 Hrečkovski, "Progoni i deportacije," pp. 36; Dušan Lazić-Gojko, *Sremsko krvavo leto 1942* (Sremska Mitrovica: Sremske novine, 1982), pp. 49–51, 298–300.; Filip Škiljan, "Stradanje Srba, Roma i Židova," *Scrinia Slavonica*, 10 (2010), pp. 349; Mihael Sobolevski, "Ustanak na dijelu kotara Ogulin 1941. i početkom 1942. godine," in: Đuro Zatezalo (ed.) *Prva godina narodnooslobodilačkog rata na području Karlovca, Korduna, Gline, Like, Gorskog kotara, Pokuplja i Žumberka* (Karlovac: Historijski arhiv, 1971.), pp. 911.
74 Ivan Karaula, "Žitelji Slakovaca stradalnici Drugog svjetskog rata i poraća," *Hrašće*, vol. 2, no. 5 (1997), pp. 74.
75 Drago Kolesar, "Gudinačke žrtve II. svjetskog rata i poraća," *Hrašće*, vol. 3, no. 12 (1998), pp. 88; cf. Hrečkovski, *Slavonski Brod u NOB*, pp. 401–402.
76 HR–HDA–246, box. 79, no. 1179/1941.
77 HR–DAOS–52, box 2, no. 25–26.
78 HR–DAOS–52, box 2, no. 29–31.
79 Ivan Balta, "Kolonizacija u Slavoniji od početka XX. stoljeća s posebnim osvrtom na razdoblje 1941.–1945. godine," *Radovi Zavoda za povijesne znanosti HAZU u Zadru*, vol. 43, 2001, pp. 469–470.
80 HR–DAKA–10, box 1944, no. 1–8927 / no. 181/44 (no. 15104/42)
81 HR–DAKA–10, box 7, no. 18655/1942.
82 HR–HDA–246, box 325, unnumbered.
83 Daniel Kovačević, "Prvi dan u logoru Jasenovac," in: Simo Brdar (ed.) *Riječi koje nisu zaklane* (Jasenovac: Spomen područje Jasenovac, 1989), pp. 117–118, 120.
84 Mario Kevo, "Počeci logora Jasenovac," *Scrinia Slavonica*, vol. 3 (2003), pp. 480; Narcisa Lengel-Krizman, *Genocid nad Romima*, pp. 67–68.
85 Milko Riffer, *Grad mrtvih: Jasenovac 1943* (Zagreb: Nakladni zavod Hrvatske, 1946), pp. 38.
86 Narcisa Lengel-Krizman, *Genocid nad Romima*, pp. 47–48.
87 Vladimir Čerkez, "Riječi o ljudskoj patnji," in: *Sarajevo u revoluciji*, vol. 4: *U borbi do punog oslobođenja (novembar 1943–april 1945)*, ed. Nisim Albahari (Sarajevo: Istorijski arhiv, 1981), pp. 558.
88 Milko Riffer, *Grad mrtvih*, pp. 154; *Zločini u logoru Jasenovac* (Zagreb: Naprijed, 1946), pp. 49.

89 Narcisa Lengel-Krizman, *Genocid nad Romima*, pp. 53; Narcisa Lengel-Krizman, "Genocid nad Romima," pp. 166.
90 Milan Bulajić, *Jasenovac: ustaški logori smrti: srpski mit?: hrvatski ustaški logori genocida nad Srbima, Jevrejima i Ciganima* (Beograd: Stručna knjiga, 1999), pp. 124–125; Milko Riffer, *Grad mrtvih*, pp. 20, 25; Mladen Iveković, *Nepokorena zemlja: zapisi iz IV i V neprijateljske ofenzive protiv narodno-oslobodilačke vojske i partizanskih odreda Jugoslavije* (Zagreb: Spektar, 1986), pp. 14–15.
91 Mira Kolar-Dimitrijević, "Sjećanja veterinara Zorka Goluba na trinaest dana boravka u logoru Jasenovac 1942. godine," *Časopis za suvremenu povijest*, XV/ 1983, no. 2, pp. 169.
92 Milko Riffer, *Grad mrtvih*, pp. 155.
93 Milko Riffer, *Grad mrtvih*, pp. 46, 58, 155–156; *Zločini u logoru Jasenovac*, pp. 22–23, 49–51; Narcisa Lengel–Krizman, *Genocid nad Romima*, pp. 51–52; Đoko Jovanović (ed.) *Lika u NOB 1941.: pišu učesnici* (Beograd: Vojno delo, 1963), pp. 172.
94 Milan Bulajić, *Jasenovac: ustaški logori*, pp. 128.
95 Dušan Lukač, *Ustanak u Bosanskoj krajini* (Beograd: Vojnoizdavački zavod, 1967), pp. 63.
96 Muhamed Džemaludinović, "Jedno svjedočanstvo naše humanosti iz ratnih dana," *Takvim*, XXXVI/1971, pp. 72–73.
97 Milan Bulajić, *Ustaški zločini*, pp. 150.
98 Džemaludinović, "Jedno svjedočanstvo," pp. 73.
99 Milan Bulajić, *Ustaški zločini*, pp. 152.
100 Muhamed Džemaludinović, "Jedno svjedočanstvo," pp. 74.
101 Ibid.
102 Mirko Peršen, *Ustaški logori* (Zagreb: Globus, 1990), pp. 158.
103 Slobodan D. Milošević, *Izbeglice i preseljenici na teritoriji okupirane Jugoslavije 1941.–1945. godine* (Beograd: Studije i monografije, 1981) pp. 241.
104 Sevasti Trubeta, "'Gypsiness,' Racial Discourse and Persecution: Balkan Roma during the Second World War," *Nationalities Papers*, XXXI/2003, no. 4, pp. 514.
105 Antun Miletić, *Ubijeni u koncentracijskom logoru Jasenovac 1941-1945* (Jagodina: Gambit, 2011), pp. 18.
106 János Bársony, "Povijest Roma u 20. stoljeću i u doba Pharrajimosa," in: János Bársony and Ágnes Daróczi (eds.) *Pharrajimos: sudbina Roma u doba Holokausta*, ed. (Zagreb: ArTresor, 2013), pp. 37.
107 Martin Kaminski, "NOP i nacionalne manjine," in: Martin Kaminski (ed.) *Slavonija u narodnooslobodilačkoj borbi (Materijali naučnog skupa 25. i 26. novembra 1966. povodom 25-godišnjice ustanka)* (Slavonski Brod: Historijski institut Slavonije, 1967), pp. 171–182; "Stenografski zapisnik," in: Jovan Mirković (ed.) *Lipovljanski susreti '81* (Lipovljani: Organizacijski odbor "Lipovljanski susreti," 1981), pp. 63; Marinko Gruić, "Romi: Neka aktualna pitanja socijalne emancipacije i nacionalne afirmacije," in Jovan Mirković (ed.) *Lipovljanski susreti '81* (Lipovljani: Organizacijski odbor "Lipovljanski susreti." 1981), pp. 26.
108 Milan Bastašić, *Bilogora i Grubišno Polje*, pp. 103.
109 Luka Šteković, *Romi u virovitičkom kraju*, pp. 49; Vladimir Dedijer, *Dnevnik: 1941–1944: Od 28. novembra 1942. do 10. novembra 1943*, book 2 (Rijeka-Zagreb: Liburnija/Mladost, 1981), pp. 469.
110 Stjepan Kokanović, *Radnički i narodnooslobodilački pokret u županjskom kraju* (Županja: Savez udruženja boraca NOR-a Hrvatske, Općinski odbor, 1985,) pp. 127.

111 Milajn Bulajić, *Ustaški zločini*, pp. 120.
112 Ibid., pp. 155–165.
113 Milan Bukvić, *Otočac i Brinje*, pp. 225; Nikola Rubčić, "Zapisi i sjećanja," in: Đuro Zatezalo (ed.) *Prva godina narodnooslobodilačkog rata na području Karlovca, Korduna, Gline, Like, Gorskog kotara, Pokuplja i Žumberka* (Karlovac: Historijski arhiv, 1971), pp. 735.
114 *Građa za historiju Narodnooslobodilačkog pokreta*, pp. 322.
115 Milan Bulajić, *Ustaški zločini*, pp. 88.
116 Ibid., pp. 168.
117 Luka Šteković, *Romi u virovitičkom kraju*, pp. 49–50.
118 Josip Benc Moser, "Akcije Prigorske partizanske udarne grupe," in: ed. Pero Popović (ed.) *Zagrebački partizanski odred: zbornik dokumenata i sjećanja* (Zelina etc.: Općinski odbor SUBNOR-a, 1976), pp. 83–84.
119 Mladen Koić and Nikola Banić, "Nema nikakvih dokaza o masovnoj likvidaciji Roma u Jasenovcu," Hrvatski tjednik (Zagreb), April 27, 2017, pp. 38–47; Veljko Kajtazi, "Vjerujem da je u Jasenovcu ubijeno više Roma nego što ih je uopće i bilo!," https://narod.hr/hrvatska/veljko-kajtazi-vjerujem-da-jasenovcu-ubijeno-vise-roma-sto-ih-uopce-bilo (accessed November 8, 2017).
120 Narcisa Lengel-Krizman, *Genocid nad Romima*, pp. 44–45; Mataušić, *Jasenovac 1941.–1945*, pp. 67; Franjo Tuđman, *Bespuća povijesne zbiljnosti: Rasprava o povijesti i filozofiji zlosilja* (Zagreb: Nakladni zavod Matice hrvatske, 1989), pp. 346; Antun Miletić, "Mrtvi u Jasenovcu 1941–1945: Prilog utvrđivanju broja usmrćenih," *Vojno-istorijski glasnik*, vol. 40, no. 1–2 (1994), pp. 147–148; Mark Biondich, "Persecution of Roma," pp. 40.
121 *Poimenični popis žrtava KL Jasenovac*, www.jusp-jasenovac.hr/Default.aspx?sid=6284 (accessed September 30, 2017).
122 Mladen Koić and Nikola Banić, *Nema nikakvih dokaza*, pp. 38–47.
123 It is important to note that the last, 2011 census certainly did not register the entirety of the Roma population in Croatia, because it is estimated that there are at least twice as many Roma living in Croatia than the official census data records; Vojak, "Romi u popisima stanovništva iz 1921. i 1931.," pp. 447–476; Danijel Vojak, "Romsko stanovništvo u popisima stanovništva u Hrvatskoj i Slavoniji u razdoblju 1850.–1910," *Časopis za suvremenu povijest*, vol. 36, no. 2 (2004), pp. 701–728.
124 HR–HDA–367, the State Institute for Statistics SRH fonds (RZZS SRH), population statistics vol. 81, box 63 (Census material from 1931 and statistics produced prior to 1941 – vol. 81).
125 Vladimir Geiger, "Ljudski gubici Hrvatske u Drugom svjetskom ratu koje su prouzročili 'okupatori i njihovi pomagači.' Brojidbeni pokazatelji (procjene, izračuni, popisi)," *Časopis za suvremenu povijest*, 43/2011., no. 3, pp. 699–749; Mihael Sobolevski, "Konzultirati dopunske izvore," *Naše teme*, vol. 30, no. 9 (1986), pp. 1281–1287.
126 Jelka Smreka, Đorđe Mihovilović, *Poimenični popis žrtava koncentracijskog logora Jasenovac 1941.–1945.* (Jasenovac: Spomen područje Jasenovac, 2007); "Pregled i pretraga poimeničnog popisa žrtava KCL Jasenovac 1941.–1945.," www.jusp-jasenovac.hr/Default.aspx?sid=7618 (accessed October 29, 2015)
127 Jozo Tomasevich, *Rat i revolucija u Jugoslaviji: okupacija i kolaboracija: 1941–1945* (Zagreb: EPH, 2010), pp. 676–677.

128 *Stanovništvo prema narodnosti po gradovima/općinama*, 2011 census, Zagreb, www.dzs.hr/hrv/censuses/census2011/results/htm/H01_01_04/h01_01_04_RH.html (accessed February 2, 2018)
129 *Poimenični popis žrtava KL Jasenovac*. Spomen-područje Jasenovac. www.jusp-jasenovac.hr/Default.aspx?sid=6284 (accessed February 2, 2018).
130 Narcisa Lengel-Krizman, *Genocid nad Romima*, pp. 60–61.
131 Antun Miletić, *Ubijeni u koncentracijskom logoru*, pp. 445–450, 793–798.
132 Milan Bulajić, *Ustaški zločini*, pp. 83; Mark Biondich, "Persecution of Roma," pp. 39; Geiger, "Ljudski gubici," pp. 699–749; Rajko Đurić, *Povijest Roma: prije i poslije Auschwitza* (Zagreb: Prosvjeta, 2007), pp. 108; Ferdo Čulinović, *Okupatorska podjela Jugoslavije* (Beograd: Vojnoizdavački zavod, 1970), pp. 324–325; Jozo Tomasevich, *Rat i revolucija*, pp. 676.
133 Mladen Ivezić, *Jasenovac: brojke* (Zagreb: self-published, 2003), pp. 67, 69, 70, 71; Vladimir Mrkoci, Vladimir Horvat, *Ogoljela laž logora Jasenovac* (Zagreb: Naklada E. Čić, 2008), pp. 20, 39.
134 Dennis Reinhartz, "Genocid nad jugoslavenskim Ciganima," in: Donald Kenrick (ed.) *Romi u Drugom svjetskom ratu: Završno poglavlje* (Zagreb: Ibis grafika, 2009), pp. 104.

Bibliography

Archival and Unpublished Sources

HR–HDA–246, Hrvatska, Hrvatski državni arhiv, Zagreb, fund Zavod za kolonizaciju NDH–Zagreb [1934.–1940.] (1941.–1945.).

HR–HDA–255, Hrvatska, Hrvatski državni arhiv, Zagreb, fund Veliki župan župe Zagorje.

HR–HDA–223, Hrvatska, Hrvatski državni arhiv, Zagreb, fund Ministarstvo unutarnjih poslova NDH / Predsjednički ured.

HR–HDA–367, Hrvatska, Hrvatski državni arhiv, Zagreb, fund Republički zavod za statistiku SRH (RZZS SRH), pp. Popisni materijal iz 1931. godine i statistike koje su vođene do 1941. godine–vol. 81; Državljanstvo za banovine Savsku i Primorsku 1931. tabele Banovinske, sreske, gradske i općinske–vol. 82.

HR–DABJ–21, Hrvatska, Državni arhiv u Bjelovaru, Bjelovar, fund Kotarska oblast Bjelovar–Bjelovar (1941.–1945.).

HR–DABJ–20, Hrvatska, Državni arhiv u Bjelovaru, Bjelovar, fund Velika župa Bilogora Bjelovar (1941.–1945.).

HR–DAV–25, Državni arhiv u Varaždinu, fund 25, Gradsko Poglavarstvo Varaždin.

HR–DAZG–1050, Hrvatska, Državni arhiv u Zagrebu, Zagreb, fund Upravna općina Kustošija.

ARSBL–74, Bosna i Hercegovina (Republika Srpska), Arhiv Republike Srpske, Banja Luka, fund Velika župa Sana i Luka, Banja Luka 1941.–1945.

VARS (Vojni arhiv Republike Srbije), Republika Srbija, Beograd, fund Nezavisne Države Hrvatske.

HR–DAOS–52, Hrvatska, Državni arhiv u Osijeku, Osijek, fund Ured za kolonizaciju Osijek.

HR–DAKA–10, Hrvatska, Državni arhiv u Karlovcu, Karlovac, fund Gradsko poglavarstvo Karlovac.

Published Sources

Albert, Gwendolyn; Dijksterhuis, Ruus; End, Markus; Hrabanova, Gabriela; Jařab, Jan; Koller, Ferdinand; Mack, Jonathan; Makaveeva, Lili; Mille, Saimir; Mirga-Kruszelnicka, Anna; Pascoët, Julie; Szilvási, Marek; Verhelst, Matthias. *Antigypsyism–a Reference Paper* (version June 2017). https://fnasat.centredoc.fr/doc_num.php?explnum_id=1178 Accessed January 7, 2023.

Baić, Dušan. *Kotar Vrginmost u NO borbi: 1941–1945*. Vrginmost: Općinski odbor Saveza boraca NOR-a Vrginmosta, 1980.

Balta, Ivan. "Kolonizacija u Slavoniji od početka XX. stoljeća s posebnim osvrtom na razdoblje 1941.–1945. godine," *Radovi Zavoda za povijesne znanosti HAZU u Zadru*, vol. 43, 2001, pp. 459–478.

Banda, Milica. "Ljudski gubici na području kotara Gračac tokom NOR-a," in: Đuro Zatezalo (ed.) *Kotar Gračac u narodnooslobodilačkom ratu 1941.–1945.*, book 1. Karlovac: Historijski arhiv u Karlovcu, 1984, pp. 841–864.

Bandžović, Safet. "Građanska odgovornost i humanizam u ratu: Odjek bošnjačkih rezolucija uz 1941. godine," *Almanah*, vol. 50, 2011, pp. 147.

Bársony, János. "Povijest Roma u 20. stoljeću i u doba Pharrajimosa," in: János Bársony and Ágnes Daróczi (eds.) *Pharrajimos: sudbina Roma u doba Holokausta*. Zagreb: ArTresor, 2013, pp. 33–58.

Bastašić, Milan. *Bilogora i Grubišno Polje 1941–1991*. Banja Luka–Beograd: Branmil, 2009.

Biondich, Mark. "Persecution of Roma–Sinti in Croatia, 1941.–1945," in: Paul A. Shapiro and Robert M. Ehrenreich (eds.) *Roma and Sinti: Under-Studied Victims of Nazism*. Washington, DC: USHMM, 2002, pp. 33–48.

Blumer, Nadine. "Disentangling the Hierarchy of Victimhood. Commemorating Sinti and Roma and Jews in Germany's National Narrative," in: Anton Weiss-Wendt (ed.) *The Nazi Genocide of the Roma*. New York and Oxford: Berghahn Books, 2013, pp. 1–26.

Bukvić, Milan. *Otočac i Brinje u NOB 1941.-1945*. Otočac: Savez udruženja boraca NOR-a, 1971.

Bulajić, Milan. *Jasenovac: ustaški logori smrti: srpski mit?: hrvatski ustaški logori genocida nad Srbima, Jevrejima i Ciganima*. Beograd: Stručna knjiga, 1999.

———. *Ustaški zločini genocida i suđenje Andriji Artukoviću 1986. godine*, book 2. Beograd: Rad, 1988.

Ciolan, Valeriu Nicolae. *The Role of Diplomacy in Achieving Representation and Participation for the Roma* (dissertation). Faculty of Arts University of Malta, 2006. www.diplomacy.edu/sites/default/files/23082010104317%20Nicolae%20(Library).pdf. Accessed October 15, 2017.

Council of Europe Descriptive Glossary of terms relating to Roma issues. http://a.cs.coe.int/team20/cahrom/documents/Glossary%20Roma%20EN%20version%202018%20May%202012.pdf. Accessed October 15, 2017.

Čerkez, Vladimir. "Riječi o ljudskoj patnji," in Nisim Albahari (ed.) *Sarajevo u revoluciji 4. U borbi do punog oslobođenja* (novembar 1943–april 1945). Sarajevo: Istorijski arhiv Sarajevo, 1981, pp. 556–564.

Dedijer, Vladimir. *Dnevnik: 1941–1944: Od 28. novembra 1942. do 10. novembra 1943.*, book 2. Rijeka–Zagreb: Liburnija, 1981.

———. *Vatikan i Jasenovac: dokumenti*. Beograd: Rad, 1987.

———. and Miletić, Antun. *Genocid nad muslimanima 1941–1945. Zbornik dokumenata i svjedočenja*. Sarajevo: Svjetlost, 1990.
Deutsche Zeitung in Kroatien (Agram/Zagreb). 1, 1941 / 2, 1942.
Dom (Zagreb), 23, 1929.
Dupalo, Adam. *Banija i Sisak u NOP-u 1941: događaji, svjedočanstva, dokumenti*. Zagreb: Savez antifašističkih boraca, 2014.
Džemaludinović, Muhamed. "Jedno svjedočanstvo naše humanosti iz ratnih dana," *Takvim*, 36, 1971, pp. 72–73.
Džinić, Mehmed. "Vraća–Stratište nepokorenih i nepobijeđenih," in: Nisim Albahari (ed.) *Sarajevo u revoluciji 4. U borbi do punog oslobođenja* (novembar 1943–april 1945). Sarajevo: Istorijski arhiv Sarajevo, 1981, pp. 632–648.
Đurić, Ljuban. *Banijski partizanski odredi: 41–45*. Beograd: Vojnoizdavački i novinski centar, 1988.
Finci, Žak. "O kontroli i ograničenju kretanja stanovništva," in: Nisim Albahari (ed.) *Sarajevo u revoluciji 4. U borbi do punog oslobođenja* (novembar 1943–april 1945). Sarajevo: Istorijski arhiv Sarajevo, 1981, pp. 191–196.
Fings, Karola. "Romi i Sinti u koncentracijskim logorima," in: Karola Fings, Herbert Heuss and Frank Sparing (eds.) *Romi u Drugom svjetskom ratu: Od 'rasne znanosti' do logora*, vol. 1. Zagreb: Institut društvenih znanosti Ivo Pilar, 2006, pp. 69–114.
Fraser, Angus. *The Gypsies*. Oxford: Wiley-Blackwell, 1995.
Geiger, Vladimir. "Ljudski gubici Hrvatske u Drugom svjetskom ratu koje su prouzročili 'okupatori i njihovi pomagači.' Brojidbeni pokazatelji (procjene, izračuni, popisi)," *Časopis za suvremenu povijest*, vol. 53, no. 3. 2011, pp. 699–749.
Goldstein, Ivo. *Hrvatska 1918.–2008*. Zagreb: Novi liber, 2008.
———. *Građa za povijest Narodnooslobodilačke borbe u Sjeverozapadnoj Hrvatskoj 1941.–1945.*, no. 1, March–December 1941, Zagreb, 1981.
Gruić, Marinko. "Romi: Neka aktualna pitanja socijalne emancipacije i nacionalne afirmacije," in: Jovan Mirković (ed.) *Lipovljanski susreti '81*. Lipovljani, 1981, pp. 21–38.
Hadžijahić, Muhamed. "Bosanski Romi 1941/1942. godine," *Naše teme*, vol. 28, no. 7–8, 1984, pp. 1313–1323.
Hancock, Ian. *We are the Romani People*. Hatfield: University of Hertfordshire Press, 2012.
Heuss, Herbert. "Njemačka politika Cigana 1870.-1945.," in: Karola Fings, Herbert Heuss and Frank Sparing (eds.) *Romi u Drugom svjetskom ratu: Od 'rasne znanosti' do logora*, vol. 1. Zagreb: Institut društvenih znanosti Ivo Pilar, 2006, pp. 1–26.
Hrečkovski, Slavica. "Progoni i deportacije slavonskih Roma u koncentracioni logor Jasenovac," in: Dobrila Borović (ed.) *Okrugli stol 21. travnja 1984*. Jasenovac: Spomen područje Jasenovac, 1985, pp. 35–38.
Hrečkovski, Slavica. *Slavonski Brod u NOB i socijalističkoj revoluciji 1941–1945*. Slavonski Brod: Historijski institut Slavonije i Baranje, 1982.
Hrvatski narod (Zagreb), 3 (1941) / 4 (1942).
Hrvatsko jedinstvo (Varaždin), 4 (1941).
Ivan, Emil. *Nepokorena mladost (SKOJ u prvim godinama ustanka)*. Zagreb: Lykos, 1961.
Iveković, Mladen. *Nepokorena zemlja: zapisi iz IV i V neprijateljske ofenzive protiv narodno-oslobodilačke vojske i partizanskih odreda Jugoslavije*. Zagreb: Nakladni zavod Hrvatske, 1986.
Jakovljević, Ilija. *Konclogor na Savi*. Zagreb: Konzor, 1999.

Janjatović, Zoran. *Deca careva, pastočard kraljeva: Nacionalne manjine u Jugoslaviji 1918–1941*. Beograd: Institut za noviju istoriju Srbije Beograd, 2005.
Jelić-Butić, Fikreta. *Ustaše i NDH*. Zagreb: Sveučilišna naklada Liber, 1977.
Jovanović, Đoko (ed). *Lika u NOB 1941.: pišu učesnici*. Beograd: Vojno delo, 1963.
Jutarnji list (Zagreb), 1936 (1938) / 28. 1939.
Juzbašić, Vinko. "Bošnjački Cigani," in: Stjepan Bogutovac, Ivan Ćosić-Bukvin, Vinko Juzbašić and Stjepan Tomislav Krčelić (eds.) *Priče iz spačvanske šume*. Gunja: Castrum Alšan, 2001, pp. 101–102.
Kaminski, Martin. "NOP i nacionalne manjine," in Martin Kaminski (ed.) *Slavonija u narodnooslobodilačkoj borbi (Materijali naučnog skupa 25. i 26. novembra 1966. povodom 25-godišnjice ustanka)*. Slavonski Brod: Historijski Institut Slavonij, 1967, pp. 171–182.
Karaula, Ivan. "Žitelji Slakovaca stradalnici Drugog svjetskog rata i poraća," *Hrašće*, vol. 2, no. 5 (1997), pp. 71–74.
Kenrick, Donal. "Holocaust," in: *Historical Dictionary of the Gypsies (Romanies)*. Lanham-Toronto-Plymouth: Scarecrow Press, 2007, pp. 109–113.
———. "Porraimos," in: *Historical Dictionary of the Gypsies (Romanies)*. Lanham–Toronto–Plymouth: Scarecrow Press, 2007, pp. 203.
Kevo, Mario. "Počeci logora Jasenovac," *Scrinia Slavonica*, vol. 3 (2003), pp. 471–499.
Koić, Mladen and Banić, Nikola. "Nema nikakvih dokaza o masovnoj likvidaciji Roma u Jasenovcu," *Hrvatski tjednik (Zagreb)*, April 27, 2017, no. 657, pp. 38–47.
Kolar, Dimitrijević, Mira. "Sjećanja veterinara Zorka Goluba na trinaest dana boravka u logoru Jasenovac 1942. godine," *Časopis za suvremenu povijest*, vol. 15. no. 2, 1983, pp. 155–176.
Kolesar, Drago. "Gudinačke žrtve II. svjetskog rata i poraća," *Hrašće*, vol. 3, no. 12, 1998, pp. 83–88.
Korb, Alexander. "Ustaša Mass Violence Against Gypsies in Croatia, 1941–1942," in: Anton Weiss-Wendt (ed.) *The Nazi Genocide of the Roma: Reassessment and Commemoration*. New York and Oxford: Berghahn, 2013, pp. 72–95.
Kovačević, Daniel. "Prvi dan u logoru Jasenovac," in: Simo Brdar (ed.) *Riječi koje nisu zaklane*. Jasenovac: Spomen područje Jasenovac, 1989, pp. 105–141.
Lazić-Gojko, Dušan. *Sremsko krvavo leto 1942*. Sremska Mitrovica: Novinsko-izdavačka radna organizacija "Sremske novine," 1982.
Lengel-Krizman, Narcisa. "Genocid nad Romima–Jasenovac 1942.," in Tea Benčić Rimay (ed.) *Spomen–područje Jasenovac*. Jasenovac: Spomen područje Jasenovac, 2006, pp. 154–169.
———, Narcisa. "Prilog proučavanju terora u tzv. NDH: Sudbina Roma 1941–1945," *Časopis za suvremenu povijest*, vol. 18, no. 1. 1986, pp. 30–32.
Lewy, Guenter. *The Nazi Persecution on the Gypsies*. Oxford: Oxford University Press, 2000.
Ljubić, Dragutin, Josip Lulik, and Emil Ludviger. "Općina Duga Resa u okupaciji i NOB-i 1941–1945. godine," in: Đuro Zatezalo (ed.) *Duga Resa: radovi iz dalje prošlosti NOB-e i socijalističke izgradnje*. Karlovac: Historijski arhiv Karlovac, 1986, pp. 385–445.
Lukač, Dušan. *Ustanak u Bosanskoj krajini*. Beograd: Vojnoizdavacki Zavod, 1967.
Margalit, Gilad. *Germany and its Gypsies: A Post–Auschwitz Ordeal*. Madison University of Wisconsin Press, 2002.
Marushiakova, Elena and Popov, Vesselin. "Holocaust, Porrajmos, 'Samudaripen ... Tworzenienowej mitologii narodowej,'" *Studia Romologica*, vol. 3, 2010, pp. 75–94.

Matijević, Pavao. "Rasna pripadnost," *Glasnik biskupija bosanske i srijemske* (Đakovo), April 15, 1942, pp. 52–53.
Matras, Yaron. "Gilad Margalit, 1959–2014," *Romani Studies*, vol. 24, no. 2, 2014, pp. 211–212.
Miletić, Antun. "Mrtvi u Jasenovcu 1941–1945: Prilog utvrđivanju broja usmrćenih," *Vojnoistorijski glasnik*, vol. 40, no. 1–2, 1994, pp. 147–148.
———. *Ubijeni u koncentracijskom logoru Jasenovac 1941–1945*. Jagodina: Gambit, 2011.
Milošević, Slobodan D. *Izbeglice i preseljenici na teritoriji okupirane Jugoslavije 1941–1945*. Beograd: Narodna knjiga, 1981.
Moser, Josip Benc. "Akcije Prigorske partizanske udarne grupe," in: Pero Popović (ed.) *Zagrebački partizanski odred: zbornik dokumenata i sjećanja*. Zelina-Zagreb: Općinski odbori SUBNOR-a, 1976, pp. 80–84.
Mrkoci, Vladimir and Horvat, Vladimir. *Ogoljela laž logora Jasenovac*. Zagreb: Naklada E. Čić, 2008.
Nikolić, Nikola. *Jasenovački logor*. Zagreb: Nakladni Zavod Hrvatske, 1948.
Nova Hrvatska (Zagreb), 2, 1942.
Novitch, Myriam. "Genocid nad Romima u nacističkom režimu," *Europski glasnik*, vol. 17, no. 17, 2012, pp. 829–833.
Obzor (Zagreb), 70, 1930.
Pavlek, Mihovil (Miškina). "K agrarnoj reformi ili- što ćemo s ciganima?" *Razgovor*, vol. 1, no. 2–3. 1920, pp. 37–38.
Pavličević, Dragutin. *Povijest Hrvatske*. Zagreb: Naklada Pavićić, 2007.
Peršen, Mirko. *Ustaški logori*. Zagreb: Stvarnost, 1990.
Peukert, Detlev J. K. *Inside Nazi Germany: Conformity, Opposition and Racism in Everyday Life*. New Haven-London: Yale University Press, 1987.
Podravske novine (Koprivnica), 9, 1938.
———. *Poimenični popis žrtava KL Jasenovac*. Spomen–područje Jasenovac. www.jusp-jasenovac.hr/Default.aspx?sid=6284. Accessed, February 2, 2018.
Potporni tim Posebnog povjerenika Glavnog tajnika Vijeća Europe za romska pitanja. *Dosta! oslobodimo se predrasuda–upoznajmo Rome!* Strasbourg, Council of Europe, 2011.
Reinhartz, Dennis. "Genocid nad jugoslavenskim Ciganima," in Donald Kenrick (ed.) *Romi u Drugom svjetskom ratu: Završno poglavlje*. Zagreb: Ibis grafika, 2009, pp. 99–109.
Riffer, Milko. *Grad mrtvih: Jasenovac 1943*. Zagreb: Naklada Pavičić, 1946/2011.
Riječ Međimurja (Čakovec), 1, 1931.
Romčević, Bogdanka. "Žrtve fašističkog terora i rata s područja kotara Vojnić 1941–1945," in: Đuro Zatezalo (ed.) *Kotar Vojnić u narodnooslobodilačkom ratu i socijalističkoj revoluciji*. Karlovac: Historijski arhiv Karlovac, 1989, pp. 1178–1325.
Rubčić, Nikola. "Zapisi i sjećanja," in: Đuro Zatezalo (ed.) *Prva godina narodnooslobodilačkog rata na području Karlovca, Korduna, Gline, Like, Gorskog kotara, Pokuplja i Žumberka*. Karlovac: Historijski arhiv Karlovac, 1971, pp. 701–739.
Skoko, Savo. "Na tragičnoj stranputici," in: Rajko Šarenac (ed.) *Hercegovina u NOB / pišu učesnici, sv. 4 (april 1941.–juni 1942) / Ratna prošlost naroda i narodnosti Jugoslavije*, book 285. Beograd: Vojnoizdavački i novinski centar, 1986, pp. 321–369.
Sobolevski, Mihael. "Ustanak na dijelu kotara Ogulin 1941 i početkom 1942. godine," u in: Đuro Zatezalo (ed.) *Prva godina narodnooslobodilačkog rata na*

području Karlovca, Korduna, Gline, Like, Gorskog kotara, Pokuplja i Žumberka. Karlovac: Historijski arhiv Karlovac, 1971, pp. 909–936.

———. "Konzultirati dopunske izvore," *Naše teme*, vol. 30, no. 9, 1986, pp. 1281–1287.

———. "Nacionalne manjine u Kraljevini Jugoslaviji," in: Hans-Georg Fleck and Igor Graovac (eds.) Dijalog povjesničara-istoričara, vol. 2. Zagreb: Friedrich Naumann Stiftung, 2000, pp. 395–410.

Sparing, Frank. "'Ciganski logori': Nastanak, karakter i značenje logora kao sredstvo progona Sinta i Roma u doba nacionalsocijalizma," in: Karola Fings, Herbert Heuss and Frank Sparing (eds.) *Romi u Drugom svjetskom ratu: Od 'rasne znanosti' do logora*, vol. 1. Zagreb: Institut društvenih znanosti Ivo Pilar, 2006, pp. 27–67.

———. *Stanovništvo prema narodnosti po gradovima/općinama, popis 2011*. Zagreb: Državni zavod za statistiku. www.dzs.hr/hrv/censuses/census2011/results/htm/H01_01_04/h01_01_04_RH.html. Accessed 29 October, 2015.

Škiljan, Filip. "Stradanje Srba, Roma i Židova u virovitičkom i slatinskom kraju tijekom 1941. i početkom 1942. godine," *Scrinia Slavonica*, vol. 10, 2010, pp. 341–365.

Šovagović, Đuro, and Cvetković Josip. *Valpovština u revoluciji (Kronika revolucionarnih zbivanja 1918–1945)*. Valpovo, 1970.

Šteković, Luka. *Romi u virovitičkom kraju*. Beograd: Radnička štampa, 1998.

———. "Stenografski zapisnik," in: Jovan Mirković (ed.) *Lipovljanski susreti '81*. Lipovljani, 1981, pp. 49–59.

Taylor, Becky. *Another Darkness, Another Dawn: A History of Gypsies, Roma and Travellers*. London: Reaktion Books, 2014.

Trubeta, Sevasti. "'Gypsiness,' Racial Discourse and Persecution: Balkan Roma during the Second World War," *Nationalities Papers*, vol. 31, no. 4, 2003, pp. 495–514.

Tuđman, Franjo. *Bespuća povijesne zbiljnosti: Rasprava o povijesti i filozofiji zlosilja*: Zagreb: Hrvatska sveučilišna naklada, 1989.

Vojak, Danijel. "Romi u popisima stanovništva iz 1921. i 1931. na području Hrvatske," *Migracijske i etničke teme*, vol. 20, no. 4, 2004, pp. 447–476.

———. *U predvečerje rata: Romi u Hrvatskoj 1918.–1941*. Zagreb: Udruga za promicanje obrazovanja Roma u RH "Kali Sara", 2013.

———. "Međunarodni dan sjećanja na romske žrtve holokausta Jasenovac, 2. kolovoza 2012.," *Povijest u nastavi*, vol. 10, no. 20, 2014, pp. 247–250.

———. "Počeci progona Roma u Nezavisnoj Državi Hrvatskoj ili o inicijativi Križevaca o potrebi 'odstranjenja' Roma," in Vojislav Vučinović (ed.) *Zbornik radova: Druga međunarodna konferencija Holokaust nad Jevrejima, Romima i Srbima u Drugom svetskom ratu*. Beograd: Fakultet za poslovne studije i pravo u Beogradu, 2015, pp. 43–51.

———. *Romi u Prvome svjetskom ratu u Hrvatskoj 1914.–1918*. Zagreb: Vojak, Danijel. *Romi u Prvome svjetskom ratu u Hrvatskoj 1914.-1918*, 2015.

———. "Izbor iz bibliografije radova o stradanju Roma u Nezavisnoj Državi Hrvatskoj," in: Danijel Vojak, Bibijana Papo and Alen Tahiri. *Stradanje Roma u Nezavisnoj Državi Hrvatskoj, 1941.-1945*. Zagreb: Institut društvenih znanosti Ivo Pilar, 2015, pp. 353–369.

———. "Anketa o kolonizaciji cigana' ili pokušaj koloniziranja Roma u Savskoj banovini," *Časopis za suvremenu povijest*, vol. 40, no. 2, 2016, pp. 431–458.

Vojak, Danijel, Papo, Bibijana and Tahiri, Alen. "Dokumenti," in: *Stradanje Roma u Nezavisnoj Državi Hrvatskoj 1941.-1945*. Zagreb: Institut društvenih znanosti Ivo Pilar, 2015, pp. 61–369.

Vranješ, Pero. "Ljudski gubici i materijalna šteta u narodnooslobodilačkom ratu od 1941.-1945. godine," in: Đuro Zatezalo (ed.) *Duga Resa: radovi iz dalje prošlosti NOB-e i socijalističke izgradnje*. Karlovac: Historijski arhiv Karlovac, 1986, pp. 818–831.

Vukobratović, Božo. "Teror i zločini fašističkih okupatora i njihovih pomagača na Kordunu 1941.," in: Dušan Čalić (ed.) *Simpozij o Petrovoj gori: u povodu 25-godišnjice III zasjedanja ZAVNOH-a, Topusko, 10.–13. studenog 1969*. Zagreb: Jugoslavenska akademija znanosti in umjetnosti, 1972, pp. 341–364.

Weiss-Wendt, Anton. "Introduction," in: Anton Weiss–Wendt (ed.) *The Nazi Genocide of the Roma*. New York–Oxford: Berghahn Books, 2013, pp. 1–26.

———. Zaključci sa sastanka Međunarodne romske unije (URU), Riga, Latvija, u: Andrea Šimek and Veljko Kajtazi (eds.) *Svjetski dan romskog jezika 03-05/11/ 2016*. Zagreb: Udruga za promicanje obrazovanja Roma u Republici Hrvatskoj "Kali Sara," pp. 86–95.

Zimmermann, Michael. *Zločini u logoru Jasenovac*. Zagreb, 1946.

———. "Zločini Nezavisne Države Hrvatske 1941.–1945," in: Slavko Vukčević (ed.) *Zločini na jugoslovenskim prostorima u Prvom i Drugom svetskom ratu*. Collection of Documents, vol. 1. Beograd: Vojnoistorijski institut, 1993.

———. "Intent, Failure of Plans, and Escalation: Nazi Persecution of the Gypsies in Germany and Austria, 1933–1942," in: Paul A. Shapiro, Robert M. Ehrenreich (eds.) *Roma and Sinti: Under-Studied Victims of Nazism*. Washington, DC: USHMM, 2002, pp. 9–21.

Part III
Describing

8 Contested Cultural Memory in Jasenovac
A Post-Communist/Post-Socialist Memorial Museum in an Era of Historical Revisionism

Vjeran Pavlaković

The violent dissolution of Yugoslavia in the 1990s resulted not only in far-reaching political and economic transformation, but also prompted new processes of state-building, identity formation, and cultural memory construction. In Croatia, the post-communist transition was thus intimately linked with its war of independence from Yugoslavia (known as the Homeland War, or *Domovinski rat*), profoundly affecting memory politics in the last two decades. Franjo Tuđman, who became Croatia's president after free democratic elections in 1990, was a pivotal figure in reasserting Croatian identity by restoring historic symbols, traditions, holidays, and suppressed collective memories in order to sever the connection with the shared Yugoslav historical and cultural narrative. Similar transformations took place in other European countries that had once been under Soviet influence. In Croatia, however, the new forms of cultural memory did not merely challenge the ideology of the former communist regime, but emphasized the Croatian ethno-national identity of the newly independent country. In addition to changing street names, erecting new national monuments, revising textbooks, and constructing a new commemorative calendar, the Croatian authorities sought to enforce the official narratives through the country's history museums and memorial parks. While other countries in the region have established national museums and private institutions that address the communist period (for example, the House of Terror in Budapest, the Museum of Genocide Victims in Vilnius, and the DDR Museum in Berlin), Croatia still lacks a permanent exhibit in the Croatian History Museum (in Croatian: *Hrvatski povijesni muzej*), which addresses the communist past. Moreover, any discussion of the communist legacy in Croatia and the former Yugoslavia inevitably requires an analysis of World War II. Yet this period of Croatian history is also effectively missing from the museological landscape.

The present chapter examines why the memorialization of the communist era and World War II in Croatia has not included the establishment of permanent exhibitions or new museums that deal with these subjects. A few sites

DOI: 10.4324/9781003326632-11

of memory (*lieux de memoire*), described in more detail below, touch upon the communist-led Yugoslav Partisan struggle, the Holocaust, and the communist legacy, but these are limited in scope and fall short of any kind of national memory politics. Instead, remembrance politics in Croatia, and debates about twentieth-century history, generally take place during commemorative events held at emotionally powerful memory sites. Symbolic politics and debates over contested histories take center stage at commemorations that pay respect to the anti-fascist struggle, as well as those that exclusively remember the communist terror that followed the defeat of the Ustaše, Croatia's pro-Axis regime during World War II.[1] Even though remembrance politics are focused on the more recent Homeland War, memories of World War II are often blurred into debates about the conflict of the 1990s and vice versa. Moreover, the cultural memory of World War II and communism in Croatia is not divided only along ideological lines. The traumas of the twentieth century have exerted enormous influence on the construction of collective memories and the ethno-national identity of both Croats and Serbs (as well as other ethnic groups) living in Croatia, further complicating the process of reaching even a minimal consensus on key moments in the past that would be enshrined in a national history museum, resistance museum, or museum of communism.

The Jasenovac Memorial Site (*Spomen područje Jasenovac*) – established in the 1960s, devastated during the war of the 1990s, and restored in 2006 – is the only permanent memorial museum dedicated to World War II in Croatia; it has also been a constant target of right-wing revisionism since Croatia's entry into the European Union in 2013. The museum, along with its publications and efforts to create a database of all victims, has long been a bastion of scientific research and education about the crimes of the Ustaša regime, which has resulted in attacks by those seeking to whitewash the Ustaše and discredit the anti-fascist Partisan movement.

Cultural Memory and Museums

The work of scholars in recent decades has clearly shown the relationship between memory and identity, both of which are constructed and reconstructed. According to John Gillis, "just as memory and identity support one another, they also sustain certain subjective positions, serial boundaries, and of course, power."[2] In analyzing the "culture of memory," its relationship with national identity – and how both of those changed after the fall of communism – it is necessary to define the three levels in which memory functions. The first level is individual memory, or the remembering of events actually experienced by individuals. Since there are still people living who experienced World War II, their oral histories contribute to the communicative memory and discourse of those events, although the death of this generation will change the way this past is remembered.[3] The second level is collective memory, a term coined by sociologist Maurice Halbwachs, who argued that group memory was socially constructed through interaction with others and reflected the dominant discourses of society.[4] Collective memory, especially in relation to museums, can be defined as "a representation of the past, both that shared by a group and that which is collectively commemorated, that enacts and gives substance to the group's identity, its present conditions, and its vision of the future."[5] Institutional memory – the way ruling elites, as well as their opponents, construct historical narratives – represents the third level of memory and is the most relevant framework for analyzing the post-communist transition in Croatia. Commemorations, textbooks, the naming of public spaces, and monuments are a few elements of institutionalized memory that states and regimes use to present their interpretation of the past in order to justify the present political order. Museums are another example of institutionalized memory that can anchor official representations of the past, yet they are also spaces where contested narratives vie for dominance. National history museums enshrine the objects, images, and narratives that transmit the values and instill loyalty to the state, or even to specific regimes. According to Carol Duncan, "museums can be powerful identity-defining machines. To control a museum means precisely to control the representations of a community and some of its highest, most authoritative truths."[6] It is not surprising, therefore, that a museum such as the Museum of the History of Catalonia – whose motto is "the memory of a country" – immediately replaced all of its Spanish-language captions with Catalan texts after the death of General Francisco Franco, who had banned the public use of Catalan during his dictatorship. This history museum in Barcelona was thus part of the process of reasserting Catalan identity in the mid-1970s. Museologist Peter Davis argues that "museums have assumed cultural significance because they have formed collections of objects in which history and attitudes are reflected," even though many traditional museums focused more on form than content and subsequently did not always influence cultural identity.[7] Museums in Croatia seem to be struggling between the traditional approach of displaying as many objects as possible, a characteristic of the communist-era museums dedicated to memorializing World War II, and implementing new, postmodernist theories that threaten to distance the audience too much from the reality of the past.

Moreover, the issue of how to incorporate Croatia's Serbs into the idealized representations of the nation-state is relevant not only for Croatian museologists, but for Croatian society at large. According to a September 2011 opinion poll, 43.4 percent of respondents believed that the institutions of Croatia's Serbs should be involved in the development of history museums dealing with the twentieth century (39.3 percent believed they should not be involved, while 17.3 percent answered that they did not know).[8] As scholars of nationalism have concluded, "cultural institutions such as museums have played a central role in the construction of a coherent historical national discourse that reinforce a sense of collective identity and social cohesion through common understandings of order, aesthetics, and symbols."[9] The disintegration of the Yugoslav state and communism in the 1990s resulted in a comprehensive rewriting of historical narratives of the twentieth century. Both World

War II and the Homeland War resulted in traumatic episodes of interethnic violence that overshadow the centuries of cooperation between Croat and Serb communities. Incorporating Serb narratives and cultural contributions into the dominant national narratives of Croatian state-building and victories over Greater Serbian ideology complicate the task of curators and museum officials. Since the Serb nationalist project was defeated during the Homeland War, Croatia's Serbs look to their role in the anti-fascist, and multiethnic Partisan movement for historical continuity. However, this is in itself problematic, because the Partisan victory resulted in the restoration of a Yugoslav state (and not Croatian independence) under a communist dictatorship, as well as in a massive postwar repression that claimed tens of thousands of lives. Reflecting on the debates surrounding controversial exhibitions in the United States, Steven Dubin argues that

> [m]useums have become places where conflicts over some of the most vital issues regarding national character and group identity – the struggle between universalism and particularism – regularly break out. These conflicts are displays of power, the result of groups flexing their muscles to express who they are or to beat back the claims of others.[10]

Although in Croatia the arenas for these kinds of contests over the past tend to be commemorative events rather than museum exhibits, the lack of history museums dealing with the twentieth century can be attributed to the sensitivity of displaying representations of interethnic bloodletting in a manner that will not perpetuate new conflicts. While art and ethnographic museums assist in the construction of national identity by displaying a nation's cultural heritage, history museums are considerably more politicized and explicitly present historical narratives. This raises the questions: Who determines the narrative, and who is the intended audience? The original history museums in Europe were established to celebrate military victories and were maintained by the state.[11] Yet new trends in international museology have expanded the range of subjects covered by national history museums. As noted by Stephen Weil, the history museum

> has shown that beyond being celebratory, it can also [...] be compensatory, and that beyond praising history's winners, be they military, political, professional, or economic, it can also seek to soothe the pain – or at least recognize, memorialize, and try to understand the losses – of history's victims.[12]

In fact, the proliferation of truth commissions and other forms of transitional justice in the last few decades has impacted the role of history museums, which increasingly serve as memorial sites in addition to places of community education and repositories of historical objects. This new role of history museums presumes that they can contribute to reconciliation in post-conflict states such as Croatia. A study of the impact of museums on reconciliation states,

> If one analyzes the reports of a range of truth commissions, memorializations and conflict-oriented museums are clearly advocated, but exactly what contribution they can make is seldom expressed. Equally, memorial museums are spoken about by those who run them as having profound educational benefits and as being instrumental in preventing human rights violations, but exactly how they do this is generally not articulated.[13]

The authors of the article concede that there are differing views on whether memorial museums should offer a single meta-narrative or present multiple narratives. However, they do agree that these kinds of museums should be accompanied by long-term investment and accompanying educational programs, as well as other transitional justice mechanisms. Although the prospect of a truth commission in Croatia in the immediate future is unlikely – the political difficulties of the RECOM (Regional Commission for Establishing the Facts about the Victims of War Crimes and Other Serious Human Rights Violations)[14] initiative is indicative of the challenges facing the implementation of transitional justice mechanisms in the region – any kind of history museum dealing with the twentieth century will have to include some references to victims and perpetrators of war crimes on all sides of the conflict. Along with the challenges facing Croatian museologists in defining the goals of museums dealing with the twentieth century (for instance, whether to present only the nation-building narratives that buttress the legitimacy of the political elites or to develop exhibitions that acknowledge the complexities of the past and contribute to building an atmosphere of interethnic tolerance), the intended audience of the history museums should be taken into account. Croatia relies heavily on the tourism industry for revenue, and international visitors' attendance at national history museums must be considered when deciding how to represent the past. For example, the House of Terror Museum in Budapest appeals to foreign visitors with its slick and innovative displays, although it has been widely criticized for manipulating the past in order to discredit left-wing political parties in Hungary.[15] In Prague, the Museum of Communism seems to be pitched exclusively to tourists, who are invited to purchase a variety of satirical communism-inspired shirts, mugs, posters, and other objects in the large gift shop.[16] Although the Adriatic coast remains the primary draw for tourists visiting Croatia, cities such as Zagreb have seen an increase in visitors and have thus made efforts to offer more museums. According to research on war, tourism, and memory by Lauren Rivera, "in its post-war tourism promotion campaign, the Croatian government omitted a crucial part of Croatian history – the war that initiated its independence."[17] This article touches upon how the Croatian state represents the recent past to the international audience, in contrast to the discourse geared towards domestic consumption. On the one hand, Croatia is marketed to potential foreign tourists as a peaceful Mediterranean country that is far removed from the instability plaguing its Balkan neighbors. On the other hand, the memory of the Homeland War is constantly evoked through commemorations and monuments, while the legacy of the conflict is omnipresent in the media, culture, interethnic relations, and regional as well as domestic politics. Any future museum dealing with the twentieth century will thus not only have to negotiate between the contested ideological and ethno-national narratives, but will also need to find a balance between serving as an institution of cultural memory involved in nation-building and presenting Croatian history to a foreign audience in line with European memory practices.[18]

Communist Legacies, Contemporary Narratives

During Yugoslavia's communist era, the regime strictly controlled the representations of the past, especially those housed in history museums across the country. Renata Jambrešić-Kirin, writing on the politics of memory related to World War II, concludes that "the Yugoslav animators of cultural memory" were important in "affirming the political order, the ideology of brotherhood and unity, and the legitimacy of the ruling party, while repressing the problem of interethnic conflicts."[19] Not only did each Yugoslav republic have its own museum dedicated to the People's Liberation Struggle (*Narodnooslobodilačka borba*, as World War II was known in Tito's Yugoslavia), but museums were also located at important sites related to the Partisan struggle, such as the battlefields of Sutjeska and Neretva, the cave in Drvar where Tito was nearly captured by German paratroopers, and the concentration camp in Jasenovac.

The World War II museum in Zagreb, housed in the pavilion designed by noted sculptor Ivan Meštrović on Victims of Fascism Square (and which briefly served as a mosque during the war), is illustrative of communist-era cultural memory policies. The Peoples' Revolution Museum (after 1960 called the Revolution of the Peoples of Croatia Museum, or *Muzej Revolucije naroda Hrvatske*) held its first exhibition in 1955. In addition to the permanent collection on the history of the Yugoslav Communist Party and Partisans, there were thematic exhibitions and an archive of materials related to World War II. In this sense the museum functioned as an archetypal *lieux de memoire* (site of memory), since it was "concerned less with establishing the veracity of historical facts than with the ways in which the past is understood and appropriated within contemporary consciousness."[20] An institution such as a museum was an ideal vessel by which to construct the communist narrative of the past, along with public rituals, holidays, school curricula, monuments, and all of the other components of the culture of memory mentioned earlier.[21] The brochure from the 1961 exhibition Croatia in 1941 states that

> this exhibition – lively, picturesque, and easily accessible – will enable our youth to become familiar with the most important events from the

beginning of the People's Liberation Struggle. By bringing these events to life, it will also be considerably easier for our educators in interpreting our revolution.[22]

Children, and the public at large, were indoctrinated about the communist version of the past through the museum exhibitions, as ultimately the regime's culture of memory about World War II served to legitimate and perpetuate its monopoly on political power. Examples of other exhibitions include Forty Years of the Communist Party of Yugoslavia (April–July 1959); Testimonies about the Uprising in Croatia in 1941 (July 1981); and Fortieth Anniversary of the People's Front (July–August 1984), which filled Meštrović's gallery spaces with materials and images buttressing the one-sided view of the past. But by the mid-1980s, growing criticism of the ruling communist ideology extended to its production of cultural memory. In 1986, on the fiftieth anniversary of the beginning of the Spanish Civil War, the museum on Victims of Fascism Square organized an exhibition honoring the nearly 1,700 Yugoslavs who joined the International Brigades to defend the Popular Front government in Spain. The official brochure for the exhibition referred to the members of the International Brigades as a "symbol" and "legends," stating that their decision to volunteer was a "heroic deed par excellence."[23] The effort to mobilize enthusiasm for the regime by reliving past exploits was no longer immune to criticism. Lucija Benyovsky, a museologist initially involved with the exhibition, issued a scathing critique of it in the journal *Informatica museologica*. She pointed out a number of factual errors (for example, the exhibition featured a large model of a Luftwaffe "Stuka," an airplane that played a very limited role in the Spanish Civil War), the lack of informative captions on pictures and displays, and the haphazard method for organizing the material on the Yugoslav volunteers.[24] More important, in Benyovsky's opinion, was the misguided decision by the exhibition's creators, Đurđa Knezević and Snježana Pavičić, to base it upon a "symbolic-thematic overview of history" due to a dearth of physical objects that could be displayed.[25] The reliance on symbols and images without the accompanying systematic historical explanations resulted in an exhibit that merely perpetuated the mythologization of the war in Spain, and by extension the construction of the Yugoslav communist past. She concludes that without the necessary background information, visitors of the exhibit

> could not get the full picture of who fought against whom, what each side's goals were, what the situation on the battlefield was like, what the source and nature of aid to the warring sides consisted of, and what kind of role in all of this the [Yugoslav] volunteers played in Spain and later in our People's Liberation War.[26]

Although part of Benyovsky's criticism can be attributed to internal disagreements among museologists, this exhibition shows that there were increasing debates and approaches in how to critically present history in museums while still staying within the Party's ideological parameters. Yet this debate over the presentation of history was confined to journals not read outside of the field. The state-controlled press rated the exhibition a "must see."

Revolutionary museums in communist Yugoslavia, which served to visually inform children and the public at large about the accomplishments of the Partisan struggle, had always presented a very black-and-white version of twentieth-century history: fascism, capitalism, and nationalism were evil, while antifascism, communism, and internationalism were good. Within this paradigm, an exhibition depicting Franco standing next to Hitler and Mussolini, or several photographs of Yugoslav communists who fought in the ranks of the International Brigades, would convey the basic idea that the Nationalists were villainous fascists and that the Yugoslav volunteers were on the side of the good, anti-fascist Republicans. But professionals such as Benyovsky were no longer content with such simplistic characterizations of history that were intended to bolster the ruling party's control of the past, and ultimately, its flagging legitimacy. In the 1980s there were plans to build a memorial center and museum to fallen Partisans and civilian victims in Dotrščina Park in Zagreb. These plans were never realized, but recently some non-governmental organizations have revived the idea of a museum at the same location that would pertain to the victims from both World War II and the Homeland War.[27] The victory of Tuđman's nationalists in multiparty elections permitted by the regime in the spring of 1990 meant that Meštrović's pavilion would once again be targeted for an ideological facelift. The new administration in Zagreb quickly shut down the museum and its communist version of the past, and the pavilion was renamed the Pantheon of Croatian Great Men (*Panteon hrvatskih velikana*). There were rumors that the building would be used to house a Croatian history museum or even that Tuđman had considered making it his mausoleum, but the war conditions and lack of funding meant that those plans were shelved. Other local museums similar to the one housed in the Meštrović pavilion dedicated to the National Liberation War were closed throughout Croatia, even in regions such as Istria and cities such as Rijeka that had leftist local governments after 1990 and continued to venerate anti-fascist traditions. The purging of communist institutions included shutting down those museums that had perpetuated the regime's monopoly over historical narratives. About seventy museums were damaged or destroyed during the war, including many history museums and memorial sites dedicated to World War II, while others were stripped of their collections during the rebel Serb occupation.[28]

The Jasenovac Memorial Site – between Holocaust Museum and Postmodern Trash?

The devastating consequences of the Homeland War and the emergence of a Croatian state resulted in a sweeping revision of the former regime's historical narratives and institutionalized memory. Instead of historical interpretations that depicted as inevitable the formation of a joint Yugoslav state under the leadership of the revolutionary communist party, textbooks,[29] monuments,[30] public spaces,[31] and museum exhibitions had to be transformed to reflect the Croatian nation-building project. Since most of the history museums had been dedicated to the People's Liberation War, one of the pillars of the regime's legitimacy during the Tito era, the exhibitions were outdated ideologically as well as methodologically. Some museums handled the transition by cutting out the exhibitions related to World War II and relying on less controversial earlier historical periods (such as the History Museum of Istria in Pula), while others ceased to display a permanent exhibition (such as the Croatian History Museum). The result is that in the three decades since independence, there has been a conspicuous vacuum in professional history museum exhibitions dealing with World War II and the rest of the twentieth century. This is particularly the case when it comes to permanent exhibitions. While the memorialization of the Homeland War is a priority for the Croatian state, since the political establishment draws on its legacy for electoral support, Croatian participation in the Partisan anti-fascist resistance movement (one of the largest in Europe) and the Croatian experience of communist rule are given scant attention in official museums.

Although not exactly a resistance or World War II museum, the Jasenovac Memorial Site is the only significant museum in Croatia dealing with any aspect of World War II, specifically the system of concentration camps built in the area by the Ustaša regime.[32] Shortly after the Independent State of Croatia was proclaimed in April 1941, a number of racial laws against Serbs, Jews, and Roma were enacted, followed by both systematic arrests of non-Croats and mass killings of Serbs by so-called "wild" Ustaše.[33] Lipa Remembers Memorial Center (*Memorijalni centar Lipa pamti*) is perhaps the only other museum that deals with World War II in a modern approach, preserving both the ruins of the village of Lipa (burned by the Nazis on 30 April 1944) and offering an interactive educational center within the museum.[34] Since the new permanent exhibition was opened in 2015, schools from Primorje regularly visit Lipa, and the museum hosts the annual commemoration for this tragedy. There are also other smaller memorial rooms (*spomen sobe*) dedicated to local histories of World War II, such as the Muzejska zbirka Kastavštine (Kastav) or Muzej oslobođenje Dalmacije (Šibenik), but these do not have the size to be considered national museums.

The narrative of World War II is thus confined to the museum of a concentration camp. In contrast to the gas chambers of the Nazi death camps, victims in Jasenovac, nearby Stara Gradiška, and other Ustaša camps were often murdered by less systematic but more brutal methods. The estimated number of victims at Jasenovac has fluctuated wildly over the years and was subject to considerable political manipulation almost immediately after the end of the war. The statistic of 700,000 victims was considered sacrosanct in communist-era Yugoslavia, and by the 1980s some scholars inflated that figure to allege that over 1 million individuals, predominantly Serbs, were killed in the camps alone.[35] The reaction of Croatian nationalists, such as Franjo Tuđman, was to minimize the numbers. Even before he became president, Tuđman argued that the total death toll for camps in Croatia was not more than 40,000, a figure he continued to cite in the 1990s.[36] The museum's website currently lists 83,845 Serbs, Jews, Roma, Croats, and individuals of other nationalities as victims,[37] although many scholars believe the final number is higher.[38]

Unlike other World War II camps in Europe that have been preserved and transformed into memorials, at the Jasenovac site no original structures remain. The Ustaše destroyed the camp and nearly all administrative records in 1945 when it became clear the war was lost, and in subsequent years the inhabitants of the town of Jasenovac scoured the ruins for building material to repair their devastated homes. In the 1950s local officials floated the idea of creating some kind of memorial at the site, but it was not until 1963 that 1,500 people participated in a "work action" to clear the terrain and a decision was made to construct a monument.[39] The Croatian People's Liberation War veterans' organization chose Belgrade architect Bogdan Bogdanović's *Stone Flower* (*Kameni cvijet*) design, symbolizing "indestructible life," as the central monument.[40] Work on the monument lasted from 1964 until the opening ceremony on July 4, 1966.[41] Construction on a museum was begun in September 1967 and completed in July 1968, the same year the Jasenovac Memorial Site was established to administer the museum. In 1983 the Jasenovac Memorial Site was expanded to include all of the outlying camps that constituted the Jasenovac system, such as Krapje, Uštica, Stara Gradiška (the location of a women's camp), and Donja Gradina. The latter location is a massive killing field across the Sava River and is currently located in Bosnia-Herzegovina (in the Republika Srpska entity), which has physically divided the once-united memorial site between two countries. The fragmentation of the memorial site has resulted in two radically different constructions of the past: the Croatian one, which offers a contemporary museum space and commemorative site, and a Bosnian Serb one that perpetuates the Jasenovac myths from the communist period.

The memorial museum's exhibition was originally established in 1968 and was updated in 1988. Both permanent exhibitions featured horrific photographs of corpses and of murders being committed by Ustaše and other pro-Axis forces, along with a large collection of objects (including many weapons allegedly used to kill the victims), which traumatized generations of students who visited Jasenovac. A book by Nataša Mataušić reveals that about half of the photographs exhibited in the museum were in fact taken in German concentration camps or locations that had nothing to do with Jasenovac or even the Ustaša perpetrators.[42] In 1991 the memorial site was occupied by rebel Serb forces who devastated the museum and looted its collection. The objects ended up in a storage facility in Banja Luka (Bosnia and Herzegovina), were transferred to Washington, DC, with the help of the United States Holocaust Memorial Museum in 2000, and were finally returned to Croatia in 2001.[43] Several thematic exhibitions[44] were organized at the memorial site, and the Stone Flower monument was restored in 2003–2004, but the most important development was the preparation and implementation of the permanent exhibition at the memorial museum.

As mentioned above, all significant museums in Croatia dealing with World War II were closed, transformed, or destroyed during the 1990s war for independence. Thus, the Jasenovac Memorial Site Memorial Museum became the litmus test for Croatia's readiness to come to terms with the dark chapters of its past after the partial rehabilitation of the Ustaše in Tuđman's Croatia.[45] Tuđman's conceptualization of the Jasenovac memorial had threatened to turn the site into a symbolic manifestation of his goal of Croatian national reconciliation. According to him, "Jasenovac could become a place for all victims of war, which would warn the Croatian people that in the past they were divided and brought into an internecine conflict, warn them to not repeat it, and to reconcile the dead just as we reconciled the living, their children, and their grandchildren."[46] After an avalanche of protests from the international community and domestic anti-fascist and human-rights organizations, Tuđman abandoned his idea for turning the site into an exclusively Croatian memorial site.

On March 8, 2001, the Croatian parliament passed a new law on the administration of the *Jasenovac Memorial Site*, which included the appointment of a nine-member advisory board, a five-member governing board, and a new director, who was tasked with developing the concept for the permanent exhibition. As Ljiljana Radonić notes in her sharp critique of the Jasenovac museum, the authors of the new permanent exhibition had to negotiate between European standards of (Holocaust) memorialization and the specificities of the Jasenovac camp and its victims.[47] In early 2006, months before the new exhibition was opened, an intense public debate erupted over the museum's conceptual design. Since 2002, the staff at the Jasenovac Memorial Site worked closely with the U.S. Holocaust Memorial Museum, and in 2005 Croatia became a regular member of the Task Force for International Cooperation on Holocaust Education, Remembrance, and Research (today the *International Holocaust Remembrance Alliance*). The debate centered on fears that Jasenovac would become exclusively a Holocaust memorial, which would obfuscate the genocidal policies of the Ustaše against Serbs (who were the most numerous victims at the camp), Roma, and other targets of the regime. Zorica Stipetić, a historian and the head of the advisory board, stated in an interview before the exhibition opened that

> [t]he symbol of the Holocaust is a gas chamber, while the symbols of Jasenovac are a dagger and the letter "U" [for Ustaše]. If those are removed or marginalized, then we will hide the true character of that camp; in other words, we will not present the full truth and educational potential of what really happened there.[48]

Moreover, the decision to focus on individual victims, rather than the collective victims who were killed only because of their religion or nationality, raised the issue that the magnitude of the murders would be minimized. The decision to list the names of all the victims on glass plates that hang in the museum was considered controversial, since their nationality was not included, so two plasma screens with all the names and nationalities were subsequently added. The controversy over the museum did not subside after the official opening of the new exhibition on November 27, 2006. Croatia's political leaders – the president, prime minister, and speaker of the parliament – gathered at the memorial site and gave speeches about the meaning of Jasenovac. Stjepan Mesić, the president at the time, emphasized the importance of the camp as a World War II site of memory:

> If there is a place in Croatia where there can be absolutely no doubt about how this country views what happened in World War II, then it is here – Jasenovac[. ...] If there exists a place where it is possible to be informed of the crimes of the Ustaša so-called state, then that place is here – Jasenovac. To be absolutely clear: this museum can not only illustrate the crimes that were committed, but it must provide information about them, completely and decently.[49]

Croatia's prime minister at the time, Ivo Sanader, went a step further and drew parallels with the war of independence and placed the museum exhibition within the context of Croatia's road towards European Union membership. In his speech he referred not only to fascist crimes but also to communist ones:

> We must speak about a Europe without divisions precisely at Jasenovac. Because Jasenovac is a tragic measure of the depth of divisions which, in the context of the old conflicted Europe, were carved deeply into the tissue of Croatian society. Few countries in Europe felt and suffered so much from the consequences of European divisions and conflicts between ideologies and peoples. In the Homeland War we overcame those divisions, we strengthened our anti-fascist foundations while simultaneously condemning communist totalitarianism, and we raised the paradigm of a newly united and reconciled Croatia that is our pledge in the new Europe. That new Europe brings values that are also part of our inheritance, such as dialogue, tolerance, peace, and democracy. Modern Croatia will be built precisely upon those values.[50]

After the speeches, the politicians toured the new exhibition along with the museum staff and several hundred visitors, but their statements afterwards were noticeably more critical than earlier. Mesić criticized the minimalist and rather avant-garde design because "it did not adequately present the brutality of the killings, even though it was good that the victims were individualized.

Perhaps I am subjective, but this was a concentration camp of horror and the most terrible kinds of death."[51] Milorad Pupovac, a parliamentary deputy and the president of the Serbian National Council (SNV – *Srpsko narodno vijeće*), stated that

> [t]his is only the first step, which needs to be built upon in collaboration with the representatives of the victims. This is more of an informational – documentary center than a museum, more of an installation that can be anywhere rather than a place that is connected to what Jasenovac really was.[52]

Zorica Stipetić, the president of the advisory board, agreed that the museum was not ideal and that efforts would be made to add to the permanent exhibition. She concluded that the problem was not the material that was displayed, but the items that were missing: "I believe that there should be one more exhibition space that could display more authentic artifacts and objects which were in the original exhibition, so as to get a feel for the truth of what happened here."[53] Other critics were even harsher in their opinions. Julija Koš, a member of the advisory board, told reporters from Republika Srpska that "even the Ustaše would have been pleased with this kind of exhibition," insinuating that the museum deliberately covered up the truth about Ustaša crimes.[54] Koš continued to attack the exhibition years later, accusing the authors of being "notoriously incompetent" and suggesting that the museum should be closed immediately.[55] Meanwhile, Efraim Zuroff, the director of Jerusalem's Simon Wiesenthal Center, called the exhibition "postmodern trash" after visiting the museum when it opened. He added that

> [i]n the new exhibition there is nothing about the ideology of Ustaša massacres. Based on the exhibition, no one can understand anything about the ideology of the Ustaše, who tried to turn Croatia into a purely Catholic country, without Serbs, Jews, and Roma. There is no context, nothing about World War II, and hardly any historical evidence of genocide and the Holocaust.[56]

Despite many of the negative comments, two staff members from the United States Holocaust Memorial Museum in Washington, DC, Diane Saltzman and Arthur Berger, blamed the museum's flaws on the small exhibition space and emphasized that it had nevertheless succeeded in "returning individual victims their identity, because that was taken away in the concentration camp."[57]

More than ten years after its reopening, the Jasenovac museum remains the main permanent exhibition in Croatia dealing with World War II. But is it effective in fulfilling its role as a history museum? After several visits to the memorial site since 2006, my opinion is that, unfortunately, it has failed to provide a clear narrative of what happened in the concentration camp and in

Croatia under the Ustaša regime. When I led a group of Italian high school students to the site as part of a study trip in 2010, many of the museum's problems became evident. First, despite promises that the exhibition would be expanded and modified following the wave of criticism in 2006, the permanent exhibit remains the same. The museum added a timeline for context in the nearby educational center, and an outdoor exhibit shows the development and construction of Bogdanović's Flower as part of the 50th anniversary of the monument.

Second, while the phrase "postmodern trash" is perhaps a bit too harsh, the exhibition has opted for an artistic design over the kind of content one would expect in a traditional history museum. From the moment one enters the museum, there is already a sense of confusion; there are two exhibition spaces, to the left and right, but no markings to indicate where to begin. In fact, the museum has no chronological order. Unlike similar museums dealing with the Holocaust (such as the Oskar Schindler Factory Museum in Kraków or the Holocaust Memorial Center in Budapest), there is no historical narrative to guide visitors through the events that led up to the construction of the camp and the political context from which the Ustaša movement emerged. Some captions are placed low, near the ground, so it is a challenge to read them, while all of the captions in English are printed in white on a gray background, rendering them practically illegible. The interior of the museum is black, dark, and oppressive, although it does not necessarily convey what the victims experienced (unlike the barracks and gas chambers visitors can walk around in Auschwitz). The proper atmosphere is certainly created, but it lacks the pedagogical techniques found in other concentration camp museums. Moreover, there are no models or maps of what the camp looked like, so one is expected to reconstruct the past through oral histories presented on video screens and a few grainy photographs. It is surprising that the objects from the 2002 exhibition on the first year of the concentration camp were not included, since they gave a much more vivid picture of what took place in Jasenovac. Although the authors argue that limited space forced them to take a multimedia approach, the several computers for visitor use are a poor substitute for featuring more images and objects that would "guide" them through the past, as is to be expected from a museum. Third, the decision to focus on the individual victims is legitimate, but barely mentioning the perpetrators gives only a partial picture of what happened during World War II. All the other museums mentioned above that served as a model for Jasenovac extensively analyze the ideology and movements that perpetuated the Holocaust and other crimes against humanity in the various countries, so it is surprising that the Jasenovac museum only acknowledgment of this topic is a single photograph of the Ustaša leader Ante Pavelić meeting with Adolf Hitler. The curator speaking to the visiting Italian students explained that not showing the perpetrators honors the victims, but the result is that visitors who have not extensively studied the subject leave more confused than enlightened. Since World War II and the subsequent communist period are not represented in museums, the contested narratives of the past are transmitted to the public primarily through commemorative events and the political speeches given at those sites. This is particularly the case regarding Croat and Serb identities, as well as interpretations of the anti-fascist struggle and the uprising against fascism in 1941. The official government position, as defined in the Constitution, is that the modern Croatian state was built on anti-fascist foundations. The state-building narrative is thus emphasized; Croats were an important part of the Partisan movement that established Croatia's current territorial borders, which were subsequently defended by the veterans of the Homeland War in the 1990s. The cultural memory of World War II plays an even more important role for Croatia's Serbs. Pupovac, the president of the Croatian Serb organization SNV, noted that participation in the People's Liberation War was a crucial element of Croatian Serb identity and cultural heritage.[58] He added that the systematic destruction of anti-fascist monuments in the 1990s served to erase that part of Croatia's cultural memory.[59] For this reason, the SNV has included the renovation of anti-fascist monuments as one of the key goals in its program.[60] Thus commemorations of the 1941 uprising against the Ustaša regime reinforce Croatian Serb anti-fascist identity (and reject Serbian extremist narratives) as well as restoring Serbs to the broader Croatian anti-fascist narrative emphasized since 2000.

New Revisionist Trends and Jasenovac

Whereas the previous analysis showed the development of the Jasenovac Memorial Site in the period of Croatia's transition from communism and in the immediate postwar era, when it was subjected to new national interpretations of the past as well as international criteria due to Croatia's EU accession, this final section provides a brief overview of some of the more recent trends in the politics of memory. Since many of the events described below can be considered current, rather than historical, inevitably the analysis tends to be more subjective and based on extensive media observations, intensive fieldwork on commemorative practices related to World War II since 2013 as part of the project "Framing the Nation and Collective Identity in Croatia: Political Rituals and Cultural Memory of 20th Century Traumas" (FRAMNAT),[61] and participation in conferences, workshops, seminars, trainings, and interviews dealing with memory politics in Croatia and Europe. In 2019 Routledge published the results of this project which, alongside several other edited volumes in recent years, provides an interdisciplinary analysis of memory politics in the former Yugoslavia.[62]

The election of Kolinda Grabar-Kitarović, the HDZ's candidate for president in 2015, precipitated a shift in the discourse used at World War II commemorations, which paralleled a more general trend in attempts by right-wing politicians and intellectuals to undermine Croatia's anti-fascist legacy. In April 2015, President Grabar-Kitarović chose to break the practice of her predecessors and did not attend the commemoration to the Jasenovac victims (she laid a wreath at the site several days earlier). She took several other symbolic actions soon after becoming president, such as removing a bust of Tito from the presidential office (which even Tuđman had kept) and then sponsoring the Bleiburg commemoration in May, which the SDP coalition had stopped funding because it felt that it contributed to the rehabilitation of the Ustaša movement. The electoral campaign prior to parliamentary elections in the fall of 2015 were notable for the HDZ's virulent anti-communist discourse, threats of imminent lustration, and the decision to include parties openly sympathetic to the Ustaše in their coalition. Once the HDZ was able to form a government in early 2016, many of its initial moves seemed to confirm fears that the radical right wing of the party was pushing an ideological agenda that mirrored some of the developments in other Central European countries such as Hungary, Poland, and Slovakia. Some of the first decisions of the new government were to appoint a controversial (some would say revisionist) historian, Zlatan Hasanbegović, as the minister of culture and restore parliamentary sponsorship over the Bleiburg commemoration.

The year 2016 saw a number of openly revisionist moves regarding Jasenovac as a broader trend of rehabilitating the Ustaše as Croatian patriots and further delegitimizing the Partisans by framing them exclusively as anti-Croat war criminals.[63] In 2015, after initial difficulty in getting registered, several right-wing scholars established the Society for Researching the Triple Jasenovac Camp (*Društvo za istraživanje trostrukog logora Jasenovac*), which challenges the number of victims in the Ustaše-led camp while positing the theory that the communist authorities were in fact the ones who committed the most crimes at a new camp that existed there after 1945.[64] Many of these arguments were articulated in the book *Jasenovac Camps* (*Jasenovački logori*, 2015) and through right-wing media outlets.[65] The questionable methodology, selective interpretation of documents, and claims bordering on Holocaust denial in this book prompted respected intellectual Slavko Goldstein to directly respond with the 2016 book *Jasenovac-tragedija, mitomanija, istina* (*Jasenovac-Tragedy, Mythomania, Truth*), while Đorđe Miholović published a book of documentary photographs taken after the camp's liberation in 1945, depicting ruins and reconstruction by the villagers of Jasenovac that debunk the theory that the communists continued to maintain a concentration camp on the site.[66]

In April 2016, the premier of Jakov Sedlar's revisionist film, *Jasenovac-Istina* (*Jasenovac – the Truth*), which included several falsifications identified by investigative journalists, was the straw that broke the camel's back and spurred an outcry from human rights NGOs, the Serb minority, Roma and Jewish organizations, the anti-fascist association of Croatia, and even the Israeli ambassador.[67] Consequently, all of these groups boycotted the official commemoration, resulting in an international scandal.[68] While the official commemoration was held on April 22, attended primarily by government ministers and parliamentary deputies, alternative commemorations were held on April 15 (organized by Croatia's Jewish community) and April 24 (organized by the Association of Anti-fascist Veterans of Croatia and the Serbian National Council), along with a protest in Zagreb organized on the same day as the official event. The rival interpretations of the nature of the Jasenovac camp were thus present not only in academic publications and the media, but in a number of commemorative rituals and official government statements.

The revisionist attacks continued through 2016 and 2017, particularly in right-wing publications such as *Hrvatski tjednik*, which regularly questions the number of victims compiled by the Jasenovac researchers at the Jasenovac Memorial Site.[69] Rather than engaging in scholarly debate that would contribute to a better understanding of the concentration camp and the Ustaša regime, the rhetoric employed by the revisionists suggests that any errors are deliberate lies, manipulations, and conspiracies by a communist elite that still holds power in Croatia and seeks to malign Croats through the guilt of Jasenovac. While the numbers of victims in Jasenovac is still manipulated in certain nationalist circles in Republika Srpska and Serbia, as evidenced by political speeches given by Milorad Dodik and Aleksandar Vučić at commemorations in recent years in Donja Gradina (Bosnia and Herzegovina), serious scholars in the region and abroad consider the figure of 80,000–100,000 total victims a reasonable estimate. Yet the systematic attacks by contributors to *Hrvatski tjednik*, such as Blanka Matković, who argues that "Jasenovac is the biggest falsification in Croatian history,"[70] seeks to undermine the entire existence of the camp by questioning the number of victims, which will never be complete.

The memorial plaque, erected on the wall of the local kindergarten by the Zagreb Association of Croatian Armed Forces/*Hrvatske Oružane Snage* (Croatian acronym: HOS) volunteers on November 5, 2016, is dedicated to the memory of eleven HOS soldiers who died in or near Jasenovac during the Homeland War. The controversy exploded when it became publicly known that the plaque contained the Ustaša salute "Za dom spremni" ("For Home/Homeland, Ready!") in the emblem of the HOS organization, which was legally registered in Zagreb. The presence of the same salute used by the perpetrators in the Jasenovac camp so close to the Jasenovac Memorial Site deeply offended families of the victims, Croatian Serb organizations, the Jewish community, anti-fascist organizations, and many other Croatian citizens who felt this was unacceptable for a country that supposedly valued its anti-fascist and European foundations. Prime Minister Plenković, at the head of a shaky coalition and already unpopular with the more radical right members of his party, opted to delay deciding and instead announced the formation of the Commission for Dealing with Totalitarian Symbols (also known as the Council for Dealing with the Legacy of Undemocratic Regimes) on December 8, 2016. Although at certain moments a controversial monument can spark a fruitful debate in society about a difficult past, in this case the polemics seemed an unnecessary distraction and merely provoked radical reactions from both the right and the left while the government appeared indecisive.

Anti-fascists, Croatian Serb politicians, and the Jewish community kept up the pressure against the government, boycotted the official Jasenovac commemoration in April and warned of encroaching fascism in Croatian society. Their argument was that they had nothing against a memorial to fallen HOS volunteers, but demanded the removal of the Ustaša salute "Za dom spremni." Right-wing pundits and HOS veterans refused to compromise, launching a campaign that claimed that not only was "Za dom spremni" a salute from the Homeland War that had nothing to do with the Ustaša movement, but that it was in fact an "old Croatian salute" going back centuries.[71] As in the case with the supporters of the HOS monument in Split, those defending this plaque attempted to erase the memory of the negative aspects of the Ustaše by reframing all of their symbols and imagery as originating in the Homeland War. As Plenković's coalition partners increased pressure on him over the summer, the government initiated direct talks with HOS veterans (but interestingly, not with representatives of the Jasenovac Memorial) and promised that the Commission would hurry with its work on controversial symbols. On September 7, over eight months after the controversial plaque was erected, workers removed it from Jasenovac and transferred it to Trokut memorial park, near the town of Novska. Although the controversial monument was no longer visible in Jasenovac, "Za dom spremni" remained on the plaque and, moreover, the new location is on the site of a devastated Partisan memorial (destroyed during the Homeland War) and ossuary of fallen Partisans[72] which, at the time of this writing, seems to only have deepened the controversy rather than resolved it.

Conclusion

While the Croatian state embarked on a broad revision of institutionalized cultural memory since independence in 1991, history museums have been sidelined during this process and can be considered part of the country's "culture of forgetting" rather than its culture of memory. As discussed above, any representation of the communist past invariably has to include an analysis of World War II, and the ongoing ideological and ethno-national divisions in everyday politics means that reaching an even minimal consensus about the recent past is nearly impossible. Croatia, which had one of the largest resistance movements in occupied Europe, is thus left with hardly any exhibition space dedicated to this period. Jasenovac, which partially plays the role of a resistance museum, remains too controversial to be an effective educational tool for displaying the history of World War II. There are initiatives to return exhibitions to some other memorial sites (Glina, Petrova Gora) and vague plans for a future museum of victims of all wars (an initiative by the NGO Documenta), but at the moment this period remains in a museological void. The daily *Slobodna Dalmacija* recently reported that a memorial center for anti-fascist fighters on the island of Vis was dismantled and the materials moved into a hallway to make room for a new bank, further evidence that there is little consideration for an appropriate relationship with the past.[73]

The creation of a permanent exhibition in the national history museum is going to be challenging and will test Croatia's ability to come to terms with the past. While for years there have been plans to move the museum to a new space and develop the permanent exhibition, no public debate about the content has taken place; all discussion has been at internal meetings in the Ministry of Culture. The committee in charge of designing the new exhibition has included representatives of broad segments of Croatian society (including the Serb minority), presumably so it does not become exclusively a state-building historical narrative of ethnic Croats.

The United States, often held to be a successful multiethnic society, likewise faced difficult challenges in developing a National Museum of African American History and Culture that would balance a narrative about the victimization of blacks in American history while also portraying how the country overcame the legacy of slavery and racism.[74] The myth of this rosy melting pot unraveled as the United States was repeatedly confronted with new eruptions of racial tension (#BlackLivesMatter, the murder of George Floyd, widespread debates and protests over the removal of Confederate monuments, etc.) and, while the museum has been hailed for its depictions of Black history, the country is increasingly divided about its controversial past. The National Memorial for Peace and Justice as well as the Legacy Museum, both in Montgomery, Alabama, offer much starker and gut-wrenching depictions in racial terror in the United States, and the current political climate seems to indicate further polarization in the aftermath of the Donald Trump presidency.

Although slavery and racial violence in the United States has significant differences from the historical legacies in the former Yugoslavia, the experiences in memorialization offer interesting comparative reflections for Croatian museums. How will Serbs in Croatia be portrayed in the national history museum? Will the narrative treat them as equal partners in forming the political and cultural heritage of the country, or as a negative factor that obstructed the Croatian state-building project? Will the exhibition move beyond the Yugocommunist and Serbo-Chetnik discourses of the 1990s, which associated all Serbs with communism, a Yugoslav state, and murderous extremism?

While the complexities of World War II and the communist period, as well as Croatia's political elites' unwillingness to undertake a process of lustration, have contributed to the lack of history museums on this period, another factor is the active memorialization of the Homeland War, from monument-building to commemorative events and the establishment of museum exhibitions dedicated to Croatia's struggle for independence. The town of Vukovar, whose capture by Serbian troops and paramilitaries after a three-month siege in 1991 became a symbol of Croatian victimization, also functions as an outdoor museum full of sites of memory (such as the heavily damaged water tower and the street known as the "Graveyard of Tanks"). There are official museum sites in and around Vukovar, such as the city hospital (Vukovar Hospital-Site of Memory Museum), the Ovčara Memorial Site (site of a massacre of over 200 Croatian soldiers and civilians), and the Memorial Cemetery. The Memorial Center for the Homeland War in Vukovar, established in 2013 and fully functioning since 2016, provides Croatian students with site visits and educational activities, focusing mostly on the military aspects of the conflict with less attention given to work on peace-building and tolerance.[75] The experiences of the Homeland War will influence how World War II and the communist era are interpreted both at the official level as well as in Croatian society at large. In a country full of memory politics, it will be important for Croatia's political elites and museologists to coordinate the creation of permanent exhibitions dealing with the twentieth century that convey a pluralistic narrative of the past in line with European Union paradigms of remembrance in dealing with the Holocaust, World War II, and communist dictatorships.

Notes

1 Croats, who felt persecuted and exploited by the Serbian regime during the first Yugoslavia (1918–1941), initially welcomed the establishment of the Independent State of Croatia (Nezavisna Država Hrvatska, or NDH) following the German invasion in April 1941. Although it was clear that the Ustaša movement, a radical Croat nationalist organization influenced by Fascist Italy and Nazi Germany and led by Ante Pavelić, was not going to create a liberal democratic regime when it took power on April 10, few could imagine the horrors of mass murder, concentration and death camps, systematic persecution of non-Croat civilians, and widespread destruction that was to ensue in the next four years of spiraling violence and retribution. See: Sabrina P. Ramet (ed.) *Nezavisna Država Hrvatska* (Zagreb: Alinea, 2009).
2 John R. Gillis, "Introduction," in John R. Gillis (ed.) *Commemorations: The Politics of National Identity* (Princeton: Princeton University Press, 1994), pp. 4.
3 Jan Assmann, *Kulturno pamćenje* (Zenica: Vrijeme, 2005), pp. 59.
4 Maurice Halbwachs, *On Collective Memory* (Chicago: University of Chicago Press, 1992).
5 Barbara Misztal, quoted in Sheila Watson (ed.) *Museums and Their Communities* (London: Routledge, 2007), pp. 375.
6 Carol Duncan, quoted in James Cuno, "Money, Power, and the History of Art," in Sheila Watson (ed.) *Museums and Their Communities* (London: Routledge: 2007), pp. 514.
7 Peter Davis, "Place Exploration: Museums, Identity, Community," in Sheila Watson (ed.) *Museums and Their Communities*, pp. 56–57.
8 The survey was conducted among 1,500 respondents throughout Croatia by IPSOS Strategic Marketing as part of the Symbolic Strategies of Nation Building in the West Balkan States project. The complete results of the survey are available at www.hf.uio.no/ilos/english/research/projects/nation-w-balkan/index.html (accessed December 20, 2017).

9 Lorena Rivera-Orraca, "Are Museums Sites of Memory?" *New School of Psychology Bulletin* vol. 6, no. 2, 2009, pp. 32.
10 Steven C. Dubin, "The Postmodern Exhibition: Cut on the Bias, or is Enola Gay a Verb?" in Sheila Watson, *Museums and Their Communities*, pp. 225.
11 Stephen Weil, "The Museum and the Public," in Sheila Watson, *Museums and Their Communities*, pp. 35.
12 Ibid., pp. 36.
13 Brandon Hamber, Liz Ševčenko, and Ereshnee Naidu, "Utopian Dreams or Practical Possibilities? The Challenges of Evaluating the Impact of Memorialization in Societies in Transition," *International Journal of Transitional Justice*, vol. 4, 2010, pp. 399.
14 Information about the Coalition for RECOM, which includes hundreds of NGOs and other organizations throughout the former Yugoslavia, can be found at www.zarekom.org/The-Coalition-for-RECOM.en.html.
15 The museum was supported by Viktor Orbán's right-wing party when it opened in February 2002 and overtly demonizes the socialists while minimizing Jewish victims and the crimes of Hungarian fascists. *Jewish News* (July 26, 2002), online version at www.jewishaz.com/jewishnews/020726/budapest.shtml (accessed August 25, 2011). See also Maria Schmidt, *House of Terror Museum* (Budapest: Public Endowment for Research in Central and East-European History and Society, 2008).
16 Prague's Museum of Communism's official website is at www.muzeumkomunismu.cz/ (accessed August 25, 2011).
17 Lauren A. Rivera, "Managing 'Spoiled' National Identity: War, Tourism, and Memory in Croatia," *American Sociological Review*, vol. 73, no. 4, 2008, pp. 620.
18 European memory was in many ways defined by the anti-fascist victory in World War II, the tragedy of the Holocaust, and the reunification of Europe after the Cold War. In the last decade this has become more complex as the European Union expanded to include former Soviet bloc countries with their experience under communism and former Yugoslav republics with new traumatic memories of war in the 1990s. These new directions in memory politics have been defined by a number of declarations and resolutions by the European Parliament, the creation of national institutions of remembrance, and several memory networking initiatives. Sara Jones, "Cross-border Collaboration and the Construction of Memory Narratives in Europe," in Tea Sindbaek Andersen and Barbara Tornquist-Plewa (eds.) *The Twentieth Century in European Memory: Transcultural Mediation and Reception* (Leiden: Brill, 2016), pp. 28–30.
19 Renata Jambrešić-Kirin, "Politička sjećanja na Drugi svjetski rat u doba medijske reprodukcije socijalističke kulture," in Lada Čale Feldman and Ines Prica (eds.) *Devijacije i promašaji: Etnografija domaćeg socijalizma* (Zagreb: Institut za etnologiju i folkloristiku, 2006), pp. 166.
20 Peter Carrier, "Places, Politics and Archiving of Contemporary Memory in Pierre Nora's Les Lieux de mémoire," in Susannah Radstone (ed.) *Memory and Methodology* (Oxford: Berg, 2000), pp. 43.
21 Joel Palhegyi, "National museums, national myths: constructing socialist Yugoslavism for Croatia and Croats," *Nationalities Papers*, vol. 45, no. 6, 2017, pp. 1048–1065.
22 *Hrvatska 1941. godine* (Zagreb: Muzej Revolucije naroda Hrvatske, 1961), inside front cover.

23 *Rat u Španjolskoj* (Zagreb: Muzej Revolucije naroda Hrvatske, 1986), pp. 1.
24 Lucija Benyovsky, "Španjolski građanski rat i naši interbrigadisti," *Informatica museologica*, no. 1–4 (1986), pp. 46.
25 Ibid. Benyovsky quotes Knezević and Pavičić from an interview in *Vjesnik* (December 19, 1986), where they explain how the conditions facing volunteers fighting in Spain (evading police, living in internment camps, illegal border crossings back into Yugoslavia) meant that few artifacts from that period survived into the present.
26 Ibid., 47–48.
27 Out of about 18,000 victims from Zagreb in World War II, some 7,000 were estimated to have been killed by the Ustaše in Dotrščina, a forested area on the edge of the city. While the park is filled with dozens of monuments dedicated to fallen civilians and Partisans, the memorial center was never built. *Večernji list* (March 14, 1981), pp. 6–7. See also Saša Šimpraga, *Zagreb, javni prostor* (Zagreb: Porfirogenet, 2011), pp. 243.
28 For details about the damage to individual museums, see the website of the Museum Documentation Center at www.mdc.hr/RatneStete/eng/fs-glavni.html (accessed August 25, 2011).
29 Stefano Petrungaro, *Pisati povijest iznova: Hrvatski udžbenici povijesti 1918.–2004.* (Zagreb: Srednja Europa, 2009).
30 Juraj Hrženjak (ed.), *Rušenje antifašističkih spomenika u Hrvatskoj, 1990.–2000.* (Zagreb: Savez antifašističkih boraca Hrvatske, 2002).
31 Dunja Rihtman-Auguštin, *Ulice moga grada* (Beograd: XX vek, 2000).
32 Several books on the history of Jasenovac include Nataša Mataušić, *Jasenovac 1941–1945* (Zagreb: Kameni cvijet, 2003); Tea Benčić Rimay (ed.) *Jasenovac Memorial Site* (Jasenovac: Spomen-područje Jasenovac, 2006); and Mišo Deverić and Ivan Fumić, *Hrvatska u logorima, 1941.–1945* (Zagreb: Savez antifašističkih boraca i antifašista Republike Hrvatske, 2008).
33 For example, the "Decree regarding Racial Affiliation and the Decree regarding the Protection of Aryan Blood and the Honor of the Croatian People" was passed on April 30, 1941, less than three weeks after the NDH was established. Hrvatski narod (Zagreb), May 1, 1941, 1. For more details on the NDH, see Jozo Tomasevich, *War and Revolution in Yugoslavia, 1941–1945: Occupation and Collaboration* (Stanford: Stanford University Press, 2001); Fikreta Jelić-Butić, *Ustaše i Nezavisna Država Hrvatska* (Zagreb: SN Liber, 1978); Tvrtko Jakovina, "The Independent State of Croatia in Hitler's Axis System," Tea Benčić Rimay (ed.) *Jasenovac Memorial Site* and Sabrina P. Ramet (ed.) *Nezavisna Država Hrvatska, 1941.–1945.*
34 http://lipapamti.ppmhp.hr/ (accessed December 20, 2017)
35 Vladimir Žerjavić, *Opsesije i megalomanije oko Jasenovca i Bleiburga* (Zagreb: Globus, 1992), pp. 11–12, 44; and Nataša Mataušić, "The Jasenovac Concentration Camp," in Tea Benčić Rimay (ed.) *Jasenovac Memorial Site*, pp. 47–48.
36 Interview with Tuđman, reprinted in *Novi list* (April 23, 1996), pp. 21. See the discussion of manipulating the number of Jasenovac victims in Franjo Tuđman, *Bespuća povijesne zbiljnosti: Rasprava o povijesti i filozofiji zlosilja* (Zagreb: Nakladni zavod Matice Hrvatske, 1990), pp. 56–58. The notion of collective guilt was one of the central tenets of Tuđman's challenging the number of Serbian victims in World War II. According to him, the number of victims was exaggerated to justify a

unified Yugoslavia and Serb dominance in key party, police, and military positions in Croatia. Franjo Tuđman, "The Sources, Changes, and Essence of the National Question in the Socialist Federal Republic of Yugoslavia," reprinted in Peter Sugar (ed.) *Eastern European Nationalism in the Twentieth Century* (Washington, DC: American University Press, 1995), pp. 330–331.

37 Tables identifying the victims at the Jasenovac camp by nationality can be found at www.jusp-jasenovac.hr/Default.aspx?sid=6711 (accessed August 1, 2011).

38 Slavko Goldstein, while not directly working on the list of victims, often used the figure of 100,000 total victims in newspaper articles and internal discussions. Archive of Javna ustanova Spomen područje (JUSP) Jasenovac, Fond SPJ–Komemoracije, A–745, Slavko Goldstein, "Procjene o približnom broju žrtava ustaškog logorskog sustava Jasenovac 1941–1945," April 21, 2005. The number of victims varies among scholars in Croatia, Serbia, the US Holocaust Memorial Museum, and Yad Vashem, and continues to be debated by politicians and revisionists. Ivo Goldstein provides a short overview of the polemics about numbers ("O broju žrtava jasenovačkog logorskog kompleksa") in Slavko Goldstein, *Jasenovac: tragika, mitomanija, istina* (Zagreb: Fraktura, 2016), pp. 103–127.

39 Duško Lončar, *Deset godina spomen-područja Jasenovac* (Jasenovac: Spomen-područje Jasenovac, 1977), pp. 13–14.

40 Bogdanović stated in an interview that "in the Jasenovac Flower I denoted life – the crimes which took place in Jasenovac were terrible, but it is important to show what comes afterwards." Quoted in Nataša Jovičić, "The Alchemy of the Flower," in Tea Benčić Rimay (ed.) *Jasenovac Memorial Site*, pp. 229.

41 Duško Lončar, *Deset godina spomen-područja Jasenovac*, pp. 13–14.

42 Nataša Mataušić, *Jasenovac fotomonografija* (Zagreb: Spomen-područje Jasenovac, 2008). Mataušić reveals how many photographs were used in different publications and exhibits with various captions to manipulate the victims for political purposes.

43 Nataša Mataušić, "The Jasenovac Concentration Camp," in Tea Benčić Rimay (ed.) *Jasenovac Memorial Site*, pp. 54. Croatian authorities estimate that about 30 percent of the collection, which in 1991 consisted of some 14,000 objects and 2,500 publications, is still missing. It is believed to be in Bosnia-Herzegovina or Serbia.

44 From April 2002 to April 2003, the memorial site hosted the exhibition "The Jasenovac Concentration Camp: An Exhibition about the Beginning of the Camp System, August 1941–February 1942," which featured numerous original artifacts, models, and photographs of the camp, and a life-sized reconstruction of the main gate. Compared to today's relatively abstract permanent exhibition, this exhibition was far more effective at conveying the look and feel of the Jasenovac camp.

45 While Tuđman never completely rejected Croatian antifascism, Tito, or his own Partisan past, since the 1990s there have been systematic efforts to portray the Ustaša, not as fascist collaborators, but as patriotic anti-communists. See Darko Karačić, Tamara Banjeglav, and Nataša Govedarica, *Re:vizija prošlosti: Politike sjećanja u Bosni i Hercegovini, Hrvatskoj i Srbiji od 1990. godine* (Sarajevo: Freidrich Ebert Stiftung, 2012); Vjeran Pavlaković, "Flirting with Fascism: The Ustaša Legacy and Croatian Politics in the 1990s," in Lorenzo Bertucelli and Mila Orlić (eds.) *Una storia balcanica: Fascismo, comunismo e nazionalismo nella Jugoslavia del Novecento* (Verona: Ombre corte, 2008); and Stevo Đurašković, "National

identity-building and the 'Ustaša-nostalgia' in Croatia: the past that will not pass," in *Nationalities Papers*, vol. 44, no. 5, 2016.
46 Interview with Tuđman, reprinted in *Novi list* (April 23, 1996), pp. 21. While Tuđman envisioned Croatian war dead from various sides being buried at Jasenovac in separate graves, opponents of that idea accused him of "mixing the bones of the dead."
47 Ljiljana Radonić, "Univerzalizacija holokausta na primjeru hrvatske politike prošlosti i spomen-područja Jasenovac," *Suvremene teme*, vol. 3, no. 1, 2010, pp. 55–58.
48 *Identitet*, no. 94 (January 2006), pp. 10.
49 Speech of former president Stjepan Mesić at Jasenovac, November 27, 2006, transcript available at www.predsjednik.hr/Default.aspx?art=13331&sec=715 (accessed on August 29, 2008).
50 Speech of former PM minister Ivo Sanader at Jasenovac, November 27, 2006, transcript in the possession of the author.
51 *Novi list* (November 28, 2006), pp. 3.
52 Ibid.
53 *Nezavisne novine* (December 2, 2006), online version at www.nezavisne.com (accessed on August 29, 2008). This daily newspaper, published in Banja Luka (Republika Srpska), also emphasized how the museum had "minimized" the victims by claiming there were "only" about 70,000 and not 700,000, the official statistic that continues to be used by the Bosnian Serb authorities.
54 *Jutarnji list* (November 28, 2006), pp. 8.
55 *Novi list* (November 22, 2008), pp. 7; *Novi list* (December 6, 2008), pp. 22–23; and *Novi list* (December 20, 2008), pp. 22. Mataušić responded to Koš's allegations; this was followed by a final article by Koš in the daily Novi list, criticizing the museum and its staff.
56 *Novi list* (November 29, 2006), pp. 5.
57 *Novi list* (December 2, 2006), pp. 6.
58 Historian Filip Škiljan's research on Croatian Serbs confirmed that the anti-fascist legacy was a crucial part of their identity. Filip Škiljan, "Identitet Srba u Hrvatskoj," *Politička misao*, vol. 51, no. 2, 2014.
59 Interview with Milorad Pupovac in Zagreb, Croatia, October 1, 2009. Pupovac admitted that some participants at World War II commemorations were not critical enough of communist Yugoslavia and Tito but rejected any suggestions that Greater Serbian ideology was glorified.
60 Saša Milošević (ed.) *Srbi u Hrvatskoj 2007* (Zagreb: Vijeće srpske nacionalne manjine grada Zagreba, 2007), pp. 20–21.
61 www.framnat.eu (accessed December 20, 2017).
62 Vjeran Pavlaković and Davor Pauković (eds.) *Framing the Nation and Collective Identity: Political Rituals and Cultural Memory of the Twentieth-Century Traumas in Croatia* (London: Routledge, 2019). See also Oto Luthar (ed.) *Of Red Dragons and Evil Spirits: Post-Communist Historiography Between Democratization and New Politics of History* (Budapest: CEU Press, 2017); Ana Milošević and Tamara Pavasović Trošt (eds.) *Europeanisation and Memory Politics in the Western Balkans* (New York: Palgrave MacMillan, 2021); Jody Jensen (ed.) *Memory Politics and Populism in Southeastern Europe* (London: Routledge, 2021); and Gruia Bădescu, Britt Baillie, and Francesco Mazzucchelli (eds.) *Synchronous Pasts: Transforming heritage in the former Yugoslavia* (New York: Palgrave MacMillan, 2021).

63 One of the trends observed at commemorations at Bleiburg and Knin was the blurring of lines between Ustaša iconography and legitimate symbols of the Homeland War, most notably the Ustaša slogan "Za dom spremni." At the Day of Victory and Homeland Thanksgiving commemoration in Knin on 5 August 2016 (as well as in 2017), HOS shirts with Za dom spremni were popular since they were "legal" to wear, even though this appeared on numerous other shirts, hats, and souvenirs sold along with images of Ante Pavelić, Bleiburg collectibles, and other iconography explicitly or more subtly alluding to the NDH. T-shirts are not necessarily an academic measure of pro-fascist affinity, but after twelve years of commemorative fieldwork it is safe to say that since 2015 there has been a dramatic increase in this kind of iconography in Knin, in addition to instances of HOS veterans marching in black shirts, singing of Ustaša songs, and other excesses which were more often associated with the concerts of Marko Perković Thompson and football matches. See Dario Brentin, "Ready for the homeland? Ritual, remembrance, and political extremism in Croatian football," *Nationalities Papers*, vol. 44, no. 6, 2016.
64 https://drustvojasenovac.wordpress.com/ (accessed, December 20, 2017).
65 Stjepan Razum and Igor Vukić (eds.) *Jasenovački logori: istraživanja* (Zagreb: Društvo za istraživanje trostrukog logora Jasenovac, 2015).
66 See Goldstein, *Jasenovac: tragika, mitomanija, istina*; and Đorđe Mihovilović, *Jasenovac 1945–1947: fotomonografija* (Jasenovac: Javna ustanova spomen područje Jasenovac, 2016).
67 *Jutarnji list*, 8 April 2016, p. 5. The Israeli ambassador to Croatia, Kalay Kleitman, stated that after seeing the film she felt that it "selectively depicted history, attempted to revise many known historical facts, and offended the feelings of people who lost their loved ones in Jasenovac."
68 The US State Department's annual *International Religious Freedom Report for Croatia* in 2016 mentioned the boycott of the Jasenovac commemoration as well as other trends which can be considered historical revisionism. US Department of State, 2016 *Report on International Religious Freedom*, www.state.gov/j/drl/rls/irf/2016/ (accessed, December 20, 2017). See also SNV Bulletin #10: *Historijski revizionizam, govor mržnje i nasilje prema Srbima u 2016*. (Zagreb: SNV, 2017).
69 Nikola Banić and Mladen Koić published almost weekly articles in Hrvatski tjednik seeking to frame the Jasenovac database as a deliberate falsification, which would then presumably lead to a new understanding of the NDH, unburdened by the dark legacy of Jasenovac. There is not enough space to fully undertake a thorough analysis of the media debates over Jasenovac, in both the right-wing as well as left-wing presses, but this merely served as an example of historical revisionism of the camp and World War II more broadly in the media.
70 *Hrvatski tjednik*, 12 January 2017, pp. 37.
71 Even a superficial examination of HOS and HSP publications, newspapers, video clips, interviews, and memoirs reveals that they were in fact very consciously drawing upon the legacy of the NDH in their choice of symbols in the 1990s, which paradoxically some veterans are now attempting to deny. However, HOS general Ante Prkačin in a number of interviews openly admitted that HOS directly took the imagery of the NDH and glorified the Ustaše when they were organizing their paramilitary units in 1991. See 7dnevno.hr, 3 September 2017, online at www.7dnevno.hr/izdvajanja/izdvojeno/da-se-ne-lazemo-hos-je-hrvatska-ustaska-vojska-nastala-na-tekovinama-hrabrih-domoljuba-iz-1941/ (accessed

October 4, 2017). While the phrase "Za dom" had appeared throughout Croatian history, most famously in the opera "Nikola Šubić Zrinski" (1876), the formulation "Za dom spremni" is beyond a doubt an Ustaša salute and thus problematic when appearing in public space.
72 For an overview of other sites where Homeland War memorials now stand on top of destroyed Partisan monuments and ossuaries, see *Novosti*, 29 September 2017, pp. 10–11, online at www.portalnovosti.com/otimaci-kostiju (accessed October 4, 2017).
73 *Slobodna Dalmacija*, 5 September 2011, pp. 10–11.
74 New York Times (22 January 2011), online version at www.nytimes.com/2011/01/23/us/23smithsonian.html?_r=1&scp=1&sq=thorny%20path%20to%20a%20national%20black%20museum&st=cse (accessed January 24, 2011). The museum opened in September 2016 in Washington, D.C.
75 Based on several site visits to the Memorial Center for the Homeland War in 2016 and 2017, conversations with curators leading the tours, discussions with human rights activists in Vukovar, and reviews of the study visits.

Bibliography

Assmann, Jan. *Kulturno pamćenje*. Zenica: Vrijeme, 2005.
Benčić Rimay, Tea (ed.). *Jasenovac Memorial Site*. Jasenovac: Spomen-područje Jasenovac, 2006.
Benyovsky, Lucija. "Španjolski građanski rat i naši interbrigadisti," *Informatica museologica*, no. 1–4, 1986.
Brentin, Dario. "Ready for the homeland? Ritual, remembrance, and political extremism in Croatian football," *Nationalities Papers*, vol. 44, no. 6, 2016, pp. 860–876.
Carrier, Peter. "Places, Politics and Archiving of Contemporary Memory in Pierre Nora's Les Lieux de mémoire," in: Susannah Radstone (ed.) *Memory and Methodology*, Oxford: Berg, 2000, pp. 37–57.
Cuno, James. "Money, Power, and the History of Art," in Sheila Watson (ed.) *Museums and Their Communities*. London: Routledge, 2007, pp. 510–518.
Davis, Peter. "Place Exploration: Museums, Identity, Community," in: Sheila Watson (ed.) *Museums and Their Communities*. London: Routledge, 2007, pp. 53–75.
Deverić, Mišo, and Ivan Fumić. *Hrvatska u logorima, 1941.–1945.* Zagreb: Savez antifašističkih boraca i antifašista Republike Hrvatske, 2008.
Dubin, Steven C. "The Postmodern Exhibition: Cut on the Bias, or is Enola Gay a Verb?," in: Sheila Watson (ed.) *Museums and Their Communities*. London: Routledge, 2007, pp. 213–227.
Đurašković, Stevo. "National identity-building and the 'Ustaša-nostalgia' in Croatia: The past that will not pass." *Nationalities Papers*, 44, no. 5, 2016, pp. 772–788.
Gillis, John R. "Introduction," in: John R. Gillis (ed.) *Commemorations: The Politics of National Identity*. Princeton: Princeton University Press, 1994.
Goldstein, Ivo. "O broju žrtava jasenovačkog logorskog kompleksa," in: Slavko Goldstein, *Jasenovac: tragika, mitomanija, istina*. Zagreb: Fraktura, 2016.
Goldstein, Slavko. *Jasenovac: tragika, mitomanija, istina*. Zagreb: Fraktura, 2016.

Halbwachs, Maurice. *On Collective Memory*. Chicago: University of Chicago Press, 1992.
Hamber, Brandon, Liz Ševčenko, and Ereshnee Naidu. "Utopian Dreams or Practical Possibilities? The Challenges of Evaluating the Impact of Memorialization in Societies in Transition," *International Journal of Transitional Justice*, vol. 4, 2010.
Hrvatska 1941. godine. Zagreb: Muzej Revolucije naroda Hrvatske, 1961.
Hrženjak, Juraj (ed.). *Rušenje antifašističkih spomenika u Hrvatskoj, 1990.–2000*. Zagreb: Savez antifašističkih boraca Hrvatske, 2002.
Jakovina, Tvrtko. "The Independent State of Croatia in Hitler's Axis System," in: Tea Benčić Rimay (ed.) *Jasenovac Memorial Site*. Jasenovac: Spomen–područje Jasenovac, 2006.
Jambrešić-Kirin, Renata. "Politička sjećanja na Drugi svjetski rat u doba medijske reprodukcije socijalističke culture," in: Lada Čale Feldman and Ines Prica (eds.) *Devijacije i promašaji: Etnografija domaćeg socijalizma*. Zagreb: Institut za etnologiju i folkloristiku, 2006.
Jelić–Butić, Fikreta. *Ustaše i Nezavisna Država Hrvatska*. Zagreb: SN Liber, 1978.
Jones, Sara. "Cross–border Collaboration and the Construction of Memory Narratives in Europe," in: Tea Sindbaek Andersen and Barbara Tornquist-Plewa (eds.) *The Twentieth Century in European Memory: Transcultural Mediation and Reception*. Leiden: Brill, 2016.
Karačić, Darko, Tamara Banjeglav, and Nataša Govedarica. *Re:vizija prošlosti: Politike sjećanja u Bosni i Hercegovini, Hrvatskoj i Srbiji od 1990. godine*. Sarajevo: Freidrich Ebert Stiftung, 2012.
Lončar, Duško. *Deset godina spomen–područja Jasenovac*. Jasenovac: Spomen–područje Jasenovac, 1977.
Luthar, Oto. *Of Red Dragons and Evil Spirits: Post-Communist Historiography Between Democratization and New Politics of History*. Budapest: CEU Press, 2017.
Mataušić, Nataša. *Jasenovac 1941–1945*. Zagreb: Kameni cvijet, 2003.
———. "The Jasenovac Concentration Camp," in: Tea Benčić Rimay (ed.) *Jasenovac Memorial Site*. Jasenovac: Spomen–područje Jasenovac, 2006.
———. *Jasenovac fotomonografija*. Zagreb: Spomen-područje Jasenovac, 2008.
Mihovilović, Đorđe. *Jasenovac 1945–1947: fotomonografija*. Jasenovac: Javna ustanova spomen područje Jasenovac, 2016.
Milošević, Saša (ed.). *Srbi u Hrvatskoj 2007*. Zagreb: Vijeće srpske nacionalne manjine grada Zagreba, 2007.
Misztal, Barbara. "Memory Experience: The forms and functions of memory," in Sheila Watson (ed.) *Museums and Their Communities*. London: Routledge, 2007, pp. 379–396.
Palhegyi, Joel. "National museums, national myths: constructing socialist Yugoslavism for Croatia and Croats," *Nationalities Papers*, vol. 45, no. 6, 2017, pp. 1048–1065.
Pavlaković, Vjeran. "Flirting with Fascism: The Ustaša Legacy and Croatian Politics in the 1990s," in: Lorenzo Bertucelli and Mila Orlić (eds.) *Una storia balcanica: Fascismo, comunismo e nazionalismo nella Jugoslavia del Novecento*. Verona: Ombre corte, 2008, pp. 115–143.
Petrungaro, Stefano. *Pisati povijest iznova: Hrvatski udžbenici povijesti 1918.–2004*. Zagreb: Srednja Europa, 2009.
Radonić, Ljiljana. "Univerzalizacija holokausta na primjeru hrvatske politike prošlosti i spomen-područja Jasenovac," *Suvremene teme*, vol. 3, no. 1, 2010, pp. 53–62.

Ramet, Sabrina P. (ed.). *Nezavisna Država Hrvatska*. Zagreb: Alinea, 2009.
Rat u Španjolskoj. Zagreb: Muzej Revolucije naroda Hrvatske, 1986.
Rihtman–Auguštin, Dunja. *Ulice moga grada*. Beograd: XX vek, 2000.
Rivera, Lauren A. "Managing 'Spoiled' National Identity: War, Tourism, and Memory in Croatia," *American Sociological Review*, vol. 73, no. 4, 2008, pp. 613–634
Rivera-Orraca, Lorena. "Are Museums Sites of Memory?" *New School of Psychology Bulletin*, vol. 6, no. 2, 2009, pp. 32–37.
Razum, Stjepan, and Igor Vukić (eds.) *Jasenovački logori: istraživanja*. Zagreb: Društvo za istraživanje trostrukog logora Jasenovac, 2015.
Schmidt, Maria. *House of Terror Museum*. Budapest: Public Endowment for Research in Central and East-European History and Society, 2008.
Šimpraga, Saša. *Zagreb, javni prostor*. Zagreb: Porfirogenet, 2011.
Škiljan, Filip. "Identitet Srba u Hrvatskoj," *Politička misao*, vol. 51, no. 2, 2014, pp. 111–134.
SNV Bulletin #10: *Historijski revizionizam, govor mržnje i nasilje prema Srbima u 2016*. Zagreb: SNV, 2017.
Tomasevich, Jozo. *War and Revolution in Yugoslavia, 1941–1945: Occupation and Collaboration*. Stanford: Stanford University Press, 2001.
Tuđman, Franjo. *Bespuća povijesne zbiljnosti: Rasprava o povijesti i filozofiji zlosilja*. Zagreb: Nakladni zavod Matice Hrvatske, 1990.
———. "The Sources, Changes, and Essence of the National Question in the Socialist Federal Republic of Yugoslavia," in: Peter Sugar (ed.) *Eastern European Nationalism in the Twentieth Century*. Washington, DC: American University Press, 1995.
Weil, Stephen. "The Museum and the Public," in Sheila Watson (ed.) *Museums and Their Communities*. London: Routledge, 2007, pp. 32–46.
Žerjavić, Vladimir. *Opsesije i megalomanije oko Jasenovca i Bleiburga*. Zagreb: Globus, 1992.

9 Jasenovac on Film

Manipulations of Identities and the Performance of Memory

Ana Kršinić–Lozica

Introduction

Many films, most of them documentaries, have been made about the Jasenovac camp system. In the period from 1946 to 2016, more than ten films were made. They are all dedicated directly to the Jasenovac camp or to the suffering related to Jasenovac. The number of films that partly refer to it is even higher.[1] As a topic belonging to a difficult legacy, the Jasenovac camp is marked by an ambivalent and problematic memory that manifested itself in a combination of various manipulations and utilitarian appropriations of collective identities in public space. It is not surprising that documentaries greatly predominate over feature films on the subject. The cause of this predominance can be sought in the 'seriousness' often attributed to documentary form[2] (and the same is expected of its reception – the documentary is to be taken as serious or authentic). Another reason can be the need to fix the traumatic memory of the camp through its reappropriation within identity categories and narratives that sometimes speak more about the moment of filming than about the camp itself. However, regardless of the different rewritings of the Jasenovac theme according to the ideological or national key, not all films are necessarily manipulative in their basic idea, nor do they treat historical facts the same way. Films are very different from each other. Among them, some refer to accurate data and incorporate equally authentic visual material, some completely manipulate or present data that are not historically grounded, while others combine both approaches.

The film is often (erroneously) understood as the medium closest to a true portrayal of reality. When accessible to a wider audience (via television broadcast or Internet, as is the case with the examples to be analyzed here), it can significantly impact the formation of public opinion on a particular topic. Although film material can provide 'evidence' of historical events, to achieve this, it is necessary to carefully analyze the film and the origin of the material being shown, as well as the narrative structure and film techniques used in the production of meaning. A critical approach that will differentiate various photographs and footage incorporated in the film is needed just as much as the differentiation between historically relevant statements and ideological

DOI: 10.4324/9781003326632-12

manipulations. I will leave this factual aspect of each film, which is in principle verifiable, to historians, and this chapter will deal with their discursive analysis and reading of the respective ideologies. Whether the depicted events correspond to the truth, that is, to the historically established facts, I will deal with as much as is necessary to understand the representational strategies used in the film. While we cannot ignore the references by which a documentary refers to the real world (events, persons, or phenomena outside the film), the way it is shot and narrative techniques are equally important for interpreting the meaning of a (documentary) film as a whole. In this sense, this chapter will focus on one aspect of the narrative and visual techniques used in the film: their role in the performance of memory and related identity politics. Building on theoretical assumptions that emphasize the importance of performance in the study of cultural memory, the text will focus on film not only as a representation of memory, but also as a work of memory, which plays an active role in forming collective identities in public space.

Writing about performance studies, Richard Schechner argues that anything can be viewed as performance, as long as practices, events, behaviors, relations, and interactions are considered, not just objects or things themselves.[3] Furthermore, Liedeke Plate and Anneke Smelik write about the performative aspect of cultural practices such as art, literature, and the media advocating focusing on the procedural and dynamic characteristics of memory. They elaborate that memory does not exist in a vacuum, and it requires a medium that will shape and transmit it.[4] Thus media-transmitted memory results in concrete objects, products, performances, and networks that people use and connect to negotiate the relationships between themselves and society, between personal and cultural memory. By linking memory to action, Plate and Smelik point to an epistemological turn in cultural memory studies shifting from understanding memory as a trace of what once was, toward memory as a performance of the past in the present moment.[5] Also, the text will build on the term "acts of memory" by Mieke Bal who theoretically explains their role in the performance of subjectivity. In her analysis of contemporary art, Bal establishes important theoretical assumptions about the interaction between performance, performativity, and memory. She emphasizes the role of the spectator as the key to the realization of the performance of memory, and she inextricably links time with it as a category which memory necessarily plays around with.[6]

The films made so far about Jasenovac share one common characteristic, which refers to the processes of forming different identity positions in relation to the narratives about the Jasenovac camp. The primary intention is to show how, although they are documentaries, their role is not only to document and show, more or less objectively, the existing corpus of knowledge about the Jasenovac camp, but also to (dis)solve certain subject positions. Although these positions are a construct of the film medium, they are directed towards the audience as a stimulus for various identification processes. It is the moment when film ceases to be merely a representational medium and becomes a performative medium that can be viewed as an act that has a role to play in creating a particular social space in Lefebvre's sense.[7] The transmission of memory through the film medium gives way here to the performance of memory, which plays an active role in forming discourses that become an integral part of the public sphere.

The text is limited to the analysis of four documentaries made about Jasenovac in different periods: the film *Jasenovac* by Gustav Gavrin and Kosta Hlavaty, the film of the same name by Bogdan Žižić, *Blood and Ashes of Jasenovac* by Lordan Zafranović, and the recent film by Jakov Sedlar, *Jasenovac – the Truth*. Most of the analysis will be devoted to the last film due to the controversy caused by its screening. Still, it will be interpreted in relation to earlier films to compare the film procedures used and to emphasize the heterogeneity of previous approaches to the topic of Jasenovac. It will try to show how Gavrin's and Hlavaty's film establishes the cohesion of a single people and calls for justice; how collective identities are dismantled to their human existential basis in Žižić's film; and how Zafranović's film reaffirms the discourse of building a new socialist society. Although produced in different periods and socio-political arrangements, the ways in which the narrative about the camp is constructed in the films are always linked to particular identity politics and memory mechanisms. These identity politics are manifested in how the detainees are talked about, showing those responsible for the formation of the camp and the crimes committed in it, defining the events in the camp, and positioning the subject of the narrative or the focalizer through whose perspective the camp is presented. The relationship between the executioner and the victim, as well as the position taken by the subject who mediates the story of the camp, are set differently in each film and form quite different constellations of subject positions between members of different ethnic, national, religious, class, and political groups. By analyzing such subject positions as a key place that makes the basic mechanism of meaning production visible, the goal is to read the ideological layer of films that determines how the story of the camp is framed meaningfully.

Gustav Gavrin, Kosta Hlavaty: *Jasenovac*

The documentary *Jasenovac* by Gustav Gavrin and Kosta Hlavaty,[8] made in 1945 after the liberation of the village and camp Jasenovac, propagates the identity construction of the united people not only as victims of the Jasenovac camp, but also as an active agent seeking justice. The film begins with the gradation of Ustaša crimes through a series of various Ustaša camps and places of mass killings (Lepoglava, Glina church, Rab, Lobor-grad, Đakovo, Pag, Jadovno, Gospić, Stara Gradiška), and the last in that series was Jasenovac, as the place of the most terrible crime. Throughout the film, Jasenovac serves as a metonymy of fascist terror as a whole, which is presented as the opposition, that is, "the enemy of every nation and every single honest man." A simple binary opposition is formed between the people on the one hand

and fascism on the other, in which, as the narrator's voice specifies, "German-fascist bandits and their servants, Ustaša-Chetnik butchers" are equated. The goal of the identity politics present in the film is to construct "people" as a unique and comprehensive category that includes different national, ethnic, religious, and class affiliations. The narrator emphasizes that in the Ustaša camp Jasenovac, Serbian peasants, Croatian workers and intellectuals, all social strata – artists, writers, students, workers, peasants, Jews, Roma, and others – found a common death. The voice that narrates very suggestively and vividly identifies, on the one hand, with the people who perished in the camp, appropriating the voice of the victims, and, on the other hand, with the people whom it is addressing. This suggests equality between the victims and the narrator speaking on their behalf ("[T]hey all cry out for revenge in the name of their own and their fallen comrades") and the viewers whom he addresses. Victims are seen in the context of the need to form cohesion between different nationalities, religions, and classes to function as a single social and political entity. At the same time, those responsible for crimes are declared enemies who tried to divide the people ("inspirers of fratricidal war"). The Ustaša authorities are thus opposed to the people and equated with the occupier wanting to exterminate the people. Similarly, the crimes in the Jasenovac camp are completely equated with "the crimes of fascism that sent the whole of Europe into mourning." Jasenovac victims (as well as other victims) became the metonymy of the entire nation, and the Ustašas who managed the camp became the metonymy of fascism.

This process of universalizing victims to equate them and use them to build a unique identity of the people will remain a characteristic of socialist remembrance practices related to Jasenovac. But what is specific here is that the film does not specify that it is about the Yugoslav people; it does not mention Yugoslavia, socialism, or communism, but the discourse is highly general. The victims, the narrator, and the viewers are members of the same, unnamed, "our people." The ideological features such as a star or a sickle and a hammer can only be seen in passing, near the end of the film, on banners held by a group of people honoring the dead. In addition to constructing the "people" as the subject of the narrative (but also the implicit viewer), the film has another important function: presenting evidence of crimes to punish the perpetrators. While the narrator specifies the horrors in the camp, collage footage and photographs of the destroyed camp and the town of Jasenovac are shown together with photos of corpses and mutilated human remains. Some of these are authentic and filmed at the Jasenovac site on May 18, 1945, and others at some entirely different locations, as shown by historians Nataša Mataušić and Filip Škiljan.[9] Footage of various origins, including Ustaša propaganda footage of Jasenovac and views of the camp immediately after liberation, was mixed with records from other locations, some of which were made even in other states and unrelated contexts). They are all placed on the same level of meaning and shown without any mutual differentiation. Although authentic aerial photographs of the camp showing corpses floating on the river and the ruins of the camp and the nearby village, as well as brief testimonies of camp survivors, testify sufficiently to the brutal nature of the camp, a series of photographs and footage from other locations contributed to the impression of horror. These different recordings are shown as part of the same whole and connected by a narration that refers to Jasenovac, so that viewers can only interpret them as depictions of the victims of Jasenovac.

The goal of such a series of explicit photographs of horror is to emphasize the brutality of the enemy, to show evidence of crimes, and to call for justice. The narrator exclaims how the ruins and corpses accuse and call for revenge. At the end of the film, excerpts from the war crime tribunal show perpetrators' faces in close-up, while the narrator calls for justice (although the names of the accused are not given). The film ends with a scene showing a procession marching through the streets with banners, seeking revenge for the victims of Jasenovac.

Lordan Zafranović: *Blood and Ashes of Jasenovac*

While the early postwar film about Jasenovac established a simple identity opposition between the people and the enemies of the people, in Lordan Zafranović's 1983 documentary *Blood and Ashes of Jasenovac*, the identity constellations are much more complex. The voice of the narrator, who speaks about the political context of the NDH and the camp, alternates with fragments of the surviving camp inmates' testimonies. At the beginning of the film, the narrator states that Roma, Serbs, Jews, Partisans, and communists were imprisoned in the camp. Then, just like the surviving witnesses, he refers to the detainees in various ways, as people brought from certain areas, from Kozara, from Potkozara and Sarajevo, or the Roma, communists, intellectuals. One witness thus explicitly declared himself a Croat and a Catholic, another testified about the organized work of Party members in the camp, and a third emphasized that the detainees were "of all nationalities, from all cities and all places in Yugoslavia." Those responsible for the crimes in Jasenovac are talked about with less passion and more precisely than in Gavrin and Hlavaty's film. Those responsible are mostly named, from Pavelić and Hitler, through Mile Budak, as the creator of the law on the basis of which they were deported to Jasenovac, and Vjekoslav Maks Luburić as the commander in chief of the camp, to individual Ustaša officials who were particularly cruel to prisoners.

The identity construction in the film is finalized through an audio recording of Tito's speech from the commemoration on the "Day of the Uprising of the People of Croatia in Glina in 1952." This speech, which gives a concise overview of World War II in the context of the NDH and Partisan struggle, brings a value judgment within which it positions the identity interpretation of the conflicting parties in the war, and functions as a retroactive explanation of everything presented in the film. The speech explains that it was not only about the national extermination of other peoples, but also about the extermination of communists, and that crimes should not be seen in a national context, but as crimes of a person against a person. He also emphasizes the role of communists in opposing national hatred and underlines that the culprits for the crimes in Jasenovac should not be sought in an entire nation, but in those who were in power at the time, and which he declares traitors to that nation. Speech incorporates time jumps that connect the past (war), the present (the moment of holding the address), and the future by emphasizing the brotherhood and unity of all peoples as the main achievement of the revolution that needs to be preserved to avoid a recurrence of such catastrophes. The crimes in Jasenovac are interpreted as a sacrifice necessary to build a socialist society ("We created a new society, a socialist society on streams of blood"), and projects a vision of a better and happier future to be built by all together. Fragmented and taken out of the original context in this way, Tito's speech was used in the film to fix subject positions related to the narrative of the Jasenovac camp. The speech was incorporated into the movie only as an audio recording. Meanwhile, the audience sees a collage of video recordings and photographs from World War II, and of the *Jasenovac Memorial Site*. The figure of Tito here acquires the status of an invisible narrator and a cognitive, unrepresentable point of view. Since the film ends with Tito's words giving a concise interpretation of the context of the Jasenovac camp and the contemporary reception of these events, one gets the impression that Tito is an implicit author who encompasses all particular positions of previous narrators and witnesses, and thus functions as the central subject position from which the story of the camp is presented. This is confirmed by the visual structure of the film which repeats the temporal constellation of relations between the past, present, and future from Tito's speech.

The film begins with footage belonging to the film's present. It shows the ceremony at the foot of Bogdanović's monument, *Stone Flower*, with the music of an orchestra playing there, a large audience as well as a series of symbolic scenes of children playing cheerfully while exiting the Memorial Museum. Parallel to this is a scene of white and dark horses playing. The idyllic landscape of the Memorial Area accompanied by the chirping of birds suddenly merges into retrospective shots of a landscape of horror with the sounds of gunfire. The film goes back to the past, during and immediately after World War II, edited as a bricolage of various photographs and footage from that time, with short interruptions of shots of witnesses who recount their memories in the present. With the final words of Tito's speech, the camera returns to the film's present in a sequence that again shows the commemoration at the Jasenovac Memorial Area with a song by the choir. The scene, which is dominated by a bright red flag fluttering as a procession of people carries it, clearly symbolizes how the film belongs to socialist society and how the mediation of the Jasenovac camp is placed in the context of building a 'new human.' The masses of people around the monument, and the children playing, embody the ideal spectator as a projection of the film structure, to whom the performative of building a new socialist society without interethnic hatred is intended. The film ends with a shot from a frog's perspective showing the *Stone Flower* monument while in the background there is the sky with the released doves flying, and an aerial view of the *Stone Flower*. In addition to the ambiguous symbolism of peace, freedom, and the ascension of the souls of the dead to heaven, the shot also suggests a focus on the future, repeating the teleological orientation of Tito's speech on the Jasenovac victims as a pledge of a bright future and creating socialist individuals.

Bogdan Žižić: Jasenovac

The poetic documentary *Jasenovac*, directed by Bogdan Žižić, was made in 1966, between the postwar *Jasenovac* and *Blood and Ashes of Jasenovac*, is one of the most valuable films on the subject and certainly the most aesthetically elaborated. This film is also one of the few films made so far about Jasenovac that does not approach this topic from the aspect of affirming, constructing, or performing collective identities. The director is filming the arrival in Jasenovac by train (and the departure by train), and the ceremonial opening of the sculptural and landscape design by the architect Bogdan Bogdanović. The complete absence of a narrator is striking, and the only narrative fragments belong to the witnesses who give their statements at the foot of the *Flower* monument. Short fragments are dissolving one into the other, and in the background of the speech one can hear the murmur of the people gathered at the ceremony. Witnesses do not declare their ethnic, religious, or ideological affiliation. The first witness emphasizes that the detainees were of all nationalities and came from all parts of Yugoslavia. Other witnesses refer to the detainees very generally, primarily as people or prisoners, women, and children. On the one hand, the detainees are presented in their universal, human dimension, and on the other, exclusively individually, through fragments of their statements. The polyphony that emerges from such a mosaic narration creates an impression of liveliness, diversity of perspectives, and the predominance of personal memories over one dominant historical (political, ideological) narrative, which is entirely absent here. The departure from the objective point of view is also suggested by the introductory sequence of the train coming to Jasenovac. We see the landscape from the train through cracks and crevices in the train windows, which narrows the field of vision, indicating a subjective shot of what prisoners see while being transported by train to the Jasenovac camp.

Žižić's film is characterized by a symbolic mode of representation combined with a classic documentary form. The film begins with the sound of a human heartbeat in the dark and ends with a white horse in a trot. The symbolism of light and darkness as a theme is carried through the entire film by visual contrasts within the same frame, or a rhythmically arranged sequence of scenes. Sound also plays an important role in shaping the meaning of the film. Instead of a voice that guides the film from beginning to end and explains the events, there are various sounds, such as the heartbeat, the crying and screaming of the grieving mother, the chirping of birds, the murmur of people, the neighing and stamping of horses, the sound of trains, an orchestra playing, the chirping of crickets or the ringing of bells, rhythmically interrupted by moments of silence. These sounds suggest the creation of meaning that takes place outside of discourse, and outside of identity processes that require verbalization and narrative cohesion. There is the avoidance of closing victims within any fixed identities, except the basic human one, which is outside all discursive and representational frameworks. By repeating the sounds of heartbeats and screams in different places in the film, humanity is presented in its universal and ultimate existential sense of bare life, outside of all its national, religious, or worldview identities. With the role of sounds (the film ends with a loud neighing of horses) and the repetition of darkened shots, the reach of the representation and narration itself is problematized and their (im)possibility can be seen as an underlying idea of the film.

An in-depth analysis of these three previous films would require more space than is devoted to them here, and this is especially true of Bogdan Žižić's film, which, due to its associative approach and complex form, certainly deserves a more detailed treatment. Here, a brief attempt has been made to sketch the films' relevance, manifested on two interrelated levels. The first level concerns the credibility, the veracity of these films, and their correspondence with the extra-film reality. In this sense, documentaries carry the burden of ethical responsibility and are subject to factual checks on the basis of which they can be valorized and, if necessary, discredited. Films often incorporate heterogeneous photographic and film material, some of it belonging to the authentic corpus of material related to the Jasenovac crimes, and the other to sites not related to Jasenovac. Thus, Gavrin and Hlavaty's and Zafranović's films use ideological discourse manifested in different ways; they show some photographs taken at other sites, but they also bring authentic footage and valuable testimonies of the Jasenovac camp survivors. The aim of showing this diverse footage is to portray the brutality of starvation, torture, and murder that took place in the Jasenovac camp, because more relevance is given to leaving the impression of horror on the viewer than to the authenticity of what is shown. This is precisely one of the arguments used in attempts to question everything that has been researched so far about Jasenovac as evidence of organized manipulations of public opinion. However, in films it is possible to distinguish authentic from non-authentic parts and with adequate contextualization they can be used, to some extent, as relevant sources of information about what was happening in the Jasenovac camp. However, the non-transparent use of various materials is not characteristic of all documentaries about Jasenovac from the socialist period. Bogdan Žižić's film is an example of the correct use of documentary material because it is based on authentic footage and testimony taken for that film, as well as transparent usage of borrowed video materials. Žižić's film is also devoid of any narrative framework that would introduce ideological interpretation. The movie uses symbolic and aesthetic procedures, thus approaching a poetic documentary film format. Its documentary value is much more pronounced than in other films adhering to simpler documentary forms.

The second level in the focus of this text concerns memory performance. Apart from (in)accurately referring to events from the past, documentaries about Jasenovac have an active role in the present (and the present is not only the moment of film production but also the moment of its reception). The films create a narrative about the past that has an impact on viewers, on the formation of collective memory and identity politics, and ultimately participate in the production of social space. Thus, the 1945 film *Jasenovac* uses the memory of the Jasenovac victims as a cohesive factor to construct the collective identity of the "people." A sign of equality is placed between the victims of Jasenovac and the narrator, who appropriates both their voice and the voice of the ideal recipients of the film. All peoples and nationalities of Yugoslavia, as well as all classes, are placed in the position of the movie subject. By analogy, this appeals to the subjects of postwar society, which are still (at least on film) not addressed as socialist, to unite against a common enemy. The film *Jasenovac* from 1966 abandons the collective approach to the victim. Victimhood is therefore represented as an individual experience viewed from an existentialist perspective. The lack of a narrator emphasized the absence of a single subject position from which to narrate the camp story. The intertwining of subjective, objective, and authorial shots, and the sound fusion of witness voices achieved multi-perspectivity. Various visual and sound signals question the idea of the (human) subject and the possibilities of representing the traumatic experience. In *Blood and Ashes of Jasenovac* from 1983, the camp is seen through the prism of the socialist revolution, and the camp inmates are thought of as victims that were necessary for building a 'new human,' who is also the ideal recipient of the film. The main subject position is occupied by the person, that is, the voice of Tito. Tito's voice functions as a metonymy of the socialist order within which a value framework for the interpretation of the Jasenovac trauma and its legacy is established.

Jakov Sedlar: *Jasenovac – the Truth*

In the context of the (documentary) film as a performance act, it is necessary to consider the recent film by Jakov Sedlar, *Jasenovac – the Truth*, from 2016, which caused numerous controversies. As a standard documentary format with a dominant voice of commentary and collaged shots and photographs taken from earlier films about Jasenovac, it is a film that does not bring anything new on a formal level. However, the film's visibility in the public space requires more attention than it might deserve based on its aesthetic or historiographical achievements. Unlike all previous films made on the Jasenovac camp that refer to events related to the camp or the broader context of its activities, Sedlar's film largely refers to the already existing discourse on Jasenovac. It refers to historiography, journalism, the media, but also much wider than that, to the entire existing corpus of knowledge about the Jasenovac camp, trying to discredit it as untrue. Expanding its field of reference, the film attempts to deal with all previous narratives about the Jasenovac camp and the identity politics they represent. It is claimed in the introductory part, in a dramatic and sensationalist way, that "the real truth about Jasenovac is hidden" and that "the purpose of this film is to get to the closest truth by presenting some less known or completely unknown details." The voice of the narrator presents the whole heterogeneous and vast[10] corpus of everything written, researched, and said so far about Jasenovac, as a myth.

The implicit author of the film, who encompasses the perspectives of the narrator and witnesses, takes on the role of a scientist who, based on the discovered documents, brings new insights about the camp. But if we look a little better at the structure of the film and the nature of the documents and arguments presented in it, it becomes evident that the alleged scientific position from which the revalued truth about the camp is presented, is not based on scientific methodology, but has a purely rhetorical function. The voice of the narrator (alternating male and female voices leading the narrative from the beginning to the end of the film, interrupted only by witness statements) explains in several places in the film that none of what is known about the Jasenovac camp so far is scientifically based. The narrator thus discredits all previous knowledge about the camp. However, the alleged evidence in the film does not support that statement. Such a straightforward rejection of everything researched so far, all the numerous testimonies of camp survivors collected over the decades from various sides – in situ excavations, demographic, anthropological, and historical research – and placing them on a par with political propaganda, ideological interpretations, speculation about the number of victims, and various media articles and other types of manipulation, of which there are also many, testifies to the highly unscientific approach used in the film. A scientifically based re-examination of everything researched so far about Jasenovac would imply an extremely differentiated approach in which various sources and methods would be valorized. Instead, we hear the narrator declaring everything a myth and conspiracy, which brings the film's argumentative position closer to conspiracy theories.

The basic structural characteristics that the film *Jasenovac – the Truth* shares with the formal aspects of conspiracy theories, as presented by Blanuša,[11] are the following: encouraging suspicion that the world is not as it seems, an attempt to leave an impression of credibility by linking information into a coherent narrative of a conspiracy, by simplifying complex social and historical phenomena, by describing political antagonisms or, even more generally, by describing society through pronounced binary oppositions. Conspiracist narratives also allegedly expose the culprits to whom they attribute immense powers, and their insidious mode of action. Finally, there is a demand to neutralize and/or remove them from society. Furthermore, Groh emphasizes the importance of a continuous time perspective according to which conspirators have performed evil in the past, are successfully active in the present, and will triumph in the future if they are not prevented from doing so.[12] There is also a complete reduction of individuals to their group belonging (in the film these groups are characterized by ethnic or ideological affiliation) with whom they share a common ground, which Moscovici attributes to the conspiracy mentality.[13] The aim of these methods in the film is to destabilize the existing corpus of knowledge about Jasenovac through an arbitrarily constructed narrative world that bases its persuasiveness on the imitation of scientific argumentation.

The film *Jasenovac – the Truth* contains two thematic units: The first deals with the Ustaša camp, Jasenovac, and the second tries to convince the viewer of the existence of the Partisan camp Jasenovac after the end of World War II. These two units differ not only thematically but also formally. The first is based on the evidence presented in large numbers, which, as I will explain later, do not have the status of authentic evidence but of rhetorical figures. The second unit is based on the absence of evidence as the final proof of the existence of a conspiracy. The status of evidence, therefore, plays a vital role on the basis of which the entire visual structure of the film, as well as the film narrative itself, is built. By focusing on alleged 'evidence,' the film imitates scientific discourse. Several procedures are used in the film to manipulate the evidence to fit it into the argumentative sequence put forth by the narrator's voice. The first procedure, which is used extensively – especially in the first half of the film dealing with the Ustaša camp Jasenovac – is to visually bombard the viewer with a rapidly alternating large amount of alleged evidence. Letters, archival documents, lists, books, newspaper headlines, and so forth are shown one after the other, but lined up too fast for viewers to truly study the document as a whole and are taken out of the context necessary for their adequate understanding. The goal of such ordering of documents in front of the camera is to fascinate, impress the viewer, and convince them by the very act of showing the document, that is, by its performative function, regardless of what the document really means and shows. At the same time, the narrator's voice conveys a handful of data, names and events at equal speed, thus creating the illusion of information. The viewer is overwhelmed with data in a short time to the extent that, without enough prior knowledge of the events in question, they may be inclined to believe what is shown. Another procedure for manipulating evidence is to falsify documents that are then presented as authentic and to provide false information.

Numerous forgeries and untruths in Sedlar's film have already been written about. Journalist Nikola Bajto published a list of many fakes and inaccurate data that are brought and presented in the film as facts.[14] Furthermore, historian Lovro Krnić analyzed in detail the front page of *Vjesnik* newspaper from 1945, which in the film serves as alleged evidence of manipulations about the nature of the Jasenovac camp that were carried out during socialism. Based on a careful study of a screenshot from the high-resolution film and its comparison with the original copy of *Vjesnik* archived at the *National University Library* in Zagreb, Krnić was able to prove that it was an evident photomontage.[15] Journalist Boris Dežulović wrote about the alleged letter of Ante Pavelić to Milo Budak, the NHD's Minister of Worship and Teaching, which is presented in the film as another important piece of evidence. Analyzing the typography, Dežulović demonstrated that it, too, was a forgery.[16] The next manipulation technique often used in film is the selective presentation of information.[17] Some accurate information is given that supports the theses presented in the film. Still, at the same time other information is omitted that would have shed a completely different light on what was shown, and thus would call into question the basic narrative thread.

For example, the uninterrupted activities of the Jewish community in Zagreb during the Independent State of Croatia are mentioned (as an argument in support of the thesis that the Ustaša leadership had respect for Jews), but there is no mention of the demolition of the Zagreb synagogue. Following the same line of argument, it is stated that the Jewish community was allowed to send packages to Jasenovac. Yet, it is omitted that these packages did not always reach the detainees, or that they arrived incomplete because the camp control[18] thoroughly inspected all packages, and then some or all of the content was confiscated. To shift the responsibility exclusively to Germany, it is stated twice that the NDH took over racial laws from Germany, emphasizing that this was the case in the whole of Europe under Hitler. It is not mentioned that the Ustaša government, along with Jews and Roma, persecuted Serbs.[19] The role of the Catholic Church in the baptism of Jews is emphasized as well. Based on that, the narrator claims that all surviving Jews managed to avoid death precisely thanks to baptizing. This is opposed by numerous research that testifies that baptism did not save Jews since they were persecuted primarily based on racial affiliation, not religion.

Furthermore, the footage of the testimony of one of the witnesses shown in the film, Zdravko Macura, was edited so that short clips were shown in which he mentions that his house in Kozara was burned by Chetniks, while the part in which he says that the house was burned several times is omitted because the second time it was burned by Ustašas. A short excerpt was also edited in which the witness talks about his stay in the Jasenovac camp complex. It can be concluded from it that he did not have a bad time there, whereas the part in which he explains the unacceptable conditions in which he was accommodated is omitted. The recording was taken from the website of the *Istrian Historical Society* without authorization, which is why the authors of the recording sued Jakov Sedlar for copyright infringement, and the court ruled in their favor.[20] The fourth method of manipulating alleged evidence can be detected in the relationship between the visual and textual parts of the film, that is, between the recordings that are shown while the narrator is speaking, without explicitly referring to them. Clips from various films and photographs illustrate the narration, although they are not authentic and do not really show what the narrator is referring to. For example, a photograph shows a football team[21] as the narrator talks about football matches held in the camp. The photograph, as Bajto shows,[22] was not taken in the Jasenovac camp. Furthermore, Ustaša propaganda photographs and recordings were manipulated to falsely depict Jasenovac as a labor camp in which satisfactory living and working conditions prevailed. Among other things, photographs taken by professional reporters of the NDH Photo Service are shown, including photographs by war reporter Edmund Stoger, intended for display at a propaganda exhibition in Zagreb in 1942 titled "Positive Work of the Ustaša Defense Camp."[23] These photographs do not show the actual situation in the camp. The staging was carefully prepared, and only newly arrived prisoners who did not yet look hungry or sick were selected. They were dressed in work suits, not corresponding to what the prisoners wore. The photographs of prisoners fit perfectly with the aesthetics of Nazi propaganda photographs based on the repetitiveness and rhythmic composition of prisoners as they work, with a sharp contrast of light and darkness.[24] Nazi propaganda photographs were taken to present concentration camps as exclusively labor camps to deceive the public. The propaganda photographs of the Jasenovac camp were created according to this template. Nowhere in the film *Jasenovac – the Truth* is it mentioned that these were propaganda photographs. On the contrary, it is continuously repeated throughout the film that the Ustaša Jasenovac was a "concentration and labor camp."[25] During the display of the propaganda photos, the narrator describes in detail the production facilities in the camp as well as the work activities of the detainees, without mentioning almost anything about the actual living conditions in Jasenovac. Existing authentic photographs that testify to the mass killings and harassment of detainees are also not shown, so both the image and the sound give the impression of a place that was primarily a labor camp. This impression is further supported by the insertion of the Ustaša propaganda footage about Jasenovac, which is repeated a couple of times in Sedlar's film. Those fragments were shot in the same way and with the same goal as the described photographs.

Sedlar's film is not the only one that uses Ustaša footage: This has been done in many films made so far about Jasenovac, as it is the only film footage from the time when the camp existed. However, in all the other films that use these shots, it is made clear in some way that they are not a depiction of the actual situation in the camp complex. In Gavrin and Hlavaty's film, the textual explanation is shown at the very beginning, and it specifies how these recordings – found in the Ustaša film archives during the liberation of Zagreb – were made to refute rumors of mass slaughter and torture. Zafranović's film does not explain the origin of these recordings, but it contextualizes them with surviving inmates' testimonies about their experience, from which viewers still get a clear picture of the actual conditions in the Jasenovac camp. In Žižić's *Jasenovac*, inserts of a propaganda film and photographs were accompanied by two witnesses testifying that they were in the camp during the filming. The witnesses explain how the cameramen chose people who looked better than the others, and that they were mostly those who had just arrived at the camp. They also said that the cameramen filmed for eight days, and that the camp leadership even organized a jazz concert to leave a good impression in front of the cameras. However, in Sedlar's film there is no such contextualization of Ustaša footage. On the contrary, the clip is used as proof that Jasenovac was primarily a collection and labor camp, perpetuating thus, with a gap of more than 70 years, the original propaganda function of that footage.

The second part of Sedlar's film, dedicated to the alleged Partisan camp in Jasenovac, differs significantly from the first. While the part about the Ustaša Jasenovac is based on documents as a rhetorical figure, the second part dedicated to the Partisan camp is based on the absence of documents.[26] The argument used is one we often encounter in conspiracy theories – that there is no evidence because it has been deliberately destroyed or carefully hidden[27] – and the viewer has no choice but to believe the unsubstantiated claim. The first part of the film achieved the desired effect and convinced the viewers of the credibility of what was stated by the force of the alleged documentation and argumentation; in the second part, however, uninformed viewers rely on the voice of the narrator, whom they should believe. No evidence is given for what is said; only diverse photographs and recordings have yet to illustrate, not demonstrate, what is being said. Among them, there are incorporated fragments of original shots of the destroyed Jasenovac taken on May 18, 1945, which Gavrin and Hlavaty showed in their film to testify to the destruction committed by the Ustašas during the retreat.[28] Sedlar shows the same materials as an illustration of the alleged Partisan crimes that purportedly occurred in Jasenovac somewhat later, so that the demolition of the camp complex and of the village is attributed to the Partisans. The only 'evidence' offered in this part of the film is the testimony of two alleged witnesses, who were presented as former guards at the Yugoslav Jasenovac camp between 1950 and 1951. With blurred faces and introduced only by initials, they tell their story, which will probably not be convincing to even an utterly uninformed viewer, due to the apparent fact that their appearance, voice, and manner of speaking reveal much younger people than those they are supposed to be.[29] The large amount of inaccurate yet easily verifiable information presented in the movie, shows that its intention is not to explore the archive material and use scientific methods to gain new knowledge, as the narrator claims, but to influence public discourse in a much simpler and more effective way. No real evidence is searched for, since the film, by the sole virtue of its presence in public space and its pronounced performativity, participates in the creation of specific memory politics. At the end of the film, individual participants in the Croatian political, literary, and cultural scene are called out and accused of participating in the conspiracy. In the final anachronistic turn, they are declared co-responsible for crimes committed in Jasenovac, in socialist Yugoslavia and in the Homeland War. In this way, it becomes evident that the film is not directed towards establishing the facts about the camp, but towards regulating the discourse about the camp.

Conclusion

As with earlier films from the socialist period, *Jasenovac – the Truth* can be valorized from the aspect of authenticity of the presented material, as well as from the aspect of memory performance. The film uses so many different types of manipulation and denial of facts that no segment of it can be considered credible. Footage and photographs of various origins are used, a significant part of which has already been shown in earlier films about Jasenovac. However, the problem is not their reproduction, but their problematic contextualization. The order of their presentation, film editing, and meaning as interpreted by the narrators' voices, is performed so that the viewers get a completely wrong impression of the nature of the Jasenovac camp. In terms of memory performance, the film approaches a radical rewriting of history from a conspiracy theory perspective. An unnamed subject position is determined in binary opposition to conspirators described as an entity that has operated continuously throughout history. It consists of various ethnically, ideologically and politically identified groups between which a sign of equality is placed (Serbs, Chetniks, Communists, Yugoslavs, and individual public figures).

The narrative constellation establishes connections that try to retroactively elaborate the idea of the Croatian people as a unique and homogeneous historical subject that is the victim of the conspirators' actions. The conducted analysis tries to show that it is necessary to consider credibility, that is, the match between film and extra-film reality when it comes to the role of cinema in the construction of collective memory. Nevertheless, the performative aspect by which memory is linked with the construction of collective identities plays an even more critical role in the film than its potential historical authenticity. The text aims to emphasize that the documentary is not just a representation of events from the past, nor a mere transfer of memory, but above all – a performance.

How the memory of Jasenovac is performed in each film is primarily related to the need to form a social space in the present that adapts the interpretation of the camp and its traumatic heritage to its vision of society. Each of these films participates in heterogeneous negotiations about the meanings that continuously take place in the public sphere in other media and disciplines. The diversity of approaches shows how dynamic the theme of Jasenovac in film is (and it should be borne in mind that only a small number of films dealing with this theme are analyzed here). Through these various approaches, we can also see how representational strategies and ideological patterns vary and participate in continuous (re)appropriations and struggles over meaning, not only of past events, but also of entirely different visions of social space. The performance of memory on film works on two levels. In the way Plate and Smelik elaborate it, performance is manifested by the very act of embodying memory in a particular medium. At this first level of performance, the distribution of film in public space, at a specific historical moment and social context, testifies to the active role that film plays in creating various representational mechanisms and discursive shifts when it comes to difficult heritage and identity politics. The film influences, thus, the rearrangement of the relationship between the visible and the invisible, the expressive and the inexpressible. The aspect of identity performance is crucial here, because it shows how any film mediation of the Jasenovac camp is related to the affirmation of different subject positions that serve to build or deconstruct collective identities that are presented as relevant in the (film) present. In this sense, this chapter analyzes those subject positions that are the film products, as well as the positions of the ideal recipients projected by the films.

But to fully view the film as an act of performance, it is necessary to consider another level of performance that is much more difficult to explore: the context of reception. Mieke Bal emphasizes that performativity is an individual act that always happens here and now. Memory takes place in that unique present. Bal writes about memory as a process of connecting the past, future and present that is realized in a specific moment of performance.[30] This process is clearly visible in all four analyzed films. The past, in this case the Jasenovac camp, was used to determine the present through a clear definition of identity positions, while the idea of the future was also, implicitly or explicitly, indicated – by calling for immediate revenge, to the building of a socialist human, by the galloping of a white horse (as a symbol of freedom), by denouncing the conspirators, and by appeals to stop their conspiracy. Yet, each individual spectator ultimately performs the act of memory and connects the act of seeing with the act of forming their subjectivity which, according to Bal, is always formed *in* time and *through* time.[31] The problem of different identity politics in the context of memory and its performativity is both an ideological and social phenomenon and an intrinsically media phenomenon concerning film communication or, more precisely, the relationship between the film and its viewer.

Notes

1 Documentary films *Jasenovac* by G. Gavrin and K. Hlavaty (1945), *Poruke* by Stjepan Zaninović (1960), *Jasenovac* by B. Žižić (1966), *Evanđelje zla* by G. Kastratović (1973), *Krv i pepeo Jasenovca* by L. Zafranović (1983), *Jasenovac* by Milan Bulajić (1995), *Jasenovac u TV-kalendaru* (2000), *Jasenovac–suština užasa* by M. Stevanović (2008), *Jasenovački memento* by B. Žižić (2015.), *Zaveštanje* by I. Jović (2016.), *Jasenovac–istina* by J. Sedlar (2016.) were all made about the Jasenovac camp. Also, the film *Kula smrti* by V. Tadej (1987) was made about the camp in Stara Gradiška; S. Mrkonjić shot *Djeca iz pakla* (1967) about Kozara children, some of whom ended up in Jasenovac, and F. Štiglic shot a feature film *Deveti krug* (1960) on the theme of Jasenovac.

2 But it should be borne in mind that a documentary is no closer to a non–film reality than a feature film. Filmologist Nikica Gilić emphasizes in his description of the documentary: "However, it is necessary to constantly emphasize a fact that even filmologists sometimes forget: although it refers to reality, the documentary does

not belong to it more than other film genres – it only establishes a different relationship with reality or, more precisely, with extra-film phenomena." Nikica Gilić, "Documentary Film," in: *Filmske vrste i rodovi. 2. izdanje* [electronic book], Zagreb, 2013. Available at: http://elektronickeknjige.com/knjiga/gilic-nikica/film ske- vrste-i-rodovi/ (accessed 27 November, 2017).
3 Richard Schechner, *Performance Studies. An Introduction* (New York, London: Routledge, 2006).
4 Liedeke Plate and Anneke Smelik, "Performing Memory in Art and Popular Culture. An Introduction," in Liedeke Plate and Anneke Smelik (eds.) *Performing Memory in Art and Popular Culture* (New York: Routledge, 2013), pp. 2–3.
5 Ditto, pp. 6, 11.
6 Mieke Bal, "Memory Acts: Performing Subjectivity," *Boijmans Bulletin*, vol. 1, no. 2 (2001), pp. 8–10.
7 According to Lefebvre's theory of space production, the space of representation, as a logical-epistemological space, consists of a physical, mental and social area. Henry Lefebvre, *The Production of Space* (Oxford: Wiley-Blackwell, 1991), pp. 41–43.
8 In the literature, G. Gavrin and K. Hlavaty are always cited as co-authors of the film, although in the film introduction Gavrin and Hlavaty are listed as the production, and Gavrin only is listed as the director.
9 Filip Škiljan states that in the film there is edited footage of various origins: Footage of Ustaša propaganda films, footage of the camp from the air immediately after the liberation, footage of detainees from other concentration camps (in the NDH and in the Third Reich), footage of civilian liquidations in Herzegovina and the shootings of anti–fascists in the Balkans by firing squads; even staged scenes filmed after World War II. See: Filip Škiljan, "A Collection of Film and Video Recordings in the holdings of the Jasenovac Memorial Area with Special Reference to the Memories of Detainees," *Dialogue of Historians*, vol. 10, no. 2 (2015), pp. 312–313. Nataša Mataušić mentions that part of the shown film material and photographs were taken on May 18, 1945, and other parts were incorporated from authentic Ustaša promotional films. See: Nataša Mataušić, *Jasenovac 1941.–1945.: Logor smrti i radni logor* (Jasenovac: Spomen–područje Jasenovac, 2003), pp. 154.
10 Nataša Mataušić states that by the year 2000, 1,188 books, 1,544 memoirs and study articles, and 108 collections of documents were published on the Jasenovac and Stara Gradiška concentration camps; cf. Nataša Mataušić, "Koncentracioni logor Jasenovac," in Benčić Rimay (ed.) *Spomen-područje Jasenovac* (Jasenovac: Spomen područje Jasenovac, 2006), pp. 54.
11 Nebojša Blanuša, *Teorije zavjera i hrvatska politička zbilja 1980.–2007.* (Zagreb: Plejada, 2011), pp. 15, 53, 79.
12 Dieter Groh, "The Temptation of Conspiracy Theory, or: Why Do Bad Things Happen to Good People? Part I: Preliminary Draft of a Theory of Conspiracy Theories," in Carl F. Graumann and Serge Moscovici (eds.) *Changing Conceptions of Conspiracy* (New York: Springer, 1987), pp. 3.
13 Serge Moscovici, "The Conspiracy Mentality," in Carl F. Graumann and Serge Moscovici (eds.) *Changing Conceptions of Conspiracy*, pp. 155.
14 Nikola Bajto, "Sve laži Jakova Sedlara," *Novosti* (2016), available at: www.portal novosti.com/sve-lai-jakova-sedlara (accessed November 27, 2017).
15 Lovre Krnić, "Otkrivamo–Jasenovac–fotošopirana istina: Sedlarov udarni argument o plivanju leševa uzvodno je loša montaža," *Lupiga* (2016), available

at: http://lupiga.com/vijesti/otkrivamo-jasenovac-fotosopirana-istina- sedlarov-udarni-argument- o-plivanju-leseva-uzvodno-je-losa-fotomontaza (accessed November 27, 2017).
16 Boris Dežulović, "Čas lobotomije," *N1* (2016), available at: http://hr.n1info.com/a116840/Kolumne/Boris-Dezulovic/Jakov- Sedlar-Cas-lobotomije.html (accessed November 27, 2017).
17 The elements of truth that appear in conspiracy theories are mentioned by Blanuša who quotes Neumann, claiming that the picture of history offered by "conspiracy theories of history" is never completely false, but must contain grains of truth in order to work convincingly. The same is noted by Arendt when describing totalitarianism, where elements from which fiction is built are chosen from reality. They are isolated and generalized so that they are no longer subject to experiential verification and become inaccessible to reasoning. See: Nebojša Blanuša, *Conspiracy Theories and Croatian Political Realit*, pp. 12–13.
18 Maja Kućan states that the packages rarely reached the prisoners in their original form, because the food, which did not get spoiled in the transport to the camp, would be partially stolen by the Ustašas who carried the packages, or partially or completely confiscated by Ustaša censors, who would inspect the packages, see: Maja Kućan, *"Jedinomoje i ostali!": Pisma iz logora* (Jasenovac: Spomen područje Jasenovac, 2010), pp. 10–12. The fact that the detainees did not receive packages at all, or would receive packages from which the Ustašas would take all the better food, is also testified by the surviving prisoner Egon Berger in his published memoirs: Egon Berger, *44 mjeseca u Jasenovcu* (Jasenovac: Spomen područje Jasenovac, 1978), pp. 21, 73.
19 Nataša Mataušić writes that immediately after the establishment of the Independent State of Croatia, political propaganda against Serbs began and numerous discriminatory provisions were passed banning certain Serbian national and religious characteristics. Other forms of pressure were applied as well (Nataša Mataušić, *Jasenovac 1941.–1945.: Logor smrti i radni logor*, pp. 19). Nevenko Bartulin explains that, unlike Jews and Roma, who were officially persecuted by racial laws adopted in late April 1941 as "non–Aryan" peoples, Serbs were not officially defined as a racial community, but were religiously defined as "Greek Orientals." The regime did not pursue a unified policy towards all Serbs in the NDH, based on the fact that the Serb population was divided into several groups. The regime's policy towards Serbs thus included three different methods: their deportation to Serbia, mass killings, and forced assimilation (conversion to Roman Catholicism or under the auspices of the established Croatian Orthodox Church) (Nevenko Bartulin, "Ideologija nacije i rase: ustaški režim i politika prema Srbima u Nezavisnoj Državi Hrvatskoj 1941.–1945.," *Radovi–Zavod za hrvatsku povijest*, vol. 39 (2007), pp. 225.
20 Information on Sedlar's unauthorized taking over of the testimony of the late witness Macura, and on the trial, is provided by journalist Boris Pavelić in the *Novi list*. See: Boris Pavelić, "Jakov Sedlar 'prilagodio' iskaz žrtve Jasenovca: Otkrili smo novu podvalu u kontroverznom filmu," *Novi list*, available at: www.novilist.hr/Vijesti/Hrvatska/Jakov-Sedlar-prilagodio-testi-mony-of-the-victims-of-Jasenovac-We-discovered-a-new-hoax-in-controversial-film (accessed November 27, 2017).
21 Regarding the mentioned football match, Ivo Goldstein writes that the year 1943 and the first months of 1944 were a period in Jasenovac in which there

were significantly fewer transports to the camp and there were not so many mass liquidations, so some sections were established which were a farce, with the aim of forming a more favorable image of the camp in public. He quotes detainee Miroslav Šalom Freiberger as claiming that in 1943 the detainees were forced to form "an amateur group, one music and one football section. The tendency was to deceive the public. They forced us to write home to send us books for the library, which never even existed." See: Ivo Goldstein, "Židovi u logoru Jasenovac," in Tea Benčić Rimay, *Spomen–područje Jasenovac*, pp. 125.

22 Nikola Bajto refers to the historian Nataša Mataušić, a researcher of Jasenovac photo documentation, who confirmed that such a photo related to Jasenovac does not exist. Bajto further states that there are indications that it could be a photograph of Jasenovac's NK Balkan from the 1970s. See: Nikola Bajto, "Sve laži Jakova Sedlara," *Novosti*, 2016. Available at: www.portal- novosti.com/sve-lai-jakova-sedlara (accessed November 27, 2017).

23 Mataušić mentions that the aim of the exhibition, organized under the motto "Their previous work was politics, our current politics is work," was to show Concentration Camp Jasenovac as a well-organized labor camp in which detainees were retrained and brought to useful work. See Nataša Mataušić, *Koncentracioni logor Jasenovac: fotomonografija* (Jasenovac: Spomen područje Jasenovac, 2008), pp. 70.

24 Very similar photographs, for example, belonging to the same shooting aesthetics and showing the prisoners of the Ravensbruck camp at work are found in the main exhibition of the Ravensbruck Memorial Center. They are exhibited there as part of an SS photo album, and it is clearly indicated that they were propaganda photographs depicting an idealized picture of reality in the camp.

25 Slavko Goldstein writes that the Jasenovac camp system was organized on the model of the German concentration camp Sachsenhausen-Oranienburg, where detainees worked for the German war industry and were systematically starved and killed. In September 1941, Vjekoslav Maks Luburić, then already the commander of all Ustaša concentration camps in the Independent State of Croatia, went through two weeks of training in Sachsenhausen. According to this recipe, Goldstein states, "he established Jasenovac as a multipurpose camp, in which the detainees would, by working, support themselves and the Ustaša guards. They also worked some for the needs of the Ustaša army and the NDH economy, and eventually were to be liquidated by a large majority." See: Slavko Goldstein and Ivo Goldstein, *Jasenovac–tragika, mitomanija, istina* (Zagreb: Fraktura, 2016), pp. 17–18.

26 Slavko Goldstein refers to the claim of the destruction of documents that would testify to the existence of the alleged Jasenovac Partisan camp and explains that it is unsubstantiated (although he does not refer to Jakov Sedlar's film, but to Vladimir Horvat's text from the book *Jasenovački logori–istraživanja*). He states that tens of thousands of documents related to Jasenovac are stored in the central archives of the states that emerged in the former Yugoslavia, and in about fifty local archives. All these documents cannot be discredited as a product of the communist regime because a significant number of documents are of Ustaša provenance, and a certain number belong to German intelligence officers who reported during the NDH, from which the deadly character of the Jasenovac camps in 1941–1945 is clearly visible. He further points out that documents of local archives in the former Yugoslavia were also recorded in "central republican archives and

were often replaced by photocopies in order to expand accessibility, so it is quite impossible that in this intertwined network someone could have 'carefully hidden' or even destroyed 'complete documentation,'" leaving no trace behind (Slavko Goldstein and Ivo Goldstein, *Jasenovac – tragika, mitomanija, istina*, pp. 11–12). The Goldsteins dedicate their entire book to refuting the thesis of the existence of a Partisan camp on the site of the Ustaša camp Jasenovac.

27 As an argument typical of the placement of conspiracy theories, Blanuša points out the claim of a lack of evidence of a conspiracy as proof of its superior organization. Thus, conspiracy theory is presented as irrefutable because all potentially refuting evidence can be understood as corroborating (Nebojša Blanuša, *Teorije zavjera i hrvatska politička zbilja*, pp. 22).

28 Mataušić states that these shots were taken on May 18, 1945 (Nataša Mataušić, *Jasenovac 1941.–1945.: Logor smrti i radni logor*, pp. 154. Đorđe Mihovilović in his photomonography publishes photographs of the same scenes of the destroyed Jasenovac town and camp buildings, and also dates them as 1945. See: Đorđe Mihovilović, *Jasenovac 1945.–1947. Fotomonografija* (Jasenovac: Spomen područje Jasenovac, 2016), pp. 118–120.

29 Journalist Sven Milekić also noticed the unconvincingness of the alleged witnesses while writing about Sedlar's film. See: Sven Milekić, "Dishonor for Zagreb Over 'Alternative Facts' About the Holocaust." BIRN, 2017, available at: www.balkaninsight.com/en/article/dishonour-for-zagreb-over-alternative-facts-about-holocaust-04-21-2017 (accessed 27th November 2017). People who were guards in the camp 65 years ago should be at least 80 years old. Both witnesses look younger than that, and especially one of them looks at least a few decades younger in stature and voice, while dark hair can be seen through the blurred circle that covers his face.

30 Meike Bal, "Memory Acts: Performing Subjectivity," *Boijmans bulletin*, vol. 1 (2001), pp. 8–9.

31 Ibid., pp. 8–18.

Bibliography

Bajto, Nikola. "Sve laži Jakova Sedlara," *Novosti*. www.portalnovosti.com/sve-lai-jakova-sedlara 2016 (accessed November 27, 2017).

Bal, Mieke. "Memory Acts: Performing Subjectivity," *Boijmans bulletin*, vol. 1. 2001, pp. 8–18.

Bartulin, Nevenko. "Ideologija nacije i rase: ustaški režim i politika prema Srbima u Nezavisnoj Državi Hrvatskoj 1941.–1945," *Radovi–Zavod za hrvatsku povijest*, vol. 39, 2007, pp. 209–241.

Berger, Egon. *44 mjeseca u Jasenovcu*. Jasenovac: Spomen područje Jasenovac, 1966.

Blanuša, Nebojša. *Teorije zavjera i hrvatska politička zbilja 1980.–2007*. Zagreb: Plejada, 2011.

Blažević, Robert and Amina Alijagić. "Antižidovstvo i rasno zakonodavstvo u fašističkoj Italiji, nacističkoj Njemačkoj i ustaškoj NDH," *Zbornik Pravnog fakulteta Sveučilišta u Rijeci*, vol. 31, no. 2, 2010, pp. 879–916.

Dežulović, Boris. "Čas lobotomije," *N1* (2016). http://hr.n1info.com/a116840/Kolumne/Boris-Dezulovic/Jakov-Sedlar-Cas-lobotomije.html (accessed, November 27, 2017).

Gilić, Nikica. "Dokumentarni film," in: *Filmske vrste i rodovi. 2. izdanje [electronic book]*. Zagreb, 2013. http://elektronickeknjige.com/knjiga/gilic-nikica/filmske-vrste-i-rodovi/ (accessed, November 27, 2017).

Goldstein, Ivo. "Židovi u logoru Jasenovac," in Tea Benčić Rimay (ed.) *Spomen-područje Jasenovac*. Jasenovac: Spomen područje Jasenovac, 2006, pp. 108–153.

Goldstein, Slavko and Goldstein, Ivo. *Jasenovac. Tragika, mitomanija, istina*. Zagreb: Fraktura, 2016.

Grubišić, Grgo. "Prijelazi Židova u Katoličku crkvu u Đakovačkoj i srijemskoj biskupiji od 1941. do 1945," *Croatica Christiana periodica*, vol. 27, no. 52, 2003, pp. 155–169.

Groh, Dieter, "The Temptation of Conspiracy Theory, or: Why Do Bad Things Happen to Good People? Part I: Preliminary Draft of a Theory of Conspiracy Theories," in Carl F. Graumann and Serge Moscovici (eds.) *Changing Conceptions of Conspiracy*. New York: Springer, 1987, pp. 1–13.

Krnić, Lovre. "Otkrivamo–Jasenovac – fotošopirana istina: Sedlarov udarni argument o plivanju leševa uzvodno je loša montaža," *Lupiga*, 2016. http://lupiga.com/vijesti/otkrivamo-jasenovac-fotosopirana-istina-sedlarov-udarni-argument-o-plivanju-leseva-uzvodno-je-losa-fotomontaza (accessed, November 27, 2017).

Kućan, Maja. *"Jedinomoje i ostali!": Pisma iz logora, Jasenovac*. Jasenovac: Spomen područje Jasenovac, 2010.

Lefebvre, Henri. *The Production of Space*. Oxford: Wiley–Blackwell, 1991.

Mataušić, Nataša. *Jasenovac 1941.–1945., Logor smrti i radni logor*. Jasenovac: Spomen područje Jasenovac, 2003.

———. "Koncentracioni logor Jasenovac," in Tea Benčić Rimay (ed.) *Spomen-područje Jasenovac*. Jasenovac: Spomen područje Jasenovac, 2006, pp. 46–72.

———. *Koncentracioni logor Jasenovac: fotomonografija*. Jasenovac: Spomen područje Jasenovac, 2008.

Mihovilović, Đorđe. *Jasenovac 1945.-1947. Fotomonografija*. Jasenovac: Spomen područje Jasenovac, 2016.

Milekić, Sven. "Dishonour for Zagreb Over 'Alternative Facts' About Holocaust," *BIRN*, 2017. www.balkaninsight.com/en/article/dishonour-for-zagreb-over-alternative-facts-about-holocaust-04-21-2017 (accessed November 27, 2017).

Moscovici, Serge. "The Conspiracy Mentality," in Carl F. Graumann and Serge Moscovici (eds.) *Changing Conceptions of Conspiracy*. New York: Springer, 1987, pp. 151–169.

Pavelić, Boris. "Jakov Sedlar 'prilagodio' iskaz žrtve Jasenovca: Otkrili smo novu podvalu u kontroverznom filmu," *Novi list*. www.novilist.hr/Vijesti/Hrvatska/Jakov-Sedlar-prilagodio-iskaz-zrtve-Jasenovca-Otkrili-smo-novu-podvalu-u-kontroverznom-filmu (accessed November 27, 2017).

Plate, Liedeke and Anneke, Smelik. "Performing Memory in Art and Popular Culture. An Introduction," in Liedeke Plate and Anneke Smelik (eds.) *Performing Memory in Art and Popular Culture*. New York: Routledge, 2013, pp. 1–24.

Schechner, Richard. *Performance Studies. An Introduction*. New York, London: Routledge, 2006.

Škiljan, Filip. "Kolekcija filmskih i video zapisa u fundusu Spomen-područja Jasenovac s posebnim osvrtom na sjećanja logoraša," *Dijalog povjesničara–istoričara* vol. 10, no. 2, 2015, pp. 309–324.

10 The International Committee of the Red Cross and Camps on the Territory of the Independent State of Croatia with Special Review of the Jasenovac Concentration Camp

Mario Kevo

Even before the outbreak of hostilities that started World War II, the Nazi authorities opened several camps inside the Third Reich (e.g., Dachau was opened in 1933) to which they sent Jews, among others.[1] Most often, the camps were surrounded by barbed wire and were used for the forced labor of detainees and for the liquidation of dissidents, of non–Aryans, and of persons undesirable to the regime. With the beginning of the armed conflict on September 1, 1939, all belligerent parties, without exception, opened concentration camps for prisoners of war, but all belligerents also opened camps for protective interment of civilians from enemy states. The topic of the camps was one of the most important aspects of the work of the International Committee of the Red Cross (ICRC) from Geneva during World War II. The grounds for the ICRC's work in wartime circumstances arises from the provisions of the *International Laws of War* (Geneva and Hague Conventions) of that time.[2] In wartime circumstances, based on the-then *International Laws of War*, there were three categories of war victims, and consequently the same types of camps. The first type was for prisoners of war (*Prisonniers de la Guerre – PG –* captured members of military forces of enemy countries). There also were camps for interned civilians (*Interne civils – IC –* protective internment of civilians of belligerent parties who were situated in the territory of the enemy state at the time of war). Finally, there were camps for civilians (*Civils – C –* internal issue of each state, that is civilians arrested in their own country for political reasons or as victims of racial persecution – Jews, Roma, political prisoners).[3]

After the establishment of the Independent State of Croatia (ISC), which enforced policies of racial and national exclusivity, the establishment of a camp system for the interment of persons "undesirable" to the regime began in the second half of April 1941. Among the first camps as a part of the camp system of the ISC (and the ISC was one of the first non-German countries in Europe to do so): Danica near Koprivnica, Gospić, Jadovno, Slana, Metajna on the island of Pag, and Kruščica near Travnik) A circular sent

DOI: 10.4324/9781003326632-13

by the Directorate of Ustaša Police (Croatian acronym: RUR) to all grand governorates shortly after the establishment of the Independent State of Croatia testifies to the persons who were undesirable to the regime. The circular requested "swift incarceration of all Jews and Serb Orthodox, known as communists, even if there was the slightest suspicion that they are prone to this movement." The same measures should have been taken against communists of the Catholic and Muslim faith, as well as others; they were to be kept in custody, whereas Serbs and Jews should have been immediately deported to the "Gospić collection point."[4] The second phase of the formation of the ISC's camp system began at the end of August 1941, when state authorities established a temporary camp near Jasenovac. Specifically, on August 19, 1941, they opened a camp near the village of Krapje while, on September 10, the authorities opened another camp near the village of Bročice. The authorities dissolved both camps in mid–November 1941, while the Jasenovac camp began to take shape in mid–October on a meadow located not far from village of Jasenovac. In early 1942, the penitentiary of Stara Gradiška was incorporated into the camp system, and the two camps, that is, Jasenovac (1941–1945) and Stara Gradiška (1942–1944/1945) were in fact the only concentration camps in the territory of the ISC that operated nearly the whole duration of World War II. In mid–1944, the penitentiary of Lepoglava was also included in the ISC's camp system. Ustaša authorities reorganized that penitentiary into a camp under the command of the Poglavnik's Bodyguard Brigade (Croatian acronym: PTS).[5]

As I have already stated, the issue of concentration camps constituted one of the most important aspects of the work of the International Committee of the Red Cross in wartime circumstances. The ICRC collected information on POW camps and internment camps for civilians from both official and unofficial sources, from individuals, institutions, national Red Cross societies and in official places in belligerent states (governments, ministries, etc.). The information was collected mainly for the work of the Central Agency for Prisoners of War of the International Committee of the Red Cross (*Agence Centrale du Prisonniers de la Guerre du Comité International de la Croix–Rouge*), which was responsible for the needs of all categories of detainees. Thus, the ICRC collected the first data on the existence of camps in the ISC from private sources, although on several occasions it unsuccessfully requested information from the ISC's authorities on the camps, the number of detainees, and their ethnic structure. However, a letter from J. Duchosal, an ICRC member, sent to the Croatian Red Cross in December of 1941, confirms the fact that the ICRC's representatives were very well acquainted with the situation in the ISC, based on the information collected from private sources. In the letter, Duchosal stated that the ICRC had information on the existence of camps in the Independent State of Croatia. He also stated that Serbs, Jews and Orthodox interned in camps near Gospić and on the island of Pag (since May 1941) were in an extremely difficult situation.[6] Looking for information, the ICRC received notice from the Italian Red Cross that all of those detainees could be considered "missing" and that they had not been transferred to camps in the Kingdom of Italy. So Duchosal asked the Croatian Red Cross leadership to confirm that intelligence so the International Committee of the Red Cross could organize an action to aid those detainees.[7] In an attempt to establish direct relations with the national organization of the Red Cross, and consequently with the ISC's authorities, in order to successfully carry out humanitarian activities in the Independent State of Croatia, the ICRC's headquarters sent Rudolf Vögeli, a liaison agent of the ICRC who operated in the territory of occupied Serbia. In talks held by Vögeli in Zagreb in early 1942, he asked for permission to visit the concentration camps, and one of the key issues was the attempt to determine how to send aid to Serbs interned in Ustaša camps, that is, the possibility of sending parcels to Serbs detained in concentration camps.[8]

In the Ustaša camps, according to the provisions of *International Laws of War*, were interned groups of people who were classified as a third category of victims. They were categorized as civilians (*Civils*), but mostly they were victims of racial persecution (Jews and Roma, as well as Serbs on whom the ISC's authorities extended the same status), and members of the Partisan movement or sympathizers of the Communist Party (political prisoners). However, it is certain that some detainees were selected to be sent to forced labor outside the borders of the Independent State of Croatia. From time to time camp inmates of Jasenovac and Stara Gradiška were selected and sent to forced labor in the Third Reich, mainly via the Sajmište (Fairground) of Zemun. Some detainees were also sent to forced labor, for example, to Norway, France, and some other countries.[9] According to former detainee Ilija Jakovljević, those kinds of detainees gathered in the concentration camp of Stara Gradiška were men and women selected to be sent in Germany, and a special German commission selected able–bodied people, exclusively of the Orthodox faith.[10] Thus, in June 1942, as part of *Operation Viking* (an operation to forcibly take detainees into the Reich for work in the military industry and agriculture), about 1,200 detainees from Jasenovac arrived at the camp of Zemun. During the war, about 10,000 Serbs, Muslims, and Croats from Jasenovac and Stara Gradiška were sent to the Reich for forced labor.[11] The ISC's consul general in Belgrade, Ante Nikšić, also provided some basic information about the camp of Zemun. Those reports were sent to the Ministry of Foreign Affairs of the Independent State of Croatia in Zagreb. For example, in a secret report dated July 4, 1942, Nikšić stated that the camp of Zemun was under German command, situated on the grounds of the former Belgrade Fairgrounds, and that it was "a gathering place for various bandits" from Bosnia.[12] Of course, they were members of the Partisan movement, but also civilians. At the same time, after the death or deportation of their parents to forced labor in the Third Reich, thousands of mostly Orthodox children up to 14 years of age remained in Jasenovac and Stara Gradiška, and in the surrounding villages of Mlaka and Jablanac. After their release, the Caritas of the Archdiocese of Zagreb, Diana Budisavljević's Action and the Croatian

Red Cross provided care for these children. The International Committee of the Red Cross also gave support in humanitarian efforts. Since early 1943, ICRC's aid for children was channeled directly through the Permanent Delegation of the International Committee of the Red Cross in Zagreb.[13]

The work of ICRC during World War II was one of the biggest controversies and subject to manipulation. Especially after the end of the war, when the Yugoslav authorities, among others, accused the ICRC of cooperating with the Third Reich and Berlin's satellite regimes. Contrary to those accusations, it is certain that after the designation of Julius Schmidlin, Jr., as the ICRC's permanent representative in the Independent State of Croatia (1943), the organization was involved in many humanitarian actions. Schmidlin's tasks were primarily connected with the carrying out activities in the favor of prisoners of war. Given the fact that there were no such prisoners in the Independent State of Croatia, Schmidlin's work was based on attempts to determine the living and working conditions in the concentration camp of Jasenovac, or to find the simplest way for providing various types of aid to those detainees, that is, especially with additional food, clothing, and medicine.[14] As early as August 22, 1941, the Croatian Red Cross asked the Directorate of Ustaša Police in Zagreb to grant detainees the right to write postcards. According to an explanation of the request, detainees had that right, that is, based on the provisions of the "Geneva Convention the detainees have the right to monthly, one to two times, communicate with their families via open postcards of the Red Cross." The Directorate of Ustaša Police granted this right in October 1941, and detainees were able to receive parcels. This right arose from the provisions of the Geneva Convention relative to the Treatment of Prisoners of War, and many inmates were able to send notifications to their families about the need for food and medicines. According to the preserved postcards, the most important needs can be identified, and it can be seen that they turned to the Red Cross for an aid. For an example, a certain Nusret Prohić, who was sent to Jasenovac on September 21, 1942, asked his parents to contact the Red Cross and make an inquire about sending vitamins to the camp.[15] In September 1941, the Zagreb Jewish Community sent 12 boxes of additional food to Jasenovac, and then, according to the request of 40 interned Jews from Bijeljina and, in the fall of 1941, a special truck with clothing was sent to Jasenovac.[16] Survivors, including Egon Berger, a Jew, and Ante Ciliga, a Croat, noticed that the Jewish community sent parcels every Thursday, and both of them confirmed the sending of hundreds of parcels at the end of 1941.[17] The application of the provisions of the *International Laws of War* extended to the interned civilians, reflects the use of food cards issued by the commands of concentration camps of Jasenovac and Stara Gradiška. Detainees used these cards to collect daily meals (breakfast, lunch, dinner).[18] The veterinarian Zorko Golub from Zagreb, a former detainee of Jasenovac, also testified to this, stating, "Not all barracks are equal. For example, in barrack 4 there is Stojan and the management of the barracks; food tickets are distributed there, people are assigned to work there."[19] It is obvious that the detainees in camps of Jasenovac and Stara Gradiška used food cards. Despite the existence of three types of cards, it could be said that all the cards were uniform and contained the name and surname and six rows for the dates and the name of the meal. The purpose of these cards was control of food retrieval, that is, each food retrieval was recorded on the card. The cards were a kind of voucher intended exclusively for food, and their usage was based on the provisions of the Geneva Convention relative to the Treatment of Prisoners of War. The provisions of the Geneva Convention were in force during World War II, and provisions were applied to prisoners of war. Conventions on the treatment of civilian internees were signed in 1949, so the belligerent parties entered World War II without any international legal regulations related to the treatment of interned civilians. Therefore, the International Committee of the Red Cross initiated an action that resulted in the extension of existing provisions to the interned civilians, which was supported by the majority of belligerent parties that decided to apply these provisions to civilian detainees as well.

Nevertheless, let us go back to Schmidlin's constant demands for the Independent State of Croatia authorities to allow visits to camps for interned civilians of belligerent parties/enemy countries (protective internment) and civilians who were political detainees or victims of racial persecution. Although Schmidlin only officially began to figure as a person taking care over the representation of the ICRC's interests in the ISC in Zagreb from the end of 1942, the Geneva Committee received certain information about the camps in the ISC (primarily about Jasenovac) from various sources, including the Catholic Church, that is, the Vatican. The increase in numbers of information about the existence of camps in the ISC also resulted in an international pressure, initially channeled through the Vatican, that is, the Secretariat of State. After multiple inquiries, the Croatian diplomat Nikola Rušinović suggested to the Secretariat of State to request information about concentration camps from their Apostolic Office in Zagreb, and so the foreign journalists were invited to visit the concentration camps.[20] As a result, on February 6, 1942, an international commission visited Jasenovac. According to Egon Berger, a survivor of Jasenovac camp, who attended the event, the commission consisted of two Vatican church dignitaries, several German, Italian, Ustaša, and Home Guard officers, Germans in SS uniforms and Ustaša journalists.[21] However, according to the testimonies of other surviving detainees, it was a staged farce organized by the camp's administration to give a better impression of the camp to the members of an international commission. Even newspaper articles about "the best-organized camp in Europe" appeared after the visit.[22] Thus, for example, very soon after the visit, an article appeared, written by the German journalist Herman Probst. In the article entitled "Jasenovac is neither a health resort nor a torture chamber." the journalist described almost idyllic scenes of the Jasenovac camp.[23] A report written by Siegfried Kasche, the German ambassador to Zagreb, and sent to the Reich Ministry of Foreign Affairs, reveals a far different composition of this commission. Kasche stated that the members of the commission were also foreign journalists, military personnel and diplomats, and then Archbishop Stepinac's secretary Stjepan Lacković and Giuseppe Carmelo Masucci, secretary to Giuseppe Ramiro Marcone, envoy of the Holy See to the Croatian Episcopate. Masucci himself confirms those allegations in his diary entries.[24] This visit by the international commission was in fact the first indication that representatives of the ICRC had visited the camp, but these were incorrect allegations, as there were no ICRC representatives there (neither the ICRC nor the League of the Red Cross Societies, that is, there were no representatives of the International Red Cross).

First, some basic information should be provided regarding the work of the International Committee of the Red Cross in relation to the issue of camps. Namely, the representatives of the Committee paid visits to the camps on the basis of Article 86 of the *Geneva Convention Relative to the Treatment of Prisoners of War*.[25] From the first information about the existence of the camp at the end of 1941, the International Committee demanded that the ISC authorities approve ICRC's work in favor of the prisoners of war and interned civilians, especially Serbs and Jews in the camps on the territory of the Independent State of Croatia. Constant requests were made at each meeting of Permanent Representative Schmidlin with representatives of the authorities and, on March 17, 1944, Frédéric Barbey, a member of the ICRC from Geneva, sent a letter to Stijepo Perić, Minister of Foreign Affairs of the Independent State of Croatia. He asked Perić to allow Schmidlin to pay visits to the camps of Jasenovac and Stara Gradiška in order to see the basic needs of the 1,200 detained Jews for whom the International Committee of the Red Cross was preparing aid consignments.[26] After several months of requests, on July 4, 1944, Schmidlin was granted a tour of Jasenovac and Stara Gradiška, and on July 13, 1944, the General Directorate for Public Order and Security of the Independent State of Croatia informed him of the authorities' favorable decision.[27] This event should certainly be viewed in the broader context of the preparations for the ISC's transition to the side of Allies, which intensified in the summer of 1944. This visit was in fact part of a deliberate plan to convince the Western Allies that the authorities treated the detainees well, and that the state adhered to the prescribed provisions of the International Laws of War. The special delegation led by Milutin Jurčić, director general of the General Directorate for Public Order and Security, and Schmidlin's inspection of the camp lasted from July 14th to 17th, 1944.[28] Schmidlin submitted a very extensive report on the visit to the International Committee, addressing it to Jean Etienne de Schwarzenberg, a member of the ICRC's Secretariat and head of the ICRC's Special Relief Division in charge of humanitarian aid. It is obvious from the report that the visit and the report were made according to the basic form for visits to the camps prepared by the legal service of the ICRC. Since the Geneva Conventions in favor of prisoners of war existed, a pattern of visits to the camps created for this purpose and the questions were based on the conventions relative to prisoners of war.[29] However, as the later provisions of the Convention were extended to the interned civilians, the usage of the form was also extended to all categories of camps. Although the form is not preserved in Schmidlin's correspondence, a comparison of his report with the questionnaire for visits to POW camps in Italy on May 20, 1941, indisputably confirms that this form was used by all ICRC representatives in inspecting the camps, and thus Schmidlin's report was made according to these standard ICRC instructions. According to the basic form – questionnaire of 66 points – during their visits to camps ICRC representatives paid special attention to, among other things, determine the description of the camp, accommodation and health and hygiene conditions, nutrition, clothing, and work conditions, religious activities, correspondence opportunities, and complaints of detainees. As Schmidlin noted in the report, during the visit he was unable to take photographs or even to talk to detainees. It was indeed contrary to the provisions of the *International Laws of War*.[30] It is interesting to note that Edmund Stöger, a Ustasha officer and a professional photographer, took the photos after all. He was an employee of the Propaganda Office of the Independent State of Croatia, who accompanied Schmidlin and other members of the delegation who visited the camps.[31]

In addition to a brief overview of the above-mentioned visit, certain information can be found in the chapter on the Jasenovac camp in the book *Holocaust in Zagreb*. The authors stated that Schmidlin received permission from the authorities to visit the camps in the spring of 1944.[32] In the chapter, they also state a somewhat vague conclusion: "Perhaps because of conformism and fear, and perhaps because the International Committee of the Red Cross had rather vague relations with the Nazis, Schmidlin's report clearly embellished the portrayed situation in the Jasenovac complex."[33] Furthermore, they stated that Schmidlin, after visiting the camps in June,

> submitted a list of proposals to enable the International Committee of the Red Cross to work more effectively. Schmidlin demanded a list of detained Jews with all information, regular information on the movement, death, and hospitalization, inclusion of commissioners from the ranks of internees in the organization, and distribution of aid, all according to the principles of the *Geneva Convention relative to the Treatment of the Prisoners of War*. It is clear that such an attempt was completely illusory and was unsuccessful, and in autumn of 1944 the International Committee gave up on sending food parcels to Jasenovac camp because the promises of Ustaša authorities could not be trusted, nor could guarantees be given that the Jewish community of Zagreb would also participate in the distribution of received aid.[34]

In these sentences, the authors stated several factual inaccuracies, which also resulted in a poor attempt to draw relevant conclusions on the above issues. It is indisputable that the camp's administration prepared the camp for the purpose of the visit, of which Schmidlin was very well aware. He had no need to improve the situation in the camp when the camp's administration had already done so before the announced visit.[35] Furthermore, it is obvious that Schmidlin visited the Jasenovac and Stara Gradiška camps in mid-July 1944. Therefore, the conclusion that in June, after a visit to the camps, he submitted a list of proposals to the ICRC's headquarters in Geneva to improve the work and to achieve greater efficiency is completely wrong. The claim that relations between the ICRC and the Nazi authorities had an impact on Schmidlin's report on the visit to the camps also remains unclear, especially since it was a highly secret report intended solely for the internal use of the ICRC's leadership and its various services. According to archival sources, the ICRC refused to send aid to the camp due to the actions of the camp's administration, that is, obstruction by the camp's administration in the delivery of aid. I shall discuss it more shortly.

Following the receipt of Schmidlin's report, the ICRC's headquarters launched a multi-directional action to help the detained Jews, with the direct participation of the permanent representative, Schmidlin himself. Primarily, an attempt was made to organize the systematic delivery of food parcels, medicine, and clothing to Jews interned in the camps of Jasenovac and Stara Gradiška. Certain contacts were established with the Geneva branch of the World Jewish Congress (*Congrès juif mondial*) and especially with Saly Mayer, president of the Union of Swiss Jewish Communities (*Fédération des communautés israélites suisses*) and representative of JOINT (American Joint Distribution Committee) for Europe.[36] They also contacted various Jewish institutions as well as non-governmental organizations in the United States, and they established relations with the War Refugee Board (WRB) in Washington. Although Schmidlin, in his secret report to the ICRC, noted that he was unable to talk to the detainees, he succeeded in his intentions and had established closer contact with the detainees. I have already mentioned that Vögeli, the ICRC's liaison agent from Belgrade, visited Zagreb in early 1942 to seek permission from the authorities to visit the camps. However, it was not until the end of 1942 that Robert Schirmer, a special ICRC's envoy, went on a special mission to Zagreb. The Ustaša authorities promised to apply the provisions of the Geneva Conventions, and they stated an intention to extend it to interned civilians.[37] A special request concerned the possibility for the ICRC to send donations and remittances to prisoners of war and interned civilians, to which the Ustaša authorities agreed.

In providing aid to all of detainees, the ICRC procured most of its funds and material goods from foreign financiers. Private individuals, various support organizations, non-governmental and non-profit associations and societies, and especially Jewish organizations, provided extremely high funding to provide aid. According to above-mentioned, it was of most importance that the supervision over the aid and its distribution be under the control of an ICRC permanent representative in Zagreb. The presence of ICRC representatives in the distribution of the received aid was also necessary in order to confirm to the financiers that the joint efforts were not in vain and that the aid reached those to whom it was sent, that is, that there was no abuse in the distribution of aid by the camp's administration. In addition, during Schmidlin's visit to the camps, he identified the most important needs of detainees: their health status, and in particular, he collected certain data required by the War Refugee Board to expedite the approval of funding for Jewish detainees. On April 11, 1944, Daniel J. Reagan, Economic Attaché at the US Embassy in Switzerland (Bern), sent a notice to the ICRC's Secretariat member, J. E. von Schwarzenberg. He noted that the War Refugee Board had asked for the number of detainees and their ethnicity to be determined, and that the ICRC's leadership should make a cost estimate as well as the list of food to be procured in Portugal. On behalf of the War Refugee Board, he also asked for guarantees that food shipments would indeed be distributed among detainees.[38] Therefore, Schmidlin's task was establishing a control mechanism for the distribution of aid among detainees. This stemmed from several provisions of the Geneva Convention, the most important of which were certainly the 43rd and 78th articles on the designation of a special detainee' commissioner chosen among inmates themselves.[39] In agreement with Schmidlin, former Jasenovac inmate Milo Bošković became the detainees' commissioner in charge of supervision over the distribution of incoming aid.[40] Despite the bans imposed by the camp's administration during a visit to the Jasenovac, Schmidlin managed to agree on the way of receiving aid parcels and records of their receipt, that is, the distribution among detainees. Bošković should have been a credible and reliable source in the field, a supervisor of the aid provided by the ICRC directly and through the Jewish community of Zagreb, and his task was to confirm aid distribution among the detainees. In order to avoid abuses of received aid by the camp's administration, Bošković was supposed to inform the ICRC's Permanent Delegation in Zagreb about the distribution of parcels. However, Schmidlin was aware that abuses of the camp's administration were common. Although, according to the 43rd Article of the Geneva Convention, the appointment of a detainee commissioner should have been agreed directly with the military authorities, in this case the camp's administration. However, Schmidlin characterized the entire operation as very dangerous and kept it secret.[41] The data thus collected enabled Schmidlin to begin distributing food, medicine and clothing for detainees in Ustaša camps, especially for detained Jews.

In wartime circumstances, the most vulnerable groups of the population were completely deprived of the protection of the provisions of the *International Laws of War*. Those groups were victims of political or racial persecutions – that is, political detainees, Jews and Roma – who were exposed to persecution, looting and liquidation within the Third Reich, as well as in the area of states occupied or directly dependent on Berlin. The same situation was present in the Independent State of Croatia, where the Archbishop of Zagreb, Alojzije Viktor Stepinac, protested against such actions of the Ustaša authorities. He later became one of the main protectors of Jews and all persecuted persons and people in need in the ISC.[42]

The supply of the camp was the responsibility of the Department of Public Supply in the Ministry of Crafts, Wholesale and Trade of the ISC, through Jewish religious communities. The communities were obliged to procure remittances to obtain the necessary contingents of food, medical, and other materials for people interned in the camps. In addition, the communities received the financial resources for this from the so-called state aid remitted to the Jewish Department at the Directorate of Ustaša Police, and originating from municipal contributions that had to be paid by all persons covered by the *Racial Relations Act*. Jews were left without funds, and Ustaša commissioners who took over the administration of Jewish companies refused, almost as a rule, to pay the full amount of the contributions. This was contrary to the Law of July 3, 1941, which allowed Jewish religious communities to collect yields in all Jewish companies in the amount they had been collecting until then. In numerous requests, Jewish communities demanded that money from frozen bank accounts or from collected contributions be made available to them for the support of the detainees. Each time such requests were denied. The three largest Jewish communities (Sarajevo, Zagreb, and Osijek) took care of the families left without the funds for living, but also took care in providing the gathering places and transports to the camps. In addition, these communities had to maintain camps in Đakovo, Loborgrad and Gornja Rijeka for which the state allocated insufficient funds.[43] In order to improve their care on the imposed obligations, the Jewish communities of Zagreb and Osijek also established special institutions through which they carried out aid activities. Thus, the support of the interned Jews fell entirely on the social organization Care for the Camps, established at the Jewish communities in Osijek and Zagreb.[44] In addition to carrying out tasks for the camps, these Jewish communities had to support all Jewish emigrants from other parts of Europe who found themselves in the ISC at the beginning of the war. The fact that the Jews had already been robbed by imposing on them numerous contributions, which further impoverished and financially destroyed them, also speaks to the exceptional burden that was imposed. Therefore, the Jewish community of Zagreb, the only one that operated in the ISC throughout the war, turned to Zagreb's Archbishop Stepinac, to the Croatian Red Cross, to Schmidlin and the ICRC, to various Jewish organizations around the world, and above all to Saly Mayer, president of the Union of Swiss Jewish Communities and representative of the JOINT for Europe. The National Red Cross Society was among the first to get involved in helping interned Jews. As early as mid-1941, the society received approval from the Directorate of Ustaša Police to receive parcels for detained Jews. Many of these parcels were plundered on their way to the destinations. At the same time, permission was granted to provide food for transports passing through the Zagreb railway station.[45] With the cold weather, living and working conditions in the camp of Jasenovac deteriorated, and nothing could be sent directly to the detainees, so their relatives often appealed to the ISC's Red Cross, which was issued a special permit to deliver necessities to the camp.[46] Historian Ivo Goldstein mentioned a few times that only the Jewish community of Zagreb sent parcels to the detainees, which is refuted by records in the memoirs of survivors. In this context the testimony of Egon Berger is very valuable. He was a Jew detained in Jasenovac for 44 months. He testified that parcels had been received from families, and there were detainees who did not receive the parcels because there was no one to send to them. In the spring of 1942, the so-called Parcels Community was founded in Jasenovac. Three detainees were appointed as a sort of customs officers, but they confiscated a certain part of the food, so new parcels were assembled and distributed in alphabetical order to detainees who had not been receiving parcels from anyone.[47]

From the beginning of May 1943, Julius Schmidlin, took control over the all actions related to providing aid for Jewish needs. Saly Mayer, as the representative of JOINT for Europe, approved a monthly loan of 10,000 Swiss francs, and he doubled that amount in early 1945 (20,000 CHF).[48] Alfred Silberschein, a representative of RELICO (Committee for the Relief of War-Stricken Jewish Population) organization in Switzerland, delivered the money.[49] It is certain that Mayer secured the funds, and Silberschein sent the money to a Swiss businessman named Hockey, paid in kunas in Zagreb. The ICRC's permanent representative in Zagreb supervised these financial transactions. The Jewish community of Zagreb complained about such an approach on August 30, 1943. Robert Glückshtal and Oskar Kišicky told Schmidlin that the payment in kunas was made according to the official exchange rate (1 CHF=100 kn), which did not correspond to the current inflationary trends. They asked Mayer to shape the exchange rate more favorably, for example, 180 kuna per 1 CHF.[50] It is unclear how Saly Mayer could comply with this request. Representatives of the Jewish community could only expect from Mayer that monthly amounts be delivered to Zagreb, where the money should be exchanged at a more realistic exchange rate. Alternatively, they could ask Mayer to send more money.

According to ICRC's representatives, Archbishop Stepinac was willing to help regardless of the political, religious or racial affiliation of people in need. Letters from the Jewish community of Zagreb were sent to Geneva, and letters received from Saly Mayer confirm that the Jewish community had held intensive negotiations with the Archbishop via Schmidlin on securing funds, food, and various forms of aid. Stepinac promised that the Archdiocesan *caritas* would take care of the interned Jews, in the way that the Jewish community already had done it before.[51] It is unnecessary even to think at all about the repercussions of the Ustaša authorities against the Archbishop's actions, but it should be added that he thereby strengthened the favorable beliefs they had acquired about him at the ICRC in Geneva. On the abovementioned issues regarding the provision of aid for detained Jews and the willingness of the *caritas* to take over their care, in mid-1943 the Archbishop of Zagreb conducted negotiations with special ICRC's representatives who visited the city.[52]

Given the war circumstances and the needs of populations around the world, the ICRC had very little possibility for funding, so the money had been secured in various ways. In terms of aid to detained Jews, the ICRC mostly contacted Jewish organizations around the world, and especially in the United States. Although smaller quantities of medicine and food had already been delivered to the Jewish community of Zagreb since December of 1943, the ICRC had been trying to secure more money to launch a more serious and extensive humanitarian action for detained Jews in concentration camps in the Independent State of Croatia. Thus, the ICRC's leadership turned to the Intergovernmental Committee on Refugees in London, asking for 300,000 CHF for the humanitarian aid which was to be delivered to the concentration camp of Theresienstadt and to Jews interned in concentration camps in ISC, Slovakia, Hungary, and Romania. The requested organization, in London, does not appear to have complied with the request. In early 1944, the War Refugee Board offered to support the project with 100,000 USD (CHF 429,000) provided by the American Joint Distribution Committee. The ICRC agreed to these proposals and all further activities were carried out in collaboration with Saly Mayer, JOINT's representative for Europe, so the WRB approved the ICRC to purchase the necessary goods in Hungary, Romania and in some neutral countries.[53]

Historian Ivo Goldstein states that JOINT sent "large and beautiful shipments" of various medicines, especially those that were in short supply in Zagreb, directly through the International Red Cross on three occasions. All shipments were forwarded to the camps, and one of these shipments ("11 boxes of pharmaceutical products"), which arrived at the Croatian Red Cross (July 1943), was distributed to the camps via the Jewish community of Zagreb.[54] This is a little bit odd because it was common that this kind of aid was addressed to the national Red Cross organization in order to avoid unnecessary payment of high postage costs. Every national Red Cross society was exempted from paying postal costs. However, the consignments were distributed via ICRC's Permanent Delegation or the work was entrusted to a national organization with the obligatory supervision of ICRC's representatives. At the end of 1943, S. Mayer paid 10,000 CHF to the Joint Aid Commission (Joint Relief Commission or originally the *Commission Mixte de Secours* – CMS). The Joint Aid Commission of the International Committee of the Red Cross and the League of Red Cross Societies were asked for an action to help the Jewish community of Zagreb (for the detainees).[55] A few days later, the community sent a list of medicines to Schmidlin asking that the specified aid be sent to detainees in the camps and to the nursing homes.[56] Schmidlin immediately reacted and sent a letter to the ICRC's Special Relief Division, suggesting that it would be best to send wagon shipments of aid to the Jewish community of Zagreb or to the Croatian Red Cross. He also stated that the distribution would be under the strict supervision of the ICRC's Permanent Delegation in Zagreb.[57] In the same letter, Schmidlin also pointed out there were about 800-interned Jews in the concentration camp of Jasenovac, while another 400 were interned in the camp of Stara Gradiška camp and at the camp's farm, Gređani.[58]

After his visit to the camps in mid-1944, Schmidlin organized the delivery of aid to Zagreb and its dispatch to Jasenovac. Earlier, certain quantities of food, clothing, vitamins, medicines, and pharmaceuticals were addressed to the Central Office of the Croatian Red Cross, which was taken over by Schmidlin after delivery and forwarded to the Jewish Community of Zagreb to be distributed among Jews detained in Jasenovac. In August and September of 1944, Schmidlin organized the shipment of larger consignments of clothing, footwear, groceries, and various medical supplies provided by the Joint Aid Commission of the ICRC and IRC.[59] According to Schmidlin's allegations, made in a letter sent to the ICRC's Ppesident, there were not too many confirmations from the camps of receiving of aid. However, the amount of aid was much larger than the preserved camp receipts for food, medicine, clothing, and footwear suggested, and Schmidlin was certain that the camp's authorities had been abusing aid shipments.[60] The most obvious example of disabling the ICRC's work in the field in favor of detainees occurred in late September 1944, when six tons of the food procured by the ICRC's Permanent Delegation of Zagreb were sent to Jasenovac; 1,200 food parcels were distributed to the inmates. Despite the fact that the truck was marked with ICRC markings, the camp's administration confiscated the truck. All Schmidlin's interventions at the Ministry of the Interior were unsuccessful.[61] The ICRC with an aid from Saly Mayer and via the Joint Aid Commission planned to send food parcels every 15 days.[62] According to the Jewish community of Zagreb, these parcels should contained dried meat, cheese, pasta, dried fruit, jam, flour, rusks, canned fish, dried vegetables, condensed milk, vitamins, lemon, candy, chocolate, and also browned flour, bread, onions, eggs and early vegetables procured on the local market.[63] These products were also part of standardized ICRC aid parcels up to 5 kilos of weight. However, all the activities in the favor of Jews interned in concentration camps were disabled with the actions of the camp's administration, that is, with requisition of the only truck of the ICRC's Permanent Delegation in Zagreb. According to the conclusions of the American historian Yehuda Bauer, Schmidlin's designation as the ICRC's permanent representative in Zagreb was a crucial event for the survival of the Jews remaining in the Independent State of Croatia. After his designation, the JDC (JOINT) helped with numerous parcels, allocation of funds, milk, and clothing, which was delivered to the interned Jews via the Joint Aid Commission (*Commission Mixte de Secours* of the ICRC and the League of RC Societies).[64] At the same time, in October of 1944, thanks to Schmidlin's intervention, leaders of the Jewish Community of Zagreb, that is, R. Glücksthal and O. Kišicky, were released, and they continued the work in favor of interned Jews, naturally, as far as the war circumstances and as well as the Ustaša authorities allowed, actions in favor of people interned in the concentration camps of Jasenovac and Stara Gradiška.[65]

After the outbreak of World War II, all belligerent parties opened camps for prisoners of war and for the protective internment of civilians of belligerent (enemy) states. The camp issue was one of the most important aspects of the work of the International Committee of the Red Cross in the field in these circumstances. In connection with this issue, after the end of World War II, one of the biggest controversies arose regarding the Wwork of the International Committee of the Red Cross. This work was reevaluated among politicians and historians, not only in the former Yugoslavia. Therefore, among others, the Yugoslav communist authorities accused the ICRC of cooperating with the Third Reich and satellite regimes. According to archival sources and scientific research, a different light is shed on this topic, especially the work in the territory of the Independent State of Croatia. It is obvious that the ICRC's leadership collected information on the existence of camps from official and unofficial sources in the belligerent states. The first data on the existence of camps in the Independent State of Croatia were acquired from private sources. According to collected information, international pressure increased on the authorities of the ISC to allow visits to the camps. At the beginning of 1942, the pressure resulted in the consent of the Ustaša authorities to organize a visit by an international commission. Members of that commission visited the concentration camp of Jasenovac on February 6, 1942.

Despite the fact that there were no representatives of the International Committee nor League of Red Cross Societies, the mentioned visit in the literature as well as in the memoirs of the survivors were connected with the work of the International Red Cross. However, only after the designation of J. Schmidlin as a Permanent Representative in Zagreb (1943), that is, after the establishment of direct relations, the ICRC's leadership could have been much more involved in attempts to implement the provisions of the International Laws of War in the ISC. Schmidlin took care for providing aid for interned people. He forwarded certain quantities of food, clothing, vitamins, and medicines to the Jewish Community of Zagreb to be distributed among Jews interned in the camps. In addition, he tried to determine the living and working conditions in Jasenovac, so he could initiate more extensive work on providing aid for the detainees. Accordingly, Schmidlin had been submitting numerous requests to the ISC's authorities to grant visits to these concentration camps. In the summer of 1944, the Ustaša authorities approved the request. In mid-July of 1944, Schmidlin visited Jasenovac and Stara Gradiška and this camp's farm, Građani.

Afterwards Schmidlin wrote an extensive secret report. His visit was the only visit to the Ustaša camps by ICRC's representatives during World War II. Following the receipt of Schmidlin's report, the ICRC's leadership made efforts to organize the systematic delivery of parcels containing food, clothing, and medicine to the inmates of the Ustaša camps. However, as the ICRC lacked financial resources, it turned to the Geneva branch of the World Jewish Congress, and to various Jewish institutions and non-governmental organizations in the United States to secure aid, primarily to be sent to the Jews detained in Jasenovac and Stara Gradiška. Thus, at the end of September 1944, the ICRC sent six tons of aid to the Jasenovac camp, where 1,200 food parcels were distributed among inmates. The mentioned aid action, which was supposed to take place twice a month, was interrupted by restrictions from the camp's administration, which seized the only truck available to the ICRC's Permanent Delegation in Zagreb. That is why the action itself was ended even before it started.

Notes

1 Catholic University of Croatia (CUC, Zagreb) funded the present chapter through an approved research project, „Humanitarni rad na području hrvatskih zemalja u ratnim okolnostima 20. stoljeća," HKS-2018-8 ("Humanitarian Work in the Territory of the Croatian Lands in War Circumstances of the 20th Century)."
2 On the most important aspects of work in war circumstances, see briefly: Mario Kevo, "Neki aspekti rada Središnje agencije za ratne zarobljenike Međunarodnog odbora Crvenog križa u korist ratnih stradalnika s područja Nezavisne Države Hrvatske," *Časopis za suvremenu povijest*, vol. 44, no. 3, 2012, pp. 651–678; Mario Kevo, "Imenovanje stalnog predstavnika Međunarodnog odbora Crvenog križa u Nezavisnoj Državi Hrvatskoj (1943.)," *Croatica Christiana Periodica*, vol. 40, no. 78, 2016, pp. 209–234; especially pp. 209–211 and 229–232. For a synthetic review cf. François Bugnion, *The International Committee of the Red Cross and the Protection of War Victims* (Geneva: ICRC, 2003).
3 For more details, see Mario Kevo, "Neki aspekti rada Središnje agencije za ratne zarobljenike Međunarodnog odbora Crvenog križa u korist ratnih stradalnika s područja Nezavisne Države Hrvatske," 2012, pp. 654 et seq.
4 Mirko Peršen, *Ustaški logori* (Zagreb: Globus, 1990), p. 18. Cf. and Mario Kevo, "Počeci logora Jasenovac," *Scrinia Slavonica*, vol. 3, 2003, pp. 471–499.
5 For a brief overview about the camps, see Zdravko Dizdar, "Logori na području sjeverozapadne Hrvatske u toku drugoga svjetskog rata 1941–1945. godine," *Časopis za suvremenu povijest*, vol. 22, no. 1–2, 1990, pp. 83–110; See also: Tea Benčić Rimay (ed.) *Spomen–područje Jasenovac* (Jasenovac: Javna ustanova Spomen–područje Jasenovac, 2006); Mirko Peršen, *Ustaški logori*; Ivo Goldstein and Slavko Goldstein, *Holokaust u Zagrebu* (Zagreb: Znanje, 2001); Mario Kevo, "Počeci logora Jasenovac," 471–499.
6 Archives du Comité International de la Croix-Rouge, Genève, Suisse, Archives générales 1918–1950, Group G.: Généralités, affaires opérationnelles 1939–1950. (Hereinafter: CH–ACICR, G.), G. 85 /Croatie. Letter from J. Duchosal dated December 22, 1941 sent to the Croatian Red Cross (CRC).
7 CH–ACICR, G. 85 / Croatia. Letter from J. Duchosal dated December 22, 1941 sent to Croatian Red Cross.
8 Mario Kevo, "Imenovanje stalnog predstavnika Međunarodnog odbora Crvenog križa u Nezavisnoj Državi Hrvatskoj, 1943," p. 219.
9 Cf. documents, minutes from the hearings and memoirs in: Nihad Halilbegović, *Bošnjaci u jasenovačkom logoru* (Sarajevo: Istraživačka publicistika. Vijeće Kongresa bošnjačkih intelektualaca, 2006), pp. 75, 211, 246, 400, 401, 416. On the structuring of the repressive apparatus of the Independent State of Croatia, as well as for a detailed overview of the formal–legal grounds for sending persons to concentration camps cf. Mario Kevo, "Lišavanje slobode i prisilni rad u zakonodavstvu Nezavisne Države Hrvatske (1941–1945)," in Vladimir Geiger, Martina Grahek

Ravančić, Marica Karakaš Obradov (eds.) *Logori, zatvori i prisilni rad u Hrvatskoj / Jugoslaviji 1941–1945* (Zagreb: Hrvatski institut za povijest, 2010), pp. 9–39 and bibliography cited there.
10 Cf. Ilija Jakovljević, *Konclogor na Savi* (Zagreb: Konzor, 1999), pp. 73–74, 83, 99.
11 Cf. Ivo Goldstein and Slavko Goldstein, *Holokaust u Zagrebu*, p. 322.
12 Aleksandar Vojinović, *NDH U Beogradu* (Zagreb: Naklada Pavičić, 1995), p. 147.
13 Fore more details, see: Mario Kevo, Uloga nadbiskupa Stepinca u zbrinjavanju i spašavanju srpske i židovske djece / Archbishop Stepinac's Role in Rescuing and Providing for Serbian and Jewish Children," in Ivan Majnarić, Mario Kevo, Tomislav Anić (eds.) *Nadbiskup Stepinac i Srbi u Hrvatskoj u kontekstu Drugoga svjetskog rata i poraća / Archbishop Stepinac and the Serbs in Croatia within the Context of World War II and Post-war Period* (Zagreb: Hrvatsko katoličko sveučilište / Zagrebačka nadbiskupija / Kršćanska sadašnjost, 2016), pp. 331–394; Cf. and Mario Kevo "Prilog poznavanju humanitarnoga rada Diane Budisavljević rođ. Obexer tijekom Drugoga svjetskog rata," in Enes S. Omerović (ed.) *Nijemci u Bosni i Hercegovini i Hrvatskoj – nova istraživanja i perspektive / Die Deutschen in Bosnien und Herzegowina und Kroatien–neue Forschungen und Perspektiven* (Sarajevo-Zagreb-Tübingen: Institut za istoriju Sarajevo, 2015), pp. 309–322. A series of data is also provided by Diana Budisavljević in her diary entries. Cf. *Dnevnik Diane Budisavljević*, in *FONTES–izvori za hrvatsku povijest* 8 (Zagreb: Hrvatski državni arhiv, 2002).
14 On the basic activities in the ISC, cf. Mario Kevo, "Neki aspekti rada Središnje agencije za ratne zarobljenike Međunarodnog odbora Crvenog križa u korist stradalnika s područja Nezavisne Države Hrvatske," pp. 651–678.
15 Nihad Halilbegović, *Bošnjaci u jasenovačkom logoru*, p. 232.
16 Ivo Goldstein "Dobrotvorno i socijalno djelovanje židovske zajednice u Zagrebu u 19. i 20. stoljeću," *Revija za socijalnu politiku*, vol. 12, no. 3–4 (2005), p. 296.
17 Ibid.; see also Egon Berger, *44 mjeseca u Jasenovcu* (Zagreb: Grafički zavod Hrvatske, 1966), pp. 18, 31, 64–65, 75.
18 More cf. Mario Kevo, "Prehrambene kartice koncentracijskih logora Jasenovac i Stara Gradiška (1941./42–1945)," *Numizmatičke vijesti*, vol. 51, no. 62 (2009), pp. 198–207.
19 "Sjećanja veterinara Zorka Goluba na trinaest dana boravka u logoru Jasenovac 1942. godine," Mira Kolar-Dimitrijević (ed.) *Časopis za suvremenu povijest*, vol. 15, no. 2, 1983, p. 161.
20 John Cornwell, *Hitlerov papa: tajna povijest pape Pija XII.* (Zagreb: Golden marketing / Tehnička knjiga, 2005), p. 278.
21 According to Egon Berger, *44 mjeseca u Jasenovcu*, p. 53.
22 Cf. Miliša, Đorđe (Jure), *U mučilištu–paklu: Jasenovac* (Zagreb 1945 / reprinted Naklada Pavičić 2011), pp. 155–157; Cf. and Egon Berger, *44 mjeseca u Jasenovcu*, pp. 52–54.
23 "Posjet koncentracionom logoru, Jasenovac nije ni lječilište ni mučilište," *Spremnost: misao i volja ustaške Hrvatske*, vol. 1, no 2, 1942, p. 4, Zagreb, March 8, 1942.
24 Cf. Antun Miletić, *Koncentracioni logor Jasenovac 1941–1945. Dokumenta*, Book. 1 (Beograd: Narodna knjiga / Spomen-područje Jasenovac, 1986), pp. 170–172; Giuseppe C(armelo) Masucci, *Misija u Hrvatskoj: Dnevnik od 1. kolovoza 1941. do 28. ožujka 1946.*, Marijan Mikac (ed.) (Madrid, 1967), pp. 54–56.

25 *Nezavisna Država Hrvatska: Ministarstvo vanjskih poslova, Međunarodni ugovori,* 1941.–1943. (Zagreb, sa), *Međunarodni ugovori 1943*, p. 44.
26 CH-ACICR, G. 85/Croatie. Letter from Dr. F. Barbey dated March 17, 1944.
27 CH-ACICR, G. 17/Camps–Listes des effectifs–Courrier des Délégations CICR, 1939–1950., G. 17/00-II, Généralités PG, Questions yougoslaves (janvier 46–juin 47). Brief notice on Schmidlin's activities in favor of interned civilians, July 24, 1946; CH-ACICR, G. 59/12/151–360.02, Israélites, Visites des camps et ghettos, 1941–1948. Visites en Croatie–Correspondance Générale (18.07.1944–12.10.1944). Schmidlin's secret notice no. 739 of July 18, 1944. For more details on the visit, together with a detailed report in the original and in translation, see: Mario Kevo, "Posjet poslanika Međunarodnog odbora Crvenog križa logorima Jasenovac i Stara Gradiška u ljeto 1944.," *Časopis za suvremenu povijest*, vol. 40, no, 2 (2008), pp. 547–585; Cf. Mario Kevo (ed.) *Veze Međunarodnog odbora Crvenog križa i Nezavisne Države Hrvatske, Dokumenti*, Book 1 (Slavonski Brod–Jasenovac–Zagreb: Hrvatski institut za povijest / Hrvatski državni arhiv / Javna ustanova Spomen-područje Jasenovac 2009), pp. 360–363.
28 More cf. Mario Kevo, "Posjet poslanika Međunarodnog odbora Crvenog križa logorima Jasenovac i Stara Gradiška u ljeto 1944," pp. 547–585. For transcription and translation of the original report see Mario Kevo (ed.), *Veze Međunarodnog odbora Crvenog križa i Nezavisne Države Hrvatske*, Book 1, pp. 379–405. Although this paper focuses on ICRC's primary sources which witness to the historical facts as well as to the complex relationship between the ICRC and the Jasenovac camp, and it is worth mentioning that precisely ICRC's visit to the Jasenovac camp was at the center of Holocaust denial and distortion, massively used by certain revisionist groups in nowadays Croatia. These groups especially use the photographs taken during the visit to the concentration camps of Jasenovac and Stara Gradiška. See more in footnote no. 31 and the basic text after footnote no. 34.
29 CH–ACICR, G. 17/74, Italie (1939–1950). Questionnaire devant servir pour les visites des camps de prisonniers de guerre par les délégués du C.I.C.R. (May 20, 1941).
30 Mario Kevo, "Posjet poslanika Međunarodnog odbora Crvenog križa logorima Jasenovac i Stara Gradiška u ljeto 1944," pp. 563, 576.
31 The photos are stored in the ICRC's Photo Library (*Centre d'information et de Documentation du CICR, Photothèque, Genève, Suisse*). The Photos have been published for the first time in Mario Kevo (ed.) *Veze Međunarodnog odbora Crvenog križa i Nezavisne Države Hrvatske, Dokumenti*, Book 1, pp. 61, 120, 121, 144, 145, 152, 153, 162, 163, 166, 167, 221, 236, 237, 272, 273, 287, 319, 327, 358, 359, 383, 387, 401, 403, 408, 409, 422, 423.
32 Ivo Goldstein and Slavko Goldstein, *Holokaust u Zagrebu*, p. 332.
33 Ibid.
34 Ibid.
35 For details and the original text of the report, see Mario Kevo, "Posjet poslanika Međunarodnog odbora Crvenog križa logorima Jasenovac i Stara Gradiška u ljeto 1944," pp. 547–585.
36 For more on S. Mayer's work, see: Yehuda Bauer, *American Jewry and the Holocaust: The American Joint Distribution Committee, 1939–1945* (Detroit: Wayne State University Press, 1982). The American Jewish Joint Distribution Committee

The International Committee of the Red Cross 293

(JOINT or JDC) is an international humanitarian aid organization for the Jews, which provided various forms of aid and assistance to detained Jews, and it was based in the United States. According to Mario Kevo (ed.), *Veze Međunarodnog odbora Crvenog križa i Nezavisne Države Hrvatske*, Book 1, p. 441.

37 CH–ACICR, G. 17/151–69, Croatie (juin 1942-juin 1943), Correspondance avec les autorités allemandes, avec la Croix-Rouge allemande, avec la Délégation du C.I.C.R. en Allemagne. Note of the ICRC's Permanent Delegation in Berlin, no. 2.766 of December 22, 1942; For more details, see Mario Kevo, "Neki aspekti rada Središnje agencije za ratne zarobljenike Međunarodnog odbora Crvenog križa u korist ratnih stradalnika s područja Nezavisne Države Hrvatske," pp. 666–667.

38 CH–ACICR, G. 59/12/151–15, Israélites, Secours et questions de principe, Secours à la Croatie (27.04.1943–18.04.1944.). Notice by Daniel J. Reagan dated April 11, 1944.

39 *NDH: MVP, Međunarodni ugovori 1943.*, pp. 31–32, 41.

40 CH–ACICR, G. 17/00/139, Généralités concernant yougoslaves, G. 17/00-6.1– - G. 17/00 III, Mémorandum au Gouvernement Yougoslave, août 46–mars 48. Schmidlin's letter addressed to the ICRC, June 18, 1947.

41 Ibid.

42 Extensively on the most important views of Archbishop Stepinac, on the position of the Catholic Church in the ISC as well as on the fundamental historiographical problems, cf. Jure Krišto, *Sukob simbola: politika vjere i ideologije u Nezavisnoj Državi Hrvatskoj* (Zagreb: Hrvatski institut za povijest, 2001). Cf. and Esther Gitman: "Nadbiskup Alojzije Stepinac, 1941.–1945., pod povećalom povjesničara i diplomata," in Željko Tanjić (ed.) *Kardinal Stepinac: Svjedok istine* (Zagreb: Glas koncila, 2009), pp. 183–212.

43 Narcisa Lengel–Krizman, "Logori za Židove u NDH," in Ognjen Kraus (ed.) *Antisemitizam, holokaust, antifašizam* (Zagreb: Židovska općina Zagreb, 1996), pp. 96–97. Cf. and a request from the Jewish Religious Community of Zagreb dated December 8, 1941 to the State *Directorate for Economic Renewal* to allocate a regular monthly amount of 2.82 million kunas to support 6,700 detainees in concentration camps. Antun Miletić, *Koncentracioni logor Jasenovac 1941– 1945: Dokumenta*, Book 1, pp. 103–104; Mario Kevo, "Počeci logora Jasenovac," p. 489.

44 Yehuda Bauer, *American Jewry and the Holocaust: The American Joint Distribution Committee, 1939–1945*, 1982, p. 295. For more details, see Ivo Goldstein and Slavko Goldstein, *Holokaust in Zagreb*, pp. 385–402.

45 Narcisa Lengel–Krizman, "Prilog proučavanju terora u tzv. NDH: Ženski sabirni logori 1941.–1942.," *Povijesni prilozi*, vol. 4, no. 1, 1985, p. 9.

46 Mario Kevo, "Počeci logora Jasenovac," p. 488.

47 Egon Berger, *44 mjeseca u Jasenovcu*, p. 65.

48 Rapport du Comité International de la Croix-Rouge sur son activité pendant la seconde guerre mondiale (1er septembre 1939 to 30 juin 1947), Volume III: Actions de Secours, Genève, Juin 1948, p. 570.

49 Yehuda Bauer, *American Jewry and the Holocaust: The American Joint Distribution Committee, 1939–1945*, 1982, pp. 283, 484.

50 CH–ACICR, G. 59/2/151–15, Israélites (1939–1961), Secours et questions de principe (1940–1961), Secours a la Croatie (27.04.1943–18.07.1945.). Confidential

letter from J. Schmidlin to J. E. Schwarzenberg, member of the ICRC's Secretariat, August 30, 1943; Cf. Mario Kevo (ed.) *Veze Međunarodnog odbora Crvenog križa i Nezavisne Države Hrvatske, Dokumenti,* Book 1, pp. 86–89.

51 CH–ACICR, G. 17 / 151–70, Croatie (juin 1942–juin 1943), Correspondance avec Monsieur Schmidlin: Lettres reçue (décembre 42–juin 43). Schmidlin's notice (No. XXVII) sent to the ICRC, April 27, 1943; G. 59/2/151–15, Israélites, Secours et questions de principe, Secours à la Croatie (27.04.1943–18.07.1945). Confidential letter from J. Schmidlin sent to the Central Agency for Prisoners of War of the ICRC, July 5, 1943; Mario Kevo, "Imenovanje stalnog predstavnika Međunarodnog odbora Crvenog križa u Nezavisnoj Državi Hrvatskoj (1943)," p. 231.

52 Mario Kevo, "Imenovanje stalnog predstavnika Međunarodnog odbora Crvenog križa u Nezavisnoj Državi Hrvatskoj (1943.)," pp. 232–233.

53 Ronald W. Zweig, "Feeding the Camps: Allied Blockade Policy and the Relief of Concentration Camps in Germany, 1944–1945," *The Historical Journal,* vol. 41, no. 3 (1998), pp. 832–833; On JOINT's activities in favor of Jews in Europe during World War II, cf. Yehuda Bauer, *American Jewry and the Holocaust: The American Joint Distribution Committee, 1939–1945,* 1982.

54 Ivo Goldstein, "Dobrotvorno i socijalno djelovanje židovske zajednice u Zagrebu u 19. i 20. stoljeću," p. 298.

55 CH–ACICR, G. 59/2/151–15, Israélites, Secours et questions de principe, Secours à la Croatie (27.04.1943–18.07.1945). Letter from the Joint Aid Commission to the ICRC's Secretariat, November 9, 1943.

56 Ibid.; Letter from the Jewish Community sent to the Permanent Delegation of the ICRC in Zagreb, November, 17, 1943.

57 Ibid.; Schmidlin's letter to the ICRC's Department for Assistance in Geneva, November 23, 1943.

58 Ibid.

59 CH–ACICR, G. 3/48s, Mission of Mrs Gloor-Marti et Siordet aux Balkans 1947–1949, Correspondance diverse 1947–1949.

60 CH–ACICR, G. 17/00 III, Mémorandum au Gouvernement yougoslave, août 46–mars 48. Schmidlin's letter of June 18, 1947, sent to the ICRC.

61 CH–ACICR, G. 17/00/139; Fasc. G. 1700–6.2 = G. 17/00 III, Généralité, Mémorandum au Gouvernement Yougoslave, March 4, 1947, p. 23.

62 CH–ACICR, G. 59/2/151–15, Israélites, Secours et questions de principe, Secours à la Croatie (27.04.1943–18.07.1945). Letter from J. Schwarzenberg sent to S. Mayer, April 3, 1944.

63 CH–ACICR, Division d'assistance spéciale [Special Relief Divison], 1940–1963. (B SEC DAS), ZA–28.02, Correspondance générale, Délégation du CICR à Zagreb (03.07.1943–27.02.1945.). *Prijedlog Židovske općine iz Zagreba o sastavu paketa (Jewish Community of Zagreb on ingredients of the concentration camps parcels),* April 6, 1944.

64 Yehuda Bauer, *American Jewry and the Holocaust: The American Joint Distribution Committee, 1939–1945,* 1982, p. 284.

65 CH–ACICR, G. 17/00/139; Fasc. G. 1700–6.2 = G. 17/00 III, Généralité, Mémorandum au Gouvernement Yougoslave, March 4, 1947, p. 23; Yehuda Bauer, *American Jewry and the Holocaust: The American Joint Distribution Committee, 1939–1945,* 1982, p. 284.

Bibliography

Unpublished Sources

Archives du Comité international de la Croix-Rouge, Genève, Suisse Archives générales 1918–1950:

Groupe G:
Généralités: affaires opérationnelles 1939–1950.

G. 3

Missions, Délégations, 1939–1950.
3/48s–Balkans–Europe Centrale – Gloor–Marti–Siordet, septembre 1947.

G. 17

Camps–Listes des effectifs – Courrier des Délégations CICR, 1939–1950.
G. 17/00 – Généralités PG, septembre 1939–juin 1947.
G. 17/74 – Italie, 1939–1950.
G. 17/139 – Yougoslavie, 1939–1950.
G. 17/151 – Croatie, 1939–1950.

G. 59

Israélites, 1939–1961.
G. 59/2 – Secours et questions de principe, 1940–1961.
– /151–15 – Secours à la Croatie, 27.04.1943–18.07.1945.
G. 59/12 – Visites de camps et ghettos, 1941–1948.
– /151–15 – Secours à la Croatie, 27.04.1943–18.04.1944.
– /151–360 – Visites en Croatie, 18.07.1944–12.10.1944.
– /151–360.01 – [Visites en Croatie: camps de Jasenovac, Stara Gradiska et Gredjani Salas], 02.08.1944–02.08.1944.
– /151–360.02 – [Visites en Croatie: correspondance générale concernant les camps croates], 18.07.1944–12.10.1944.
G. 85
Gouvernements, 1939–1950.
Croatie, 1939–1950.

B SEC DAS:

Division d'assistance spéciale [Special Relief Divison], 1940–1963.

B SEC DAS1

ZA – Correspondance générale

28 – Délégation du CICR en Yougoslavie [y compris Croatie]: [correspondance générale], 03.07.1943–27.02.1945.
28.02 – Délégation du CICR à Zagreb, 11.04.1944–21.02.1945.

Published Sources and Literature

Bauer, Yehuda. *American Jewry and the Holocaust: The American Joint Distribution Committee, 1939–1945.* Detroit: Wayne State University Press, 1982.

Benčić Rimay, Tea (ed.). *Spomen područje Jasenovac – katalog-monografija.* Jasenovac: Javna ustanova Spomen–područje Jasenovac, 2006.

Berger, Egon. *44 mjeseca u Jasenovcu.* Zagreb: Grafički zavod Hrvatske, 1966.

Bugnion, François. *The International Committee of the Red Cross and the Protection of War Victims.* Geneva: ICRC, 2003.

Cornwell, John. *Hitlerov papa: tajna povijest pape Pija XII.* Zagreb: Golden marketing/ Tehnička knjiga, 2005.

Dizdar, Zdravko. "Logori na području sjeverozapadne Hrvatske u toku drugoga svjetskog rata 1941–1945. godine," *Časopis za suvremenu povijest*, vol. 20, no. 1–2 (1990), pp. 83–110.

———. Dnevnik Diane Budisavljević. FONTES – izvori za hrvatsku povijest, 8, Zagreb, 2002.

Gitman, Esther. "Nadbiskup Alojzije Stepinac, 1941.–1945., pod povećalom povjesničara i diplomata," in Željko Tanjić (ed.) *Kardinal Stepinac: Svjedok istine, Zbornik radova s međunarodnoga simpozija.* Zagreb: Glas koncila, 2009, pp. 183–212.

Goldstein, Ivo. "Dobrotvorno i socijalno djelovanje židovske zajednice u Zagrebu u 19. i 20. stoljeću," *Revija za socijalnu politiku*, vol. 12, no. 3–4, 2005, pp. 285–300.

Goldstein, Ivo and Slavko Goldstein. *Holokaust u Zagrebu.* Zagreb: Znanje, 2001.

Halilbegović, Nihad. *Bošnjaci u jasenovačkom logoru.* Sarajevo: Istraživačka publicistika. Vijeće Kongresa bošnjačkih intelektualaca, 2006.

Jakovljević, Ilija. *Konclogor na Savi.* Zagreb: Konzor, 1999.

Kevo, Mario. "Počeci jasenovačkog logora," *Scrinia Slavonica*, no. 3. 2003, pp. 471–499.

———. "Posjet poslanika Međunarodnog odbora Crvenog križa logorima Jasenovac i Stara Gradiška u ljeto 1944.," *Časopis za suvremenu povijest*, vol. 40, no. 2. 2008, pp. 547–585.

———. (ed.). V*eze Međunarodnog odbora Crvenog križa i Nezavisne Države Hrvatske, Dokumenti*, book 1. Slavonski Brod-Jasenovac-Zagreb: Hrvatski institut za povijest-Javna ustanova Spomen-područje Jasenovac-Hrvatski državni arhiv, 2009.

———. "Prehrambene kartice koncentracijskih logora Jasenovac i Stara Gradiška (1941./42.–1945.)," *Numizmatičke vijesti*, vol. 11, no. 62, 2009, pp. 198–207.

———. "Lišavanje slobode i prisilni rad u zakonodavstvu Nezavisne Države Hrvatske (1941.–1945.)," in Vladimir Geiger, Martina Grahek Ravančić, Marica Karakaš Obradov (eds.). *Logori, zatvori i prisilni rad u Hrvatskoj / Jugoslaviji 1941.–1945.* Zagreb: Hrvatski institut za povijest, 2010, pp. 9–39.

———. "Neki aspekti rada Središnje agencije za ratne zarobljenike Međunarodnog odbora Crvenog križa u korist ratnih stradalnika s područja Nezavisne Države Hrvatske," *Časopis za suvremenu povijest*, vol. 44, no. 3, 2012, pp. 651–678.

―――. "Prilog poznavanju humanitarnoga rada Diane Budisavljević rođ. Obexer tijekom Drugoga svjetskog rata," in Enes S. Omerović (ed.) Nijemci u Bosni i Hercegovini i Hrvatskoj–nova istraživanja i perspektive / Die Deutschen in Bosnien und Herzegowina und Kroatien–neue Forschungen und Perspektiven, Zbornik radova / Konferenzbeiträge. Sarajevo–Zagreb–Tübingen: Institut za istoriju Sarajevo, 2015, pp. 309–322.

―――. "Imenovanje stalnog predstavnika Međunarodnog odbora Crvenog križa u Nezavisnoj Državi Hrvatskoj (1943.)," *Croatica Christiana Periodica*, vol. 40, no. 78, 2016, pp. 209–234.

―――. "Uloga nadbiskupa Stepinca u zbrinjavanju i spašavanju srpske i židovske djece / Archbishop Stepinac's Role in Rescuing and Providing for Serbian and Jewish Children," in Ivan Majnarić, Mario Kevo, Tomislav Anić (eds.) *Nadbiskup Stepinac i Srbi u Hrvatskoj u kontekstu Drugoga svjetskog rata i poraća / Archbishop Stepinac and the Serbs in Croatia within the Context of World War II and post-war period.* Zagreb: Hrvatsko katoličko sveučilište – Zagrebačka nadbiskupija – Kršćanska sadašnjost, 2016, pp. 331–394.

Kolar-Dimitrijević, Mira (ed.). "Sjećanja veterinara Zorka Goluba na trinaest dana boravka u logoru Jasenovac 1942. godine," *Časopis za suvremenu povijest*, vol 15, no. 2, 1983, pp. 155–176.

Krišto, Jure. *Sukob simbola: politika vjere i ideologije u Nezavisnoj Državi Hrvatskoj.* Zagreb: Hrvatski institut za povijest, 2001.

Lengel–Krizman, Narcisa. "Logori za Židove u NDH," in Ognjen Kraus (ed.) *Antisemitizam, holokaust, antifašizam.* Zagreb: Židovska općina Zagreb, 1996, pp. 91–103.

Lengel–Krizman, Narcisa. "Prilog proučavanju terora u tzv. NDH: Ženski sabirni logori 1941.–1942.," *Povijesni prilozi*, vol. 4, no. 1, 1985, pp. 1–38.

Masucci, C(armelo) Giuseppe. *Misija u Hrvatskoj: Dnevnik od 1. kolovoza 1941. do 28. ožujka 1946.* Marijan Mikac (ed.). Madrid, 1967.

Miletić, Antun. *Koncentracioni logor Jasenovac 1941–1945. Dokumenta*, I. Beograd, 1986.

Miliša, Đorđe (Jure). *U mučilištu–paklu: Jasenovac.* Zagreb: Naklada Pavičić, 1945/2011.

Nezavisna Država Hrvatska, Ministarstvo vanjskih poslova, Međunarodni ugovori, 1941.–1943. Zagreb (without year mark).

Peršen, Mirko. *Ustaški logori.* Zagreb: Globus, 1990.

Pröbst, Herman. "Posjet koncentracionom logoru, Jasenovac nije ni lječilište ni mučilište," *Spremnost: misao i volja ustaške Hrvatske*, vol. 1, no 2, 1942.

Rapport du Comité International de la Croix-Rouge sur son activité pendant la seconde guerre mondiale (1er septembre 1939–30 juin 1947), volume III: Actions de Secours. Genève: CICR, Juin, 1948.

Vojinović, Aleksandar. *NDH u Beogradu.* Zagreb: Naklada Pavičić, 1995.

Zweig, W. Ronald. "Feeding the Camps: Allied Blockade Policy and the Relief of Concentration Camps in Germany, 1944–1945," *The Historical Journal*, vol. 41, no. 3 (1998), pp. 825–851.

Index

Note: Page numbers in **bold** indicate tables; those in *italics* indicate figures, end of chapter notes are denoted by a letter n between page number and note number.

Abakunoa, Anna 189
About, Ilsen 189
Albania 203
Alexander, Harold 109
Alexander, Jeffrey C. 19n6
Alliance of Anti-Fascist Fighters and Anti-Fascists of Croatia 110, 116–117
Almuli, Jaša 42
American Jewish Joint Distribution Committee (JOINT) 283, 285–287
antigypsyism 188
anti-Semitism 34, 42, 68n6; racial laws 56, 58–59, 63, 65
April War 139–140
Arendt, Hannah 3, 272n17
Artuković, Andrija 37, 58, 88
Asseo, Henriette 189
Association of Anti-fascist Veterans of Croatia 243
Association of Croatian Armed Forces (HOS) 243–244
Association of Fine Artists of Serbia 35
Association of Former Detainees of Jasenovac 48
Association of Jewish Communities of Yugoslavia 51n28
Association of People's Liberation War Veterans (SUBNOR) 46, 99, 180n4
Auschwitz: as central representational axis of Holocaust 4; as contested term 9; Jews 64; memorialisation 240; Roma 189, 211n25
Avramov, Smilja 37, 104

Babić, Josip 204
Bajto, Nikola 265–266

Bal, Mieke 256, 270
Banić, Nikola 107, 251n69
Banjica 42
Banovina of Croatia 190–191, 194
Barbarić, Ilija 105
Barbey, Frédéric 281
Bartulin, Nevenko 272n19
Basta, Milan 88n3
Bauer, Yehuda 288
Benyovsky, Lucija 233–234, 248n25
Berčić, Vojdrag 79
Berger, Arthur 239
Berger, Egon 272n18, 279–280, 286
Black Legion 76
Blanka Matković, Blanka 108
Blanuša, Nebojša 264, 272n17, 274n27
Bleiburg and the "Way of the Cross" 74–77, 87–88, 242; victim numbers 75, 97, 108–119, **120**
Blood and Ashes of Jasenovac (Zafranović) 257, 259–263, 267, 270
Boban, Ljubo 104
Bodyguard Division 77
Bogdanović, Bogdan 236, 240, 260–261
Bojović, Edo 43
Bošković, Milo 284
Bosnia and Herzegovina: Bosnian war xvi; memorialisation 236; Roma 188, 195, 198, 202–203, 205–208; symbolic use of Jasenovac 5; victim numbers 101–102; *see also* Republika Srpska
Bosniak Institute 104–105
Bosniaks 113, 116
Bosnians 40, 112
Boursier, Giovanna 189
Brdar, Simo 11, 14, 16

Breznik, Dušan 180n7
British 74, 80, 82–83, 108–109
Brzica, Petar 41
Buchenwald 15
Budak, Mile 58–59, 63, 259, 266
Budisavljević, Diana 278, 291n13
Bulajić, Milan 13, 16, 104, 207; Sajmište memorial 37–42, 44, 46, 48, 49
Bulatović, Radomir 104
Bulgaria 198, 203
Bušić, Bruno 104
Bužđon–Slomić, Marija/Maja 84–85, 87

Care for the Camps 285
Catholicism/Catholic Church: anti-Serb orientation 104; Bleiburg and the "Way of the Cross" 76; Filipović 77–79; International Committee of the Red Cross 280; memorialisation 239; racial laws 62, 63; role in genocide 42; Roma 190; Sedlar's *Jasenovac – the Truth* 266, 272n19; symbolic use of Jasenovac 5; victim numbers 105; Zafranović's *Blood and Ashes of Jasenovac* 259
censorship of research on World War II crimes xvi
censuses 12–13, 25n70, 97, 121n3; 1931 139, 194, 205; 1940s 99–102, 180n4, 83n23, 206; 1950 99–102, 1964 99–102, 104, 138–178; 2011 206
Čerkez, Vladimir 200
Chetniks: Bleiburg and the "Way of the Cross" 108–112, 115; Croatian Commission for the Identification of War and Postwar Victims 76; and Filipović 80; Gavrin and Hlavaty's *Jasenovac* 258; historical revisionism 7; and Roma 204; Sedlar's *Jasenovac – the Truth* 266, 269; victim numbers 100, 103, 108–112, 115
Churchill, Winston 3
Ciglana 78, 82, 84, 85, 104
Ciliga, Ante 81, 279
Ciolan, Valeriu Nicolae 208n1
Clendinnen, Inga 15
Cohen, Philip 41
collective traumas 3–4
commemoration *see* memorialisation
Commission for Dealing with Totalitarian Symbols 243–244
Commission for the Census of War Victims of the Federal Executive Council (SIV) 99–101, 104

Commission for the Identification of War and Post-War Victims of the Republic of Croatia (RH) 101–102, 113, 115
Commission for the Investigation of the Crimes of the Occupiers and Their Accomplices 12, 18n4, 98–99, 206; Sajmište 36, 38, 39, 43
Commission for the Secret Graves of Those Killed After September 12, 1944 in Serbia 116
Committee for the Relief of War-Stricken Jewish Population (RELICO) 286
communists/communism: 1964 census 180n7; Bleiburg and the "Way of the Cross" 110, 113, 116; Gavrin and Hlavaty's *Jasenovac* 258; historical revisionism 7, 8; International Committee of the Red Cross 277–278, 289; memorialisation 227–230, 232–235, 238, 240–242, 245–246; political prison, Jasenovac as xvii, 10, 13; racial laws 59; and Roma 192; Sedlar's *Jasenovac – the Truth* 269; victim numbers 12, 106–107, 110, 113, 116; Zafranović's *Blood and Ashes of Jasenovac* 259–260
conspiracy theories 264–265, 268–270, 272n17
Coordinating Committee for the Preservation of Revolutionary Traditions 35–36
Ćosić, Dobrica 37
Council for Dealing with the Legacy of Undemocratic Regimes 243–244
counting *see* victim numbers
Croatian History Museum 227, 235, 245
Croatian Muslim Society 202
Croatian Orthodox Church *see* Orthodox Church
Croatian Party of Rights 5
Croatian People's Liberation War Veterans 236
Croatian Red Cross 277–279, 285, 287–288
Croatian State Archives 102, 113
Croatian War of Independence/Homeland War: historical revisionism xvi–xviii, 4–5, 12, 76; memorialisation 227–230, 232, 234–235, 237, 241, 243–246; Sajmište 34, 46, 47; Sedlar's

Jasenovac – the Truth 268; symbolic use of Jasenovac 5
Croats: 1931 census 139, 182n14; 1964 census 181n9; attitudes towards Jews 41–42; Bleiburg and the "Way of the Cross" 74–75, 110, 112–116; circumstances of suffering 146–147, **146**, *147*, 183n21; civil losses *142*, 142–145, **143**, *143*, **144**, *145*; Gavrin and Hlavaty's *Jasenovac* 258; historical revisionism xvii, 6–14, 16–18, 34; International Committee of the Red Cross 278–279; Jasenovac's role in destruction of different nationalities 162–165, **163**, *164*, 172–173, **174**, *175*; memorialisation 227–230, 236, 241; national structure of Jasenovac victims 154–161, *154*, **155**, *156*, **157**, *158*, *159*, **160**, *160–161*; racial laws 55–67; Sajmište 40, 42–44, 48; symbolic use of Jasenovac 5; victim numbers 98, 100–107, 110, 112–116, 118–119, 173–178, 236; Zafranović's *Blood and Ashes of Jasenovac* 259
Ćulibrk, Jovan 33
Čulinović, Ferdo 207
cultural memory: films 256–257, 263, 269–270; memorialisation 227–246
cultural traumas 3–4
Cvijanović, Željka 11
Czech Republic 231

Dachau 276
Danica 276
Davis, Peter 229
DDR Museum, Berlin 227
Dead Opening the Eyes of the Living exhibition 17
Dedijer, Vladimir 37, 104
Democratic Party, Serbia 49
describing: historical revisionism 4, 14–17, 18; symbolic use of Jasenovac 6
Dević 5
Dežulović, Boris 266
Đilas, Dragan 49
Đilas, Milovan 114–115
Đinđić, Zoran 48
Divjak, Joca 82
Dizdar, Zdravko 112
Documenta 244
Dodik, Milord xviii, 11, 243
Donja Gradina 16, 40; Memorial Site xvii–xviii, 11, 14, 18, 26n87, 236, 243

Döringy, Hans-Joachim 189
Dubajić, Simo 110
Dubin, Steven 230
Duchosal, J. 277–278
Đujić, Duke Momčilo 88
Duncan, Carol 229
Đurić, Rajko 207

Eastern Orthodox Church *see* Orthodox Church
Ekmečić, Milorad 37
European Union 208n1, 228, 238, 241, 246, 247n18

Federal Institute for Statistics (SZS) 181n9
Federal Yugoslav Commission for the Registration of War Victims 13
Federation of the Association of Veterans of the National Liberation War of Yugoslavia (SUBNOR) 46, 99, 180n4
Fifth Ustaša Coalition 76
Filipescu, Teodor 202
Filipović-Majstorović, Miroslav 77–81, 85–87
films 255–257, 269–270; Gavrin and Hlavaty's *Jasenovac* 257–259, 262–263, 267–268, 270; Sedlar's *Jasenovac – the Truth* 242, 257, 263–270; Zafranović's *Blood and Ashes of Jasenovac* 257, 259–263, 267, 270; Žižić's *Jasenovac* 257, 261–263, 267–268, 270
Floyd, George 245
food cards 279–280
"Framing the Nation and Collective Identity in Croatia" project 241
France 75, 203, 278
Franco, Francisco 229, 234
Freiberger, Miroslav Šalom 273n21
Fumić, Ivan 109, 117
Fund for Genocide Research 13

Gams, Andrija 42
Gavrin, Gustav, and Kosta Hlavaty, *Jasenovac* 257–259, 262–263, 267–268, 270
Geiger, Vladimir 10, 12, 14, 57–58
Geneva Conventions 111, 116, 276, 279–284
genocide, use of term 9, 17–18, 19
Genocide Convention xvii, 17

Index 301

Germans: 1931 census 139, 182n14; 1964 census 181n9; Bleiburg and the "Way of the Cross" 113–116; Gavrin and Hlavaty's *Jasenovac* 258; Partisans 203; Roma 205
Germany: Bleiburg and the "Way of the Cross" 108; concentration camps 159, 184nn25, 35, 235–236, 267, 273n25, 276, 278; DDR Museum 227; and Filipović 78; International Committee of the Red Cross 279–281, 283–284; Lipa Remembers Memorial Centre 235; NDH civil losses 141; racial laws 56, 58–64, 67, 68n6, 69n27, 70n63, 266; recognition of NDH 57; reparations xvi, 12, 75, 98–99, 139; Roma 189, 191–193, 197; Sajmište 34–35, 40–43, 45–48; Sedlar's *Jasenovac – the Truth* 266; suffering by nationalities 173; and Ustaše regime 8; victim numbers 98–100, 103, 106
Gilić, Nikica 270–271n2
Gillis, John 228
Gilsenbach, Reimar 189
Glamočanin, Radojka 77
Glück, Leopold 202
Glückshtal, Robert 286, 288
Gobineau, Joseph Arthur de 68n6
Goldstein, Ivo 103, 108, 115, 207, 249n38, 272–273n21, 274n26, 285, 287
Goldstein, Slavko 103, 105, 108, 115, 242, 249n38, 273–274nn25–26
Golub, Zorko 200–201, 279
Gomen, Janko 203
Gordon, Clive 26n87
Gorganc, Milan 117
Gospić 183n24, 184nn30, 34, 276–277
Government Commission of the Republic of Slovenia 115
Grabar-Kitarović, Kolinda 241–242
Gradina 79, 86, 99, 104
Grahek Ravančić, Martina 12, 14
Greece 203
Greif, Gideon 16
Groh, Dieter 264
Gutić, Viktor 77
Gypsies *see* Roma

Hague Conventions 276
Halbwachs, Maurice 228
Hancock, Ian 211n25
Handžić, Mehmed 202
Hasanbegović, Zlatan 242

Heuss, Herbert 189
Hilberg, Raul 9
Himmler, Heinrich 192
historical revisionism xv, xvii, xviii, 3–19, 34; Bleiburg and the "Way of the Cross" 75; International Committee of the Red Cross 292n28; memorialisation 241–244; Sajmište 38–41, 43, 44
History Museum of Istria, Pula 235
Hitler, Adolf 68n13, 234, 240, 259, 266
Hlavaty, Kosta, and Gustav Gavrin, *Jasenovac* 257–259, 262–263, 267–268, 270
Holocaust: Auschwitz as central representational axis of 4; deniers xvii, 5, 19, 242, 292n28; "Gorgon effect" 15; historical revisionism 7–8, 11, 17–18, 34; Israeli–Serbian scientific exchange 48; Jasenovac's central role 168, 178; memorialisation 47, 228, 237, 239–240, 246, 247n18; NDH civil losses 141, 143, 145; Roma 188, 192; Sajmište 41–44, 49; suffering by nationalities 173; use of term 9; victim numbers 80n4; Yad Vashem 34
Holocaust Memorial Centre, Budapest 240
Holocaust Memorial Museum, Washington 13, 237, 239, 249n38
Homeland War *see* Croatian War of Independence/Homeland War
Horvat, Vladimir 108, 273n26
House of Terror Museum, Budapest 227, 231
Hrečkovski, Slavica 190, 206
Hrvatska Stranka Prava (Croatian Party of Rights) 5
Hrvatski tjednik 13, 243
Hrženjak, Juraj 117
Hubert, Marie-Christine 189
Hungarians 139, 182n14, 203, 205
Hungary: Holocaust Memorial Centre 240; House of Terror Museum 227, 231; International Committee of the Red Cross 287

identity: films 255–259, 261–264, 269–270; and memory 227–230, 241
Independence War *see* Croatian War of Independence/Homeland War
Institute for Colonisation 194–197
Institute for Statistics 194–195

Intergovernmental Committee on Refugees 287
International Brigades 233–234
International Commission for the Truth on Jasenovac 14, 105
International Committee of the Red Cross (ICRC) 180n4, 276–290
International Court of Justice xvii, 17
International Holocaust Remembrance Alliance (IHRA) 189, 209n1, 237
International Laws of War 276, 278–279, 281–282, 284, 289
International Memorial Museums Charter 15
International Reparations Commission *see* reparations
International Tribunal, Nuremberg 12
Irish 109
Israel: Righteous Among the Nations medal 70–71n70; Sajmište memorial 41, 48; Yad Vashem 34, 44, 249n38
Istrian Historical Society 266
Italy: concentration camps 159; and Filipović 78; International Committee of the Red Cross 277–278, 282; racial laws 58–60, 63, 67; recognition of NDH 57; Roma 197, 203, 205; suffering by nationalities 173; victim numbers 100, 103
Ivezić, Mladen 108, 116

Jadovno 43, 183n24, 184nn30, 34, 276
Jakovljević, Ilija 80, 84, 190, 278
Jambrešić-Kirin, Renata 232
Jasenovac: cultural memory 232; films 255–270; historical revisionism 4–19; importance xv–xviii; International Committee of the Red Cross 277–290; Roma suffering 190, 198–201, 203–208; and Sajmište 33–34, 37–41, 43–49; victim numbers 97–108, 118–119, **119–120**, 138–139, **142**, 147–178; war criminals 74–88
Jasenovac (Gavrin and Hlavaty) 257–259, 262–263, 267–268, 270
Jasenovac (Žižić) 257, 261–263, 267–268, 270
"Jasenovac – A Right Not to Forget" exhibition 16
Jasenovac Memorial Site xvii; cultural memory 228, 234–244; Roma 189, 205–207; and Sajmište memorial 33–34, 48; *Stone Flower* monument xvi, 236, 237, 240, 260–261; victim numbers 13, 101; Zafranović's *Blood and Ashes of Jasenovac* 260–261
Jasenovac – the Truth (Sedlar) 242, 257, 263–270
Jasenovac Research Institute 11, 14, 16, 104
Jasenovac Triple Camp Research Society 9–10, 107, 242
Jelić, Ivan 104
Jevtić, Atanasije 37
Jews xvi; 1931 census 139, 182n14; 1964 census 180n7; circumstances of suffering 146–147, **146**, *147*, 183n21; civil losses *142*, 142–145, **143**, *143*, **144**, *145*; and Filipović 80; Gavrin and Hlavaty's *Jasenovac* 258; historical revisionism 7, 10, 13; International Committee of the Red Cross 277–279, 281–289; *International Laws of War* 276; Jasenovac's role in destruction of different nationalities 162–163, **163**, *164*, 167–168, **169**, *170*, **171**; memorialisation 236, 239, 243–244; national structure of Jasenovac victims 154–161, *154*, **155**, *156*, **157**, *158*, *159*, **160**, *160–161*; pre-war concentration camps 276; and Pudić 85–86; racial laws 56, 58–67, 69n28, 192–192, 235; and Roma suffering 190, 198; Sajmište 34, 41, 43, 45–49; and Šantić 87; Sedlar's *Jasenovac – the Truth* 266; Serb vs Croat attitudes towards 41–42; symbolic use of Jasenovac 4; victim numbers 64, 98, 101–103, 105, 173–178, 180n4, 236; Zafranović's *Blood and Ashes of Jasenovac* 259; *see also* anti-Semitism
JOINT 283, 285–287
Jonić 10
Jonjić, Tomislav 64
Jovanović, Aleksandar S. 106
Jovanović, Dragi 43
Jovičić, Nataša 17
Jurčević, Josip 115–116
Jurčić, Milutin 281
Juretić, Augustin 4

Kantardžić, Muhamed 202
Karađorđević dynasty 55
Karamarako, Milivoj 82
Kasapović, Mirjana 8, 10
Kasche, Siegfried 62–63, 280–281

Katalinić, Kazimir 106, 113
Katić, Anđeo 77
Kelso, Michelle 189
Kisić, Radivoje 43
Kišicky, Oskar 286, 288
Kleitman, Kalay 251n67
Kluger, Ruth 9
Knežević, Ante 41
Knezević, Đurđa 233, 248n25
Kočović, Bogoljub 5, 103
Koić, Mladen 107, 251n69
Kolanović, Nada Kisić 62
Koljanin, Milan 41
Kordić, Tihomir/Tiho 83, 87
Korkut, Derviš M. 202
Koš, Julija 239
Košak, Vladimir 63, 66–67
Koštunica, Vojislav 48
Kovačević, Daniel 200
Krapje 236
Kreševljaković, Hamdija 202
Krestić, Vasilije 104
Krnić, Lovro 265
Krušćica 276
Kućan, Maja 272n18
Kvaternik, Eugen Dido 39, 88
Kvaternik, Slavko 56, 63, 68n9

Lefebvre, Henri 257
Legacy Museum, Montgomery, Alabama 245
Leljak, Roman 107
Lemkin, Raphael 9
Lengel-Krizman, Narcisa 190, 206–207
Lepoglava 277
Levi, Aleksandar 42
Lewy, Gunter 189–190
Lilić, Zoran 47
Lipa Remembers Memorial Centre 235
List of Individual Victims of Jasenovac Concentration Camp 101, 206–207
Lithuania 227
Ljotić, Dimitrije 49
Luburić, Vjekoslav Maks 76–78, 81–85; Roma 200–201; training 273n25; Zafranović's *Blood and Ashes of Jasenovac* 259
Lukić, Dragoje 37

Macedonia 203
Maček, Vladko 68n9, 83
MacIntyre, Alasdair C. 19n4
Macura, Zdravko 266, 272n20

Marcone, Legate 78
Margalit, Gilad 190
Marushiakova, Elena 189
Masucci, Giuseppe Carmelo 281
Mataija, Josip 83, 87
Mataušić, Nataša 10, 236, 250n55, 258, 271nn9–10, 272n19, 273nn22–23, 274n28
Matković, Blanka 5, 107, 243
Matković, Ivica 77, 80–83, 86–87
Mayer, Saly 283, 285–288
McDonald, Bruce 9
Memorial Cemetery, Vukovar 246
Memorial Centre for the Homeland War, Vukovar 246
memorialisation 227–246; Bleiburg and the "Way of the Cross" 75, 76; divisions xvii–xviii; historical revisionism 11; Roma 189, 211n25; Sajmište 33–34, 36, 38–41, 44–49; *see also specific locations and museums*
Mesić, Stjepan 238–239
Meštrović, Ivan 232–234
Metajna 276
Mihalović 85
Mihovilović, Đorđe, *Jasenovac 1945–1947: The Photomonograph* 107–108, 242, 274n28
Milekić, Sven 274n29
Miletić, Antun 14, 101, 104, 207
Miliša, Đorđe 81
Miloš, Ljubo 77, 79–81, 83, 85–87, 106
Milošević, Slobodan xvi, 38, 48
Ministry for Internal Affairs 194–198, 202
Ministry of Culture 245
Mitrović, Andrej 37
Mojzes, Paul 4, 5, 14
Montenegrins: Bleiburg and the "Way of the Cross" 110, 112–116; and Roma deportations 198; victim numbers 110, 112–116
Montenegro 203
Montevideo Convention 57
Moscovici, Serge 265
Museum of Communism, Prague 231
Museum of Genocide Victims, Sajmište 33–34, 36, 38–41, 44–49; 1964 census 181n9; victim numbers 13, 101, 104
Museum of Genocide Victims, Vilnius 227
Museum of the History of Catalonia 229

Index

museums: communist legacies and contemporary narratives 232–234; historical revisionism 15–17; *see also* memorialisation; *specific museums*
Muslims: 1931 census 139, 182n14; 1964 census 181n9; Bleiburg and the "Way of the Cross" 113; circumstances of suffering 146–147, **146**, *147*, 183n21; civil losses *142*, 142–145, **143**, *143*, **144**, *145*; International Committee of the Red Cross 277–278; Jasenovac's role in destruction of different nationalities 162–165, **163**, *164*, 172–173, **176**, *177*; national structure of Jasenovac victims 154–161, *154*, **155**, *156*, **157**, *158*, *159*, **160**, *160–161*; Roma 188, 202–203, 208; Serbian Academy of Sciences and Arts Genocide Committee 37; victim numbers 103, 113, 173–178
Mussolini, Benito 68n13, 234
Muzej oslobođenje Dalmacije (Šibenik) 235
Muzejska zbirka Kastavštine (Kastav) 235

Nađ, Kosta 109
naming: historical revisionism 4, 9–11, 17–18; symbolic use of Jasenovac 6
National Committee for the Liberation of Yugoslavia (NKOJ) 98–99
National Memorial for Peace and Justice, Montgomery, Alabama 245
National Museum of African American History and Culture 245
nationalisation of Jewish property 65–67
Nečas, Ctibor 189
Nedić, Milan 42–43, 49
Nikolić, Danica 203
Nikolić, Josip-Joka 203
Nikolić, Nikola 190
Nikolić, Štefan 203
Nikolić, Vinko 4
Nikšić, Ante 278
Nobilo, Anto 117
Norway 100, 278
Nuremberg Laws 193
Nuremberg Tribunal 12

Obradović, Božica 84
Orbán, Viktor 247n15
Orthodox Church: forced assimilation 272n19; Institute for Colonisation 194; International Commission for the Truth on Jasenovac 105; International Committee of the Red Cross 277–278; and Majstorović 80; racial laws 56; Roma 202; Sajmište 37, 41; victim numbers 77
Oskar Schindler Factory Museum, Kraków 240
Ovčara Memorial Site 246

Pag 183n24, 184nn30, 34, 276–277
Pajić, Aleksandar 16–17
Papo, Bibijana 190
Paris Conference on Reparations 12
Partisans: 1964 census 181n9; Bleiburg and the "Way of the Cross" 113, 115–116; Croatian Commission for the Identification of War and Postwar Victims 76; historical revisionism 13; International Committee of the Red Cross 278; and Jews 64; memorialisation 228, 230, 232, 234–235, 241–242, 244; narratives 35; and Roma 192, 197, 200, 203–204; Sajmište 34, 43; Sedlar's *Jasenovac – the Truth* 265, 268; victim numbers 100, 103, 107, 113, 115–116, 119, 138; and war criminals 74, 79, 82, 85–86; Yugoslav Army 97, 114, 116; Zafranović's *Blood and Ashes of Jasenovac* 259
Pavelić, Ante 55–57, 246n1; exile 88; and Filipović 78; and Matković 82; meeting with Hitler 240; memorialisation 251n63; and Pavlović 84; Poglavnik title 57, 68n13; racial laws 58–59, 62–64; Roma 192; Sajmište camp 39; Sedlar's *Jasenovac – the Truth* 266; Zafranović's *Blood and Ashes of Jasenovac* 259
Pavelić, Boris 272n20
Pavelić, Mara 56
Pavičić, Snježana 233, 248n25
Pavlaković, Vjeran 12
Pavlović, Marko 81, 83–84, 87
Pečarić, Josip 41, 43–44
People's Liberation Army 97, 114, 116
People's Liberation War 35–36, 99, 232–233, 235–236, 241
Peoples' Revolution Museum, Zagreb 232–234
Perić, Stijepo 281
Perica, Vjekoslav 4

Index   305

Petranović, Branko 37
Pilić, Stipe 107, 108
Pilsel, Drago 117
Plate, Liedeke 256, 269
Plenković, Andrej 243–244
Poglavnik's Bodyguard Brigade (PTS)/ Division/Battalion (PTB) 76, 277
Poland 240
political prison, Jasenovac as xvii, 9–11
Popov, Vesselin 189
Popović, Miodrag 44
Portmann, Michael 113
Prkačin, Ante 251n71
Probst, Herman 280
Progressive Party, Serbia 49
Prohić, Nusret 279
propaganda xvi, xvii–xviii; attitudes towards Jews 42, 63; Bleiburg and the "Way of the Cross" 76; Gavrin and Hlavaty's *Jasenovac* 258; Sajmište 43, 44; Sedlar's *Jasenovac – the Truth* 264, 267; Serbian Academy of Sciences and Arts Genocide Committee 37; Stöger's photographs 282; victim numbers 97
Pudić, Dragutin 85–87
Puk, Mirko 58, 69n28
Pupovac, Milorad 239, 241

Quislings 180n7

race: historical revisionism 10, 11, 18; laws 55–67, 142, 145, 168, 192–195, 235, 266, 285
Radojković, Stefan 13
Radonić, Ljiljana 237
Radosavljević, Milan 203
Ravensbruck Memorial Centre 273n24
Razum, Stjepan 10, 64, 106–107
Reagan, Daniel J. 284
Red Cross 180n4, 276–290
Regional Commission for Establishing the Facts about the Victims of War Crimes and other Serious Human Rights Violations (RECOM) 231
Reinhartz, Dennis 207
reparations xvi, 12, 75, 98–99, 139
Republic of Serbian Krajina 46
Republika Srpska: memorialisation xvii–xviii, 236; historical revisionism 11, 18; victim numbers 103, 105, 243
revisionism *see* historical revisionism
Revolution of the Peoples of Croatia Museum, Zagreb 232–234

Riffer, Milko 81, 190
Ritter, Robert 192
Rivera, Lauren 231
Roma xvi, 188, 207–208; 1931 census 139, 182n14; 1964 census 180n7, 181n9; academic research 188–190; circumstances of suffering 146–147, **146**, *147*, 183n21; civil losses *142*, 142–145, **143**, *143*, **144**, *145*; colonisation and registration 193–197; deportations 198–199; expropriation of property 199–200; and Filipović 80; Gavrin and Hlavaty's *Jasenovac* 258; historical revisionism 7, 10, 13; International Committee of the Red Cross 278, 284; *International Laws of War* 276; Jasenovac's role in destruction of different nationalities 162–164, **163**, *164*, 167–170, **169**, *170*, **171**, 200–201; mass killings 197; memorialisation 237, 239, 243; national structure of Jasenovac victims 154–161, *154*, **155**, *156*, **157**, *158*, *159*, **160**, *160–161*, 184n29; and Partisan movement 203–204; pre-war history 190–192; and Pudić 85; racial laws 56, 59–61, 64, 67, 192–193, 235; Sajmište 43, 45–46; and Šantić 87; Sedlar's *Jasenovac – the Truth* 266; symbolic use of Jasenovac 4; victim numbers 98, 100–103, 105, 173–178, 197, 204–207, 204–207, 236; "White Gypsies" 188, 202–203, 208; Zafranović's *Blood and Ashes of Jasenovac* 259
Romania 198, 202, 287
Rubinić 85
Runjaš, Mirko 85
Rušinović, Nikola 280
Rušinović, Stjepan 281

Sachsenhausen-Oranienburg 273n25
Sajmište 34–49, 278; *see also* Museum of Genocide Victims, Sajmište
Saltzman, Diane 239
Samardžić, Radovan 37
Sanader, Ivo 238
Šantić, Josip 86–87
Schechner, Richard 256
Schirmer, Robert 283
Schmidlin, Julius, Jr. 279–289
Schon, Arnold 86
Schwarzenberg, Jean Etienne 281, 284

Section of Former Inmates of Sajmište 35
Sedlar, Jakov, *Jasenovac – the Truth* 107, 242, 257, 263–270
Seitz, Aleksandar 82
Serbia: Day of Remembrance for the Victims of Genocide in Yugoslavia 45, 47; Genocide Convention violations xvii; Ministry of Culture 47, 48; Ministry of Foreign Affairs 42; nationalism xvi, 5, 6, 34, 36–38, 42, 46, 103, 105–106; Operation Flash 46–47; Roma 195, 203; Sajmište 34, 48; victim numbers 103, 105, 243
Serbian Academy of Sciences and Arts (SANU): Genocide Committee 37–38; Historical Section 37; "Jasenovac 1945–1988" conference 37–38; Sajmište memorial 39; victim numbers 104
Serbian–Jewish Friendship Society 42
Serbian National Council 243
Serbian Orthodox Church *see* Orthodox Church
Serbs: 1931 census 139, 182n14; 1964 census 181n9; attitudes towards Jews 41–42; Bleiburg and the "Way of the Cross" 110, 112–116; Bosnian war xviii; circumstances of suffering 146–147, **146**, *147*, 183n21; civil losses *142*, 142–145, **143**, *143*, **144**, *145*; and Filipović 77–81; Gavrin and Hlavaty's *Jasenovac* 258; historical revisionism xvii, 6–14, 16–19, 34; International Committee of the Red Cross 277–278, 281; Jasenovac's role in destruction of different nationalities 162–163, **163**, *164*, 165–167, **166**, *167*; and Mataija 83; memorialisation 228–230, 234, 236–237, 239, 241, 243–245; national structure of Jasenovac victims 154–161, *154*, **155**, *156*, **157**, *158*, *159*, **160**, *160–161*; and Pudić 85; racial laws 55–56, 59, 192–192, 235; and Roma deportations 198; Sajmište 33, 36, 38–49; and Šantić 87; Sedlar's *Jasenovac – the Truth* 266, 269; symbolic use of Jasenovac xvi, 4, 5; victim numbers 98, 100–105, 110, 112–116, 118–119, 173–178, 236; Zafranović's *Blood and Ashes of Jasenovac* 259; and Zrinušić 86
Šešelj, Vojislav 38
Shelah, Manachem 207

Silberschein, Alfred 286
Sinti 189, 191
Škiljan, Filip 250n58, 258, 271n9
Slana 276
Slišković-Slomić, Mirko 85, 87
Slovakia/Slovaks 203, 287
Slovenia/Slovenes 74, 109–116, 139, 182n14, 198
Smelik, Anneke 256, 269
Sobolevski, Mihael 118
socialists/socialism: attitudes towards Jews 42; Gavrin and Hlavaty's *Jasenovac* 258; historical revisionism 7; postwar retribution 117; representation of Jasenovac xvi; Sajmište 36, 43, 45; Sedlar's *Jasenovac – the Truth* 265, 268; victim numbers 99, 138; Zafranović's *Blood and Ashes of Jasenovac* 257, 260–261, 263
Society for Researching the Triple Jasenovac Camp 9–10, 107, 242
Sontag, Susan 3
Soviet Union: antigypsyism 208n1; cultural memory 227, 247n18; postwar retribution 117; recognition of Yugoslavia 57
Spain: Civil War 233–234; Museum of the History of Catalonia 229
Sparing, Frank 189
Stara Gradiška: Buždon–Slomić 84; Filipović 78, 80; International Committee of the Red Cross 277–281, 283, 287–289; Kordić 83; memorialisation 235–236; Mihovilović's *Jasenovac 1945–1947: The Photomonograph* 108; victim numbers 98–101, **119**
Staro Sajmište 35, 36, 38–39, 44
Štefan, Ljubica 41, 43, 44
Stepinac, Alojzije Viktor xvii, 281, 284–286
Stipetić, Zorica 237, 239
Stöger, Edmund 267, 282
SUBNOR 46, 99, 180n4

Tahiri, Alen 190
Task Force for International Cooperation on Holocaust Education, Remembrance, and Research 237
Theresienstadt 287
Thurner, Erika 189
Tito, Josip Broz: Bleiburg and the "Way of the Cross" 109–110, 114–116;

death 35; Jasenovac closure 107; memorialisation 232, 235, 242, 250n59; and Tuđman 242, 249n45; victim numbers 106; Zafranović's *Blood and Ashes of Jasenovac* 259–261, 263
Tomašević, Jozo 207
Topovske Šupe 42
Totten, Samuel 9
tourism 231
Trump, Donald 245
truth commissions 230–231
Tuđman, Franjo 44, 46, 104–105; memorialisation 227, 234, 237, 242; victim numbers 236; *Wastelands of Historical Reality* 38

Union of Fighters of the People's Liberation Wars 35, 36
Union of Soviet Socialist Republics *see* Soviet Union
Union of Swiss Jewish Communities 283, 285
United Kingdom 57
United Nations, "Jasenovac – A Right Not to Forget" exhibition 16
United States of America: Holocaust Memorial Museum 13, 237, 239, 249n38; International Committee of the Red Cross 283, 287, 289; Jasenovac commemoration boycott 251n68; memorialisation 230, 245, 251n68; recognition of Yugoslavia 57; victim numbers 105
Ustaša Defense Brigade (UOZ) 76
Ustašas: attitudes towards 246n1; Bleiburg and the "Way of the Cross" 108–112, 117; civil losses 141; Gavrin and Hlavaty's *Jasenovac* 257–259, 267–268; historical revisionism 8, 14, 16, 42; International Committee of the Red Cross 277–289; Jasenovac's role in destruction of different nationalities 162, 167, 185n39; memorialisation 228, 235–244, 248n27; national structure of Jasenovac victims 154; partial rehabilitation 237, 242; racial laws 55–67; Roma suffering 188, 192–208; Sajmište 39, 40, 41, 43, 47, 49; Sedlar's *Jasenovac – the Truth* 265–268; Stepinac's reluctance to speak against xvii; suffering by nationalities 173; symbolic use of Jasenovac 4, 5; victim numbers 100, 103, 105–111, 119; war criminals 74–88; Zafranović's *Blood and Ashes of Jasenovac* 259–260, 267; Žižić's *Jasenovac* 261–262, 267–268
Uštica 236

Veesenmayer, Edmund 68n9
Vesić, Goran 33
victim numbers xv–xviii, 4, 6, 8, 11–14, 18; based on 1964 census 138–178; Bleiburg and "Way of the Cross" 75, 97, 108–119, **120**; Chetniks 100, 103, 108–112, 115; communists 12, 106–107, 110, 113, 116; Croatian Commission for the Identification of War and Postwar Victims 76; Croats 98, 100–107, 110, 112–116, 118–119, 173–178, 236; of Filipović 77, 79–80; Germany 98–100, 103, 106; Holocaust 80n4; Italy 100, 103; Jasenovac 97–108, **119–120**; Jews 64, 98, 101–103, 105, 173–178, 180n4, 236; of Mataija 83; of Matković 81–82; memorialisation 235–236, 242–243; Muslims 103, 113, 173–178; Partisans 100, 103, 107, 113, 115–116, 119, 138; of Pudić 85; reparation demands xvi, 12, 75, 98–99, 139; Roma 98, 100–103, 105, 173–178, 197, 204–207, 204–207, 236; Sajmište 34–35, 40, 41, 43–44; of Šantić 87; Serbian Academy of Sciences and Arts Genocide Committee 38; Serbs 98, 100–105, 110, 112–116, 118–119, 173–178, 236; symbolic use of Jasenovac 6; of Zrinušić 86
Vjesnik 265
Vögeli, Rudolf 278, 283
Vojak, Danijel 190
Vučić, Aleksandar 49, 243
Vukić, Igor 108
Vukovar Hospital-Site of Memory Museum 246
Vuković, Tomislav 41, 43

War of Independence *see* Croatian War of Independence/Homeland War
War Refugee Board (WRB) 283–284, 287
"Way of the Cross" *see* Bleiburg and the "Way of the Cross"
Weil, Stephen 230
Whitaker, Benjamin 9

"White Gypsies" 188, 202–203, 208
World Jewish Congress 283, 289

Yad Vashem 34, 44, 249n38
Yugoslav Army 97; Bleiburg and the "Way of the Cross" 108–111, 116; and Mataija 83, 87; and Matković 82, 87; NDH army's surrender 74
Yugoslavia: April War 139–140; attitudes towards Jews 42; Bleiburg and the "Way of the Cross" 74–75; civil losses 140, *140–141*; historical revisionism 7; International Committee of the Red Cross 289; memorialisation 227, 230, 232, 235, 241, 245; postwar retribution 117; representation of Jasenovac xvi; Roma pre-war history 190–192; Sajmište 36, 43, 45; Sedlar's *Jasenovac – the Truth* 268; victim numbers 97–104, 118–119, 180n7

"Yugoslavs in Fascist Prisons, Prison and Concentration Camps, and Resistance movements of Other Countries in the Second World War" project 178n1

Zafranović, Lordan, *Blood and Ashes of Jasenovac* 257, 259–263, 267, 270
Zatezalo, Đuro 37
Zavadlav, Zdenko 111
Žerjavić, Vladimir 102–104, 113, 115
Židovec, Vladimir 62
Zimmermann, Michael 189, 190
Živanović, Srboljub 14, 16, 37, 104, 105
Živković, Jovan 201
Žižić, Bogdan, *Jasenovac* 257, 261–263, 267–268, 270
Zrinušić, Ante 86–87
Zuroff, Efraim 26n82, 239